9/99

 St. Louis Community College

Forest Park
Florissant Valley
Meramec

Instructional Resources
St. Louis, Missouri

TENNESSEE WILLIAMS

A Guide to Research and Performance

Edited by
PHILIP C. KOLIN

Greenwood Press
Westport, Connecticut • London

Library of Congress Cataloging-in-Publication Data

Tennessee Williams : a guide to research and performance / edited by
  Philip C. Kolin.
      p.   cm.
    Includes bibliographical references (p.   ) and index.
    ISBN 0–313–30306–1 (alk. paper)
    1. Williams, Tennessee, 1911–1983—Criticism and interpretation—
  History.   2. Williams, Tennessee, 1911–1983—Stage history.
  3. Williams, Tennessee, 1911–1983—Bibliography.   I. Kolin, Philip
  C.
  PS3545.I5365Z8452   1998
  812'.54—dc21   98–13972

British Library Cataloguing in Publication Data is available.

Library of Congress Catalog Card Number: 98–13972
ISBN: 0–313–30306–1

First published in 1998

Greenwood Press, 88 Post Road West, Westport, CT 06881
An imprint of Greenwood Publishing Group, Inc.

Printed in the United States of America

The paper used in this book complies with the
Permanent Paper Standard issued by the National
Information Standards Organization (Z39.48–1984).

10 9 8 7 6 5 4 3 2 1

Copyright Acknowledgment

The editor and publisher are grateful to the following for granting permission to reprint from their
materials:

Jac Tharpe, ed., *Tennessee Williams: A Tribute* (Jackson: University Press of Mississippi, 1977),
reprinted courtesy of University Press of Mississippi.

For Tammie
and
JC and His Mom

Contents

Preface

PHILIP C. KOLIN

The plays of Tennessee Williams have led to some of the greatest triumphs in and of the American theatre. If Williams is not the most important American playwright, he certainly is one of the most celebrated, rivaled only by Eugene O'Neill and Arthur Miller. In a career that spanned almost five decades (from the 1930s to the 1980s), Williams created an extensive canon of over seventy plays, not to mention two collections of poetry, two novels, and four collections of stories, memoirs, and scores of essays. His contributions to the American theatre are revolutionary and inestimable. *The Glass Menagerie* (1945) introduced a new, energized dramatic technique—poetic realism—in the American theatre; *A Streetcar Named Desire* (1947), perhaps his most famous work, explored issues of sexuality and psychology that had never been privileged before in American culture; *Camino Real* (1953), which premiered the same year as Samuel Beckett's *Waiting for Godot*, brought existential absurdity full force into the realism-accustomed New York theatre; *Cat on a Hot Tin Roof* (1955) dared to challenge the political and sexual mores of the Eisenhower Era and captured the anxieties of the Cold War Era; *Orpheus Descending* (1957), perhaps the quintessential Williams work, layered myth upon myth to foreground the dilemma of all fugitive artists; and Williams's plays of the 1970s, once considered derivative or opaque, are among his most innovative works produced on the American stage.

The time is ripe for a reference work such as *Tennessee Williams: A Guide to Research and Performance*. The 1990s ushered in a renaissance of Tennessee Williams research. Lyle Leverich published his magisterial biography, an invaluable resource, sanctioned by Williams himself, for anyone researching the plays or the life of the playwright. In 1995, George Crandell's *A Descriptive Bibliography of*

Tennessee Williams offered a clear, complete, and accurate catalogue of the numerous editions, printings, and states through which Williams's works progressed. During the 1990s, too, scores of critical books—by David Savran, John Clum, Anne Fleche, Thomas P. Adler, C. W. E. Bigsby, Brenda Murphy, Jacqueline O'Connor, and others—reinvestigated the Williams canon and offered readings that challenged the more traditional approaches. The 1990s also saw radicalized productions of the plays, including the cross-gendered performance of *A Streetcar Named Desire* titled *Belle Reprieve* and black and multicultural productions of *Glass Menagerie* and *Streetcar*. Williams's influence continued to extend to other media in the 1990s, such as André Previn's operatic version of *Streetcar*, with a libretto by Philip Littell, in San Francisco in 1998 or the Simpsons's parody of Stanley and Stella. A new journal begun in the winter of 1998, the *Tennessee Williams Annual Review*, and special issues of journals devoted to Williams's work (e.g., the Fall 1995 issue of *Mississippi Quarterly* and the Fall 1997 issue of *Louisiana Literature*) also signaled a renewed scholarly interest in the playwright. During the 1990s, two vibrant Williams Festivals, one in his Delta boyhood hometown of Clarksdale, Mississippi, and the other in his spiritual home, New Orleans, continued to attract faithful fans and scrupulous scholars united in their goal of understanding and appreciating the plays. The 1999 University of Alabama's Symposium on English and American Literature will be devoted to Williams.

Ultimately, though, Tennessee Williams scholarship in the 1990s should be seen as part of a long critical legacy. The last fifty years have witnessed an enormous range of critical and scholarly responses to Williams and his works. Documenting this critical response, *Tennessee Williams: A Guide to Research and Performance* provides the first scholarly, in-depth study of the state of research as well as a history of performance of the varied Williams canon. This reference book contains twenty-two analytical and bibliographic chapters that together assess the playwright's reputation and individually classify, survey, and evaluate the scholarly, critical response to key plays or groups of works. The chapters were written by scholars of the American theatre whose credentials and academic affiliations represent the interdisciplinary talent required to write knowledgeably about the complex and catholic Williams.

The organization of each chapter reveals how the aims of this Williams *Guide* are accomplished. Each chapter follows a structured format that divides information into eight major areas of research, described as follows:

BIOGRAPHICAL CONTEXT

To know the plays is to know Tennessee Williams. Perhaps no dramatist more intimately and more incessantly inscribed his personal life within his scripts. Williams theatricalized and sexualized himself through his work. This introductory section, therefore, explores the relationship of the text to Williams's life. Each chapter begins, appropriately, with comments on book-length biographies as well as on chapters of books and relevant articles that significantly focus on biographical details influencing, or being influenced by, Williams's work. The identification of and commentary on key interviews containing pertinent biographical information will also be invaluable to anyone interested in Williams's life.

BIBLIOGRAPHIC HISTORY

Williams was an inveterate rewriter as well as a literary pack rat. He repeatedly fused one work into another and often transformed earlier works (short stories, one-act plays) into later, full-length plays. He then often revised these works long after they were published and/or performed. Rarely did he allow a work to remain static. *Cat on a Hot Tin Roof*, for example, has two different endings; and over a seventeen-year period, Williams reworked *Battle of Angels* (1940) until he thought he got it right, retitling it *Orpheus Descending* (1957). This section of each chapter supplies a short bibliographic history of the text, focusing on the versions in which the play or work appears and the relationships among the diverse versions. Major changes that Williams made in a text are succinctly outlined, and their overall impact is evaluated.

CRITICAL APPROACHES

Critical studies in this section are grouped according to relevant topics arranged into four related subsections. Each chapter cites what contributors believe are the most valuable studies of a particular play or work. Throughout this section important titles—books, articles, and so forth—are analyzed with pertinent quotations to give readers an unmistakable sense of a particular critic's argument.

Themes

Each chapter provides a summary of the major ideas or themes that the work has elicited among the critics and supplies illustrative quotations from the literature about the work's moral, historical, religious, psychic, gendered, or philosophical centers.

Characters

In a tribute to Williams at Lincoln Center in the early 1970s, Elia Kazan, who directed and collaborated with Williams on five of his major plays, identified the playwright's characters as his most lasting contribution to theatre. This section of each chapter assesses what has been thought about characters in a given play or plays, with attention going to the most significant representative views. Contributors point out how views of Williams's characters have changed over the decades. This section is further subdivided depending on the number of major characters a work contains, for example, Blanche, Stanley, Stella, Mitch in *Streetcar*.

Symbols

Williams once said that without his symbols he would have never left the St. Louis shoe factory to which his father condemned him. Understanding Williams's symbols—for example, Blanche DuBois's lantern or Laura Wingfield's glass menagerie—is central to the critical discourse on the plays. Accordingly, this part of every chapter surveys the critical reaction to Williams's most important symbols, with attention again going to highlighting conflicting opinions and probable reasons for them.

Plot

The section on plot focuses on Williams's sources, narrative techniques, and the structural paradigms he was fond of using and recycling.

MAJOR PROBLEMS THE WORK POSES FOR CRITICS

Williams and his canon were frequently the target of critical attack. Each chapter judiciously identifies those elements of the work that have puzzled or frustrated critics and describes the ways in which critical views have changed over the decades.

CHIEF PRODUCTIONS

Relying on theatre reviews, published stage histories, and biographies, contributors in this section sketch in the history of a premiere of the Williams play and/or the first time it appeared on the New York stage, identifying the accomplishments of directors, actors, and scenographers. Where appropriate, key revivals and foreign productions, incorporating pertinent quotations from leading, representative reviewers, are also surveyed. Special attention goes to the overall critical reception of the play, its ideas and language, theatrical innovations, directorial approach and influence, staging, and the actors who are so often linked to the Williams characters they played.

FILM AND TELEVISION VERSIONS

This section identifies any film or televised versions of the Williams play(s) and carefully surveys what has been lost or gained through various cinematic productions. In most chapters, this section is necessarily brief, given the inclusion of David H. Goff's separate and highly detailed chapter devoted exclusively to scholarship on the film versions of the play(s).

CONCLUDING OVERVIEW OF THE WORK

After surveying the critical responses to the Williams work(s), each contributor offers her or his own original interpretation, responding to the work in light of recent critical/cultural theories. These carefully constructed overviews are an invaluable part of *Tennessee Williams: A Guide to Research and Performance*. Contributors have built upon previous critical reactions to interpret the work in a fresh, innovative way. Each overview demonstrates the continuing variety of responses to the rich possibilities of understanding the Williams canon. Some concluding interpretations are based on a cultural reading of the work, for example, *Streetcar* as collection of American icons or *The Red Devil Battery Sign* as Williams's *Catch-22*, or on an aesthetic or psychoanalytic reading, for example, memory and art in *The Glass Menagerie*.

BIBLIOGRAPHY OF SECONDARY SOURCES

The final section of each chapter contains a bibliography of all the sources cited throughout the chapters.

A bibliography of some of the most essential biographical and critical works on Williams is to be found at the end of this volume.

Given the signal importance of Tennessee Williams to the American (and world) theatre over the last sixty years, I believe that *Tennessee Williams: A Guide to Research and Performance* will be as welcome as it is essential. No similar reference guide to Williams's stage history and critical and scholarly studies exists, though one has been needed for some time. Despite their usefulness for plot summaries and capsule biographies, general reference works on contemporary drama have offered limited bibliographic information and meager assessment of Williams's scholarship and performance history. Unlike these general reference works, *Tennessee Williams: A Guide to Research and Performance* should be an invaluable companion for readers who want to know what scholarly and critical resources are available for a study of Tennessee Williams, the playwright and his work. I hope this book will be a useful and frequently consulted reference work for anyone interested in one of America's most distinguished writers or for anyone eager to know more about American literature and drama, and American studies; for librarians concerned about developing or supplementing a collection; and for individuals charting the course and methods of critical opinion in contemporary America. Finally, this collection of bibliographic essays should also prove helpful to anyone teaching Tennessee Williams's plays, poems, fiction, and films.

Acknowledgments

Many people have helped to make this book a reality, and I gratefully recognize their help here. I have received the support and encouragement of the University of Southern Mississippi and want especially to thank President Horace Fleming, Vice President Karen Yarbrough, Associate Vice President for Academic Affairs James G. Hollandsworth, Dean of the College of Liberal Arts Glenn T. Harper, and Michael Salda, Chair of the Department of English. I owe an enormous debt of gratitude to Mary Lux, of the Medical Technology Department at USM, for preparing the index to this volume. I also thank my research assistant Diane Keene for her help.

I was the recipient of excellent editorial guidance from George Butler and David Palmer at Greenwood, and thank them for their patience and bonhomie.

To all my contributors I say thanks for their endurance and thoroughness as we worked for nearly two years on this book.

Editors do not live on bread alone, and I benefited immensely from the prayers and good wishes I received from my extended family, including Sisters Carmilita Stinn and Annette Seymour; Margie and Al Parish; and Colby H. Kullman.

My family deserves crowns with laurel wreaths for enduring a father who likes to read and prepare bibliographies—Kristin, Eric, Theresa, and Evan Philip, God love you.

Finally, I thank Tammie Brown for all things hoped for.

27 Wagons Full of Cotton and Other One-Act Plays

NEAL A. LESTER

BIOGRAPHICAL CONTEXT

Characteristically set in the South with its many cultural and aesthetic contradictions and complexities, many of the plays in Tennessee Williams's *27 Wagons Full of Cotton and Other One-Act Plays* (1945) are closely autobiographical. Falk clarifies that these plays collectively include details and sentiments from Williams's life in New Orleans in the late 1930s and early 1940s (31). Some of the plays allude to Williams's self-acknowledged strained family relations and his own fragile connection to a world that neglects and even punishes its dreamers. Biographers identify echoes of the alleged incest of Rose and Williams in some of the plays in *27 Wagons*. Leverich comments on the specific autobiographical implications of the plays (448), while Spoto accentuates the autobiographical strand, arguing that "The Purification" "is a shout of outrage about the Williams family madness, a cry of hatred against [Williams's] parents for what they had done to Rose," and perhaps also includes a subtext for his own guilt about his "feelings toward his sister" (75).

Spoto speculates that "The Long Goodbye" combines some experiences Williams had with his sister Rose and a close girlfriend, Hazel Kramer, explaining that the relationship between Hazel Kramer and Tennessee Williams was a kind of "romantic but sexually unconsummated love . . . that . . . lasted eleven years" (23–24). "Hello from Bertha" also alludes to "the physical and mental conditions of both his sister and his friend" (24).

Williams inscribes himself into "The Lady of Larkspur Lotion" as the Writer, and Mr. Charlie Colton in "The Last of My Solid Gold Watches" is believed to be fashioned after Williams's own father, "satirized" in the play (36). Boxill notes Williams's self-identification as a southern writer with Willie, the socially abandoned and neglected adolescent female in "This Property Is Condemned." Appropriately, in his *Memoirs*, Williams admits having as a youth a female sensibility and a spiritual affiliation with females: "Somewhere deep in my nerves there was imprisoned a young girl, a sort of blushing school maiden" (17). Leverich provides relevant biographical information relating to the years when Williams wrote *27 Wagons* (516, 541).

BIBLIOGRAPHIC HISTORY

Crandell identifies and describes various editions and printings of *27 Wagons Full of Cotton and Other Act-One Plays* (21–32). "27 Wagons Full of Cotton," the title play of the collection, was written as a short story in 1935 and published as such in *Manuscript* magazine in 1936, is included in *The Best One-Act Plays of 1944*, and was produced on Broadway and in New Orleans in 1955. "The Purification," Williams's attempt to emulate Federico García Lorca, "could almost be mistaken for a translation of Lorca" (Londré 42). Boxill believes that "the complementary plays 'Auto-Da-Fé' and 'The Purification' . . . foreshadow *The Glass Menagerie*" (58).

Londré notes parallels between "The Last of My Solid Gold Watches" and Arthur Miller's *Death of a Salesman* (45–46). Spoto and Leverich (437) claim that "Portrait of a Madonna" emerged from Williams's play *Port Mad, or The Leafless Block* (87). "The Strangest Kind of Romance" is a dramatization of Williams's 1945 short story "The Malediction" (Vidal 147–62). "The Long Goodbye" was Williams's first "memory play" and his first New York production (Spoto 78; Londré 50). Boxill notes that " 'This Property Is Condemned' was first published with 'At Liberty' under the joint title of *Landscape with Figures*" (50).

"Something Unspoken," which was billed with *Summer and Smoke* under the combined title *Garden District* in 1958, left most spectators unenthusiastic. A *Time* reviewer describes this shorter play as "a warm-up piece that leaves the spectator cold" (Rev. of *Garden District* 42). Londré notes character and situation parallels between this play and Williams's short story "Happy August the Tenth" from his volume *Eight Mortal Ladies Possessed* (54; see Williams, *Eight Mortal Ladies Possessed* 3–18). A *Theatre Arts* reviewer of the 1958 New York production described the play as "an allusive, evanescent and unpretentious little theatrical come-on that served to raise both the curtain and our hopes" (quoted in Londré 54).

MAJOR CRITICAL APPROACHES

Themes

Perhaps here more than in his earlier collection *American Blues*, Williams tests the powers of suggestion and controversy with tales of adultery and sexual violence, brother-sister incest, crimes of passion, bestiality, lesbianism, and mental strain. Spoto notes that *27 Wagons Full of Cotton* as a volume met with "generally unenthusiastic reviews" by New York critics. For instance, Joseph Wood Krutch found the collection full of "romantic pessimism," and W. P. Eaton at the *New York Times Book Review* declared that the plays offered "sentimental . . . disembodied emotionalism" (8). The title play "27 Wagons Full of Cotton" is a complex portrait of seduction, loyalty, and lust, complicated by an element of sexual violence. It is a "controversial" study in southern white female liberation full of Williamsian sexual suggestion, adultery, and possible rape that allegedly "repulsed" too many New Orleans theatregoers (Bentley 22). The play exposes the real world of southern deceptions—deceptions that empower a woman who dares to control the actions in her own life. Described as well as a "comedy of sorts," "27 Wagons" is a "comedy of almost matchless squalor and degradation, resembling not only most of the author's longer works but also Erskine Caldwell's masterpiece of graveyard humor called 'Tobacco Road' " (Rev. of "27 Wagons," *New Yorker* 69).

Londré identifies "The Lady of Larkspur Lotion" as one of Williams's most popular plays because it legitimizes characters' "romantic fantasies against a squalid [moral] background" (43). "The Last of My Solid Gold Watches" affirms the dignity of the human spirit as it transcends class and race. Kolin reads the play in terms of Williams's own subversive racial politics: "Williams does some fairly revolutionary things through the porter to unsettle white nostalgia and to override and deconstruct history-bound stereotypes. The way the porter is presented valorizes a black timeless experience over a white legacy of compressed time" (" 'Night, Mistuh Charlie' " 216). "Portrait of a Madonna" highlights the artificial separation individuals make between spirituality and sexuality, specifically as Christianity and its doctrines of morality lead women to deny themselves pleasures of the flesh. Essentially about social and moral prescriptions for living and loving, this play challenges the insanity behind religious principles that cause undue inner conflict for individuals struggling to accept them.

Falk believes that "Auto-Da-Fé" "anticipates Williams's later studies in decadence" (52). For Prenshaw, both "The Purification" and "Auto-Da-Fé" "illustrate very well self-condemnation and guilt that attach to sexuality" (20). According to Boxill, " 'Auto-Da-Fé' (literally, 'act of faith') takes its title from the religious ceremony that accompanied the condemnation of the heretic by the Inquisition prior to his execution at the stake. The violence in 'Auto-Da-Fé' and 'The Purification,' however, is subordinate to their brooding elegiac mood" (58). Londré connects the play's title with Eloi's final act of alleged purification (47). Corrigan insists that the dialogue in this play "resembl[es] telegraphic utterances of German Expressionism" (386).

"Lord Byron's Love Letter" is an amusement on the naïveté and willingness of people to romanticize the past to the extent that others profit. Connecting this play's emphasis on memory and the past, Boxill claims, "Seeing through the lens of the past into a still more remote past in 'Lord Byron's Love Letter' is like containing memory within memory in *The Glass Menagerie*" (45). Boxill also notes that the play, with its focus on unrevealed secrecy, seems modeled on Henry James's *Aspern Papers* (43). Londré sees the play as a study in contrasts between the Old Woman's "idealized" past and the rapacious present (49); "It is Mardi Gras time, and the . . . carnival noises intrude upon the . . . genteel world of a Spinster and an Old Woman" (48).

Draya concludes that compared to its short-story version "The Malediction," "The Strangest Kind of Romance" shows more strongly "Williams's skill in evoking the loneliness and terror of a vulnerable individual" (651). "The Long Goodbye" demonstrates the need for individuals to liberate themselves from life's disappointments, their own and the responsibility they feel for others. The play is layered in rituals involving dysfunctional family relationships, career dead ends, and aborted childhood innocence.

"Hello from Bertha" foregrounds the despair of the fugitive. Highlighting the paradox of the title's suggestive greeting, Londré claims that this one-act play displays Williams's sympathy for outcasts (51).

In "This Property Is Condemned," Williams attacks privilege and wealth. Identifying this play as "a delicate tone-poem," Londré concludes that in this work all the elements express a "lyrical effect of decadence" (51). Director Hume Cronyn says that "This Property Is Condemned" is a companion to American artist Edward Hopper's painting *A House by the Railroad*: "[Williams's] stage direction was that [the play] should be set against Hopper's portrait of 'A House by the Railroad.' It isn't a portrait. It's a drawing of a house by the railroad track and one of the best works by Hopper. Great one. Wonderful mood. Nostalgia and sadness about it" (Steen 165). Seeing parallels between Willie and Blanche DuBois, Boxill suggests that the condemned property is like a forlorn Belle Reve (50). Of "Talk to Me like the Rain and Let Me Listen," Scheick maintains that "the play both emphasizes the essential circularity of all human communication and shows that talking and touching never really satisfy the desire of completeness" (771). In the elliptical "Something Unspoken," Williams challenges a society that deems certain companionships immoral and unnatural to the extent that individuals who participate in such relationships feel compelled to keep their lives secret and protected. A *Catholic World* reviewer dismissed the play as "a trite little sketch" (Rev. of *Garden District* 469). According to Londré, "Something Unspoken" admits widely contradictory themes, including lesbian desire and bitter contempt in the two ladies' relationship (53).

Characters

Typically, Williams compassionately portrays southern white women assumed to be faded and passive in their patriarchal environs and who endeavor to construct the terms of their own psychological and emotional survival. Flora in "27

Wagons Full of Cotton," for example, seems the innocent seducee, "a somewhat stupid slattern who manages to be pathetic" (Zolotow 23), but Flora deceives her husband to satisfy her own sexual and emotional needs.

Londré notes that Williams's choice of character names in "The Purification" connects with the character naming in Lorca's *Blood Wedding*: "Williams employs the same device, designating his major characters as the Judge, the Son, the Mother, the Father, the Rancher from Rojo" (42). In this generic naming, Williams achieves an allegorical focus on potential universal experience rather than on character specifics.

According to Nelson, "The Lady of Larkspur Lotion" is Williams's fugitive poem personified (196–97). Mrs. Harwicke-Moore, in personality and circumstance, anticipates Blanche DuBois in *A Streetcar Named Desire*. As two social "derelicts" nurture each other's illusions of grandeur, Williams attacks the cruelty of individuals unsympathetic to the sensitivity of creative geniuses (*27 Wagons* 69). Like Blanche DuBois, who survives on "the kindness of strangers" when family members turn away, the Writer and alcoholic prostitute create their own survival rituals (Wolf 257–58).

Kolin (" 'Night, Mistuh Charlie' ") studies the theological implications behind the Negro porter in "The Last of My Solid Gold Watches." Mr. Charlie represents the dying Old South. Though separated by social prescriptions for behavior and attitude, two men from different sides of life participate in one historical moment to demonstrate a triumph of the human spirit.

Miss Lucretia Collins in "Portrait of a Madonna" is like Williams's other dynamic female fugitives—Blanche DuBois, Amanda Wingfield, Maggie the Cat, and the Lady of Larkspur Lotion (Spoto). Londré notes parallels between Miss Collins and Alma Winemiller in *Summer and Smoke* and Blanche DuBois in *A Streetcar Named Desire* (47). Director Hume Cronyn believes that Miss Lucretia Collins anticipates the more developed character of Alma Winemiller in *Summer and Smoke* rather than Blanche DuBois in *A Streetcar Named Desire*: "A lot of people feel that 'Portrait of a Madonna' is a sort of blueprint for *Streetcar*, which it is not. At least I don't believe it is so. . . . [T]he character of Miss Collins is really a lot closer to the character of Alma Winemiller in *Summer and Smoke*" (Steen 161). Boxill emphasizes the connection between Alma and Miss Lucretia (40), as does Wolf.

An abbreviated version of the Amanda/Tom relationship in *The Glass Menagerie* and the mother/son relationship in "Auto-Da-Fé," is plagued by misunderstanding and miscommunication. Prenshaw observes that Eloi "serves as scapegoat for the world's corruption by the flesh, and his auto-da-fé is an act of faith and redemption" (21).

Each character in "The Strangest Kind of Romance" suffers because of lost love or lovelessness. A woman who moves viciously against social grains, Bella lives for the moment and accepts her dependency on "the kindness of strangers" without self-pity or regret. Yet Bella is unable to compete with Nitchevo, the cat, who becomes "the other woman" mysteriously attracting Bella's men.

Wolf discusses the parallels between Joe Bassett in "The Long Goodbye" and Tom Wingfield in *The Glass Menagerie* (254–55). Neither Joe nor Tom is able to free himself from the guilt of feeling emotionally and psychologically responsible for the suffering and disappointments in family members' lives. The aging prostitute Bertha in "Hello from Bertha" struggles against time, death, and dying. Kolin maintains that "Bertha's plight approximates that of Blanche DuBois; in fact, 'Hello' suggests both the larger contours and the smaller details of *A Streetcar Named Desire*" (" 'Hello from Bertha' " 6). Boxill concludes that like "Portrait of a Madonna," "Hello from Bertha" depicts the final days of a Williams faded belle (46).

Alone and condemned by mainstream social standards—dirty, uneducated, morally loose—Willie, in "This Property Is Condemned," is one of Williams's youngest fugitives, the personification of America's cyclical physical and psychological sacrificing of its innocents. An adolescent female forced by social and family circumstances into a life of "tragic abandon" (*27 Wagons* 197) and not fully aware of or able to grasp the magnitude of her plight as an abandoned orphan being sexually abused by her deceased elder sister's grown johns, Willie—"a kind of child Blanche DuBois" (Boxill 50)—fashions her own survival physically and psychologically. While her physical survival in a condemned shack along the railroad tracks affords her shelter and even refuge from a social investigator, it is her imagination that enables her not to see her predicament self-pityingly as abnormal. Willie is convinced that her life and death can be as beautiful as she and Alva imagined. Even as she soothed her dying sister with myths of waiting gentlemen callers, Willie demonstrated a maturity beyond her years; she became her sister's protector and showed an understanding of the power of dreams and dreaming in making life and death more palatable. As she inherits her sister's lifestyle, she also inherits her sister's dreams. That both Alva and Willie are dreamers means that they do not allow themselves to become the bad elements that society would have them believe they are.

A young couple tries to find themselves amid the all-consuming forces of big-city living, personal longing, and mutual emotional neglect in "Talk to Me Like the Rain and Let Me Listen." As the nameless Man and Woman are confined to a small apartment in New York City, they realize the gravity of their personal alienation and isolation. Choices, temptations, economics, and ritual render them somnambulists retreating to the security of their own private worlds. The Man drinks to unconsciousness, and the Woman, implicitly a former drunk, sits, sips, and dreams. Even their desperate efforts to find themselves and each other through sexuality fail, rendering efforts at physical intimacy as impassioned choreographed performances. Londré maintains that the Man and the Woman are "rooted hopelessly in an unchanging present" (53).

More than "simply a sketch of the interplay of contrasted personalities" (Tischler 250), "Something Unspoken"—described by Williams as a "tragicomedy" and "an adventure in drama" (*Memoirs* 174–75)—offers a glimpse into the private performance rituals of two elderly women with an unnamed and unspoken, presumably lesbian, attraction. Cornelia Scott's need and willingness to articulate her romantic feelings for her younger female employee and longtime companion are repeatedly aborted by external circumstances that form an ironic backdrop to the socially dangerous would-be professions. While Grace Lancaster acknowledges her mutual feelings for Cornelia, their romantic bond is never vocalized. In this last play in the collection, Williams complicates an unspeakable social taboo. Not only is Cornelia and Grace's a presumably lesbian attraction, but it is an attraction between older women, stereotypically assumed to be without passion or desires for physical intimacy. Additionally, the women come from different worlds economically and socially. That they have found and sustained a fifteen-year unsanctioned intimacy amid the dangers of social exposure, expectation, tradition, and decorum is Williams's celebration. Dennis describes the play as "a dandy little one-act piece, demonstrating nicely Mr. Williams's understanding of the Southern gentlewoman" (138).

Symbols

These early plays are rich in Williams's symbols. Analyzing Williams's experimentations with form and symbolism in *27 Wagons Full of Cotton and Other One-Act Plays*, Falk maintains that symbolism was early on Williams's hallmark, a viable way for him to communicate with his audiences (31). Nature's rain at the end of "The Purification" brings with it an alleged cleansing of moral conscience and a move toward accepting the wildness and uncertainty that define human behavior and the human condition. Londré notes that like Lorca's plays of the 1930s, Williams's early plays use the symbols of water, moon, earth, blood, and "the horse as a symbol of masculinity" (41).

Actor Jessica Tandy adds that not only is Williams's attention to music in "Portrait of a Madonna" revealed in his ear for the lilting lyricism of southern speech but that he also celebrates music as a conscious part of his stage and set: "I am sure that there is music in [Williams's] head [when he writes] because there is a great deal of music in all of his plays. Music plays a great part in 'Portrait of a Madonna,' with those old, old records" (quoted in Steen 177). Boxill explicates Williams's ironic title, which associates the Roman Lucretia with the Virgin Mary (41).

In "Auto-Da-Fé," Mme. Duvenet's position—literally on the outside of the house and life looking in—symbolizes the futility of those unable to separate themselves from a world that is itself imperfect. Both "The Strangest Kind of Romance" and the story version "The Malediction" are laced with biblical imagery that further creates the mood of mystery and magic defining the characters' relationships with the cat. Londré identifies symbolism in the furnished room itself, the autographs on the wall, the windows, and seasonal changes (49).

According to Londré, the imagery in "Talk to Me Like the Rain and Let Me Listen" "is based on water" (53). Williams's use of water images in "Talk to Me Like the Rain"—the impending rain, the rain itself, the bathtub of ice cubes, and the woman's water drinking—reiterates the couple's need for spiritual and emotional awakening. While the restoring rain may be hope for the couple's survival, it might equally represent their entrapment in a city and circumstance that confine them to their small space.

Plot

Falk offers elementary summaries of the following plays in *27 Wagons Full of Cotton* (31–36): "This Property Is Condemned," "Hello from Bertha," "The Lady of Larkspur Lotion," "The Long Goodbye," "Lord Byron's Love Letter," "The Strangest Kind of Romance," "Auto-Da-Fé," "Portrait of a Madonna," "The Last of My Solid Gold Watches," "27 Wagons Full of Cotton," and "The Purification." Londré comments on the dramatic action and structure of "The Lady of Larkspur Lotion," which she sees as being indebted to Chekhov in its comic punchline (43).

Williams's "tragedy" subtitle for "Auto-Da-Fé" is ambiguous; Eloi's suicidal act is more likely one of selfishness than self-sacrifice. His tragedy, then, is his failure to realize the complexities of the human condition and of his own emotional needs and physical desires.

In "Lord Byron's Love Letter," the Spinster and the Old Woman engage in deceptions at the heart of the plot. They deceive their customers as breaks from their social isolation and for profit. In this instance, however, the women themselves are deceived by a husband unmoved by his wife's romanticized visions of Lord Byron. Described as "little more than a prolonged conversation between a domineering dowager and a browbeaten secretary," "Something Unspoken" is Williams's "trick . . . to create tension without action, and to give dramatic climax to a lifetime in half-an-hour's worth of his sensitively written dialogue" (Rev. of *Garden District*, *Newsweek* 84).

MAJOR PROBLEMS *27 WAGONS FULL OF COTTON AND OTHER ONE-ACT PLAYS* POSES FOR CRITICS

Falk recognizes the variety in *27 Wagons Full of Cotton and Other One-Act Plays* and the thematic variations of the one-act plays developed into longer works. Falk also notes that Williams displayed his talent to write well-crafted plots with pleasing dialogue, but also his "weakness—an artificial, more contrived style" (36).

CHIEF PRODUCTIONS

One reviewer describes "27 Wagons Full of Cotton" as "a brief but sharply etched episode of need, greed, cunning and cruelty, stupidity, spite and sadism in a Southern town. . . . This sketch, both laconic and evocative, reveals Williams in his incipient talent" (Rev. of "27 Wagons Full of Cotton," *Nation* 189).

Another reviewer says that "27 Wagons Full of Cotton"—with a plot that is "rowdy Erskine Caldwell with a crueler edge"—"reveals that for Tennessee Williams, life had dirty fingernails from the outset" (Rev. of "27 Wagons Full of Cotton," *Time* 78). In a review of the 1955 New York production, Bentley maintains: "['27 Wagons Full of Cotton'] is Williams at his best and worst: at his best in portraying another Southern girl . . . , at his worst in portraying the two men of the cast (they are merely ideas—and, of course, nasty ideas). . . . At the Playhouse, the mention of flagellation produces knowing chuckles, delighted gurgles, and even outright belly laughs. . . . The play had been tried out in New Orleans and found by many too repulsive" (22). Gill maintains that the play "shows a youthful Williams in an impish mood; he is telling a tall tale—actually, it is a subspecies of the traveling-salesman joke—and his and our delight come from the telling and not from the tale" (78). The narrator in his introduction to the 1989 televised version warns that because of "its adult themes, the play may be unsuitable for family viewing."

"The Purification" was presented in Dallas, Texas, in 1954 and later produced as a ballet in Westport, Connecticut, in 1957. Commenting on the Dallas production, under the directorship of Margo Jones, Brooks Atkinson concluded, "The play was 'staged as if it were a religious ritual by Margo Jones in her best form and it is acted with grace and devoutness by a company inspired by what they are playing.' "

"Something Unspoken" was produced in New York and London in 1958. "The Lady of Larkspur Lotion" was produced in New York in 1947 and in London in 1968. "The Last of My Solid Gold Watches" was staged in Los Angeles in 1946 and in New York in 1958. "Portrait of a Madonna" was produced in Los Angeles in 1946 and in New York in 1959. "Auto-Da-Fé" was produced in New York in 1947, in Bromley, Kent, in 1961, and in London in 1979. "Lord Byron's Love Letter" was produced in New York in 1947 and directed by Raffaello de Banfield as an opera in New Orleans in 1955. "The Strangest Kind of Romance" was produced in London in 1969. "The Long Goodbye" was produced in New York in 1940. "Hello from Bertha" was staged in Bromley, Kent, in 1961. "This Property Is Condemned" was produced in New York in 1946, in London in 1948, and was performed as a ballet in 1957. "Talk to Me Like the Rain" was presented in Westport, Connecticut, in 1958, in New York in 1962, and in London in 1978. Director Hume Cronyn lamented that few of Williams's one-act plays reached the early commercial stage: "It's a matter of eternal shame and regret that those . . . one-act plays which were written by Tennessee and all of which, I think, finally comprised the *27 Wagons Full of Cotton* collection were plays that I never managed to get on the stage [in the 1930s]. . . . It's difficult to persuade people to invest in a bill of one-acts" (Steen 159).

FILM AND TELEVISION VERSIONS

Several of the one-act plays in *27 Wagons* have been televised, including "Portrait of a Madonna" in 1948 and "Lord Byron's Love Letter" in 1953.

Williams's screenplay *Baby Doll* (released and published in 1956) uses details in character and situation from the early one-act plays "27 Wagons Full of Cotton," which itself was televised in 1989, and "The Long Stay Cut Short, or, The Unsatisfactory Supper," included in *American Blues* (published in 1948). Kahn (292–309) and Goff in his chapter on Tennessee Williams films in this volume supply relevant information on *Baby Doll*.

In 1966, "This Property Is Condemned" was made into a film starring Natalie Wood and Robert Redford. Yacowar compares the play and the film and posits that such bold liberties are taken in the extended film version that the play seems but a loose suggestion (113–21). Londré describes this film version as "a critical failure" (52).

CONCLUDING OVERVIEW

In his introduction to *27 Wagons Full of Cotton and Other One-Act Plays*, Williams defends his position that responsible theatre has an obligation to make noise, to stir up things long neglected or purposely left dormant. His comments reiterate his commitment to creating theatre that interrogates social ideals and provokes audiences beyond their comfortable social and individual expectations. Although not thematically connected in terms of the ordering of the plays in the collection, *27 Wagons*—described by Falk as "increasingly devious personal expressions" (31)—is social commentary that tellingly solicits compassion and understanding for Williams's championed fugitives. While some of the plays in the volume may seem like self-serving efforts on Williams's part to exorcise deep-seated personal issues—"The Purification," "The Last of My Solid Gold Watches," "Auto-Da-Fé," "The Long Goodbye," and "Something Unspoken"—others appear to be his personal pleas for those like himself trapped in the contradictions of loving and living—"27 Wagons Full of Cotton," "The Lady of Larkspur Lotion," "Portrait of a Madonna," "Lord Byron's Love Letter," "The Strangest Kind of Romance," "Hello from Bertha," "This Property Is Condemned," and "Talk to Me Like the Rain."

In addition to their value as psychic biography or impassioned social criticism, the plays in *27 Wagons* show the promise and the genius of the young Williams. Whether they represent an experiment in the verse form of Lorca, the mirrored performance of a visual art piece by Hopper, subverted Christian ideology, or a challenge to the myth of faded southern belles, these early plays are "essential and seminal works" (Boxill 60). Falk adds that the early plays in *27 Wagons* "justify the enthusiastic support given the playwright" (36). Hale describes Williams's one-act plays as "gems of characterization, compassionate, observant, funny and sad," adding that "these one-acts would never go out of repertory" (26). Speaking specifically about "Portrait of a Madonna," Jessica Tandy perceptively assessed the overall achievement of this early volume: " 'Madonna' is really a superb play. It's got everything in it. It's a perfect little jewel of a play. A lot of Tennessee's one-act ones are. He really mastered the one-act play" (Steen 178).

WORKS CITED

Atkinson, Brooks. "The Purification." *New York Times* 29 May 1954.

Bentley, Eric. "Theatre." *New Republic* 2 May 1955: 22.

Boxill, Roger. *Tennessee Williams.* New York: St. Martin's, 1987.

Corrigan, Mary Ann. "Beyond Verisimilitude: Echoes of Expressionism in Williams's Plays." *Tennessee Williams: A Tribute.* Ed. Jac Tharpe. Jackson: UP of Mississippi, 1977. 375–412.

Crandell, George. *Tennessee Williams: A Descriptive Bibliography.* Pittsburgh: U of Pittsburgh P, 1995.

Dennis, Patrick. "Theatre: Tennessee off Broadway." *New Republic* 27 Jan. 1958: 20.

Draya, Ren. "The Fiction of Tennessee Williams." *Tennessee Williams: A Tribute.* Ed. Jac Tharpe. Jackson: UP of Mississippi, 1977. 647–62.

Eaton, W. P. *New York Times Book Review* 24 Feb. 1946: 8.

Falk, Signi Lenea. *Tennessee Williams.* New York: Twayne, 1962.

Rev. of *Garden District. Catholic World* Mar. 1958: 469–70.

Rev. of *Garden District. Newsweek* 20 Jan. 1958: 84.

Rev. of *Garden District. Time* 20 Jan. 1958: 42.

Gill, Brendan. "The Theatre: Two Fly into the Phoenix's Nest." *New Yorker* 9 Feb. 1976: 78.

Hale, Allean. "Early Williams: The Making of a Playwright." *The Cambridge Companion to Tennessee Williams.* Ed. Matthew C. Roudané. Cambridge: Cambridge UP, 1997. 11–28.

Kahn, Sy. "*Baby Doll*: A Comic Fable." *Tennessee Williams: A Tribute.* Ed. Tharpe Jackson: UP of Mississippi, 1977. 292–309.

Kolin, Philip C. " 'Hello from Bertha' as a Source for *A Streetcar Named Desire."* *Notes on Contemporary Literature* 27 (Jan. 1997): 6–7.

———. " 'Night, Mistuh Charlie': The Porter in Tennessee Williams's 'The Last of My Solid Gold Watches' and the Kairos of Negritude." *Mississippi Quarterly* 47 (Spring 1994): 215–220.

Krutch, Joseph Wood. *New York Herald Tribune Weekly Book Review* 19 May 1946: 24.

Leverich, Lyle. *Tom: The Unknown Tennessee Williams.* New York: Crown, 1995.

Londré, Felicia Hardison. *Tennessee Williams.* New York: Ungar, 1979.

Nelson, Benjamin. *Tennessee Williams: The Man and His Work.* New York: Obolensky, 1961.

Prenshaw, Peggy W. "The Paradoxical Southern World of Tennessee Williams." *Tennessee Williams: A Tribute.* Ed. Jac Tharpe. Jackson: UP of Mississippi, 1977. 5–29.

Scheick, William J. " 'An Intercourse Not Well Designed': Talk and Touch in the Plays of Tennessee Williams." *Tennessee Williams: A Tribute.* Ed. Jac Tharpe. Jackson: UP of Mississippi, 1977. 763–73.

Spoto, Donald. *The Kindness of Strangers: The Life of Tennessee Williams.* Boston: Little, Brown, 1985.

Steen, Mike. *A Look at Tennessee Williams.* New York: Hawthorn, 1969.

Tischler, Nancy. *Tennessee Williams: Rebellious Puritan.* New York: Citadel, 1961.

Rev. of "27 Wagons Full of Cotton." *Nation* 222 (14 Feb. 1976): 189–90.

Rev. of "27 Wagons Full of Cotton." *New Yorker* 30 Apr. 1955: 69–71.

Rev. of "27 Wagons Full of Cotton." *Time* 2 May 1955: 78.

Vidal, Gore. *Tennessee Williams: Collected Stories*. New York: New Directions, 1985.

Williams, Tennessee. *Eight Mortal Ladies Possessed*. New York: New Directions, 1974.

———. *The Script for the Film Baby Doll*. New York: NAL, 1956.

———. *Memoirs*. New York: Doubleday, 1975.

———. *27 Wagons Full of Cotton*. Televised production. Arts and Entertainment Network, 1989.

———. *27 Wagons Full of Cotton and Other One-Act Plays*. New York: New Directions, 1945.

Wolf, Morris Philip. "Casanova's Portmanteau: *Camino Real* and Recurring Communication Patterns of Tennessee Williams." *Tennessee Williams: A Tribute*. Ed. Jac Tharpe. Jackson: UP of Mississippi, 1977. 252–76.

Yacowar, Maurice. *Tennessee Williams and Film*. New York: Ungar, 1977.

Zolotow, Maurice. "The Season on and off Broadway: All in One." *Theatre Arts* 39 (July 1955): 22–23, 93.

American Blues

NEAL A. LESTER

BIOGRAPHICAL CONTEXT

Tennessee Williams's self-identification as a "fugitive" helps to explain his stead-fast commitment to writing about characters on the other side of the social and moral tracks. Demonstrating his "obsession with the pariah theme" (Tischler 87) and daring to present in their rawest forms the lives of individuals trapped and defined by less than desirable circumstances, the one-act plays in *American Blues* (1948), like Williams's full-length plays, celebrate the complexities of the human condition. Winning a one-act-play contest and $100 award from the New York Theatre Guild in 1939 for three plays—"Moony's Kid Don't Cry," "The Dark Room," and "The Case of the Crushed Petunias," collected as *American Blues* and expanded in 1948 to include two other plays, "The Long Stay Cut Short, or, The Unsatisfactory Supper" and "Ten Blocks on the Camino Real"—first brought Williams to the attention of New York agent Audrey Wood and launched his dynamic career on the American stage (Leverich 306). Williams admits a kind of self-plagiarizing: "My longer plays emerge out of earlier one-acters and short stories. . . . I work them over and over again" (quoted in Cohn 45).

Williams wrote "The Long Stay Cut Short, or, The Unsatisfactory Supper"—his "favorite one-act play" (*Memoirs* 99)—when his health was failing and while he was living a relatively plush life in the New Orleans' Garden District. The character Aunt Rose may be based on Williams's sister Rose, who was emotion-ally and psychologically "abandoned" by the family because of her alleged mental imbalance. Williams's sympathetic portrait of Aunt Rose parallels his own sympathy for the sister with whom he felt a special kinship and shared a profound spiritual connection. "Ten Blocks on the Camino Real: A Fantasy" was written while Williams was convalescing (Falk 31). Spoto, who calls "Moony's Kid Don't Cry" a "family melodrama" (33), suggests that Williams's play may have been "inspired" by August Strindberg's "The Stronger" and/or by Eugene O'Neill's *Before Breakfast* (33). Hayman and Leverich offer brief biographical commentary on *American Blues*. Hale sketches in many relevant biographical details about Williams's early plays.

BIBLIOGRAPHIC HISTORY

Berney's *Contemporary Dramatists* includes publication and production dates for these one-act plays (848–51). "Moony's Kid Don't Cry," written in May 1930, produced in 1932, and first published in 1940, was originally titled "Hot Milk at Three in the Morning" (Spoto 33), and identified as a "kitchen sink" drama popularized thirty-five years later by John Osborne (Hale 14). "Moony's Kid Don't Cry" is included in *The Best One-Act Plays of 1940*.

Williams wrote "The Dark Room" as a short story in 1940 before it was published in play form in 1948; the narrative, which appears for the first time in *Collected Stories* (93–98), is full of dialogue and makes its way to play form smoothly. Both versions have nearly identical lines, though there are minor textual changes. Londré notes parallels thematically and structurally between "The Dark Room" and *Suddenly Last Summer* and emphasizes how past ghosts haunt the present in both works (40).

The extended version of "Ten Blocks on the Camino Real" uses ideas from two other one-acts, "The Purification" and "Lord Byron's Love Letter," both published in *27 Wagons Full of Cotton and Other One-Act Plays* (1945). Williams's Foreword to the longer play *Camino Real*—written before the Broadway premiere of the play and published in the *New York Times* on 15 March 1953—has become a much-anthologized defense of his artistic and creative energies (Meserve 138–40; Cole 277–81).

Some of the one-act plays in *American Blues* have been televised, anthologized, included in Margaret Mayorga's *Best One-Act Plays* series, expanded, revised, regrouped, and republished. Crandell documents editions and printing history of *American Blues* (56–59).

MAJOR CRITICAL APPROACHES

Themes

The one-act plays collected in *American Blues* focus thematically on the circumstances of survival against a multitude of racial, gender, economic, social, and personal odds. Williams described *American Blues* as "plays as close to social consciousness as any" he ever wrote (quoted in Gould 236). Specifically,

"Moony's Kid Don't Cry" and "The Case of the Crushed Petunias" "reflect the influence of the social action plays of the 1930s" that criticized "the factory and the city, . . . the plight of the working class[,] and the dehumanizing conditions of modern life" (Corrigan 387). Londré recognizes in "Moony's Kid Don't Cry" that the chief theme is that of the artist (or dreamer) at the mercy of the impersonal metropolis (38).

"The Dark Room," which shows an unsympathetic social worker's indifference to an immigrant Italian-American family, attacks American capitalism and its power to reduce human lives to someone else's simplest terms. Williams questions a society of individuals without moral integrity who are privileged to make decisions and determinations about others' lives. A critique of the American Dream as it relates to family and aging, "The Long Stay Cut Short, or, The Unsatisfactory Supper" attacks negative social perceptions of aging and shows the callousness and self-absorption of youth. Tensions between Archie Lee and Baby Doll arise from their resentment at having to care for the aging Aunt Rose, whom they see as a costly burden. Tischler comments that the almost poetic treatment of Aunt Rose, who, comforted by her Christian faith, walks into the threatening storm, achieves a "characteristic Williams . . . mingl[ing] of a fragile and sweet poignancy with a biting cruelty" (221).

"Ten Blocks on the Camino Real" is a metaphorical dissection of the American Dream of a single communal society to show that this alleged ideal is full of disappointments, pretense, alienation, and unrealized selfhood. Structured as an all-American Everyman's epic journey toward spiritual self-destruction, this early one-act play critiques American capitalism and a society of individuals ruled by the fortunate few who are financially and hence socially endowed.

Characters

American Blues presents a gallery of characters struggling against the obstacles that impede their peaceful spiritual existence. Williams highlights their struggle as his own efforts to make his life an American ideal. From his own battles with drugs, poverty, and self-validation (see Leverich), Williams emerges as a champion of "little people" or the "fugitive kind"—those "strange, crazed, queer, damned, brilliant and deformed. Lovely misfits" threatened by the circumstances of surviving a malevolent earth ready to "destroy her crooked child" (Nelson 196–97). Jackson reiterates Williams's recurring attention to the lives of characters with unraveling threads connecting them to human understanding and compassion (134). Nelson asserts that "Williams's characters in the one-acts struggle for freedom in the face of hopeless odds" (40).

In "Moony's Kid Don't Cry," Moony and Jane's survival comes in their shared revelries of past moments when life was fresh and ideals were clear. For Jane, whom Londré describes as "a frail, sickly creature" (39) and Wolf sees as "romantically retrospective" (261), certain satisfaction comes in her maternal nurturing, "mocking" (Londré 39), and even chastising of Moony, who throughout the play demonstrates a childlike restlessness and a need for instant gratification and self-validation. Wolf notes that Moony's personality and masculine strength parallel Stanley Kowalski's in *A Streetcar Named Desire*: "Moony [as a] young, strong workman[,] shares many physical qualities with Stanley . . . : pride in bodily prowess; a conqueror's attitude toward women; energetic awareness of his would-be independence" (264). Londré also points out connections between Moony and the muscular Stanley Kowalski and the romantic Tom Wingfield in *The Glass Menagerie* (39). Matthew contends that Moony is victimized by "an inevitably self-inflicted fate" as he tries and fails to "escape the morass of the self-satisfied middle class" (179). Hale claims that Williams was influenced by O'Neill and D. H. Lawrence in creating Moony (14–15).

In "The Dark Room," the Pocciottis embody Miss Morgan's stereotyping of those who are not from her self-perceived "all-American stock." Unwilling to accept personal responsibility for the ways and actions of others, even her own family members, Mrs. Pocciotti, who is validated in Williams's eyes because she admits and accepts the reality of life's unanswerables, accepts her predicament with dignity, passing judgment on no one and holding no one responsible for her circumstances. Falk concludes that Williams deftly incorporates the "verbal conflicts between [Miss Morgan and Mrs. Pocciotti] with considerable humor" (30).

Dorothy Simple, the heroine in "The Case of the Crushed Petunias," is initially restricted from living a fulfilled life because of her entrepreneurial position in her morally upright and culturally stagnant community of Primanproper, Massachusetts. Dorothy's cherished petunias afford her an opportunity to flirt with unbridled passion and to accept life's myriad uncertainties. According to Londré, "Dorothy Simple becomes what Williams once called himself—a rebellious puritan" (41). Falk describes Aunt Rose of "The Long Stay Cut Short, or, The Unsatisfactory Supper" as "a tragic figure . . . [with] childlike religious faith" (30).

At each stop along their journey toward spiritual self-realization in "Ten Blocks on the Camino Real," Kilroy and the other characters move closer to spiritual drought as symbolized in the "dried-up fountain" (*American Blues* 43). With each block or station, Kilroy is given an opportunity to realize his spiritual waywardness, his worldly seduction by a vainglorious boxing past. Yet with no one to identify him (*American Blues* 73), Kilroy, before and even after death, becomes Everyman who loses his soul in worldly pursuits.

Symbols

The chief symbol in "Moony's Kid Don't Cry" is the child who, despite the fact that the unplanned pregnancy "forced" Moony and Jane to marry, validates the couple spiritually, reminds them of happier times, and gives them hope for still happier times. Wolf contends that Moony's "pride of fatherhood, nourishing his vanity, blocks the temptation" (264) to abandon his family in pursuit of his own selfish dream. Matthew believes that the child, conceived during a time of

Moony's adult malehood freedom, is also part of Moony's subsequent enslavement (179). Matthew reads phallic symbolism in Moony's lumberjack desire to "swing [his] axe . . . throughout the world" (*American Blues* 11). Another key symbol, the rocking horse, is for Moony an illusion of his manhood and his ability to give his child a piece of the world. The moving yet stationary horse also comments on Moony's futile efforts to construct a clear masculine self-identity.

Prevalent symbols in "The Case of the Crushed Petunias" concentrate on heterosexual intercourse as a metaphor for life and living. As the allegorical Dorothy Simple proves that her frustrated existence is anything but simple, her experiences are revealed in sexual terms. For Dorothy, life unfulfilled equals death; hence, "hellbent for heaven, she searches for a dynamic male and new adventure" (Wolf 257). The dominant symbol of crushed petunias assumes gender-specific connotations of man as crusher and woman as crushed. Though suggestive of a phallocentric approach to life and living, the symbol does signal Dorothy Simple's acceptance and liberation of self.

Gascoigne points out that the abbreviated title, *Camino Real*, of the extended version of "Ten Blocks on the Camino Real" means royal roadway in Spanish, and he notes that "the play's action takes place at the point where the roadway of life changes from royal to real" (170) for Kilroy and the other characters who meet with various misfortunes. In addition to the journey motif, the other central symbol is the dry fountain that represents the characters' spiritual drought. Finally, the characters' physical sicknesses symbolize their spiritual sicknesses also.

Plot

Falk offers perfunctory summaries of each play in *American Blues* (30–31). Londré adds interpretive details on "Moony's Kid Don't Cry," "The Dark Room," and "The Case of the Crushed Petunias" (38–41). While *American Blues* foregrounds individuals in conflict with society, many of the one-act plays display Williams's free experimentation with various dramatic structures, experimentation that was less possible commercially and economically in his longer works. Through his early one act plays Williams experimented with a variety of dramatic techniques and an artistic freedom that was censored by a larger mainstream audience.

In "Moony's Kid Don't Cry," a young couple see themselves as stagnant and restless. The plot reflects that their lives fall short of the American Dream. Spoto adds that "the [play] is strident and expresses the motif of emotional confinement that would emerge in all his great full-length plays" (33). Londré sees "The Dark Room" as "the least successful piece of dramatic writing" in *American Blues*, insisting that "the characters are lifeless and the conclusion is limp" (40).

Described as "an experiment in comedy . . . and perhaps parody" (Falk 31), and subtitled a "lyrical fantasy" by Williams himself, "The Case of the Crushed Petunias" is an allegory that unravels much like a detective story. The mystery solved early in the play—the culprit who crushed the petunias—is less important than the mystery of life that Dorothy comes to accept as the essence of existence. Londré contends that "The Case of the Crushed Petunias" is different from the other plays in *American Blues* because of its "gentle humor" (40).

Commenting on the structure of "Ten Blocks on the Camino Real" as a dream to help explain its action as well as its prevailing themes and symbols, Tischler provides one of the most helpful examinations of the longer play, offering background on Williams's desolate Mexico living during its writing and concluding that Williams considered *Camino Real* "a purgation for his despair" (182). Falk maintains that the play demonstrates Williams's "literary posturing" that appears in his later works (31).

MAJOR PROBLEMS *AMERICAN BLUES* POSES FOR CRITICS

Speaking about the Williams canon up to 1961, Nancy Tischler observed, "Williams critics have never been quite comfortable with the poetic tone in his work" (179). That "poeticizing" started with the early plays, especially in the "juvenilia" (Londré 40) of *American Blues*. The problems later critics found in the longer plays based upon the shorter ones in *American Blues* come back to haunt Williams's earlier works. Using the same dramatic action and forms of the one-act "Ten Blocks on the Camino Real" (1948), Williams's *Camino Real* was pronounced a failure by many critics. Alluding to the earlier "Ten Blocks," Hayes called *Camino Real* a "dramatic abortion . . . another tragic illustration of the malign state of our present cultural climate" (52).

Perhaps, though, the biggest problem these plays present to the critics is that they too often get lost in the shadows of the longer works and are not judged fairly on their own terms. Audrey Wood's injunction to Williams about "Ten Blocks on the Camino Real"—"Do not let anybody else see it" (quoted in *Memoirs* 10)—sadly relates to many of the other plays in *American Blues* as far as the critics are concerned.

CHIEF PRODUCTIONS

The production history of the one-act plays in *American Blues* is not extensive. Gunn records major productions of Williams's plays. The social and critical acclaim of Williams's great Broadway successes (and not a few misses) repeatedly kept him from doing more with his one-act plays. "The Dark Room" was produced in London in 1966, and "The Case of the Crushed Petunias" was staged in Cleveland in 1957, in New York in 1958, and in Glasgow in 1968. Williams's *Camino Real*, which premiered on Broadway in 1953, was a "radical reworking" (Davis 197) and expanded version of "Ten Blocks on the Camino Real." In his *Memoirs*, Williams discusses revising the one-act play into the longer play and also comments at length on the hostile reception of the Broadway production (165–67).

FILM AND TELEVISION VERSIONS

"The Long Stay Cut Short" was incorporated into Williams's film *Baby Doll* in 1956 (see the chapter on Williams's films by David Goff). Londré points out that on 16 April 1958, "Moony's Kid" was shown on NBC TV's "Kraft Theatre" along with "This Property Is Condemned" and "The Last of My Solid Gold Watches" (39).

CONCLUDING OVERVIEW

Playwright Horton Foote said that Tennessee Williams's one-act plays were "some of the most effective theater [he] had ever seen" (Foote xi). Williams communicates in *American Blues* an implicit identification of his characters with the spiritual plights of oppressed black people in American history, a history of disappointment, denial, and social, political, and economic neglect. Tellingly, the plays in *American Blues* connect with nineteenth- and twentieth-century American folk-song traditions—spirituals, slave songs, work songs, and the blues—that dissect the American Dream by celebrating the struggles of those teetering on life's edge. A response to social injustices politically, morally, and economically, the collection itself is a kind of blues rendition wherein personal testimonials become communal experiences, and liberation for the characters— at least for Moony and Jane, Mrs. Pocciotti, Aunt Rose, and Dorothy Simple— and the audience is achieved through the telling or singing of their stories of survival. Deconstructing American ideals, Williams demonstrates the deceptive nature of the American Dream for all in pursuit of it. He foregrounds in this volume his version of American blues and the resilience of those who refuse to stop gazing at the stars.

A celebration of the common folk whose lives are subject to public disapproval and pity, each play in *American Blues* is a note in a blues tune. In "Moony's Kid Don't Cry," Moony can stop crying for the moment as he loses himself in the world of possibilities for his infant son. In "The Dark Room," Mrs. Pocciotti refuses to let the judgmental Miss Morgan define her existence and the truths in her life although the Pocciotti family may be disintegrating around her. Conversely, Dorothy Simple, in "The Case of the Crushed Petunias," is not denied material wants; it is her materialism and the social prescriptions that come with it that restrict her living. Hers is a song of rejuvenation and rebirth that comes after bemoaning gender and class restrictions in her life. That her behavior may bring about undesirable consequences may cause her to sing the blues again, but at the play's end she is willing to accept life on its own unpredictable and exciting terms. "Ten Blocks on the Camino Real" allows Williams the artist and self-identified fugitive to lament the spiritual loss of individuals, who, like the unconverted Dorothy Simple, are controlled by the entanglement of fortune and fame. While Kilroy does not emerge from his journey with any sense of spiritual identity, Williams nonetheless contends that individual spiritual peace is possible for those willing to establish community with others unconditionally.

WORKS CITED

Berney, K. A., ed. *Contemporary Dramatists*. 5th ed. London: St. James, 1993.

Cohn, Ruby. "The Garrulous Grotesques of Tennessee Williams." *Tennessee Williams: A Collection of Critical Essays*. Ed. Stephen S. Stanton. Englewood Cliffs, NJ: Prentice-Hall, 1977.

Cole, Toby. *Playwrights on Playwriting*. New York: Hill and Wang, 1960.

Corrigan, Mary Ann. "Beyond Verisimilitude: Echoes of Expressionism in Williams's Plays." *Tennessee Williams: A Tribute*. Ed. Jac Tharpe. Jackson: UP of Mississippi, 1977. 375–412.

Crandell, George. *Tennessee Williams: A Descriptive Bibliography*. Pittsburgh: U of Pittsburgh P, 1995.

Davis, Joseph K. "Landscapes of the Dislocated Mind in Williams' *The Glass Menagerie*." *Tennessee Williams: A Tribute*. Ed. Jac Tharpe. Jackson: UP of Mississippi, 1977. 192–206.

Falk, Signi Lenea. *Tennessee Williams*. New York: Twayne, 1962.

Foote, Horton. "Author's Preface." *Selected One-Act Plays of Horton Foote*. Ed. Gerald C. Wood. Dallas: Southern Methodist UP, 1989. ix–xi.

Gascoigne, Bamber. *Twentieth-Century Drama*. New York: Barnes and Noble, 1966.

Gould, Jean. *Modern American Playwrights*. New York: Dodd, Mead, 1966.

Gunn, Drewey Wayne. *Tennessee Williams: A Bibliography*. 2nd ed. Metuchen, NJ: Scarecrow, 1991.

Hale, Allean. "Early Williams: The Making of a Playwright." *The Cambridge Companion to Tennessee Williams*. Ed. Matthew C. Roudané. Cambridge: Cambridge UP, 1997. 11–28.

Hayes, Richard. "The Stage." *Commonweal* 17 Apr. 1953: 51–52.

Hayman, Ronald. *Tennessee Williams: Everyone Else Is an Audience*. New Haven: Yale UP, 1993.

Jackson, Esther Merle. *The Broken World of Tennessee Williams*. Madison: U of Wisconsin P, 1965.

Leverich, Lyle. *Tom: The Unknown Tennessee Williams*. New York: Crown, 1995.

Londré, Felicia Hardison. *Tennessee Williams*. New York: Ungar, 1979.

Matthew, David C. C. " 'Towards Bethlehem': *Battle of Angels* and *Orpheus Descending*." *Tennessee Williams: A Tribute*. Ed. Jac Tharpe. Jackson: UP of Mississippi, 1977. 172–91.

Meserve, Walter, ed. *Discussions of Modern American Drama*. Boston: Heath, 1965.

Nelson, Benjamin. *Tennessee Williams: The Man and His Work*. New York: Obolensky, 1961.

Spoto, Donald. *The Kindness of Strangers: The Life of Tennessee Williams*. Boston: Little, Brown, 1985.

Tischler, Nancy. *Tennessee Williams: Rebellious Puritan*. New York: Citadel, 1961.

Vidal, Gore. Introduction. Tennessee Williams. *Collected Stories*. New York: New Directions, 1985.

Williams, Tennessee. *American Blues*. New York: Dramatists Play Service, 1976.

————. *Collected Stories.* New York: New Directions, 1985.

————. *Memoirs.* Garden City, NY: Doubleday, 1975.

Wolf, Morris Philip. "Casanova's Portmanteau: *Camino Real* and Recurring Communication Patterns of Tennessee Williams." *Tennessee Williams: A Tribute.* Ed. Jac Tharpe. Jackson: UP of Mississippi, 1977.

Battle of Angels and Orpheus Descending

ROBERT BRAY

BIOGRAPHICAL CONTEXT

Tennessee Williams's first major production, *Battle of Angels*, was a calamitous debut for the playwright yet to turn thirty. The haphazard decision to move the opening from New Haven to Boston in December of 1940 left Williams faced with a priggish audience unprepared to entertain his juxtaposition of sexual and religious themes. The play ran for less than two weeks, closing after backstage feuds and sloppy staging. Yet Williams did not give up; he would continue reworking the play for thirty-five years. In 1957, Williams wrote of his "new" play, *Orpheus Descending*, "I have never quit working on this one, not even now" (*Orpheus* ix). Despite the similarities between the two plays, Williams affirmed that "about 75 per cent of it" was new (ix). He obviously intended *Orpheus* to be viewed as being somewhat independent from its ill-fated predecessor.

In constructing *Battle/Orpheus*, Williams returned to the landscape of his early youth—Clarksdale, in the northern Mississippi Delta. He set some of his work outside of the Delta (most notably in New Orleans), but as with Faulkner's Oxford, Clarksdale and the surrounding environs remained the imaginative locus of much of Williams's writing. As Williams wrote of *Battle of Angels*, "The stage or setting . . . was the country of my childhood. Onto it I projected the violent symbols of my adolescence" (quoted in Leverich, *Tom* 383). Although one can only speculate about the specific cultural "symbols," the preponderance of violence in *Battle/Orpheus* most probably referred to racial injustices that would have been disturbing to the impressionable Tom. As he said in a 1968 interview, the closest he came to "writing directly" was in *Orpheus*, where he expressed his views about the South (Devlin 128). Williams's early and subsequent years spent in the South created in him an ambivalence that he was never able to resolve fully. On the one hand, Two River County, the setting for *Battle/Orpheus*, became, according to Roger Boxill, a reflection of Williams's "elegiac sensitivity" (168) as well as a barometer of the South's violence, xenophobia, and racism. As C. W. E. Bigsby notes, although Williams did not portray an abundance of African-American characters, "he made clear his contempt for the racist" and associated "bigotry with sterility and death" (37).

Like Faulkner, Williams was an expert listener, and the voices of his early youth reemerged in *Battle/Orpheus* as well as in his numerous short stories set in the Delta. As his brother Dakin remembers, "He was always listening to those stories. He had big ears, and that's what people did . . . they sat on verandahs and told stories" (Bray, "Interview" 781). It is unlikely that young Tom ever heard a story about Val Xavier, a mysterious snakeskin-clad drifter, or about a fallen aristocrat named Cassandra, though he certainly knew the Cutreres, whose mansion was close to his grandfather's church in Clarksdale. As Leverich notes, "It was seldom that anything he wrote grew directly out of an experience. . . . The *impressions* of things past, more than his re-creation of events, were what prompted him to write" (*Tom* 447). With *Battle/Orpheus*, then, Williams re-creates "myths in the context of our own time"—the Mississippi Delta of the 1940s (Traubitz 57). The first volume of Leverich's monumental biography examines *Battle* (*Tom* 381–86), and the second volume focuses on the relative success of *Orpheus*, testifying to the lasting power of these works and to Williams's belief in their centrality in his life.

BIBLIOGRAPHIC HISTORY

As with so many of Williams's apparently "finished products," his plays exist in a variety of forms. Williams's earliest title for *Battle of Angels* was *Opus V— Written on Subways* (fall 1939), the writing of which he called "terrifically wasteful" (Leverich, *Tom* 330). A later provisional title was *Shadow of My Passion*, and though it was but a rough draft, the nascent play's focus was very clear: "I have only one major theme for all my work which is the destructive impact of society on the sensitive, nonconformist individual" (Leverich, *Tom* 333). According to Allean Hale, other trial titles included *The Memory of an Orchard*, *The Snakeskin Jacket*, and *Something Wild in the Country* ("Early Williams" 21). *Battle* was first published in *Pharos* in 1945 and included Williams's essay "The History of a Play." George Crandell's bibliography offers detailed information on the printings and editions of *Battle* and *Orpheus* (166–75).

Although *Orpheus* is similar to *Battle* in setting, plot, and character, Williams's revisions and rewrites resulted in significant changes; in "the later version he submerges . . . discursive content in his mythic structure" (Jackson 145). Significantly, the title change points to "Greek mythological materials" in *Orpheus* (Londré 63). *Orpheus* dispenses with *Battle*'s epilogue and also merges the prologue with the present action, establishing a greater sense of immediacy at the start of *Orpheus*.

A significant bibliographic difference in plot between *Battle* and *Orpheus* occurs in what might be called the "Jonathan West" version. In 1946, Williams expanded the civil rights confrontation between Val and the Sheriff into a new scene. In this version, Val arrives in Two River County. He finds a man named Jonathan West, whom he had met five years earlier. Here Val learns that West, a black socialist preacher, has been killed by the Klan and that West's church has been transformed into Jabe's store. As it turns out, the Conjure Man has memorized all of West's sermons, so Val plans to study them and "spread the gospel of racial brotherhood" (Wallace 327). These different versions add up to a play that is "as sharply political as anything Williams had written since his days with the Mummers in St. Louis" (Bigsby 60). Tischler (*Tennessee Williams* 233–40) and Thompson (95–98), among others, discuss differences in the plots between the two plays, but Matthew provides the most thorough comparison of the two versions.

MAJOR CRITICAL APPROACHES

Themes

Critics readily acknowledge *Orpheus*'s seminal significance in the Williams canon because it contains so many reemerging themes. For example, Costello theorizes that *Battle/Orpheus* serves as a "compendium of all of Williams's favorite images, thematic concerns, and dramatic devices" (quoted in Londré 55). Thompson sees the play as an early "repository of images, symbols, themes, place names" that would further unfold throughout Williams's career (96). Adler similarly finds that "the play introduces virtually all of the motifs that become central in the Williams canon" and goes on to list some ten themes, among them a "romantic valorization of the poetic misfit"; the diminution of the artist; the importance of dreams in sterile existences; repressed sexuality and "the redemptive power of sexual love"; the necessity to communicate; and the need to counterbalance masculine power with the feminine and humane (*American Drama* 132).

Critics frequently comment on *Orpheus*'s mythic dimensions. Traubitz distinguishes five mythic loci: "the loss of Eden, the battle of angels, Christ, Orpheus, and Adonis" (57). According to King, these myths demonstrate Williams's "Manichaean vision" in the struggle between the powers of "light and darkness" (19). Bigsby further notes that *Orpheus* "is Williams's version of the myth of Sisyphus" (61). Thompson is especially helpful in cataloguing the myths upon which Williams drew.

Characters

As Jackson observes, Williams expanded characters from his earlier work *Battle* in *Orpheus*. The major characters in *Battle/Orpheus* are quintessential Williams misfits. Most suffer from loneliness and society's unwillingness to understand them. Unrequited love, a sense of loss, regret, and castigation burden their psyches. They battle with a poetic imagination coupled with the conviction of their dreams. Equally revealing in *Battle/Orpheus* are the many faces of the author. Hale finds that with *Battle* "Williams first uses his hallmark technique of splitting the authorial self into several characters." She concludes that these "characters seldom win; in his existential world it is the struggle that counts" ("Early Williams" 23).

Val

Val Xavier, whose name suggests both love (St. Valentine) and Christ (Londré 57), is at the symbolic age of thirty in *Orpheus*. Perhaps this maturation prods him to surrender "his wild freedom for security" (Falk 132), for he now "denies his eroticism" (Quirino 32). He is the "rural Orpheus, the artist archetype" (Donahue 83) sent to rescue Myra/Lady (Eurydice) from Jabe (Pluto). According to Clum, Val is a "sexual free agent" (136) yet "in a strange sex reversal, Val is in heat and arouses all the females who come near him" (138). Val, who is "searching for a beautiful, uncorrupted way of life" (Donahue 228), "finds it impossible to survive in a world of cruelty, injustice, and harshness" (226). He is "a southern re-creation of the nineteenth century's romantic concept of the freedom-seeking artist" who is killed "as much for his nonconformity as for his sexual appeal to the town's lovelorn women" (Herron 355). According to Chiari, Val is a "typical specimen of feminine man dear to Tennessee Williams" (145); for Jackson he is "a dark god . . . a dying god" (145). He may be the "representation of [Williams's] inner self" (King 30).

At times, however, Val seems less a viable character than a somewhat contrived symbol, less a dying god than a mass of human contradictions. Williams himself called Val a "honky tonk guitar player and singer" (Devlin 42). Val is supposed to be a lyrical poet, yet he cannot get his subjects and verbs to agree; he minimizes his animal magnetism, yet likens himself to a febrile dog when he says that his temperature is always a few degrees hotter than normal. Perhaps Val is best understood as a prototypical D. H. Lawrence hero, for, as Bigsby observes, *Orpheus* "dramatises the immolation of a Lawrentian fox set loose in a South dying of its own narcissism" (59).

Vee

Vee Talbot, the sexually repressed wife of the Sheriff of Two River County, is perhaps the most curious character in the play. She is "as much misunderstood by the shallow busybodies as by her sadistic husband" (Herron 355). Williams invests her with equal parts of bathos and pathos, and one is left wondering precisely what to make of her. Her sexual repression leads her to confuse religious iconography with male sexuality to the extent that she transforms Val into Christ. She "struggles to come to terms with the anarchic violence which she witnesses by turning it into art" (Bigsby 62). Consequently, her primitive art allows her to express both her desire and her faith, which seem to become one and the same with the painting of Val as Christ. Her "lack of physical outlet and emotional fulfillment has resulted in a confusion of erotic fantasies and mystical experience" (Adler, *American Drama* 135). Vee thus becomes voice for the spiritual/sensual dichotomy in much of the Williams canon.

Myra/Lady

In the stage directions for *Battle*, Williams describes Myra as suffering from "emotional disaster in her girlhood" and still enduring the pain (20), referring to her being rejected by her former lover David Cutrere. Lady's reveries about David represent perhaps Williams's earliest dramatic depiction of a character's suffering from loss and a profound sense of regret. These memories are made even more poignant when she "enters into a state of legal prostitution by a loveless marriage" to Jabe (Herron 352). Myra's love-starved venture into Val's world leads to brief happiness, a fleeting sexual satisfaction. Fortunately, Williams's extensive rewrites gave Lady in *Orpheus* a much greater tragic dimension than that of Myra in *Battle*.

Cassandra/Carol

Tischler thinks that Cassandra in *Battle*/Carol Cutrere in *Orpheus* is "perhaps the most exciting character" in the story but has little to do with advancing the plot (*Tennessee Williams* 76). Sandra, "woefully misunderstood by her hypocritical, and perhaps jealous, associates" (Herron 355), exhibits a "resolute bohemianism" that is a "deliberate affront to the southern mores which condemn her" (Bigsby 59). She is an apparent alcoholic whose only consolation (aside from booze and sex) comes from visiting with her dead ancestors; her suicide over Val's death seems to indicate that he represented the one last hope of her achieving happiness. As the prophetess of doom whom no one takes seriously, she offers Val transportation at the play's end but fails to extricate him from the mob. Both characters' lives are controlled by past forces—family history in Cassandra's case and poor judgment in Val's situation—that ultimately determine their deaths.

Town Residents

Dolly and Beulah, who help frame the play, are standard Williams rustics, his "clowns," as he called them. "Stereotyped and gossipy expositors" (Herron 357), they function as the Two River County equivalent of a Greek chorus by providing background and bits of conversation reflective of popular opinion. Their husbands are equally inane and are really interchangeable; in fact, Williams himself seems inadvertently to mix up husbands and wives in scene 1 of *Orpheus*, once when Beulah, who is married to Pee Wee, shouts for Dog, and Dolly, who is married to Dog, shouts after Pee Wee (42), and in another instance when Beulah and Dolly confuse the names (36).

The Conjure Man

The Conjure Man, whose "magic is from another era" (Bigsby 61), was a well-known folk icon in the Mississippi Delta of this era, and it is fitting that Williams adapted this figure into the mythic landscape of the play. He has few lines but an important part in *Orpheus*. Less of a presence in *Battle*, he literally conjures up Val for Carol with his cry in *Orpheus*, and at the end of the play he passes on the snakeskin jacket to Carol, the only person who shows him any sympathy. Thompson labels him a "shaman" (87), and Boxill wisely concludes that Uncle Pleasant (Conjure Man) symbolizes "something wild in the country" (123).

Symbols

Tom, the narrator in *The Glass Menagerie*, said, "I have a poet's weakness for symbols," and Williams seems to have indulged this weakness in *Battle of Angels*. Most of the *Battle/Orpheus* symbols complement the mythic structure of these plays. Thompson writes that the play is "based on a mythicized story . . . reenacted in a demythicized version" and is thus "complicated" (84). Specific symbols used to help structure the play are less subtle than obvious—and therefore, it might be argued, contrived. For example, the setting, Two River County, suggests a parallel with the Tigris and Euphrates, the mythic cradle of civilization. Val's snakeskin jacket, symbolic of his "wildness," "evokes multiple associations relevant to Val's characterization and roles" (Thompson 90). Other symbols, such as the confectionery, the red steeple, the guitar, and the legless bird serve as keys to Williams's meaning (Hale, "Early Williams" 22–23). Even so, some critics find the combination of pagan and Christian symbols confusing, ponderous, and ultimately superfluous. Among these is Herron, who argues that "for all its undeniable power of psychological penetration and occasional poetic effects, the play is symbol-ridden" (355). Similarly, John Simon mused of the London *Orpheus*'s move to New York, "I wonder what freighter or cargo plane was sturdy enough not to sink under the weight of all that symbolism" (86).

Plot

The themes of *Battle/Orpheus* help to propel the plot and set up conflict among other characters. Most of the conflict arises from their inability or refusal to tolerate or understand differences. Cassandra becomes ostracized for her profligate lifestyle; Myra lives an oppressed, stultifying existence as Jabe's wife; Vee is chastised for her visionary paintings; Loon dares to agitate the Sheriff and gets threatened with jail time. All pay for their nonconformity with penalties ranging from ridicule to death.

According to Hale, although the Orpheus-Eurydice plot "forms the legendary background" of *Battle/Orpheus*, the "contemporary plot" relates to Lawrence's

Lady Chatterley's Lover, "in which a barren woman, tied to an invalid husband, meets a virile man who unlocks her passion and gets her with child" ("Early Williams" 22). The similarity of plot construction was perhaps a result of Williams's later borrowing from his voracious reading as a child.

In comparing the second published version of *Orpheus* in 1958 with the 1940 *Battle of Angels*, one is struck by how Williams's artistic persistence brought about a much more mature work. The plot is less melodramatic and contrived; the characters' motivations are better understood; and the lyrical passages—Williams's trademarks as a dramatist—are more inspiring. Stage directions, which stress "nonrealistic" sets, show that Williams was again working within the constructs of the "plastic theatre," his response to European expressionism that he first displayed in *The Glass Menagerie*. For the most part, however, the play remains in the mode of poetic realism, the art of expression that suited Williams so well and for so long.

MAJOR PROBLEMS *BATTLE OF ANGELS* AND *ORPHEUS DESCENDING* POSE FOR CRITICS

Critical reactions to *Battle*, Williams's first major production, were generally unfavorable, foreshadowing the critics' later problems with *Orpheus*. Initial reviews focused on the play's seemingly odd mix of religious and sexual content. Readers respond to the play's heavy-handed religious symbolism either by imploring us to accept it allegorically or by castigating the young author's reliance on the obvious. Thompson maintains that *Battle* contains "excessive symbolism, extraneous anecdotes, and theatrical pyrotechnics" (95). Tischler sums up the reaction of many critics to *Battle/Orpheus* when she writes that "there is too much of it" (*Tennessee Williams* 76). Adler, for example, finds that *Battle* "may be gothic and overwrought, yet is not lacking in raw power" (*American Drama* 132). Pease notes that in creating Val, "Williams the writer actually began his dramatic career with the invention of the writer as his hero" (832). Of course, the writer as chief protagonist would figure in a number of his works. At one point, Williams considered using the name Valentine Xavier as his nom de plume, after a relative from his father's side who descended from the east Tennessee Seviers, regarded by some as heroes for their early skirmishes with the Cherokees.

Questions about the plays' genre and symbolism also plague the critics. Quirino sees *Battle of Angels* as an amalgamation of tragedy, melodrama, morality play, and romantic mood play (27). According to Quirino, *Orpheus* and its predecessor *Battle* "reveal . . . the author's frantic ambition to make each of them a compendium of almost everything he believed about life and its artistic reflection in drama" (44). If this assessment does not reflect critical consensus, it nonetheless represents a leading critical sentiment, for readers generally believe that Williams simply tried to do too much in the two plays. Pagan even makes a case for another ingredient that Williams included—the Orphic connection with the blues (57). Although Williams said that *Battle* concentrates on what he regarded as "corrupt in life" (quoted in Devlin 42), Bigsby feels that "the relationship between personal and public corruption is mystified rather than clarified" (97). Williams's "exploitation of Christian mythology" (Jackson 57), combined with the two legends of Orpheus, results in a tangled symbolism that ultimately fails (Falk 135).

The problematic issues that *Battle/Orpheus* raise may ultimately reside in Williams himself. He was his own victim of the play's myriad layers of myth, symbol, and social consciousness, for, as Donahue notes, the creative strain, in addition to the play's various failures, drove him in 1957 to consult a New York psychoanalyst (93).

CHIEF PRODUCTIONS

Battle of Angels premiered at the Wilbur Theatre in Boston with a short run from 30 December 1940 to 11 January 1941, starring Miriam Hopkins as Lady. Reviews were mixed. The *Boston Evening Transcript* found *Battle* to be a "stumbling, pointless affair," and the *Boston Globe* review said that "the play gives the audience the sensation of having been dunked in mire" (quoted in McCann 2–3). The most vitriolic critiques of Williams's premiere came from the Boston City Council, which demanded censorship; one outraged assemblyman asserted, "This show is a crime to be permitted to run in the City of Boston" (McCann 4). For the most thorough discussions of the ill-fated opening of *Battle*, see Leverich (*Tom* 389–96) and Barringer.

Some sixteen years later, *Orpheus Descending*, a greatly revised version, opened in New York at the Martin Beck Theatre on 21 March 1957, with Maureen Stapleton as Lady and Cliff Robertson as Val. Brooks Atkinson found that "Mr. Williams is in a more humane state of mind than he has been in several years" (quoted in McCann 105). Walter Kerr, on the other hand, found that the play represented a "serious loss in sustained power" (McCann 113). Writing for the *Saturday Review*, Henry Hewes saw the earlier Philadelphia tryout and concluded that "Williams's poetic notions and symbolism tend to emerge as too obvious or too unrelated to the action." This lack of symmetry "puts an awful strain on the performers," and "the result is . . . a superimposition of unmatched images" (26). Two years later, productions were staged in London at the Royal Court Theatre and in Paris. *Orpheus* was also performed at the Moscow Central Theatre of the Soviet Army in 1977. Shaland's lengthy discussion of this production highlights the interpretive changes that led to characters being "dramatically deprived of their major meanings" (63). A revival was staged at the Gramercy Arts Theatre in 1959–1960, which Judith Crist found to be "a lesser Tennessee Williams work . . . in the hands of a less than inspired cast" (quoted in McCann 143).

The 1980s witnessed a number of other revivals of *Orpheus*. In December 1988 the Peter Hall Company staged the play first in London at the Haymarket and then, nine months later, at the Neil Simon Theatre in New York, with Vanessa Redgrave leading the cast as Lady in both productions. The reviewers were gen-

erally positive, with some notable exceptions. Robert Brustein thought that Redgrave's accent "seemed more Polish than Italian" (25). The Peter Hall production
in New York, which Disch of the *Nation* termed "unearthly and anesthetizing
[in] atmosphere" (610), was nevertheless, according to *Commonweal* reviewer
Weales, a "conventional" reading by Redgrave and the directors (642). Weales
offered this dismissive summary: "This *Orpheus Descending* certainly recognizes
what Williams wanted to say, but it is never demanding enough to compel me
to listen" (643). While acknowledging that his review rubs against "a critical
reception that has been virtually unqualified in praise of the play," Brustein was
also disappointed with the New York production, summing it up as a "long,
tedious circumnavigation of Williams's dream life, with a plot not far removed
from gothic soap opera" (26). Simon found the play "awash in . . . overloaded
imagery" (86), concluding, "Who would have thought that Orpheus could de-
scend *this* low?" (87).

Considerably revised, *Battle of Angels* opened thirty-four years after its Boston
premiere at the Circle Theatre in New York on 3 November 1974. This revival,
which was produced off-Broadway by an off-off-Broadway repertory, presented
"an evening of renewal and reclamation," according to Mel Gussow. This script
omitted the prologue and epilogue and also dispensed with the fire at the play's
end that had gotten out of control in Boston.

FILM, TELEVISION, AND OPERATIC VERSIONS

Kalson argues that the play contains shaping cinematic influences. A filmed
stage version of *Orpheus*, both directed and adapted by Peter Hall, premiered on
TNT (the Turner Network) on 24 September 1989. Tone of *Variety* found that
"the small screen emphasizes the play's excesses," but that "the saving grace of
the drama is Redgrave" (12). Although *Battle* was never made into a film, *Orpheus*
was released in 1960 under a different title, *The Fugitive Kind* (bearing no relation
to an early Williams play by the same title), directed by Sidney Lumet and
starring Marlon Brando as Val and Anna Magnani as Lady. This was one of the
few films that met with Williams's satisfaction. He "loved what was done with
Orpheus Descending on the screen" (quoted in Devlin 119). The following excerpts from reviews indicate that, as with the play on which it was based, there
was no consensus of critical opinion: "pretentious performances" with a laborious
plot (quoted in McCann 156), "one of the most important American films so
far this year" (156), "highly predictable" (160), "a disappointment" (171), and
"aswarm with symptoms and symbols for amateur psychiatrists to figure out and
snigger at" (171).

Orpheus was also transformed into an opera in June 1994 at the Lyric Opera
Center for American Artists in Chicago. In a recent interview, composer Bruce
Saylor and librettist J. D. McClatchy spoke about transforming the play into an
opera. Finding the play "verbally extravagant" (Holloway 18), McClatchy concluded that the transformation was natural. The adaptation was assisted by its

own "verismo tradition" of "mad scenes, murder, passionate love scenes. But underneath it's a pure, strong myth holding up the material" (19). Ultimately, the librettist found that "the whole emotional arc of the dramatic action seems to me operatic" (18). Reviewing it for *Opera News*, John Von Rhein found the operatic result "a taut, sinewy piece of music theatre with a distinctively American voice, a worthwhile opera" that emerged as "a skillful distillation of classic myth and Southern Gothic melodrama" (51). See also Kerner's review for additional commentary.

CONCLUDING OVERVIEW

These two kindred plays lend themselves to a multiplicity of approaches, all synergistically a part of Williams's *oeuvre*. In *Battle/Orpheus*, he comes closest to espousing a deterministic view of the past as it affects his characters. Most of the plays' ingredients, including plot, setting, and character, reflect the lingering dominance of the past. In *Battle*, the prologue and epilogue take place in a tourist museum that freezes the past with its macabre exhibition of articles pertaining to the deaths of Val and Myra. To a great extent the plot hinges on past events, especially the appearance of the "Woman from Waco." Also important is Williams's recurring theme of characters trapped by their personal pasts, for the lives—and for that matter the deaths—of at least two characters are determined in varying degrees by elements of their pasts. Williams uses the metaphor of the hunted fox to depict how Val's past relentlessly pursues him. Like Val, Cassandra/Carol is haunted by her past; unlike Val, she may not be as responsible for her present fate. She has inherited a run-down plantation, and the inheritance is more a curse than a blessing. People see her as an overprivileged harlot whose self-indulgent ways ill befit a lady of her lineage. But Cassandra/Carol, the decadent aristocrat, realizes that freedom will ineluctably escape her because of her family history. Cassandra's misguided life and "accidental" death are fulfillments of prophecies foretold by her ancestors, themselves representatives of the past. Val's fugitive existence and violent death are also the results of a past that flight can neither mitigate nor obviate.

This strong interest in things past in *Battle/Orpheus* reflects Williams's persistent interest in politics as well. Recent studies (Adler, "Culture"; Bray, *Streetcar*; Hale, "Tom Williams"; and Kolin) have profitably focused on Tennessee Williams's political views, which also surface strongly in *Battle/Orpheus*. Both *Battle* and *Orpheus* problematize a sleepy southern landscape with a political climate typical of the pre–civil rights era. Quite aside from the mythic dimensions and melodrama they contain, the plays fairly accurately depict race relations and what Williams saw as the necessity for change. In both *Battle* and *Orpheus*, Williams explores a political agenda by showing just how brutal racism was in the Mississippi Delta of the 1940s. These plays chronicle a Delta zeitgeist. This climate of violence and oppression doubtless assumes great importance from the perspective of the New Historicism as it interrogates the Williams canon.

Feminist approaches to the plays can also very profitably reevaluate past relationships among the major characters to explore the role that gender plays in
the various conflicts. Tischler observed that "if nothing else, *Battle* is remarkable
for its variety of women" (interview). As Hale eloquently stated, these two Williams plays, especially *Orpheus*, "would shatter the stereotypic chaste heroine/
whore dichotomy to show women in their complexity, just as his subject matter
would bring maturity to the American stage" ("Early Williams" 22). It is also
worth noting that any attempt to balance the white phallocentric power structure
in Two River County with the appropriation of feminine desire results only in
desperation, frustration, or violence. Armed with pistols, lynching rope, and
blowtorches, the Bubbas handily win these battles.

WORKS CITED

Adler, Thomas P. *American Drama, 1940–1960: A Critical History*. New York: Twayne,
       1994.
———. "Culture, Power, and the (En)gendering of Community: Tennessee Williams and
       Politics." *Mississippi Quarterly* 48 (Fall 1995): 649–65.
Barringer, Milly S. "*Battle of Angels*: Margaret Webster Directs Tennessee Williams." *Jour-
       nal of American Drama and Theatre* 4 (Winter 1992): 63–77.
Bigsby, C. W. E. *Modern American Drama, 1945–1990*. Cambridge: Cambridge UP, 1992.
Boxill, Roger. *Tennessee Williams*. New York: St. Martin's, 1987.
Bray, Robert. "An Interview with Dakin Williams." *Mississippi Quarterly* 48 (Fall 1995):
       777–88.
———. "*A Streetcar Named Desire*: The Political and Historical Subtext." *Confronting
       Tennessee Williams's A Streetcar Named Desire: Essays in Critical Pluralism*. Ed. Philip
       C. Kolin. Westport, CT: Greenwood, 1993. 183–98.
Brustein, Robert. "Orpheus Condescending." *New Republic* (30 Oct. 1989): 25–27.
Chiari, J. *Landmarks of Contemporary Drama*. London: Jenkins, 1965.
Clum, John M. "The Sacrificial Stud and the Fugitive Female in *Suddenly Last Summer*,
       Orpheus Descending, and *Sweet Bird of Youth*." *The Cambridge Companion to Ten-
       nessee Williams*. Ed. Matthew C. Roudané. Cambridge: Cambridge UP, 1997. 128–
       46.
Crandell, George. *Tennessee Williams: A Descriptive Bibliography*. Pittsburgh: U of Pitts-
       burgh P, 1995.
Devlin, Albert J., ed. *Conversations with Tennessee Williams*. Jackson: UP of Mississippi,
       1986.
Disch, Thomas M. "Orpheus Descending." *Nation* 249 (20 Nov. 1989): 609–11.
Donahue, Francis. *The Dramatic World of Tennessee Williams*. New York: Ungar, 1964.
Falk, Signi Lenea. *Tennessee Williams*. New York: Twayne, 1962.
Gussow, Mel. "*Battle of Angels*." *New York Times* 4 Nov. 1974: 51.
Hale, Allean. "Early Williams: The Making of a Playwright." *The Cambridge Companion
       to Tennessee Williams*. Ed. Matthew C. Roudané. Cambridge: Cambridge UP, 1997.
       11–28.
———. "Tom Williams—Proletarian Playwright." *The Tennessee Williams Annual Review*
       1 (Winter 1997): 13–22.

Herron, Ima Honaker. *The Small Town in American Drama*. Dallas: Southern Methodist UP, 1969.

Hewes, Henry. "Tennessee Revising." *Saturday Review* 30 (Mar. 1957): 26.

Holloway, Deborah Seabury. "Orpheus Ascending." *Opera News* (June 1994): 18–19.

Jackson, Esther Merle. *The Broken World of Tennessee Williams*. Madison: U of Wisconsin P, 1965.

Kalson, Albert E. "Tennessee Williams at the Delta Brilliant." *Tennessee Williams: A Tribute*. Ed. Jac Tharpe. Jackson: UP of Mississippi, 1977. 774–94.

Kerner, Leighton. "Orpheus Unburnt." *Village Voice* 5 July 1994: 80.

King, Kimball. "The Rebirth of *Orpheus Descending.*" *Tennessee Williams Literary Journal* 1.2 (Winter 1989–90): 18–33.

Kolin, Philip. "Sleeping with Caliban: The Politics of Race in Tennessee Williams's *Kingdom of Earth.*" *Studies in American Drama, 1945–Present* 8.2 (1993): 140–62.

Leverich, Lyle. *Tenn: The Timeless World of Tennessee Williams*. Vol. 2 (forthcoming).

———. *Tom: The Unknown Tennessee Williams*. New York: Crown, 1995.

Londré, Felicia Hardison. *Tennessee Williams*. New York: Ungar, 1979.

Matthew, David C. C. " 'Towards Bethlehem': *Battle of Angels* and *Orpheus Descending.*" *Tennessee Williams: A Tribute*. Ed. Jac Tharpe. Jackson: UP of Mississippi, 1977. 172–91.

McCann, John. *The Critical Reputation of Tennessee Williams: A Reference Guide*. Boston: Hall, 1983.

Pagan, Nicholas. *Rethinking Literary Biography: A Postmodern Approach to Tennessee Williams*. Cranbury, NJ: Associated U Presses, 1993.

Pease, Donald. "Reflections on Moon Lake: The Presences of the Playwright." *Tennessee Williams: A Tribute*. Ed. Jac Tharpe. Jackson: UP of Mississippi, 1977. 829–47.

Quirino, Leonard. "Tennessee Williams' Persistent 'Battle of Angels.' " *Modern Drama* 11 (1968): 27–39.

Shaland, Irene. *Tennessee Williams on the Soviet Stage*. Lanham: UP of America, 1987.

Simon, John. "To Hades and Beyond." *New York* 9 Oct. 1989: 86–87.

Thompson, Judith J. *Tennessee Williams' Plays: Memory, Myth, and Symbol*. New York: Lang, 1987.

Tischler, Nancy. Telephone interview with Robert Bray. 20 Sept. 1997.

———. *Tennessee Williams: Rebellious Puritan*. New York: Citadel, 1961.

Tone. "Orpheus Descending." *Variety* 22 Oct. 1989: 72.

Traubitz, Nancy Baker. "Myth as a Basis of Dramatic Structure in *Orpheus Descending.*" *Modern Drama* 19 (Mar. 1976): 57–66.

Von Rhein, John. "*Orpheus Descending.*" *Opera News* (Nov. 1994): 51–52.

Wallace, Jack E. "The Image of Theatre in Tennessee Williams's *Orpheus Descending.*" *Modern Drama* 27 (1984): 324–35.

Weales, Gerald. "Orpheus." *Commonweal* 116 (17 Nov. 1989): 642–43.

Williams, Tennessee. *Battle of Angels*. *The Theatre of Tennessee Williams*. Vol. 1. New York: New Directions, 1971.

———. *Orpheus Descending*. *Tennessee Williams: Four Plays*. New York: Signet, 1976.

The Glass Menagerie

THOMAS P. ADLER

BIOGRAPHICAL CONTEXT

Because of the heavily autobiographical nature of *The Glass Menagerie*, the first volume of Lyle Leverich's authorized biography, *Tom: The Unknown Tennessee Williams*, might almost be said to be as much the story of that play as it is of the playwright. As Leverich remarks, "For the first thirty years of his life, [Williams] was living *The Glass Menagerie*" (xxiii). In Leverich's reconstruction of the dramatist's formative years, the father who is largely written out of the play—absent except for the large photograph in the stage set—was much more central; Leverich argues, in fact, that Tom Williams's unrequited love for his father resulted in a rage against him that helped fuel the son's artistic rebellion and passion to create, and that the son's hatred was actually sublimated love. So life among a dysfunctional family that the biographer terms an "actual menagerie" (xxvi) may have been altogether darker, as might the play itself, than one at first suspects, particularly given the dramatist's description of *Menagerie* in his letters to Donald Windham as a "quiet little play" that, furthermore, "lack[ed] the violence that excites him" (60, 94).

The concluding fifty pages of Leverich's volume specifically concern *The Glass Menagerie*, and the book as a whole is rich in details that bear upon the play, from the unearthing of a real Miss Wingfield in Clarksdale, Mississippi—where Williams lived in his grandfather's rectory before the family moved to St. Louis—who displayed a collection of glass figurines in her window to the establishing of 1943 rather than 1937 as the date for the prefrontal lobotomy of Williams's sister Rose. Allean Hale has pinpointed several actual locations in St. Louis—the place she terms "the catalyst that transformed [Williams] into a writer" (609)—that have importance in this "least disguised work" (611), including the Westminster Place apartment where the action occurs.

BIBLIOGRAPHIC HISTORY

Ronald Hayman provides a succinct rundown of the genesis of *The Glass Menagerie* (86–87). More detailed discussion of the several drafts and revisions—housed primarily in the Harry Ransom Humanities Research Center at the University of Texas in Austin and in the C. Waller Barrett Library at the University of Virginia—and the complex relations among them can be found in the work of Lester Beaurline (45) and especially in R. B. Parker's two essays; he finds the discarded drafts "more sexually charged, more violent, more blackly humorous" ("Circle" 121) than the final version. Gilbert Debusscher examines three other seemingly unrelated Williams manuscripts in the collection at Austin that "reveal . . . their close connection with the final text" ("New Texas Light" 53). Although *Menagerie* owes something to Williams's 1943 short story "Portrait of a Girl in Glass," it was his film treatment and unproduced screenplay for MGM, entitled "The Gentleman Caller," that led most directly to the play. It is little wonder, then, that his first successful Broadway drama—and this will be true of several later plays as well—is imbued with certain cinematic techniques that bear on both the play's fluid structure and its elegiac mood as established by lighting and music; these have been analyzed in detail by George Brandt and Albert Kalson, and to a lesser extent by Frank Durham, Delma Presley, and Harry Smith. More recently, George Crandell has applied feminist film theory and analysis to demonstrate how the narrator's "gaze reveals the extent to which *The Glass Menagerie* replicates the organizational structures of the classic cinema, which in turn, reflect the ideology of a patriarchal society" (2).

The text of *The Glass Menagerie* exists in both a reading version (published by Random House in 1945 and reprinted by New Directions in 1949) and an acting script (published by Dramatists Play Service in 1948 and revised in 1950); the latter has generally been followed as the basis for major productions of the play, and Beaurline argues that the academic critic "ignores [it] . . . at his peril" (46). Although Charles Watson perceives subtle changes in the 1948 version to Jim's characterization that render him "more sympathetic" (76), and James Rowland judges the rethought Amanda and Tom superior to their earlier characterizations, the central difference between reading text and acting text comes, as Geoffrey Borny notes, from omitting the Piscator-like expressionistic devices, which render the playscript more in keeping with the "realistic predilection" of mainstream American theatre, though at the same time reducing it to "a kind of sentimental soap opera" that is less universal and philosophical (102, 107).

Works that have been detected as literary influences on *The Glass Menagerie* include several poems by Hart Crane that "pervade [the play's] texture" (Debusscher, "Crane" 34); Virginia Woolf's "memory novel" *The Years*, whose Sara

Pargiter has been paralleled to Laura (Diemert); and most convincingly Chekhov's *The Sea Gull*, adapted by Williams as *The Notebook of Trigorin* in the late 1930s (first performed in 1996), in which Drewey Gunn discerns not only thematic and tonal links but specific character likenesses as well. Bert Cardullo teases out the meanings of Williams's specific use of lines from Villon, Dickinson, and e. e. cummings in *Menagerie* (85–87, 89–91). Gary Konas has pointed out similarities between Williams and fellow Missourian playwright Lanford Wilson. Critics have likewise noticed possible influences of *Menagerie* on individual works as various as Paul Zindel's *Effect of Gamma Rays on Man-in-the-Moon Marigolds* and Marsha Norman's *'night, Mother*, as does Kimball King (647) when he situates Williams's theatre in the context of modern southern drama.

MAJOR CRITICAL APPROACHES

Themes

The stage set's grinning photograph of the father who left would seem to encapsulate what has most often been proposed as the central motif of *The Glass Menagerie*: escape—from a too-possessive love; from responsibility (personal, familial, and social); from reality; from time; and even from an indifferent universe. Much of the play's tension arises, as Tom Scanlon suggests, from the contradictory "quest for relatedness and independence" (107). Felicia Londré and Gene Phillips both discern the potentially hurtful and destructive nature of an overly possessive love such as Amanda's, which "threaten [s the] freedom" (Schneiderman 102) that may be "essential to creative activity" (Debusscher 39). Yet to refuse the call to love results in betrayal; Rita Colanzi, for example, applies the notion of Sartrean bad faith to the characters' actions. Not only fear of responsibility to the other, but more generally fear of "time and its demands" (Blufarb 513), which often may appear "malignant and malevolent" (Durham 71), or fear of death itself may prompt flight. For the writer, this might even take the form of resistance to narrative closure, which C. W. E. Bigsby terms the "final victory for death" (49). So escape need not be spatial; it may be into interiority: the solipsism of the mind, or the world of illusion or art—though that may ultimately prove little more than "sublimat[ion of] animal drives" (Cohn 101) or "a feeble consolation" (Boxill 66). A number of critics link art and sexuality in the play, with Harold Bloom finding an "absolute identification between [Williams's] artistic vision and his homosexuality" (4), and Parker reading the motif of brother and sister incest as a "revolt against existential isolation and awareness of death" ("Circle" 132).

Several commentators find evidence for suggesting that a bleak vision undergirds Williams's play; Benjamin Nelson calls the playwright's universe "fragmented" and "determined" (94–95), while Roger Stein names it "damned" (141). M. A. Corrigan posits a Manichean world where "quotidian existence [is] debasing" (158), while Bigsby discerns a "Spenglerian vision" of history at work

(45). Taking the absent father as a kind of *deus absconditus*, Judith Thompson particularly argues for an almost Beckettian world "devoid of transcendent goals" where (wo)man is alienated and alone, faced with the "loss of all heroes, the death of all gods, the disillusionment of all hope" (20, 22).

Both Nancy Tischler and Paul Nolan posit, respectively, that sociopolitical issues such as pre–World War II isolationism are "irrelevant" and "meaningless" (*Tennessee Williams* 27; 145) in the play; John Lahr, on the other hand, feels that it reflects "the transformation of the nation's collective unconscious from war-effort sacrifice to post-war self-involvement" (124), with others finding the Wingfields "both victims and representatives of a dark chapter in the social history of America" (Presley 73). Konas regards the work as an "indictment of urban America in the 1930s" (31), as does Bigsby, who finds in the narrative opening "an implicit attack on America" (*Introduction* 47). He makes perhaps the strongest argument for seeing the play as a social drama about "lost innocence" and how "the animating myths of America" form "the root of a destructive materialism or deceptive illusion," concluding that for the performative imagination to abstract the self "from its social environment . . . leads into a cul-de-sac" ("Entering" 35–36, 40). Stein, however, employs a Marxian analysis to argue that Williams evades writing "trenchant social drama" and "shift[s] responsibility for the human condition to the divine" (142). It is left largely to W. Geiger Ellis and Arthea Reed in their study guide to call attention to the ethnicity and socioeconomic class of the characters who either appear or are mentioned in *The Glass Menagerie* (17).

Characters

Amanda

Laurette Taylor's uncannily truthful and incandescent performance as Amanda in the original Broadway production of *The Glass Menagerie* made it seem as if it were her play—and, indeed, successive actresses (Gertrude Lawrence on film, followed by Maureen Stapleton, Jessica Tandy, Shirley Booth, Katharine Hepburn, Ruby Dee, Julie Harris, and Joanne Woodward, among others, in various media) have solidified that impression for audiences and reviewers of the play on stage and screen and, to some extent, even for academic critics. For Ruby Cohn, the play's "stage viability" rests on Amanda (101), for Joseph Davis, she is the work's "pivotal character" (198), and for Foster Hirsch (37) as well as for Marc Robinson, this "subtly observed" woman, "presented from all angles, just this side of grotesque," is a "mass of contradictions" who forms the drama's "center" (34)—contradictions that Nelson tries to capture by applying terms such as "appalling," "shrewish," "nagging," and "vulgar," yet also "noble," "strangely tender," and "valor[ous]" to her (90).

Commentary tends to center on Amanda in her roles as mother and as perpetrator, and perpetuator, of myth. As wife and martyr to motherhood, she is usually seen as a mixture of the "Good" and the "Terrible" (Thompson 17), wanting the best for her children and even "playing their fairy godmother" to get it, yet deceiving herself in not realizing that to effect her dreams and regain her lost youth, she would willingly "absorb [her] children's freedom" (Colanzi 455, 459); in this, according to Presley, she "reflects the extremely complex nature of human love" (39)—a love that Robinson is not alone in characterizing as "suffocating" (36). As mythmaker, Amanda is regarded as unable to "face reality" (McGlinn 511) and thus immaturely retreating to a "world of imagination" (Jones 217), but the falsified myth she fabricates of a "paradise now lost" is, Davis asserts, "counterfeit," a "hardly credible . . . 'pseudo-history' " (200–02). Amanda is "by nature" an actress or a role-player (Gunn 316); however, her attempts to theatricalize life as a substitute for emotional estrangement and emptiness (Robinson 35) or to make life "become art" (Colanzi 459) cannot succeed, finally rendering her, in the opinion of Robert Jones, more "pathetic" than "tragic" (212, 219), although Sam Blufarb judges the pity she "invites" as the "truest and deepest" (517) of any of the play's characters.

Tom (The Narrator)

One of the central questions about The Glass Menagerie has always been: Whose play is it? The emotional response generated during a performance has usually prompted audiences—and even some critics—to respond either "Amanda" or "Laura" when asked. The play's formal structure, however, militates seeing Tom as the focal character, since the play occurs within his memory, with his mind the site of the action (making it analogous to a first-person limited-point-of-view fictional narrative, or the camera eye that controls one's gaze in cinema). Thus Presley calls Tom's "role . . . pivotal" (25), while Roger Boxill declares that the play is his "from a dramatic critic's point of view" (72). Thomas King, reminding readers that Williams's own life formed the "raw material" for the work, goes further by claiming that Tom is really the play's "only character" and "the Prospero of Glass Menagerie" (76).

The role of Tom Wingfield—originated by Eddie Dowling, who also directed the first production, and later played by James Daly, George Grizzard, Rip Torn, Bruce Davison, and John Malkovich, among others—is, of course, a dual one: that of central character and of narrator of the action. As a character in action that occurred in the past, he has been seen as "passive" and "dependent" (Sievers 372), an "incredibly bored" (Stern 134) "dreamer" (Presley 52) whose poetic inclinations make him a freakish "outsider" (Konas 28) in the warehouse where he works—in short, an image of the alienated "existential man" (Thompson 20) and "voyager" in quest of meaning (Presley 84). The central conflict Tom faced in the past was between duty to self and responsibility to family; he particularly needed, in Thomas Scheye's formulation, to discover whether and how he might "leave without shattering Laura's fragile self" (208). Eric Levy expresses this tension in terms of "fear of being trapped . . . in intimacy founded on love," with "loneliness" as his only "protect[ion] from vulnerability" (533–34).

As narrator in the present stage time, Tom seems compelled endlessly to relive the past "in order to forget" that past (Scheye 207), and so the act of remembering becomes either confession of guilt, exorcism of that guilty past by "excessive reliving" (Parker, "Circle" 133), or transmuting it into art through "the creation of the play" (T. King 85). Whereas Nancy Cluck distinguishes between two kinds of narrators in Williams's dramas, which she categorizes as "undisguised" and "disguised," the latter being the "persona" behind the stage directions who is "like the narrator in prose fiction" (93), Davis differentiates between what he calls "nondirected" or more spontaneous and unconscious thinking as opposed to "directed" or "logical thinking," finding Tom's narrative passages an example of the former (193). Robinson claims that Tom is an "unreliable" narrator (34), while Adler posits that an audience more willingly accepts Tom as reliable both because he does not easily absolve himself of guilt and also because the dramatic form itself, where remembered events are acted out and seen, helps reduce the solipsistic effect ("(Un)reliability" 7). Some critics find the narrative segments— which are apparently designed to increase the impression of objectivity (Presley 27)—"pretentious" (Nelson 93) or, what is worse, "extraneous and tiresome" (Young 17). Thomas King, however, emphasizes the crucial importance of recognizing the absolutely essential presence of Tom's narrative framework and interjections to prevent the play's becoming "a sentimental tract," as well as the humorous, nostalgic, and ironic modes in which these passages are couched (75).

Finally, the question not only of whether Tom's act of remembering has been therapeutic, but also of what has perhaps been repressed or closeted rather than revealed—things that in other Williams plays would "erupt unchecked in a lava-flow of violence" (Dervin 183)—has been attended to by recent critics. Stewart Stern reflects on Tom's "self-disgust" over a homosexuality about which he lacks "complete openness" (12, 115); Parker ("Circle" 122), Dervin (156), and Schneiderman (98) all situate what is hidden in an incestuous desire for the sister, Laura; and Adler suggests that the formal structure of the play may create an artificial sense of closure where much is left unspoken and, further, that Tom's leaving Laura condemned to a virginal state is tantamount to Tennessee's keeping Rose to himself, forever inviolate, as the object of his art ("Tennessee Williams's 'Personal Lyricism' " 178).

Laura

Because of Laura's slight physical disability, it is easy for directors to make her the emotional or sentimental core of a production; based on Williams's text, Davis judges her the play's "lyrical and symbolical center" (194). Levy considers her burdened by self-consciousness caused through Amanda's need to "flatter her own self-image" (533), which only increases Laura's sense of worthlessness when she is rejected by Jim. Georges-Michel Sarotte discusses Laura as different, as Other, interpreting her nickname "Blue Roses" as indicative of "sickness metamorphosed into a flower" (144), which coincides with Dervin's symbolist perception of Laura as pairing "beauty and disease" (156). Cardullo, on the other hand, tracing the imagery of the blue flower back to German romanticism, interprets it as symbolizing Laura's "yearning for . . . ideal or mystical beauty and spiritual or romantic love" as well as "absolute emotional and artistic fulfillment" (82–83). Repeatedly, Laura is seen as resigned to "isolation" (Presley 141), as prone to "deadening withdrawal" and "introversion" (McGlinn 511), as "a virtual Proustian hypochondriac" who lacks "the will-to-live" (Stavrou 28). Crandell regards Laura, in her encounter with Jim, as momentarily "resist[ing] the male gaze," but ultimately—under the pressure of Tom's final command—"lacking the power to subvert it" (10). Stern speaks of her facing the "abyss" and "ultimate entombment" after Jim fails to rescue her (101), while Colanzi terms her the "ultimate symbol of nothingness" (457). Jacqueline O'Connor infers from images of entrapment and "enclosed spaces" that the final destiny of the mentally fragile Laura will "likely" be institutionalization—a fate Tom avoids by his turn to artistic creativity (83, 87). Nelson, apparently sharing the sense of Laura as objectifying these abstract conditions, concludes atypically that she "never emerges as a human being in her own right," though he still believes that "her plight is given luminous expression" (87).

Jim (The Gentleman Caller)

Although described by Tom in his narrative opening as "an emissary from a world of reality" postponed but always welcomed (23), the outsider who enters (invades is certainly too strong a word since his visit is devoutly wished for by Amanda) the illusion-filled womb of the Wingfield apartment is himself also prone to self-delusion, for Jim is a character for whom surface and substance, aspiration and achievement, do not mesh. Thus, as Colanzi astutely notices, the wall mirror becomes his prop as he "adjusts [his] image" (457); Levy also notes his "narcissism" and need to have his "self-love" buoyed up by a "flattering image" (533). On the exterior, Jim is a cliché-ridden "complete American male, both artistic and athletic" (Sarotte 142), the "apotheosis of the all-American boy" who equates happiness with success (Thompson 21); in actuality, of course, as several critics have noticed, his disappointing present situation is an immense diminishment of past promise, what Cohn terms a "retrogression" (100). The "social poise" (Presley 58) that he thinks will ensure an entry to power masks a submission to a false notion of what industry and technology can attain that finally dehumanizes him (Konas 32; Reynolds 525; Beaurline 51).

The legend "Annunciation" may announce his arrival, but he proves to be, as has been widely noted, a false savior for Laura. Assuming that the name James Delaney O'Connor is Irish Catholic, the Wingfields serve fish, the "symbol of Christ," to this "sham" and "failure" (Stein 138–39) at the Friday meal when he declines to sacrifice himself, though Sarotte finds in the "ethnic difference" of Jim's marginalized Irishness some reason for sympathizing with him. More broadly, Thompson summarizes him as the failed figure not just of religion but of fertility myths, of fairy tales, of heroic stories in general (21).

Symbols

In his opening narration, Tom Wingfield confesses to "a poet's weakness for symbols" (23); his creator, however, regarded them as "the language of plays" (*Where I Live* 66). As is frequently the case with Chekhov, Williams titles his play after a physical object that carries heavy symbolic resonance. While Richard Vowles cleverly associates the aqueous properties of glass as "arrested water" with the play's "fluid, dissolving movement" (53), most critics settle for a more mundane reading, seeing the collection of miniature animals as analogous to the "breakable" family unit (Stern 25) and, most particularly, to Laura's fragility (Cohn 100; Sievers 374). Others connect Laura's private world of the miniature animals more generally with a retreat from an "imperfect reality" (Bigsby 48) into the realm of art or illusion that easily "may be shattered" (Durham 62); sometimes, the world's "mundan[ity]"—as signified by the second half of the Wingfield surname (Thompson 16)—is attributed to the impact of secular urban life (Davis 194) or to advances in communication technology (Reynolds 525). Specific locations in the city assume dark overtones: for Borny, the fire escape and alleys suggest "the awfulness of . . . non-being" (117), while for Stein, the Paradise Dance Hall is a "Waste Land" (140). Finally, Levy focuses on glass as it appears literally in the wall mirror and metaphorically in the father's photograph that becomes a "mirror" for Tom in order to suggest the way in which to break glass is to repudiate the (self-)image that mirrors are designed to sustain.

Just as there will be two violent wrenchings off of the paper lantern in *A Streetcar Named Desire*, there are two breakings of glass in *Menagerie*, one by Tom and the second by Jim, of the unicorn, mythologically the lover of virgins and icon of chastity and the chief visual symbol in the play. Debusscher (40) and Scheye (211) both connect the loss of the unicorn's horn with the prefrontal lobotomy undergone by Williams's sister, Rose. Signi Falk understandably sees it as a symbol of Jim's having "broken [Laura's] heart" (85), especially since Laura then gives it to him as one of the several "souvenirs" exchanged in the play, others being Jim's autograph and kiss and the magician's scarf given her by Tom. Many commentators explore the sexual connotations of the unicorn: for Sarotte, it signifies Laura's own "castration" out of difference or otherness (144), and for Stavrou, her renunciation of "one of the surrogate objects of her erotic fantasies" means an embrace of greater reality (29); for Boxill, on the other hand, its broken horn represents Jim's "collapse of male ardour upon the removal of maidenly defense" (70). Adler similarly reads the extinction of candles in the play as a loss of phallic potential, condemning Laura to a condition of perpetual virginity ("Setting" 51); he, along with Parker, notes the possible allusion to Othello's putting out the light before he enters the bridal chamber to snuff out Desdemona's life.

The candles form a part of *Menagerie*'s vast network of religious imagery as well (Cardullo 85–86, 88, 90). For Stein, the interrupted meal becomes a "Christian ceremony . . . lack[ing] religious significance" (139), while Beaurline (52) finds elements of a mock communion ceremony in the sharing of wine. Davis (204–5) uncovers a reverse Dantean *Commedia* of Paradise (Old South), Purgatory (Depression), and Hell (World War II), and Thompson suggests that the Wingfields, with the absent Father, are a "fragmented" Holy Family; she uncovers the patterns of fertility rite (pagan), Communion (Christian), and chivalric courtship (romance), but regards their use as symbols "divorced from substance" (21).

Plot

Perhaps because, as Tom Scanlon remarks, "the plot is light stuff" (99), there has been only scant attention paid to that aspect of *The Glass Menagerie* in the critical literature. If one removes the narrative framework, then what remains in the scenes that occurred in the past is a fragile, melodramatic tale of a mother's thwarted efforts, with the hesitant aid of her son, to find a beau for her mildly disabled daughter, a kind of reverse fairy tale: Sleeping Beauty awakened by a kiss, Cinderella asked to the ball, only to be deserted by the Prince. The family conflict, as Londré notes, is a generational one, with the "parent destroying the child" (73). If the focus is shifted from the sister, Laura, to the brother, Tom, then the conflict becomes more clearly the tension the incipient artist faces, what Davis delineates as the "Orphian quest for unification of man's animal and intellectual dimensions through artistic means" (196). Because the dinner party turns into disaster and the family breaks up with Tom's desertion, escaping like the long-gone father from a restrictive "coffin," Boxill sees the play as incorporating Williams's two "archetypal actions": "the spoiled occasion" and "the eviction or loss of home" (71).

By taking into consideration, however, the narrative framework occurring in the present, the play becomes something else: in Stern's and Adler's words, respectively, "a confessional" (17) and an "examination of conscience" ("(Un)reliability" 7) undertaken by a man haunted by guilt over his failure to put others before self. The play's plot becomes, then, an objectification of the mind working, and the question arises whether replaying the past in memory leads to a therapeutic forgetting or to being frozen in time, condemned to a sort of Yeatsian purgatorial endless repetition without release. Adler, furthermore, sees the authorial character's opening narration, which includes lines that might be construed as incorporating aesthetic theory, as turning the alternation of the play's action between past and present into a consideration of the difference between realistic or representational theatre, on the one hand, and illusionistic or nonrepresentational theatre, on the other, so that the audience is forced to consider the nature of dramatic art itself ("Setting" 48–49).

MAJOR PROBLEMS *GLASS MENAGERIE* POSES FOR CRITICS

Williams's formal experimentation in *The Glass Menagerie*, as described in his "Production Notes" to the reading version and crystallized in the play's stage directions, has generated considerable critical debate. The "Production Notes," one of the chief aesthetic statements by an American dramatist, issue a clarion call for a "new, plastic theatre" (7), a "sculptural drama" highly visual and multimedia in nature and thus, as Adler notes, sharing something with the Artaudian distrust of a drama that is essentially language based ("Tennessee Williams's 'Personal Lyricism' " 175). Boxill terms the "Notes" a "manifesto of the cinematic stage" (68); in them, Borny sees Williams as insisting that slice-of-life realism is deficient (107), while Prasad, following Jackson, sees him opting for a "theatre language" composed of "a system of connotative signs" that are "rational equivalents for . . . individual vision" (51–52). Jackson, in fact, has commented most extensively on the distinct nature of Williams's theatrical style as a "transformation into concrete symbols" of a "subjective vision" (28), going on to conclude that he has done nothing less than "rewoven the complete fabric of the performing arts" (156) into a signature theatrical form, "not realistic . . . either in theory or in practice" but "so effective in its use of a singular iconography that it appears to many spectators to copy reality" (104), a form possessing, in Alan Chesler's formulation, "increased flexibility" through the "utilization of expressionistic and impressionistic techniques within a realistic form" (850). The result, according to Nolan, is "probably closer to romantic lyric poetry than to objective drama" (153), to what Londré terms "symbolist drama" (73).

Williams's decision to include images and legends projected onto a screen, similar, as both Boxill (68) and Borny (111) note, to titles in silent film—ostensibly (according to the playwright's "Notes") to mute and offset the episodic nature of his play, which audiences might find disorienting—has proven the most controversial element, provoking widely different judgments. If Nelson feels that the devices reveal their creator's doubt about the "power of the written word" (92), while Tischler finds them simply "unnecessary visual reinforcements" (*Tennessee Williams* 27), others attribute greater complexity. Recalling the " 'epic' form of Piscator and Brecht," Jackson defines the "screen as a symbol of consciousness" (91), as does Prasad, echoing the same words (53). Presley sees the device as "recapturing the impressionistic qualities of the human memory" (80), as does Smith (224), and as undercutting oversentimentality, as does Boxill (67). Others, including Adler ("Setting" 49) and Smith (226), explicitly link these devices that decrease any excess of feeling to Brechtian alienation effects.

Finally, if for Corrigan the projections on the screen capture the characters' " 'fantasy' worlds" (157), for Jo Mielziner, the designer who realized Williams's textual directions in designing the original stage setting, the "use of transparent and translucent scenic interior walls was not just another trick [but] a true reflection of the contemporary playwright's interest in—and at times obsession with—the exploration of the inner man" (124). Adler proposes strategies for approaching the teaching of the play in the classroom through focusing on the set designs ("Setting" 47–51), which can be found reproduced in Mielziner's volume (125, 127).

CHIEF PRODUCTIONS

The original production of *The Glass Menagerie* was the stuff of which legends are made, for it restored a former star (Laurette Taylor as Amanda) to glory; immediately secured its author a place among the pantheon of a new generation of major American playwrights; and, perhaps most remarkably, was kept alive by a Chicago theatre reviewer (Claudia Cassidy) after its pre-Broadway opening in the Windy City on 26 December 1944. At its New York premiere on 31 March 1945 (five days after the dramatist's thirty-fourth birthday), it was greeted by twenty-four curtain calls; it won the New York Drama Critics' Circle Award for Best Play, as well as the Donaldson and Sidney Howard Memorial awards, and achieved an initial run of 561 performances. In his anecdotal *Memoirs*, Williams recounts events surrounding *Menagerie*'s opening (81–91); Leverich provides more extensive detail (582–84); Parker reprints several reviews, including Stark Young's, that greeted various productions (*Twentieth Century Interpretations* 15–25); and Margaret Van Antwerp and Sally Johns collect news stories, critical notices (including Cassidy's), interviews, and photographs relevant to the original staging (58–71). The 1948 London opening of the play starred Helen Hayes, who would play Amanda in the 1956 Broadway revival.

The twenty-fifth anniversary of the play's premiere was marked by a New York revival featuring Maureen Stapleton as Amanda. It was, however, not until 1983, almost forty years after the play's initial opening, that Broadway audiences saw a version, starring Jessica Tandy—who had been *Streetcar*'s original Blanche—that employed the screen device that had been omitted from the original production; Frank Rich lauded director John Dexter's "notion of fighting against a maudlin" reading through using the "distancing" devices (C3). (In 1964, Tandy had read the role of Amanda for the Caedmon recording of the play, directed by playwright Howard Sackler with Montgomery Clift as Tom.) The images and legends appeared again in Frank Galati's 1994 revival, this time featuring Julie Harris (the Caedmon recording's Laura) as Amanda; David Richards felt the device "redundant" since "the poetry is already in the text" (B6), while Lahr found that even "subtly employed," it diminished "immediacy" and "leach[ed] intensity," though the interpolated photo of Williams that was projected on the back wall before the play "boldly announc[ed]" the dramatist's "power as an artist . . . and his romantic literary personae" (125). In a 1965 interracial production at the renowned Karamu House Theatre in Cleveland, Ohio, the Wingfield family was black, but a white actor was cast in the role of the Gentleman Caller. Two other revivals, both on the West Coast, deserve mention: in 1991, the Lorraine Hansberry Theatre in San Francisco under the direction of Whitney

LeBlanc produced *The Glass Menagerie* with a black cast (its first play ever by a non–African-American writer), which capitalized on the relevance of the absent father to the black experience and on Laura's physical infirmity as an "implied metaphor of skin color" and discovered through using a photograph of "an obviously white father who had abandoned the family" a historical allusion richly resonant of miscegenation (Kolin, "Interview" 311, 317). Kolin ("Black") offers a critical survey of many African-American productions of *The Glass Menagerie* that radicalize Williams's script. Heidi David, directing a 1994 Los Angeles production, "boldly" split Tom "into two separate characters": an "older narrator who unobtrusively react[s]" and a "younger self" who "reenacted [his] memories" (Brandes F26).

FILM AND TELEVISION VERSIONS

Williams himself abhorred the 1950 screen version of *The Glass Menagerie* as the "most awful travesty . . . horribly mangled" (quoted in Yacowar 114). Maurice Yacowar, who finds that the screen version lacks any "equivalent for the poetic techniques of the play," criticizes the film—directed by Irving Rapper, with Gertrude Lawrence as Amanda and Jane Wyman as Laura—for diminishing the play to "standard romantic melodrama" by "sacrific[ing]" its "poetic spirit," "reduc[ing]" its "complexity," and tacking on a happy Hollywood ending with mother and daughter awaiting additional gentlemen callers (9, 11, 12, 14). Phillips judges it the "first and worst" adaptation of a Williams play to the screen (50), though he reports that Williams was much happier with Anthony Harvey's 1973 teleplay starring Katharine Hepburn, with Michael Moriarity turning in an exceptionally impressive interpretation of Jim, which deleted some of the text's narrative passages. Stern has written a book-length diary detailing the rehearsal and shooting of Paul Newman's expressive and most effective sepia-toned 1987 film version (widely available on video), starring Joanne Woodward; as the film's Tom, John Malkovich is intuitive about the character's homosexual subtext and, after the opening frame, interestingly narrates the rest of the first-person passages from the persona of his past rather than his present self.

CONCLUDING OVERVIEW

The nature of memory, and how it works, has been one of the abiding subjects and structuring devices of twentieth-century literature, from the novels of Proust to the works of Pinter. As a deeply autobiographical "memory" play that is confessional in nature, *The Glass Menagerie* belongs in that tradition and so raises questions both of textuality and of its link with sexuality. How much of the past, which no longer exists except in one's lasting impressions of it, can be recovered? How much has time inevitably distorted or human agency suppressed or denied? How much of the text that Tennessee Williams/Tom Wingfield writes is only partial and thus inherently unreliable? The contemporary novelist V. S. Naipaul would argue that the transmutation of life into art results in something altogether truer: "An autobiography can distort, facts can be realigned. But fiction never lies. It reveals the writer truly." Williams's *Glass Menagerie*, however, might—from the perspective of Michel Foucault, who argued the impossibility of ever containing in words one's sex, "a universal secret, and omnipresent cause"—just as accurately be said to have as its chief concern trying to write what can never adequately be written. Much of the play focuses upon psychosexual difference (not only Laura's but Tom's as well) and the perhaps futile, even destructive, attempt to normalize it, as is foregrounded in the scene between Laura and her Gentleman Caller and in Tom's concluding narrative frame, which seems designed rather desperately to keep hints of homosexuality and incestuous desire masked and to give a false sense of closure where only doubt and ambiguity reside. The candles—autobiographical, artistic, and even analytical in nature—that this play lights are finally resistant to ever being fully extinguished.

WORKS CITED

Adler, Thomas P. "Setting as Meaning: A Scenic Approach to Teaching *The Glass Menagerie*." *Alabama English* 4.1–2 (Spring & Fall 1992): 47–51.

———. "Tennessee Williams's 'Personal Lyricism': Toward an Androgynous Form." *Realism and the American Dramatic Tradition*. Ed. William Demastes. Tuscaloosa: U of Alabama P, 1996. 172–88.

———. "The (Un)reliability of the Narrator in *The Glass Menagerie* and *Vieux Carré*." *Tennessee Williams Review* 3.1 (Spring 1981):6–9.

Beaurline, Lester A. "*The Glass Menagerie*: From Story to Play." *Twentieth Century Interpretations of "The Glass Menagerie."* Ed. R. B. Parker. Englewood Cliffs, NJ: Prentice-Hall, 1983. 44–52.

Bigsby, C. W. E. *A Critical Introduction to Twentieth-Century American Drama*. Vol. 2. Cambridge: Cambridge UP, 1984. 40–52.

———. "Entering *The Glass Menagerie*." *The Cambridge Companion to Tennessee Williams*. Ed. Matthew C. Roudané. Cambridge: Cambridge UP, 1997. 29–44.

Bloom, Harold, ed. *Tennessee Williams's "The Glass Menagerie."* New York: Chelsea, 1988.

Bluefarb, Sam. "*The Glass Menagerie*: Three Visions of Time." *College English* 24 (Apr. 1963): 513–18.

Borny, Geoffrey. "The Two *Glass Menageries*: Reading Edition and Acting Edition." *Tennessee Williams's "The Glass Menagerie."* Ed. Harold Bloom. New York: Chelsea, 1988. 101–17.

Boxill, Roger. *Tennessee Williams*. New York: St. Martin's, 1987. 61–75.

Brandes, Philip. "Illuminating the Complex Facets of *Glass Menagerie*." *Los Angeles Times* 19 Aug. 1994: F26.

Brandt, George. "Cinematic Structure in the Work of Tennessee Williams." *American Theatre*. Ed. John Russell Brown and Bernard Harris. London: Arnold, 1967. 162–87.

Cardullo, Bert. "The Blue Rose of St. Louis: Laura, Romanticism, and *The Glass Menagerie*." *The Tennessee Williams Annual Review* 1 (1998): 81–93.

Cassidy, Claudia. "On the Aisle." *Chicago Sunday Tribune* 7 Jan. 1945, "Books": 3.

Chesler, S. Alan. "Tennessee Williams: Assessment and Reassessment." *Tennessee Williams: A Tribute*. Ed. Jac Tharpe. Jackson: UP of Mississippi, 1977. 848–80.

Clayton, John Strother. "The Sister Figure in the Plays of Tennessee Williams." *Twentieth Century Interpretations of "The Glass Menagerie."* Ed. R. B. Parker. Englewood Cliffs, NJ: Prentice-Hall, 1983. 105–19.

Cluck, Nancy Anne. "Showing or Telling: Narrators in the Drama of Tennessee Williams." *American Literature* 51 (1979): 84–93.

Cohn, Ruby. "The Garrulous Grotesques of Tennessee Williams." *Dialogue in American Drama*. Bloomington: Indiana UP, 1971. 98–102.

Colanzi, Rita. "Caged Birds: Bad Faith in Tennessee Williams's Drama." *Modern Drama* 35.3 (Sept. 1992): 451–65.

Corrigan, M. A. "Memory, Dream, and Myth in the Plays of Tennessee Williams." *Renascence* 28.3 (Spring 1976): 155–67.

Crandell, George W. "The Cinematic Eye in Tennessee Williams's *The Glass Menagerie.*" *The Tennessee Williams Annual Review* 1 (1998): 1–11.

Da Ponte, Durant. "Tennessee Williams' Gallery of Feminine Characters." *Tennessee Studies in Literature* 10 (1965): 7–26.

Davis, Joseph K. "Landscapes of the Dislocated Mind in Williams' *The Glass Menagerie.*" *Tennessee Williams: A Tribute*. Ed. Jac Tharpe, Jackson: UP of Mississippi, 1977. 192–206.

Debusscher, Gilbert. "Menagerie, Glass and Wine: Tennessee Williams and Hart Crane." *Twentieth Century Interpretations of "The Glass Menagerie."* Ed. R. B. Parker. Englewood Cliffs, NJ: Prentice-Hall, 1983. 31–43.

———. "'Where Memory Begins': New Texas Light on *The Glass Menagerie.*" *The Tennessee Williams Annual* 1 (1998): 53–62.

Dervin, Daniel A. "The Spook in the Rainforest: The Incestuous Structure of Tennessee Williams's Plays." *Psychocultural Review* 3.2 (Summer/Fall 1979): 153–83.

Diemert, Brian. "Tennessee Williams's *The Glass Menagerie*: A Possible Source in Virginia Wolf's *The Years.*" *English Language Notes* 29.4 (June 1992): 79–81.

Durham, Frank. "Tennessee Williams: Theatre Poet in Prose." *Tennessee Williams's "The Glass Menagerie."* Ed. Harold Bloom. New York: Chelsea, 1988. 50–73.

Ellis, W. Geiger, and Arthea J. S. Reed. *A Teacher's Guide to Tennessee Williams's "The Glass Menagerie."* New York: New American Library/Penguin, 1988.

Falk, Signi Lenea. "The Southern Gentlewoman." *Tennessee Williams's "The Glass Menagerie."* Ed. Harold Bloom. New York: Chelsea, 1988. 79–87.

Gunn, Drewey Wayne. "'More Than Just a Little Chekhovian': *The Sea Gull* as a Source for the Characters in *The Glass Menagerie.*" *Modern Drama* 33.3 (Sept. 1990): 313–21.

Hale, Allean. "Tennessee Williams's St. Louis Blues." *Mississippi Quarterly* 48.4 (Fall 1995): 609–25.

Hayman, Ronald. *Tennessee Williams: Everyone Else Is an Audience*. New Haven: Yale UP, 1993.

Hirsch, Foster. *A Portrait of the Artist: The Plays of Tennessee Williams*. Port Washington, NY: Kennikat, 1979. 35–39.

Jackson, Esther Merle. *The Broken World of Tennessee Williams*. Madison: U of Wisconsin P, 1965.

Jones, Robert Emmet. "Tennessee Williams's Early Heroines." *Modern Drama* 2.3 (Dec. 1959): 211–19.

Kalson, Albert E. "Tennessee Williams at the Delta Brilliant." *Tennessee Williams: A Tribute*. Ed. Jac Tharpe. Jackson: UP of Mississippi, 1977. 774–94.

King, Kimball. "Tennessee Williams: A Southern Writer." *Mississippi Quarterly* 48.4 (Fall 1995): 627–47.

King, Thomas L. "Irony and Distance in *The Glass Menagerie*." *Twentieth Century Interpretations of "The Glass Menagerie."* Ed. R. B. Parker. Englewood Cliffs, NJ: Prentice-Hall, 1983. 75–86.

Kolin, Philip C. "Black and Multi-Racial Productions of *The Glass Menagerie*." *Journal of Dramatic Theory and Criticism* 9 (Spring 1995): 97–128.

———. "An Interview with Whitney J. LeBlanc." *African American Review* 26.2 (1992): 307–17.

Konas, Gary. "Tennessee Williams and Lanford Wilson at the Missouri Crossroads." *Studies in American Drama, 1945–Present* 5 (1990): 23–41.

Lahr, John. "The Haunted Menagerie." *New Yorker* 21 Nov. 1994: 124–28.

Leverich, Lyle. *Tom: The Unknown Tennessee Williams*. New York: Crown, 1995.

Levy, Eric P. " 'Through Soundproof Glass': The Prism of Self-Consciousness in *The Glass Menagerie*." *Modern Drama* 36.4 (Dec. 1993): 529–37.

Londré, Felicia Hardison. *Tennessee Williams*. New York: Ungar, 1979. 67–77.

McGlinn, Jeanne M. "Tennessee Williams' Women: Illusion and Reality, Sexuality and Love." *Tennessee Williams: A Tribute*. Ed. Jac Tharpe. Jackson: UP of Mississippi, 1977. 510–24.

Mielziner, Jo. *Designing for the Theatre: A Memoir and a Portfolio*. New York: Bramhall, 1965. 124–27.

Nelson, Benjamin. "The Play Is Memory." *Twentieth Century Interpretations of "The Glass Menagerie."* Ed. R. B. Parker. Englewood Cliffs, NJ: Prentice-Hall, 1983. 87–95.

Nolan, Paul T. "Two Memory Plays: *The Glass Menagerie* and *After the Fall*." *Twentieth Century Interpretations of "The Glass Menagerie."* Ed. R. B. Parker. Englewood Cliffs, NJ: Prentice-Hall, 1983. 144–53.

O'Connor, Jacqueline. *Dramatizing Dementia: Madness in the Plays of Tennessee Williams*. Bowling Green, OH: Bowling Green UP, 1997.

Parker, R. B. "The Circle Closed: A Psychological Reading of *The Glass Menagerie* and *The Two-Character Play*." *Tennessee Williams's "The Glass Menagerie."* Ed. Harold Bloom. New York: Chelsea, 1988. 119–36.

———. "The Texas Drafts of *The Glass Menagerie*." *Twentieth Century Interpretations of "The Glass Menagerie."* Ed. R. B. Parker. Englewood Cliffs, NJ: Prentice-Hall, 1983. 53–61.

———, ed. *Twentieth Century Interpretations of "The Glass Menagerie."* Englewood Cliffs, NJ: Prentice-Hall, 1983.

Phillips, Gene D. *The Films of Tennessee Williams*. Philadelphia: Art Alliance, 1980. 33–64.

Prasad, Hari Mohan. "Plastic Theatre of Tennessee Williams." *Indian Scholar* 2.1 (Jan. 1980): 51–56.

Presley, Delma E. *"The Glass Menagerie": An American Memory*. Boston: Twayne, 1990.

Reynolds, James. "The Failure of Technology in *The Glass Menagerie*." *Modern Drama* 34.4 (Dec. 1991): 522–27.

Rich, Frank. "Depression Dreams." *New York Times* 2 Dec. 1983: C3.

Richards, David. "From Tennessee Williams with Love, Fury, and Pain." *New York Times* 16 Nov. 1994: B1, B6.

Robinson, Marc. "Tennessee Williams." *The Other American Drama.* Cambridge: Cambridge UP, 1994. 29–59.

Rowland, James L. "Tennessee's Two Amandas." *Twentieth Century Interpretations of "The Glass Menagerie."* Ed. R. B. Parker. Englewood Cliffs, NJ: Prentice-Hall, 1983. 62–74.

Sarotte, Georges-Michel. "Fluidity and Differentiation in Three Plays by Tennessee Williams." *Staging Difference: Cultural Pluralism in American Theatre and Drama.* Ed. Marc Maufort. New York: Lang, 1995. 141–56.

Scanlon, Tom. "Family and Psyche in *The Glass Menagerie.*" *Twentieth Century Interpretations of "The Glass Menagerie."* Ed. R. B. Parker. Englewood Cliffs, NJ: Prentice-Hall, 1983. 96–108.

Scheye, Thomas E. "*The Glass Menagerie*: 'It's No Tragedy, Freckles.' " *Tennessee Williams: A Tribute.* Ed. Jac Tharpe. Jackson: UP of Mississippi, 1977. 207–13.

Schneiderman, Leo. "Tennessee Williams: The Incest Motif and Fictional Love Relationships." *Psychoanalytic Review* 73.1 (Spring 1986): 97–110.

Sievers, W. David. "Tennessee Williams and Arthur Miller." *Freud on Broadway: A History of Psychoanalysis and the American Drama.* New York: Hermitage, 1955. 370–99.

Smith, Harry W. "Tennessee Williams and Jo Mielziner: The Memory Plays." *Theatre Survey* 23.2 (Nov. 1982): 223–35.

Stavrou, Constantine N. "The Neurotic Heroine in Tennessee Williams." *Literature and Psychology* 5 (May 1955): 26–34.

Stein, Roger B. " '*The Glass Menagerie*' Revisited: Catastrophe without Violence." *Twentieth Century Interpretations of "The Glass Menagerie."* Ed. R. B. Parker. Englewood Cliffs, NJ: Prentice-Hall, 1983. 135–43.

Stern, Stewart. *No Tricks in My Pocket: Paul Newman Directs.* New York: Grove Weidenfeld, 1989.

Tharpe, Jac, ed. *Tennessee Williams: A Tribute.* Jackson: UP of Mississippi, 1977.

Thompson, Judith J. *Tennessee Williams' Plays: Memory, Myth, and Symbol.* New York: Lang, 1987. 13–23.

Tischler, Nancy M. "*The Glass Menagerie*: The Revelation of Quiet Truth." *Tennessee Williams's "The Glass Menagerie."* Ed. Harold Bloom. New York: Chelsea, 1988. 31–41.

———. *Tennessee Williams.* Austin, TX: Steck-Vaughan, 1969. 25–27.

Van Antwerp, Margaret A., and Sally Johns, eds. *Tennessee Williams.* Detroit: Gale, 1984. 58–74.

Vowles, Richard B. "Tennessee Williams: The World of His Imagery." *Tulane Drama Review* 3.2 (Dec. 1958): 51–56.

Watson, Charles S. "The Revision of *The Glass Menagerie*: The Passing of Good Manners." *Southern Literary Journal* 8.2 (Spring 1976): 74–78.

Weales, Gerald. "Tennessee Williams's Fugitive Kind." *American Drama since World War II.* New York: Harcourt, Brace, and World, 1962. 18–39.

Williams, Tennessee. *The Glass Menagerie.* New York: New Directions, 1945.

———. *The Glass Menagerie* (Acting Edition). New York: Dramatists Play Service, 1948.

———. *Memoirs.* Garden City, NY: Doubleday, 1975.

———. "Portrait of a Girl in Glass." *Tennessee Williams: Collected Stories.* Ed. Gore Vidal. New York: Ballantine, 1985. 115–24.

————. *Tennessee Williams' Letters to Donald Windham, 1940–1965*. Ed. Donald Windham. Athens: U of Georgia P, 1996.

————. *Where I Live: Selected Essays*. Ed. Christine R. Day and Bob Woods. New York: New Directions, 1978.

Yacowar, Maurice. *Tennessee Williams and Film*. New York: Ungar, 1977. 9–14.

Young, Stark. "The First Production of *The Glass Menagerie*." *Twentieth Century Interpretations of "The Glass Menagerie."* Ed. R. B. Parker. Englewood Cliffs, NJ: Prentice-Hall, 1983. 15–19.

A Streetcar Named Desire

PHILIP C. KOLIN

BIOGRAPHICAL CONTEXT

Like everything else Tennessee Williams wrote, A Streetcar Named Desire is intensely autobiographical. Williams himself admitted that it was his favorite play because it "said everything I had to say" (quoted in Rice). Earlier biographies by Spoto (146–56), Rader, and Hayman (110–17) have been conclusively supplanted by Leverich's second volume, which studies the events in Williams's life that led up to and resulted in the production of Streetcar in 1947. Van Antwerp and Johns as well as Leavitt (71–85) collect important biographical documents—letters, playbills, and telegrams—relating to Streetcar.

Williams invited comparisons between his life and the characters in Streetcar, especially Blanche. In one of his most controversial interviews, he asserted, "I can identify completely with Blanche . . . we are both hysterics" (Jennings 72). Tischler (Tennessee 137), Asselineau (160), and Holditch ("Broken World" 151), among others, identify the links between Williams and Blanche. In a letter (21 July 1970) to Audrey Wood, his agent, Williams further noted: "I was and still am Blanche . . . [but] I have a Stanley in me, too" (quoted in Tischler, "Sanitizing" 55). As Jack Kroll eloquently stated: "In this play as in no others, Williams was able to do his particular thing, to take the fragments of his divided self and turn them into the dramatis personae of an ideal conflict" (109). More specifically, Bigsby points out that Williams and his creation Blanche are both alienated, both create fictions, and both use "precipitate flight" as their "central strategy" (Critical Introduction 67–69).

The connections between Williams and Blanche are not always uncomplicated, for Blanche is the site of significant contradictions not easily mediated by reading her as Williams's surrogate. Blanche's relationship to Stanley reflects the contours of Williams's own life for many critics. Gone are the days when critics could confidently and simply associate Blanche with the Old South and with Williams and Stanley with industrialism and barbarism. As Homan puts it, "Like Blanche, perhaps even like her playwright . . . we see Williams's own complex life and personality divided between his two protagonists" (123). Separating Williams from Blanche, Cohn argues that "Blanche never understands the deep division within her [Puritan/Cavalier], as Tennessee Williams understands that division in himself" (*Dialogue*). Distancing Blanche even more caustically from Williams, Bedient insists that in preferring the "law" (represented by Stanley) to Blanche's "archaic Phallic mother," Williams inevitably "injures and humiliates part of himself" (56).

Studies by Clum, Lilly, and Savran see Williams projecting homoerotic desires through Blanche and Stanley. Claiming that Williams is "dramatizing the closet" in *Streetcar*, Clum finds that "Williams's protection of his homosexual subtext is achieved by hiding it within the action of a heterosexual female character" (151). Accordingly, Blanche mirrors Williams's homoerotic indeterminacy, though carefully subterfuged to avoid disclosure. According to Lilly, Stanley is a "stereotyped homoerotic icon for Williams" (114) and thus is "closely connected to the gay penchant for rough trade" (118). Concentrating on the invisible Allan Grey, Blanche's homosexual husband who commits suicide after she discovers him with another man, Savran documents Williams's obligatory containment of the homosexual: "Absenting the homosexual subject (and drawing attention to his absence), another homosexual subject, Tennessee Williams, is allowed to . . . speak" (110). Earlier, Boxill similarly pointed out that Williams "invests himself in the . . . young poet whose sexuality is rejected" much as Williams's request for maternal approval was rejected by Edwina Dakin Williams (83).

For a Foucaultian, postmodern approach to Williams's biography, see Pagan's provocative assault on traditional biographical assumptions (e.g., the life unlocks the work). Pagan cogently argues that the plays, especially *Streetcar*, do not bear a "filiate" relationship to life or to one another. *Streetcar* helped Williams perform his life as much as the other way around.

BIBLIOGRAPHIC HISTORY

Like most of Williams's works, *Streetcar* presents an intricate textual history, evolving over several years. The idea first came to him in the early 1940s when he outlined, in letters to his agent Audrey Wood, the basic story line and scenario for a film version of this script. The play began as a one-act drama. Altogether there are twelve different manuscript versions of *Streetcar* (housed at the Harry Ransom Humanities Research Center at the University of Texas), variously titled (*Blanche's Chair in the Moon, The Poker Night, The Moth*) and set in Chicago, Atlanta, and finally New Orleans. Influenced by Elia Kazan (see "Chief Productions"), Williams altered the script through and after production.

Two essential articles by Dickinson and Burks explore and interpret the *Streetcar* drafts. Dickinson meticulously documents the transformation of *Streetcar* from "a romance to a tragedy." In the process, Williams made "changes in characters' nationality" and their "conception and motivation." Two large problems Williams encountered in the drafts center on the relationship between Blanche and Stanley and the varying degrees and onset of Blanche's madness. According to Dickinson, Williams "seldom discarded material which would help define characters or increase their complexity" (165). Burks reviews all the early drafts, including one in which Blanche, sleeping with Stanley, "loses much of her sympathy as a character." Burks concludes that "Williams' painstaking revisions of *Streetcar* refocused the play, discarding the cynical, melodramatic impulses of the early drafts in which a villain crushes a heroine . . . [to find] the proper balance between Blanche and Stanley" (39). Further, Burks sheds light on how casting and production affected the evolution of the *Streetcar* script. Murphy studies the preproduction scripts in light of the cuts and additions director Elia Kazan made (20–25). Isaac studies one early draft in particular—"the four-page *Streetcar* scene found on the verso" of the piece entitled "The Angel in the Alcove"—which displays "a different Blanche and a different Stanley from those we know" (11). In this fragment, a wanton Blanche, morally tainted, enjoys sex with Stanley, who vows to follow her after she leaves New Orleans.

Four early one-act plays, dating from around 1945, also influenced *Streetcar*. Three of these are "This Property Is Condemned," involving a young girl's dreamy desires to be like her dead sister, Alva, a prostitute; "Portrait of a Madonna," in which Miss Lucretia Collins, an old maid, is sent to an asylum after hallucinating that her former lover has impregnated her; and "The Lady of Larkspur Lotion," in which a faded southern belle turned prostitute is evicted from a roach-infested boarding house in the French Quarter. According to Kolin, the one-act play "Hello from Bertha," about a dying prostitute summoning her ex-lover to rescue her, also parallels *Streetcar* (" 'Hello' ").

Among published versions of *Streetcar*, significant differences exist among the reading (New Directions) and the acting (Dramatists Play Service) editions. Substantial variations are found between the British and American editions as well, the former avoiding the issue of Allan Grey's homosexuality (scene 6) in response to the Lord Chamberlain's censorship order. In the British editions, *Streetcar* is printed in three acts, while in the New Directions versions it unfolds in eleven successive scenes. Crandell succinctly describes and briefly illustrates each edition—up to the sixth American and fourth British—and printing of the published texts (*Tennessee Williams* 40–55).

CRITICAL APPROACHES

Themes

Since *Streetcar*'s premiere in 1947, critics have proposed a bewildering variety of themes. Many of these themes also explain the larger Williams canon: the power and destruction of sex/desire; time as enemy; and the vulnerability of the artist. Adler usefully reviews others: "the need for mutuality among human beings"; "acceptance of fallibility"; "beauty over use"; and art as a "secular sacrament" (*Streetcar*, chapter 11). Kolin interviewed thirty-six playwrights who identify still other *Streetcar* themes ("*Streetcar* Forum").

According to Williams, the message of *Streetcar* was "If we don't watch out, the apes will take over" (quoted in Tischler, *Tennessee* 137). In his *Notebook*, Kazan elaborated: "The crude forces of violence, insensibility, and vulgarity" can overpower the embodiment of "light and culture" (364), which became a typical pronouncement of *Streetcar*'s message. Kazan saw the main conflict in *Streetcar* as between Old South gentility and a brutal new order. Echoing Kazan's sentiments, Holditch found the play to be "a classic study of the destruction of a Romantic protagonist committed to the ideal but living in the modern age, a broken world, a wasteland growing . . . more animalistic" ("Broken World" 147). Conceding the importance of Kazan's interpretation, Bigsby maintained that Williams's director "over-simplifies both sides of the conflict" between the Old South and the New South and that emphasizing the "death of a tradition" is only partially correct because it "ignores a crucial ambiguity" that "Blanche's problem is that she can operate in neither system" (*Critical Introduction* 64).

In their feminist reading, Gilbert and Gubar argued that *Streetcar* is Williams's "scathing critique of the heterosexual imperative which is driving Blanche mad" (51). Acknowledging the play as "being as close to genuine tragedy as any modern drama," Miller praised Blanche's "defiant courage trying to survive with some shred of human dignity . . . in a hostile world" (11–12). Seeing Blanche's plight as central to Williams's purpose, Bigsby found that "loss became a central theme" (*Modern American Drama* 45); qualifying such a view, Boxill contended that *Streetcar* mourns Blanche's dream of an ideal world more than the one into which she was born (92). For Sievers, the destruction of the mind—the depiction of schizophrenia—is Williams's most important thematic statement (quoted in Miller 90). Jacqueline O'Connor focuses on schizophrenia, too.

Theological and ethical issues have also occupied critics who have variously addressed the presence of a transcendent, higher power in *Streetcar*. Golden, for example, found that the most elemental conflicts in *Streetcar* are "the primitive struggle between light and dark, between god and the devil, between innocence and corruption, between illusion and reality" (125). Kunkle, on the other hand, faulted Williams for his lack of theological commitment, which produced "a literature of exhausted romanticism" (614). According to Robinson, however, "Other Williams plays are more explicitly concerned with religion, but in Blanche, Williams finds his first and most probing seeker after grace" (41). Adler claimed that Blanche and Stanley "assumed the role of a wrathful God and passed judgement on another person"; yet both needed the "assurance that a loving God exists" ("Search" 50). Asselineau found that "the dichotomy of body-soul is usually toned down in his plays" and that "Tennessee Williams' belief in God and the soul remains vague and undogmatic" (157–58). Refusing to choose

Blanche over Stanley, Jackson insisted that "neither of these protagonists represents an even remotely acceptable moral choice" (137). Persuing the *via media*,
Roderick honored *Streetcar* as a "brilliant tragicomedy" because of Williams's
"ambivalent admiration" for both protagonists; even though Blanche's "epiph-
any" was "tainted," it nonetheless offered a "positive force on the spiritual level"
(125). For the critics, as for Blanche, "Sometimes—there's God—so quickly."

Political readings of *Streetcar* inevitably differ, too. Bray examines Williams's
script in light of Marxist views on the passing of property and changes in power
from agrarian to industrial control, as does Bernard. Kelly proposes that Stanley
is an "intruder" whose "immigrant arriviste ambitions" challenge the idea of
America as a melting pot. More theoretically, Savran locates in *Streetcar* "the
liberal problematic": "All of Williams' drama . . . hovers uneasily between the
two conventions insistently destabilizing the liberal, while not yet quite able to
formulate a structure that could be called . . . socialist" (92).

A variety of opinions on *Streetcar* are found in three collections of essays
devoted to the play—in Miller, Bloom, and Kolin (*Confronting*). Only Kolin
offers original, not reprinted, essays.

Characters

Blanche

Unquestionably, Blanche DuBois is Williams's most famous character and perhaps his "finest creation" (Tischler, *Tennessee* 140). Kazan built the tragedy of
Streetcar around her (Murphy 62); the spine of Blanche's character—and a source
of her tragedy—for Kazan was her quest to "find protection" which "must be
through another person" (366). Yet for many readers *Streetcar* is the drama of
mighty opposites, divided into the warring camps of Blanche and Stanley. The
view of one character has invariably influenced how the other is seen in the
numerous dichotomies, in which Blanche is the first and Stanley the second:
artist/brute; spirit/flesh (Quirino); puritan/sensualist; "female warmth"/"masculine libido" (Hodgson 548); feminine virtues/"dark masculine forces of society"
(Brustein); desire/law (Hulley); culture/chaos; Old South/new industrialism; un-
reason/reason (Bedient); and death/desire (Kleb). Admitting that *Streetcar* deals
with "the clash between two different models of human behaviour," Bigsby nonetheless insisted that when the audience is "offered a choice between decadence
and brutality . . . [it] can hardly enter into an alliance with either" (*Critical Introduction* 67).

Criticism has grappled with Williams's own sympathies. Berlin proposed that
"Williams wishes to keep the sides balanced" (97). More recently, Abbott similarly reminded readers that "there must be a fine balance in the audience's
sympathies between Stanley and Blanche, for unless we see Blanche as a tragic
figure, then the play loses impact" (143). Chesler's survey of *Streetcar* criticism
in the early 1970s generally placed Williams in Blanche's camp, but Lacan- and

Foucault-inspired readings of the 1980s and 1990s do not always concur. Stanley has, as we shall see, moved from brute to sensitive and threatened husband. Blanche, too, has been unseated as Williams's favorite for some readers. Lant, in fact, indicted Williams for his "unacknowledged, unconscious misogyny [that] weakens his development of Blanche as a strong, exciting character . . . Blanche is damned no matter how she behaves" (233).

Undeniably, Blanche has equally strong supporters and detractors. According to Nelson, Blanche's "plight is that she is in some way on the side of what is civilized . . . when both a civilization in which to live and a tradition . . . are . . . denied human beings" (149), a view endorsed by Gassner. One of Blanche's strongest supporters is Isaac, who sees *Streetcar* "as a modern tragedy" and who characterizes Blanche as "a sexual Joan of Arc, who listens to the voices of her body; she is a prophet and poet, morally superior to her adversaries" (26). In her feminist reading, Hulley argued that to choose Stanley's text over Blanche's is to destroy those things "which make art and love possible" (96). In contrast, Brown claimed that Blanche's "abiding tragedy . . . is sprung from her own nature. . . . From her controllable duplicity. From her pathetic pretensions" (92). Berkowitz holds out even less hope: Blanche's "values and attributes" are "life-draining rather than life-supporting." For Bedient, Blanche is, bluntly speaking, the figure of death.

Responding to Blanche's ambiguity/indeterminacy, critics often have assigned her intensely contradictory roles. As Adler (*Streetcar* 36) and Murphy (44) demonstrate, Kazan took full advantage of Blanche's role-playing, and, not surprisingly, critics have labeled her a consummate actor. Cohn (103–04) and Robinson (38–39) carefully outline Blanche's various disguises: grand dame, sex kitten, and so on. In the eyes of many critics, Blanche is foremost the southern gentlewoman (Falk; Robert Emmet Jones; Boxill; Bigsby, *Modern American Drama* 45). Wright claims that Blanche is based on Birdie in Lillian Hellman's *Little Foxes*, since both are genteel southern women (295). Like Amanda in *The Glass Menagerie*, Blanche's aristocratic aspirations exceed her circumstances for Falk. Yet in contrasting these two Williams heroines, Robinson finds Blanche to be "more volatile" and "more alert to the subtleties of the moment" than Amanda (38). Emblematizing Blanche as the representative of the Old South, many critics locate her in Williams's own divided feelings as he admires the gallantry yet rejects the illusions of the region (Prenshaw 15). Porter emphasizes the ambiguities in Blanche's characterization as a southern belle: "She is caught between two worlds, one gone with the wind, the other barely worth having" (176). Sensitive to Blanche's gentility, Holditch stresses her status as a romantic idealist, comparable to Edna Pontellier in Kate Chopin's *Awakening* ("Broken World"). Robert Emmet Jones contextualizes that southern aristocratic society abused women like Blanche, "making them the passive pawns of social forces" (218). Melman claims that Blanche is an "anachronism, forced to live in a world that has discarded all adherence to her . . . tradition" (126).

Blanche is also regarded as the guardian of the arts and even portrays herself as an artist: she "pours out her creative energy on herself, attempting to re-create herself as an art object" (Harris 85). Studying Blanche in terms of Williams's "preoccupation with mental illness" and commitment practices and procedures, Jacqueline O'Connor classifies her as one of Williams's "captive maidens" whose "mental instability is clear throughout the play" (45). O'Connor links Blanche's inevitable institutionalization with her female sexuality, powerlessness, confinement, and lack of "economic resources." For O'Connor, Blanche "stands as the supreme example of how the playwright dramatizes the intersection of women and madness. Nowhere else does he succeed in balancing the madwoman's culpability and vulnerability in such equal proportions" (50). While Tischler lauded Blanche in this capacity (*Tennessee* 140), Homan denounced her "verbal imagination" and, contrasting her with Stanley, declared that "in the midst of Williams' own high art, she represents a fraudulent art—an unrealized artist" (130). Bedient dubbed her the "Mona Lisa of dread" (50).

Blanche has been apotheosized for her love yet spurned for her lust. Associating her with the spiritual, Quirino lamented her status as the soul trapped in a flesh-celebrating world. Schvey rejoiced that because of her "tragic destruction" she underwent a "heroic transcendence" (75) and linked her, through "Della Robbia blue . . . in the old Madonna pictures," to the Blessed Virgin. Extending this association, Kolin identified parallels between Blanche and Mary through historical and biblical allusions and by having Blanche's birthday (15 September) fall on the Virgin's feast as the Mater Dolorosa ("Our Lady"). Other critics find models for Blanche among classical figures: Aphrodite (Vlasopolos 334); Eurydice (Bedient 46); and Persephone, Psyche, Philomela, and a host of others (Thompson 27–28; 47). Jackson compares Blanche and Orestes: making a "guilty choice," she comes to realize her own responsibility for suffering, "aware that she suffers more for her own transgressions than for the actions of her guilty ancestors" (81). Kelly traces Blanche's roots to the White Goddess. For Kolin, Blanche is linked imagistically to Cleopatra, another tragic victim of love ("Cleopatra"). One British reviewer labeled her "a sort of Madame Bovary of the Southern States" (Mosely 2). But refusing to see Blanche as the forlorn romantic heroine, Clum insisted instead that she is "in many ways the quintessential gay character in American closet drama" (150).

Blanche is both moth (spirit) and tiger (flesh). Branding her love as dangerous lust, critics have frequently condemned her as a nymphomaniac (Trewin), a beguiling witch, or a sexual deviant (Kleb 30–31). Falk points out that Blanche wears white, like all of Williams's sexual deviates. Yet for many reviewers, her red satin wrap brands her as a common tart. Siphoning off any romance from Blanche's affairs of the heart, Davis accused her of playing hardball in the game of sexual politics to acquire power (77). Incapable of achieving intimacy, Blanche, for Berkman, bears an "irrevocable responsibility" for her actions (256). Others portray Blanche as an intruder infecting and destroying the health and sanity of Stanley's home (Kleb 29–30; Bedient).

Among Blanche's strongest supporters, though, are feminist critics (e.g., Vla-

sopolos; Schlueter, " 'We've Had This Date' "; Hulley) who promote her text/
script over Stanley's to correct the historical record that has marginalized and
stereotyped her. Vlasopolos's article is one of the most influential of the 1980s.
Lant portrays Blanche as the victim of the masculine society and of Williams's
own "misogynous attitudes" (233).

Stanley

In a letter to Kazan explaining the dynamics of *Streetcar*, Williams emphasized
that "there are no 'good' or 'bad' people, just individuals who misunderstand
each other" and warned Kazan not to cast Stanley as a "black-dyed villain"
(quoted in Murphy 24, 56). Accordingly, Kazan developed Stanley "as a character . . . most interesting in his 'contradictions,' his soft moments, his sudden
pathetic little-tough-boy tenderness toward Stella" (*"Notebook"*). In the history
of Stanley criticism, Stanley vacillates from absolutes to contradictions, with
numerous qualifications in between. Isaac identifies four sources for Stanley—
Pancho Gonzales, Williams's Mexican lover in the early 1940s; John Garfield,
who originally was to play the role; O'Neill's Yank from *The Hairy Ape*; and
Williams's own pugnacious father, Cornelius.

Critics have not always heeded Williams's admonition about Stanley. Like
Blanche, he has been given a multiplicity of rigid roles, some of them contrary
to Williams's (and Kazan's) intentions. Many readers have stressed the "apelike"
Kowalski, stereotyping Stanley for cruelty and vulgar and villainous behavior.
Dworkin, for example, assaulted Stanley as a "beast" who has "no interior life"
and who brutally suppresses his sister-in-law (41–42). He has been characterized
as an aggressor (Adler, *Streetcar* 53), an animal (Holditch, "Broken World" 161),
and, of course, Blanche's executioner. Vlasopolos maintains that Blanche is victimized by a "gender-determined exclusion from the larger historical discourse"
and because she is a threat to "the dominant discourse of patriarchy" (325).
Building upon Vlasopolos's argument, Schlueter destabilized any interpretations
of *Streetcar* based upon Stanley's account of what happens (scene 10) by establishing that through a retrospective reading, his patriarchal fictions of events in
Elysian Fields seduce the reader "into a hegemonically masculine and conventionally generic reading of the play," thus undermining Blanche's tragedy
(" 'We've Had This Date' " 78).

Against such readings, Kleb maintains that Stanley (and Stella) are the "guardians of the Same" (30), protecting their home and ensuring the "re-establishment
of society" (40) by removing Blanche—the "Other," the insane, unhealthy
one—to the madhouse. According to Kolin, Stanley behaves as if he were
Napoleon (and Napoleon's heir Huey P. Long) by invoking legal codes to defend
his French Quarter domain ("Bonaparte Kowalski").

A fairly large group of supporters has gloried in the sexual prowess of Williams's
"gaudy seed bearer," though there has been considerable debate about whether
Stanley is a Lawrentian character or not. Bigsby votes yes (*Critical Introduction*
66), while Ganz decides no. Departing from many who reviewed the Broadway

premiere, Krutch claimed that Stanley's "virility, even orgiastic virility, is the proper answer to decadence." Hirsch asserted that Williams "celebrates the sensual vigor and pride that Stanley so spectacularly incarnates" (31). Crandell contextualizes Stanley's sexuality, arguing that "by means of a racialized discourse, [Williams links] a descendant of Polish immigrants with imagery traditionally associated with black characters . . . [and thus] broaches the topic of miscegenation in a play ostensibly without an Africanist presence" ("Misrepresentation" 345). In an eloquent defense of Stanley as Pan-Dionysius, Riddell entoned, "Stanley and Stella move freely between elemental sex and mystical experience, and Williams lends to their relationship every possible symbolic device to enforce the mystical oneness of their union." Popkin concurred that "Adonis reigns in Stanley's world where Blanche must be seen as the dreaded destructive Gargoyle." For Tischler, "Stanley is all that keeps Stella from decaying like Blanche" (*Tennessee* 137). Stanley's sexuality earns him kudos as a popular hero for Winchell. In light of mass-audience appeal, Stanley is "cheered" by Winchell as "the bad boy . . . [who] proves that the sententious schoolmarm is really a secret nympho" (140). Ganz, on the other hand, links Stanley's sexuality to Williams's homoeroticism. Stanley "becomes the avenger of [Blanche's] homosexual husband" and appropriately is "identified with the lonely homosexual."

Challenging Blanche and Stanley dichotomies, several critics have valorized the "contradictions" Kazan strove to include in the role. Adler, for instance, reminds us that there is a "Blanche-side to Stanley" (*Streetcar* 54), meaning that Mr. Kowalski also displays tenderness and claims his own set of illusions—through colored lights and red pajamas. Bigsby likewise admits Stanley's tenderness (*Critical Introduction* 106). Brando's monumental performance greatly influenced *Streetcar* criticism. "With Marlon Brando's performance, Stanley, a sneering bully, became an American icon" (Hodgson 547). Gronbeck-Tedesco studies Brando's body language as part of the Group Theatre tradition and as a reflection of Stanley's attractiveness. Brando's devoted love for Stella and his own "feminine side" have surely created a "kinder" Stanley. Bentley, however, faulted Kazan, and Brando, for an interpretation that "distorted" the text by having Brando's "tough talk" basically be the "mask of a suffering human soul" (87). Some critics, it seems, want their Stanleys on the raw side.

Stella

Stella (for "star"), Blanche's younger sister, is the prize over which Blanche and Stanley strategize. She is implicated in the central problems of the play. According to Tischler, "Stella is the key figure" in *Streetcar* (*Tennessee* 137). Correspondingly, Robinson claims that "Stanley's behavior doesn't rankle Blanche as much as Stella's" since with her "achieved sexuality, Stella unintentionally mocks Blanche's failure to be the woman she hoped to be" (39). Stella must make two crucial choices in *Streetcar*: coming to terms with her Belle Reve heritage and responding to Blanche's/Stanley's view of the truth at the end of the play. Almost all of the criticism about Stella centers on these two issues.

Stella's escape from the world of Belle Reve represented by Blanche has won her applause or contempt. For Quirino, Stella sold out, accepting the "sex-glutted death in life of Elysian Fields" (83) and, with Stanley, became "one of the living dead narcotized by sex, gaming, and comic books" (86). Echoing these sentiments, Melman arraigned Stella because she "drugs herself on sex in order to forget the blatant emptiness of her existence" (137), a view endorsed by Lant's reading (229). Louise Blackwell finds Stella is in the predicament of many Williams's women "who have subordinated themselves to a domineering and often inferior person to attain reality and meaning through communication with another person" (102). According to Davis, who discards Robinson's sympathy for Blanche's sister, Stella is a plucky and revengeful doxy who wants to display "her victory, thereby reassuring herself that she has escaped her sister's 'fate.' " Stella eagerly "wants her sister to hear and to play the voyeur so she can shine as happily married pregnant sexual exhibitionist" (69). Harris estimated that Stella could have had "a creative potential even greater than that of Blanche, [but] is so acclimatized to this unwritten but very palpable code [Stanley's patriarchy] that she never questions it" (94). Perhaps more understandingly, Cohn classified Stella, like Mitch, as "part-victim and part-brute" (107). Londré insightfully concludes that although Stella chose to "be trapped in marriage to a man who makes messes for her to clean up" ("A *Streetcar* Running" 56), she will "now have to live with illusion, as Blanche did . . . [she] and Mitch have been . . . changed by Blanche's passage; perhaps they will find it in themselves to stand up against the hegemony of the apes" (62).

Many critics respect Stella for accepting "her dual nature," blending sex and soul (Asselineau 154). According to Bigsby, "Stella's compassion is real. She negotiates a middle ground. Her actions are dictated by a blend of necessity and love." Unlike Blanche, she "has the chance to rebuild" and can bring out Stanley's gentler side (*Critical Introduction* 62). For Winchell, Stella is the true star of the play for her honest sexuality. From his cultural perspective, K. Balachandran hails Stella as "a typical Indian Woman—an obedient daughter, a considerate sister, an affectionate wife and a responsive mother" (74). Absolving Stella from any wrongdoing, Kernan holds that "Stella, like most humans, participates in both [ways of life], kin to the 'romantic' and married to the 'realist.' Her moral sense is still active" (112). In Sievers's view, Stella is "a healthy housewife adjusted to reality, expecting a child, and serenely happy. . . . With unconscious jealousy, Blanche tries to split them apart" (quoted in Miller 91).

Stella's behavior in scene 11—watching as Blanche goes off to the asylum—ameliorates or frustrates closure for the critics. Abbott upholds Stella's "vital lie": "she must believe that she has done the right thing," since "there is no room for both" Stanley and Blanche in her world (144). Focusing on Stella's dilemma over believing Stanley or her sister about the rape, Adler concludes that the ending is uncertain: "Whether or not Stanley is victorious in imposing upon Stella an identity that defines her by submission remains satisfyingly ambiguous as the curtain closes" (*Streetcar* 66). Far more censorious, Lant blames Stella more than Blanche for not facing the facts; it is Stella who "constantly refuses to look at things . . . or even tell the truth" (229). Bray damns Stella with faint praise as practical, "synthetic"; through her choice at the end of *Streetcar*, Stella is "guaranteed relative economic and familial security in the future" with Stanley because she has "successfully adapted to his world" (194).

Many readers, however, predict no such tranquility for the Kowalskis. Though she has "chosen to accept reality" and forsake Belle Reve, Stella for Tischler "may never love Stanley as she did in the past; she may now devote herself to her children" (*Tennessee* 139). In two articles, Cardullo argues that the marriage bond has been severely shaken and that the child will be the wedge between Stella and Stanley ("Role," "Birth"). Stella's absence from the script in scene 11 is, for Cardullo, "indicative of the essential silence that will permeate the rest of their lives" ("Birth" 174). Faulting Stella, Melman believes that she "must consciously . . . compromise the truth to 'keep on going,' thus trapping herself within illusion, just as her sister is trapped" (128). According to Hulley, though, by taking a stand in sending Blanche to the madhouse, Stella helps to separate truth from illusion and propel the play from "discourse" to action (94).

Mitch

Unlike Blanche or Stanley, about whom a variety of critical opinion flourishes, Mitch has not fared well. He is often dismissed as pathetic at best and criticized for his lack of manliness symbolized by his being a "mama's boy" and working in the "spare parts department" at Stanley's factory. Mitch is "too much a bungler to be a hero" (Bedient). Several critics link him with the Gentleman Caller of *The Glass Menagerie* (Falk; Adler, *Streetcar*; Bray), but even so, Mitch's faults are glaring. Characterizing him as an "effete foil of the bestial Stanley," Bray believes that Mitch, like Jim O'Connor, "compensates for his insecurity with a somewhat pathetic attempt at machismo" (191). In 1955, Sievers characterized Mitch's psychological problem as that of a "boy with an Oedipus Complex, wanting to escape his mother yet loyally worshiping her" (quoted in Miller 91). Forty years later, Kleb intensified and expanded Mitch's problems: "Unmanly sensitivity, disease, arrested adolescence, even sexual confusion, have all symbolically planted their seeds in Mitch" (33). Mitch has been unfavorably contrasted with Stanley's vigorous animalism and even linked to Allan Grey and, temperamentally, to Blanche (Kleb 33; Adler, *Streetcar* 68–69).

Beyond dispute, Mitch is both Blanche's victim and oppressor. She "plays him like a fish" (Harris 91); and he is so "full of pent-up sexuality" that he becomes an easy "prey to Blanche's allure" (Adler, *Streetcar* 69). According to Cardullo, Blanche creates a "make-believe" world for Mitch (painting herself as "an old fashioned girl"), yet "without Mitch's love," she enters another make-believe world where the Doctor is Shep ("Birth" 170–71). Although some positive things have been said of Mitch for his differences from Stanley's crowd, he is more frequently attacked for his phoniness, most blatantly by Davis, who believes that if Mitch "tried to be like Stanley, he'd fail miserably" (71). He gets Blanche to admit the truth but is unable to rape her, leaving the job to the more manly Stanley. Adler, however, shows how Mitch "resembles Stanley" (*Streetcar* 70). Mitch's fate is, according to Miller, to go "back to home and mother, to a spiritual death of his own" (14).

Eunice

Eunice Hubbell, the Kowalskis' upstairs neighbor, and her husband Steve have often been marginalized as stereotypical comic foils to Stanley and Stella; the Hubbells are a burlesque team in the "satyr play" within *Streetcar* (Debusscher 151). According to Vlasopolos, Eunice lacks individuality and, together with the other characters, functions as "a chorus, a fairly undifferentiated unit that is swayed by the exercise of authority in scene 11" (328). The most detailed, sympathetic reading of Eunice is by Kolin, who argues that she has been wrongly trivialized. As a pivotal character, she "symbolizes the compassionate virtues that lie at the core of Williams's belief system—feminine friendship, feminine sense of place, and a hardy realism that triumphs amid so much pain" ("Eunice Hubbell" 119).

Allan

Though a ghost, Allan Grey is central to any discussion of Blanche's past and her presence in *Streetcar*. The most rewarding assessment of Allan Grey, and the problems this character raised in the script, the film version, and for the censors, is Gene D. Phillips, S. J.'s "Blanche's Phantom Husband." Other discussions of him are found in Adler (*Streetcar* 44–45; 68–69), Bedient (51–52), and Thompson (29–30). Bigsby alone suggests that Blanche married Allan "because he would not force her to acknowledge her own sexuality" (*Critical Introduction* 65). Susan Koprince studies Allan as one of Williams's "unseen" characters, a "consistent" character type in the canon (87).

Symbols

The most important symbols in *Streetcar*—Blanche's paper lantern, the naked lightbulb, mirror, the moth, the streetcar, food and drink, the rape, and the use of colors, place, and costume—have received intensive attention. Quirino focuses on the symbolism behind the card games and water in *Streetcar*. For brief overviews of these and other symbols, consult Boxill (83–85); Bigsby (*Critical Introduction* 59); Griffin (69–73); Falk (55–56); and Londré (*Tennessee* 94–95). Jackson claims that the symbols in *Streetcar* display Blanche's progressive madness.

For Adler, the lantern is "perhaps the major" symbol of the play. It represents Blanche's "vulnerability and subjugation to time's decay" but is also a sign of her creativity that shields her "from the grimness and cruelty of reality" (*Streetcar* 30). Kernan had earlier explicated the lantern as an "artificial light, not a natural one, which reveals Blanche as old and cheap" (112). Discussing the lantern and

Blanche's mirror, Fleche observes, "When Blanche shatters her mirror, she . . . shows that her identity has already been fractured; she doesn't see herself in the mirror; she sees the mirror as herself" (102). Cohn usefully comments on the symbology of the names in *Streetcar*, while Kolin explicates the mythic and gaming allusions behind Jax Beer ("Why Stanley"). Kolin also explores the network of paper signifiers in and underneath the script in *Streetcar*, including poetry, legal documents, and artifacts, and concludes that for Williams paper is "both script and Scripture" (" 'It's Only a Paper Moon' " 455).

New Orleans, Williams's "spiritual home," is his signature symbolic landscape. As Stella tells her visiting sister, "New Orleans isn't like other cities." Helpful articles by Barranger ("New Orleans") and Richardson explicate the city's symbolic roles in *Streetcar*. By gathering documents about Williams's residences in New Orleans, Holditch offers much primary evidence pertinent to an interpretation of *Streetcar* ("Last Frontier"). The sounds of the city, exclusive of its music, also have great symbolic import. For example, Kolin points out that the vendor's cries at the end of scene 2 summarize what has happened and project what will come (" 'Red Hot!' ").

Plot

Early reviewers criticized the *Streetcar* plot as episodic and disjointed, not understanding that in Williams's plastic theatre, realism, expressionism, and naturalism coalesce to (re)present Blanche's illusions. Several critics—for example, Corrigan, Adler, and Murphy—explore *Streetcar* as a lyrical drama with nonrealistic staging. Yet, as Adler points out, *Streetcar* "easily adapts itself to the three-act structure common to the commercial theater of its day" (*Streetcar* 19). Tischler called *Streetcar*'s plotting "outstanding" yet "simple" at the same time (*Tennessee* 140). Londré (*Tennessee*; "A *Streetcar* Running"), Griffin, and Falk offer careful plot summaries.

Critics variously explain how Williams's plot works. For Adler, it is built around "a pattern of arrival and departure" (*Streetcar* 26), while the "pattern of bonds between people maimed and broken functions as Williams's chief structural device" (23). According to Boxill, *Streetcar* is "built" around "the eviction and spoiled occasion" (85). Though Thompson sees *Streetcar* as "a romantic tragedy . . . [and] also as a dark, ironic comedy" (50), many readers, following Kazan, have defined *Streetcar* as a tragedy, in part because of its plot—Harwood, Berkman, and Miller, in particular. Atkinson thought that *Streetcar* was "almost unbearably tragic" (2:1). Also emphasizing *Streetcar*'s tragic dimensions, Falk maintained that Williams's plot is worked out through a series of "clashes" building to "fever pitch" with Blanche's rape. Callahan, on the other hand, evaluated the polarities and dualities in *Streetcar* in terms of good and evil. Lant points to events through which Williams has intentionally undercut Blanche's tragedy (228). Mood perceptively analyzed "the structural development and design of the play" (9) in light of the directions Blanche receives to Stella's apartment.

More recent criticism focuses on the problematics of Williams's plot, especially "the strain in the play's sense of closure" (Fleche 123). Savran believes that Williams's endings are "as inconclusive" as Chekhov's, "suspending rather than resolving contradictions" (90). Hulley and Schlueter, as we saw, track the competing scripts that Stanley and Blanche incorporate into the plot. Approaching *Streetcar* from reader-response theory, Schlueter (" 'We've Had This Date' ") argues for and re-creates a dual reading of the play's plot(s). Demanding comparison with Schlueter's reading, Londré observes that "a dramaturgical analysis that takes Blanche as the protagonist would logically place her crisis not in Scene 9, as Kazan did (making her a passive figure who is acted upon in the last two scenes), but in Scene 11, when (as the active agent of her own destiny) she finds a way to salvage her dignity" ("A *Streetcar* Running" 61). The most theoretical (and complex) analysis of the *Streetcar* plot, though, is in Fleche's poststructural analysis. Dismantling the traditional sense of an unfolding, tragic plot, Fleche posits that in *Streetcar* Williams was "visualizing the restless discourse of desire, that uncontainable movement between inside and outside, soul and body" (99). Arguing that "closure was [for Williams] always just next door to entrapment" (100), Fleche finds that *Streetcar*'s realistic, moralistic ending is almost perversely "forced" and that the "theatrical release [Blanche going mad] isn't purifying" at all (106).

PROBLEMS A *STREETCAR NAMED DESIRE* POSES FOR CRITICS

Streetcar has left readers perplexed about its characters, genre, ethical/gender issues, and whether it presents a consistent point of view. The play for many abounds in ambiguity. Blanche's stature is undoubtedly one of the most disconcerting elements for critics: is she tragic or manipulative, victim or aggressor, heterosexual female or homosexual male? Does she exhibit transcendent saving grace or infectious madness at the end of the play? Tied to Blanche's status, of course, is Stanley's, and a long, contentious chorus of critics has raised the vexatious question of whose play it is: who has control and where do Williams's sympathies lie? According to Lant, *Streetcar* fails because it "is rent . . . by a thematic inconsistency" (232), reflecting Williams's "double attitude toward Blanche"; "it is difficult to feel pity and terror for Blanche's plight (when we know we should) and . . . it is difficult not to feel vindicated by Stanley's brutal ascendancy (when we know we should not)" (227).

Recent discussions of gender by Clum, Davis, Hulley, Lant, Lilly, Savran, and Schlueter may differ in their conclusions, but each has problematized the script in ways radically different from an earlier generation of critics. The result is a much more complex view of Williams's own presence in the play. A closely related problem for critics deals with *Streetcar*'s genre. Is the play a tragedy or not? Some critics have faulted Williams for not being more faithful to the pristine standards of realism, while others have praised him for being unctuously repetitive and derivative. To what genre does *Streetcar* belong? Homan, for example, claims that it starts out as a comedy and then turns into a tragedy.

Another recurrent problem in *Streetcar* criticism concentrates on how to read the play. While earlier critics neatly wrapped up the ending as spiritual triumph (Schvey, Quirino) or, more recently, sexual celebration for the Kowalskis (Kleb, Bedient), other readers have stressed that Williams intentionally thwarts any attempt at easy closure or comfortable rapprochement between realism and expressionism (Fleche, Davis).

CHIEF PRODUCTIONS

Streetcar may be the most frequently produced American play. It premiered on 3 December 1947, ran for 855 performances on Broadway, and was the first play to win the Pulitzer Prize, the New York Drama Critics Award, and the Donaldson Award. Williams was thirty-six years old. Adler celebrates *Streetcar*'s achievement in light of the Pulitzer Prize (*Mirror*). The play's phenomenal success was attributed to the creative energies of Williams, Kazan, and scenographer Jo Mielziner, whose collaboration changed the American theatre.

Required reading on *Streetcar*'s progress from script to stage is Kazan's *Notebook*. Contextualizing the *Notebook*, Murphy's second chapter, "Subject and Object: A *Streetcar Named Desire*" (16–63), surveys the dynamics and aesthetics of the Williams/Kazan collaboration as well as the director's concept and realization of the characters. Arguing for a greater role than director for Kazan, Murphy cogently documents his intimate and extensive influence on the entire creative process, including props, gestures, costume, and music, and their implications for character and actors. Burks also supplies important information on the casting, acting, and staging, while Downing sheds light on the stage manager's responsibilities in producing *Streetcar*. Worth consulting, too, are studies of Kazan by David Richard Jones, Ciment, and Pauly. Pauly (77–87), for instance, concludes that in directing *Streetcar*, Kazan was fulfilling his own "professional identity"— his "sympathy for victims of social injustice" and his emphasis on the "disturbed psychology of this condition." Brief, rewarding overviews of *Streetcar* on stage can be found in Tischler (*Tennessee* 140–49), Falk (60–61), Londré (*Tennessee* 95–96), Boxill (88–93), and Griffin (74–78).

Kolin gathers and evaluates reviews of the *Streetcar* tryouts in Boston, Philadelphia, and New Haven ("First Critical"). Miller (29–47) and Hurrell provide a generous sample of the Broadway reviews. With few exceptions (e.g., Mary McCarthy, who accused Williams of "careerism"), the *Streetcar* reviews were rave. Williams was heralded as the new Eugene O'Neill and *Streetcar* as a masterpiece (Atkinson). Watts isolated "two characteristic traits of Mr. Williams' morbid imagination" that would continue to occupy critics and directors alike: "a lyrical originality in his pessimism" and "doomed heroines . . . so helplessly enmeshed in their fate that they cannot put up a proper dramatic battle against it" (43).

The original *Streetcar* cast, young and relatively unknown, earned stardom for their work. Williams was to say that Brando's Stanley ruined the role for all other actors. From a twenty-five-year retrospective, Wilson observed, "Even today it is difficult to tell where Stanley Kowalski ends and Marlon Brando begins; Stanley seems to have entered Brando almost as much as he defined the part" (12). Tough yet tender, Brando, under Kazan's direction, stole audience sympathy away from Jessica Tandy's Blanche (Clurman). Praised for her gracefulness and fragility, Tandy nonetheless lacked the feistiness of her successor Uta Hagen or the humor and coquetry of Vivien Leigh. Spector and Barranger ("Three Women") assess differences in performance and interpretation of these first Blanches.

From late 1948 through the early 1950s *Streetcar* went through a dazzling series of European premieres in which a variety of distinguished directors and designers left their mark on the play. In December 1948 *Streetcar* premiered in Brussels and in Amsterdam. Kolin examines the Italian premiere (21 January 1949) in depth (" 'From Coitus' "). The production, performed by the Rina Morelli–Paolo Stoppa Company in Rome, was enormously successful because of three Italian figures from the world of film. Count Luchino Visconti, whose extraordinary film credits include *Ossessione* and *The Leopard*, directed Vittorio Gassman as a savage Stanley and Marcello Mastroianni as a young "dear tender boy," a "nice boy from a working man's background." Franco Zeffirelli designed a realistic, un-Mielziner set that foregrounded the Kowalski bed as the central symbol of the production. A diminutive Rina Morelli (barely five feet tall) may have been the shortest Blanche on record, and her size won her immediate sympathy from the Italian audiences. In March the play opened in Gothenburg, Sweden, directed by Ingmar Bergman, who transformed the *Streetcar* setting, intercutting a movie theatre and dance hall from *The Glass Menagerie* to represent desire "as illusion, escape, entrapment . . . the key to Blanche's tragedy" (Kolin, "On a Trolley" 281). In October 1949, Sir Laurence Olivier directed his wife Vivien Leigh in the London *Streetcar* two years before her film debut as Blanche. Olivier cut Williams's script (and justified his decision) in a version that held the British boards for over twenty years (Kolin, " 'Affectionate and Mighty' "). British critics were less enthusiastic about Williams's play than were their American counterparts. Though Williams was praised for his characters and symbolism, several London reviewers deplored his sordid subject matter: "All we saw . . . was a squalid anecdote of a nymphomaniac's decay in a New Orleans slum" (Trewin 7).

The French premiere, also in October 1949, was a debacle. Falb briefly surveys the French reception (28–30). Adapted by Jean Cocteau, Williams's *Streetcar* was transformed into "a risible piece of entertainment" (MacColl 94). A half-naked black "shimmy dancer" performed in the background before Blanche's rape, pantomimed behind a scrim. French critics decried the production; Paris audiences rioted. Yet Cocteau's adaptation unsuspectingly prepared the way for alternative productions in the 1980s and 1990s. The German premiere, chronicled and interpreted by Wolter, took place in Pforzheim in March 1950, using a translation mandated by the American censor but not faithful to the nuances of Williams's poetry. Studies of other national premieres from 1953 to 1987 include Moscow (Shaland); Norway (Skei); Mexico; Japan (Kolin, "Japanese Premiere"); Spain (Kolin, " 'Cruelty and Sweaty' "); Cuba (Kolin, "*Streetcar* in Havana"); Italy (Kolin, " 'Coitus' "); and China (Kolin and Shao).

A *Streetcar* revival at the Coconut Grove Playhouse in Miami in 1956 and later that year at the City Center in New York, starring Tallulah Bankhead (Williams's friend and bête noire), was disastrous. Although Williams originally wrote Blanche with Bankhead in mind, she was quickly rejected for the role in 1947 because, as Burks pointed out, Williams realized that "a Blanche who is brilliant in the 'big scenes,' but misses the subtleties of mood in other scenes, would leave audiences unmoved and unimpressed by the tragedy of her situation" (29). Bankhead's breezy, comic, and boisterous interpretation projected a completely different Blanche from the graceful or vulnerable ones before. Israel's biography chronicles Bankhead's performance (301–7), as does Leverich.

To celebrate *Streetcar*'s twenty-fifth anniversary, bicoastal productions were staged in April 1973 at Lincoln Center in New York, with Ellis Rabb directing Rosemary Harris as Blanche and James Farentino as Stanley, and in Los Angeles at the Ahmanson Theatre, with James Bridges directing Faye Dunaway as Blanche and Jon Voight as Stanley. Though these productions affirmed *Streetcar*'s continuing power as a masterpiece, they were not enthusiastically received. While Harris captured Blanche's humor and dignity, critics complained that she either "lacks the fragile vulnerability" (Wilson) or "overstresses the quivering and shaken Southern belle" (Clurman 636). Farentino's Stanley was judged barely competent; he had the build but not the "demon"; he lacked the "complicated seductive terror of the clash" between Stanley and Blanche (Kroll 109).

If the critics found Farentino's Stanley lacking, they despaired of Voight's interpretation altogether. Offering a non-Brando Stanley, Voight "underplayed" the role, offering a "quiet, halting Stanley," which was disastrous. "He even throws dishes politely," mocked Farber (15). Sullivan complained that Voight's "boyishness" (10) interfered with the control that Stanley displays at the poker table. Voight did not wear a T-shirt, preferring a buttoned shirt and Soho vest. Dunaway's Blanche was more resourceful—stronger than Harris's—in part because of her background in comedy, affording even more laughs than Stanley (Farber 15). But she missed Blanche's "white-moth magic" (Sullivan 1).

A London revival with Claire Bloom in a blond wig was staged from 14 March to May 1974, giving critics occasion to comment on how British *Streetcars* and Blanches had changed since Olivier's interpretation twenty-five years earlier. Overall, the production was judged "superb," "effective," "stunning." Unlike Vivien Leigh's more hysterical and comic Blanche, Bloom played the role with an "elegance that never deserts her" (Young 3C). Wardle described Bloom as "delicately dispensing Southern coquetry over an undertow of hysterical panic" (15D). Kingston concurred, observing that "Bloom presents Blanche's pitiful gestures of refinement [with a] sustained tension" (519). Gone was Blanche's "comic fantasy," and even "her promiscuous past" seemed hard to imagine (Wardle 15D). In Bloom's interpretation, Blanche became an elegant British lady. Martin Shaw's Stanley also departed from Brando's "dumb-ox" interpretation; he was a "young, fluent, ruthless destroyer" (Wardle 15D). Kingston even affirmed that Stanley's prowess was glorified over Blanche's "futile romancing" (519), though Young claimed that there was "little likeable about [Shaw's Stanley] but his body" (3C). Director Edwin Sherin won rave reviews, and scenographer Patrick Roberts was praised for a set that captured New Orleans and also "eliminates any sense of privacy" for Blanche, leaving "her feeling naked" (Wardle 15D).

In August 1986, Nikos Psacharopoulos, the director of the Williamstown Theatre Festival, staged a revival of *Streetcar* starring Blythe Danner and Christopher Walken. It clearly was Danner's show; she portrayed an earthy, not delicate, Blanche whose sexual candor was closer to what Williams had intended, though *Streetcar* was prevented from such displays by the production code of the early 1950s. If Walken wanted to undo the Brando influence, he failed miserably by not "giv[ing] off any sexual heat," and his rape of Blanche came closer to "a gallant kiss" (Vineberg 235).

Psacharopoulos staged a second revival of *Streetcar* in New York's Circle in the Square Theatre from 10 March to 22 May 1988. While Humm extolled *Streetcar* as "always worth reviving," this particular production tampered so much with the "play's . . . values" as understood by the "popular perception of Williams's characters" that it was judged a failure. Critics claimed that this *Streetcar* dismantled the script because it was miscast—Danner starred as Blanche, but now with Aidan Quinn as Stanley. While Danner, whose Dixie accent was faulted, was "successful in the hightoned affectation side" of Blanche, she "never seems like a real person" (Humm), and "you never see that she is both attracted and repelled by Stanley" (Hodgson 547). Quinn's Stanley was worse. Cast more often as a "clean-cut young man," Quinn had neither the build nor the temperament to play the turbulent Kowalski. "There's no powerful animal magnetism . . . no aura of danger" in his portrayal (Hodgson 548). Without a battle of the sexes, *Streetcar* is no *Streetcar*. Like Voight, Quinn challenged a Brando-ized Kowalski and turned audiences off. Equally disappointing for the reviewers was the round stage, which hardly suggested the cramped squalor of the Kowalski apartment or the sleazy New Orleans milieu.

On 12 April 1992, Alec Baldwin and Jessica Lange, directed by Gregory Mosher, staged a revival of *Streetcar* at the same theatre, the Barrymore, where the play had premiered forty-five years earlier. Running for 160 performances, this *Streetcar* disappointed the critics, most of whom cited Lange's acting as the main problem. In her Broadway debut, Lange portrayed Blanche as a "sacrificial victim" (Richards 2: 5), consistent with the screen roles (e.g., Francis Farmer) that made her famous, but she drained power from the role. Rich complained that Lange's Blanche was "weepy" and had "no layers of personality" (C1); she was "spaced out" and did not project Blanche as the tiger or the moth (C18). Concluding that Baldwin and Lange were mismatched, the critics gave his Stanley higher marks than her Blanche; because of her weakness, Baldwin was "forced to rein in his efforts" (Richards 2:5). Like Brando, Baldwin exuded animal sexuality yet made Stanley funnier and more ingenious. Timothy Carhart inappropriately played a "glamorous" Mitch, and "glamour . . . is the last thing you want of Mitch" (Richards 2:5).

Also a vital part of *Streetcar*'s stage history are alternative productions. *Streetcars* with all-black casts open up the script to themes and interpretations never privileged in white productions (Kolin, "Williams in Ebony"). A cross-gender adaptation, *Belle Reprieve* (1991), staged by gay and lesbian theatre companies, reversed expectations of social and sexual roles, revealing *Streetcar*'s "tensions, attractions, and sexual politics" (Leonard 386). Blanche was played by the famous drag queen Bette Bourne and Stanley by lesbian actress Peggy Shaw. A reviewer for *Theater Week* observed that this production with its "gendered role playing" proved that "cross-dressed roles in the 1990's America can attain the artistic heights of cross-dressed Kabuki or Peking opera" ("Bloolips" 38). Even this very free adaptation of *Streetcar* establishes the play's powerful contribution to American culture and sexuality.

FILM AND TELEVISION VERSIONS

The classic 1951 Warner Brothers film of *Streetcar* starred the original Broadway cast with one notable exception: Vivien Leigh replaced Tandy, no doubt so producer Irene Selznick could capitalize on Leigh's film success as Scarlett O'Hara, another southern belle. Kazan opened Williams's script when he directed the film, and one of the key critical inquiries has been to see how the film and the play differ. Assessments of Kazan's methods, the film's symbols, and the problems of censorship are discussed in the *Streetcar* chapters in Phillips (*Films*) and Yacowar and in Phillips's subsequent essay ("*Streetcar*"). Ciment also usefully details Kazan's changes of the script for the film.

Censorship hounded *Streetcar* on stage and in film. Tischler ("Sanitizing") perceptively assesses the problems Williams's script raised—homosexuality and Blanche's sexual behavior—which were "far beyond the boundaries of acceptability in the 1940s" (50). Furthermore, Tischler claims, that "Blanche may be asking Stanley to rape her . . . [to] expiate her sins against Allan . . . turn[ing] sexual violence into a ritual act. Williams knew that combining sex and religion was anathema to American audiences" (50). Tischler discovered that Irene Selznick, Williams's producer, hired Lillian Hellman to prepare a more acceptable "shooting script" for the film version, but Hellman's solutions to the censorship problems—dispensing with homosexuality entirely; making Blanche's marriage problems indefinite; casting doubt on the rape itself—were clearly unacceptable to Williams, who saw himself as both Blanche and Stanley. Nonetheless, "Hellman's scenario was to triumph in the actual filming" (55) until the recently restored version reflected Williams original intentions. Studying the film in light of the industry's "censorship board" and the Catholic church's Legion of Decency, Cahir stressed that "the success of the film, oddly, is due in part to the way in which Kazan and Williams turned the tables and made potentially destructive constraints work constructively in the movie" (72). Yet Dowling claimed that theatre audiences saw a far different *Streetcar* than those who attended the film: "Blanche was made to appear much more 'virginal' in the film. . . . Conversely, Stanley was made to appear much more brutal, unattractive and villainous" (237). Also studying the production history of the film version, R. Barton Palmer found that in creating Stanley, Williams "contributed centrally to a radical transformation of what Americans had previously valued as ideal, male qualities" (220). Eroticizing the male body through Brando, Williams, according to Palmer, turned man from the "bearer of sexual desire" to its "object" (219–20). Exploring the film from "a semiotic point of view," Schnathmeier, on the other hand, insisted on a basic unity between film and play. Restored clips of the ending (first made available in 1994) show that the reconciliation between Stanley and Stella was far less problematic and tentative than in the 1951 film (Londré, "A *Streetcar* Running" 62). McCraw's interview with composer Luigi Zaninelli provides invaluable commentary on Alex North's haunting musical score.

On 4 March 1984, director John Erman's teleplay for ABC TV offered a much more racy and heavily adapted *Streetcar*. Starring Ann-Margret and Treat Williams, Erman's *Streetcar* was judged far less successful than Kazan's. The most helpful analysis of the 1984 televised *Streetcar* is in Schlueter ("Imitating an Icon"), who argues that though Erman sacramentalized "Blanche's wish for purification" (146), Ann-Margret "convert[ed] Leigh's coyness into shameless flirtation." Interviews with Ann-Margret by Hodges and Turan are also essential reading.

A second teleplay of *Streetcar* aired on 29 October 1995 on the CBS "Playhouse 90" series. Lange and Baldwin repeated their 1992 Broadway *Streetcar*, now directed by Glenn Jordan, who also produced the teleplay, but with two major cast changes, John Goodman as Mitch and Diane Lane as Stella. "This *Streetcar* is the first on-screen adaptation faithful to Williams' text (it runs three hours), including the ending that the 1951 production code deemed shocking for Kazan's film" (Schultz). Referring to the Kazan film, John O'Connor praised the Lange-Baldwin teleplay because the "production does not . . . get trapped in the memorable Kazan interpretation of the play" (D22). Overall, Lange received much better reviews for her televised *Streetcar* than for the stage production three years earlier. Rosenberg affirmed that "whatever her flaws, if any, they are not evident here" (F21). Lange's Blanche was far less fragile than Leigh's, and Baldwin's Stanley was seen as Lange's match at last. Reviewers emphasized that Baldwin brought credibility to the role, portraying a Stanley more complex than brutish.

CONCLUDING OVERVIEW

Everything American pours in and out of the seams of *Streetcar*, the quintessential American play. *Streetcar*'s production history stamps it as our most sought-after dramatic export, a monument to our theatre in the world, our world in the theatre. *Streetcar* is a chautauqua of American idea(l)s—desires, anxieties, national contradictions. American indeterminacies of time, place, and event are the collage of Williams's dramaturgical ideologies. Speaking of the "violent interplay" of his characters, Williams celebrates in theatre the characteristic American trait of random restlessness: "Every moment of human existence is alive with uncertainty. . . . I want them [audiences] to leave . . . feeling that they have met with a vividly allusive as well as disturbingly elusive experience" (*Where I Live* 73). In *Streetcar*, the American allusive is the other side of the American elusive. America is unfixedly situated everywhere in *Streetcar*.

The protean American character saturates *Streetcar*. Blanche Leigh in a Scarlett wrapper typifies our past and future simultaneously. Blanche is Old World charm and New Age desuetude. Her spiritual ancestors rode on the Mayflower, and her congeners are in the employ of the Mayflower madame. She is Walt Whitman, Edna Pontellier, and Mae West, masculine and feminine, and sometimes both. She has high tea with Miss Amanda for a William Paxton canvas yet gives the masculine gaze the slip in the Thomas Hart Benton painting. She is the southern belle on Black Tuesday, 1929, and a bag lady, one of the forlorn homeless (as in a 1991 Seattle production, described in Kolin, "Reflections" 3). She is one of the best cover girls in all of American drama. She courts intimacy to the point of parody.

But so does Stanley. He is Young Goodman Kowalski, the liquor-swilling traveling salesman and also the groom carrying his bride into the new frontier of squalid American flats. "He fills the play with the America of big-shouldered urban industrialism of brute strength and vulgar humors" (Rich C1). He is a post-Hiroshima Teddy Roosevelt and a 1950s Dixie Democrat venerating a placard written by Huey P. Long. In the 1990s he may even wear a Tommy Hilfiger shirt.

Streetcar is rich in the place(less)ness of America, too. It entertains us in quaint drugstores and boisterous neighborhood bars, bowling alleys, amusement parks, and casinos. It feeds us at toney restaurants and at hot-dog stands. It is a play at work as well. We hear the cries of street vendors; the sound of dynamos (in Kazan's interpolated factory scene); the clang of streetcars; and the whispers of small shopkeepers—like Kiefaber—and the rumors in hushed laughter at schools. We hear barge traffic on America's longest and most vital river. Old Man River, the Mississippi, divides the American river god from his votaries in Faubourg-Marigny. Even the smell of the god's incense, redolent coffee, is indeterminately American. It comes from somewhere else before it becomes café au lait at the Café du Monde.

Two cemeteries simultaneously reverence and repudiate the American experience in *Streetcar*: the smaller one at Belle Reve and the larger, more engulfing one in New Orleans where a Mexican threnodist sings of *flores* that last yet still rust. The play takes us on a streetcar ride to eternity and/or to extinction, and we cannot be sure who is riding at any one time. Blanche is not the only one assured a ticket; Stanley has purchased one, too. New Orleans streetcars become buses bound for Laurel that are transformed into black sedans that instinctively know the way to the charnel house. "Perhaps we all ride the *Streetcar* without knowing it," says Davis (76).

Streetcar is America's *Hamlet*, filled with mystery and demystification, figures and figuration. The opening and central question of *Hamlet*—"Who's there?"—is often asked in and of *Streetcar*. The answers chronicle the anxieties of its creator and country alike. It is Tennessee Williams who is Pan and panderer; he is St. Sebastian and a resident of Ritz Men Only. But we as audience are also inscribed and implicated in *Streetcar*, even though the play denies us the comfortable predictability of a tidy explanation or self-justification. Icons change. To ride the streetcar is to ride the critical whirlwind and the whisper of rumor. Even so, we have seen more of America in *Streetcar* than we ever could from a 1950s Greyhound Scenic Cruiser or from the latest Tom Cruise film.

WORKS CITED

Abbott, Anthony S. *The Vital Lie: Reality and Illusion in Modern Drama.* Tuscaloosa: U of Alabama P, 1989.

Adler, Thomas P. *Mirror on the Stage: The Pulitzer Plays as an Approach to American Drama.* West Lafayette, IN: Purdue UP, 1987.

———. "The Search for God in the Plays of Tennessee Williams." *Renascence* 26 (Autumn 1973): 48–56.

———. *"A Streetcar Named Desire": The Moth and the Lantern.* Boston: Twayne, 1990.

Asselineau, Roger. "The Tragic Transcendentalism of Tennessee Williams." *The Transcendentalist Constant in American Literature.* New York: New York UP, 1980. 153–62.

Atkinson, Brooks. " 'Streetcar' Tragedy—Mr. Williams's Report on Life in New Orleans." *New York Times* 14 Dec. 1947, sec. 2: 1.

Balachandran, K. "Marriage and Family Life in Tennessee Williams." *Notes on Mississippi Writers* 21, no. 2 (1989): 69–76.

Barranger, Milly S. "New Orleans as Theatrical Image in Plays by Tennessee Williams." *Southern Quarterly* 23 (Winter 1985): 38–54.

———. "Three Women Called Blanche." *Tennessee Williams Literary Journal* 1 (Spring 1987): 15–30.

Bedient, Calvin. "There Are Lives That Desire Does Not Sustain: *A Streetcar Named Desire.*" *Confronting Tennessee Williams's A Streetcar Named Desire: Essays in Critical Pluralism.* Ed. Philip C. Kolin. Westport: Greenwood, 1993. 45–58.

Bentley, Eric. *In Search of Theater.* New York: Atheneum, 1975.

Berkman, Leonard. "The Tragic Downfall of Blanche DuBois." *Modern Drama* 10 (Dec. 1967): 249–57.

Berkowitz, Gerald. *American Drama of the Twentieth Century.* New York: Longman, 1992.

Berlin, Normand. "Complementarity in *A Streetcar Named Desire*." *Tennessee Williams: A Tribute*. Ed. Jac Tharpe. Jackson: UP of Mississippi, 1977. 97–103.

Bernard, Kenneth. "The Mercantile Mr. Kowalski." *Discourse* 7 (Summer 1964): 337–40.

Bigsby, C. W. E. *A Critical Introduction to Twentieth-Century American Drama*. Vol. 2. *Tennessee Williams, Arthur Miller, Edward Albee*. Cambridge: Cambridge UP, 1984.

———. *Modern American Drama, 1945–1990*. Cambridge: Cambridge UP, 1992.

Blackwell, Louise. "Tennessee Williams and the Predicament of Women." *Tennessee Williams: A Collection of Critical Essays*. Ed. Stephen S. Stanton. Englewood Cliffs, NJ: Prentice-Hall, 1977. 100–106.

"Blanche and the Boys." *New Yorker* 28 Mar. 1988: 81–82.

"Bloolips and Split Britches." *Theater Week* 4 Mar. 1991: 38.

Bloom, Harold, ed. *Tennessee Williams's A Streetcar Named Desire*. New York: Chelsea, 1988.

Boxill, Roger. *Tennessee Williams*. New York: St. Martin's, 1987.

Bray, Robert. "*A Streetcar Named Desire*: The Political and Historical Subtext." *Confronting Tennessee Williams's A Streetcar Named Desire: Essays in Critical Pluralism*. Ed. Philip C. Kolin. Westport, CT: Greenwood, 1993. 183–98.

Brown, John Mason. *Dramatis Personae*. New York: Viking, 1963.

Brustein, Robert. "Williams's Nebulous Nightmare." *Hudson Review* 12 (Summer 1959): 155–60.

Burks, Deborah G. " 'Treatment Is Everything': The Creation and Casting of Blanche and Stanley in Tennessee Williams' 'Streetcar.' " *Library Chronicle of the University of Texas at Austin* 41 (1987): 16–39.

Cahir, Linda Costanzo. "The Artful Rerouting of *A Streetcar Named Desire*." *Literature/Film Quarterly* 22 (1994): 72–77.

Callahan, Edward F. "Tennessee Williams's Two Worlds." *North Dakota Quarterly* 25 (Summer 1957): 61–67.

Cardullo, Bert. "Birth and Death in *A Streetcar Named Desire*." *Confronting Tennessee Williams's A Streetcar Named Desire: Essays in Critical Pluralism*. Ed. Philip C. Kolin. Westport, CT: Greenwood, 1993. 167–82.

———. "The Role of the Baby in *A Streetcar Named Desire*." *Notes on Modern American Literature* 14 (Mar. 1984): 4–5.

Chesler, S. Alan. "*A Streetcar Named Desire*: Twenty-Five Years of Criticism." *Notes on Mississippi Writers* 7 (1974): 44–53.

Ciment, Michael. *Kazan on Kazan*. New York: Viking, 1974.

Clum, John. *Acting Gay: Male Homosexuality in American Drama*. New York: Columbia UP, 1992.

Clurman, Harold. "Theatre." *Nation* 14 May 1973: 635–36.

Cohn, Ruby. *Dialogue in American Drama*. Bloomington: Indiana UP, 1971.

Corrigan, Mary Ann. "Realism and Theatricalism in *A Streetcar Named Desire*." *Modern Drama* 19 (Dec. 1976): 385–96.

Crandell, George W. "Misrepresentation and Miscegenation: Reading the Racialized Discourse of Tennessee Williams's *A Streetcar Named Desire*." *Modern Drama* 40 (1997): 337–46.

———. *Tennessee Williams: A Descriptive Bibliography*. Pittsburgh: U of Pittsburgh P, 1995.

Davis, Walter A. *Get the Guests: Psychoanalysis, Modern American Drama, and the Audience*. Madison: U of Wisconsin P, 1994.

Debusscher, Gilbert. "Trois images de la modernité chez Tennessee Williams: Un microanalyse d'*Un tramway nommé Desir*." *Journal of Dramatic Theory and Criticism* 3 (Fall 1988): 143–56.

Dickinson, Vivienne. "*A Streetcar Named Desire*: Its Development through the Manuscripts." *Tennessee Williams: A Tribute*. Ed. Jac Tharpe. Jackson: UP of Mississippi, 1977. 154–71.

Dowling, Ellen. "The Derailment of *A Streetcar Named Desire*." *Literature/Film Quarterly* 9 (1981): 233–39.

Downing, Robert. "*Streetcar* Conductor: Some Notes from Backstage." *Theatre Annual* 8 (1950): 25–33.

Dworkin, Andrea. *Intercourse*. New York: Free Press, 1987.

Falb, Lewis W. *American Drama in Paris, 1945–1970: A Study of Its Critical Reception*. Chapel Hill: U of North Carolina P, 1973.

Falk, Signi. *Tennessee Williams*. Rev. ed. Boston: Twayne, 1978. 2nd ed. Boston: Twayne, 1978. 53–62.

Farber, Stephen. "Blanche Wins the Battle." *New York Times* 1 Apr. 1973, sec. 2: 1, 15.

Fleche, Anne. *Mimetic Disillusion: Eugene O'Neill, Tennessee Williams, and U.S. Dramatic Realism*. Tuscaloosa: U of Alabama P, 1997.

Ganz, Arthur. "The Desperate Morality of the Plays of Tennessee Williams." *American Scholar* 31 (Spring 1962): 278–94.

Gassner, John. *The Theatre in Our Times*. New York: Crown, 1954.

Gilbert, Sandra, and Susan Gubar. *No Man's Land: The Place of the Woman Writer in the Twentieth Century*. Vol. 1. New Haven: Yale UP, 1988.

Golden, Joseph. *The Death of Tinker Bell*. Syracuse: Syracuse UP, 1967.

Griffin, Alice. *Understanding Tennessee Williams*. Columbia: U of South Carolina P, 1995.

Gronbeck-Tedesco, John. "Ambiguity and Performance in the Plays of Tennessee Williams." *Mississippi Quarterly* 48 (Fall 1995): 735–49.

Hanks, Pamela Anne. "Must We Acknowledge What We Mean? The Viewer's Role in Filmed Versions of *A Streetcar Named Desire*." *Journal of Popular Film and Television* 14 (Fall 1986): 114–22.

Harris, Laurilyn J. "Perceptual Conflict and the Perversion of Creativity in *A Streetcar Named Desire*." *Confronting Tennessee Williams's A Streetcar Named Desire: Essays in Critical Pluralism*. Ed. Philip C. Kolin. Westport, CT: Greenwood, 1993. 83–104.

Harwood, Britton J. "Tragedy as Habit: *A Streetcar Named Desire*." *Tennessee Williams: A Tribute*. Ed. Jac Tharpe. Jackson: UP of Mississippi, 1977. 104–15.

Hayman, Ronald. *Tennessee Williams: Everyone Else Is an Audience*. New Haven: Yale UP, 1993.

Hirsch, Foster. *A Portrait of the Artist: The Plays of Tennessee Williams*. Port Washington, NY: Kennikat, 1979.

Hodges, Ann. "Interview with Ann-Margret." *Houston Post*, "TV Chronilog," 4–10 Mar. 1984: 4–5.

Hodgson, Moira. "*A Streetcar Named Desire*." *Nation* 16 Apr. 1988: 547–48.

Holditch, W. Kenneth. "The Broken World: Romanticism, Realism, and Naturalism in *A Streetcar Named Desire*." *Confronting Tennessee Williams's A Streetcar Named Desire: Essays in Critical Pluralism*. Ed. Philip C. Kolin. Westport, CT: Greenwood, 1993. 147–66.

———. "The Last Frontier of Bohemia: Tennessee Williams in New Orleans, 1938–83." *Southern Quarterly* 23 (Winter 1985): 1–37.

Homan, Sidney. *The Audience as Actor and Character*. Lewisburg, PA: Bucknell UP, 1989.

Hulley, Kathleen. "The Fate of the Symbolic in *A Streetcar Named Desire*." *Themes in Drama 4 (Drama and Symbolism)*. Ed. James Redmond. Cambridge: Cambridge UP, 1982. 88–99.

Humm. "Blanche and the Boys." *Variety* 16 Mar. 1988.

Hurrell, John D., ed. *Two Modern American Tragedies: Reviews and Criticism of "Death of a Salesman" and "A Streetcar Named Desire."* New York: Scribner's, 1961.

Isaac, Dan. "No Past to Think In: Who Wins in 'A Streetcar Named Desire'?" *Louisiana Literature* 14 (Fall 1997): 8–35.

Israel, Lee. *Miss Tallulah Bankhead*. New York: Putnam's, 1972.

Jackson, Esther Merle. *The Broken World of Tennessee Williams*. Madison: U of Wisconsin P, 1965.

Jennings, C. Robert. "Interview with Tennessee Williams." *Playboy* Apr. 1973: 69–84.

Jones, David Richard. *Great Directors at Work: Stanislavski, Brecht, Kazan, Brook*. Berkeley: U of California P, 1986.

Jones, Robert Emmet. "Tennessee Williams's Early Heroines." *Modern Drama* 2 (Dec. 1959): 211–19.

Kalem, T. E. "Beast v. Beauty." *Time* 7 May 1973.

Kazan, Elia. "*Notebook* for *A Streetcar Named Desire*." *Directors on Directing: A Source Book of the Modern Theatre*. Ed. Toby Cole and Helen Krich Chinoy. 2nd (rev.) ed. Indianapolis: Bobbs-Merrill, 1976. 364–79.

Kelly, Lionel. "The White Goddess, Ethnicity, and the Politics of Desire." *Confronting Tennessee Williams's A Streetcar Named Desire: Essays in Critical Pluralism*. Ed. Philip C. Kolin. Westport, CT: Greenwood, 1993. 121–32.

Kernan, Alvin. "Truth and Dramatic Mode in the Modern Theatre: Chekhov, Pirandello, and Williams." *Modern Drama* 1 (Sept. 1958): 111–14.

Kingston, Jeremy. "*Streetcar* Blooms." Punch 27 Mar. 1974: 519.

Kleb, William. "Marginalia: *Streetcar*, Williams, and Foucault." *Confronting Tennessee Williams's A Streetcar Named Desire: Essays in Critical Pluralism*. Ed. Philip C. Kolin. Westport, CT: Greenwood, 1993. 27–44.

Kolin, Philip C. " 'Affectionate and Mighty Regards from Vivien and Me': Sir Laurence Olivier and the London Premiere of *A Streetcar Named Desire*." *Missouri Review* 13.3 (1991): 143–57.

———. "Bonaparte Kowalski: Or, What Stanley and the French Emperor Have in Common (and What They Don't) in *A Streetcar Named Desire*." *Notes on Contemporary Literature* 24 (Sept. 1994): 6–8.

———. "Cleopatra of the Nile and Blanche DuBois of the French Quarter: *Antony and Cleopatra* and *A Streetcar Named Desire*." *Shakespeare Bulletin* 11 (Winter 1993): 25–27.

———, ed. *Confronting Tennessee Williams's A Streetcar Named Desire: Essays in Critical Pluralism*. Westport, CT: Greenwood, 1993.

———. " 'Cruelty and Sweaty Intimacy': The Reception of the Spanish Premiere of *A Streetcar Named Desire*." *Theatre Survey* 35 (Nov. 1995): 45–56.

———. "Eunice Hubbell and the Feminist Thematics of *A Streetcar Named Desire*." *Confronting Tennessee Williams's A Streetcar Named Desire: Essays in Critical Pluralism*. Ed. Philip C. Kolin. Westport, CT: Greenwood, 1993. 105–20.

———. "The First Critical Assessments of *A Streetcar Named Desire*: The *Streetcar* Tryouts and the Reviewers." *Journal of Dramatic Theory and Criticism* 6 (Fall 1991): 45–68.

―――. "The First Polish Productions of *A Streetcar Named Desire.*" *Theatre History Studies* 12 (1992): 67–88.

―――. " 'From Coitus to Craziness': The Italian Premiere of *A Streetcar Named Desire.*" *Journal of American Drama and Theatre* 10 (Spring 1998): 74–92.

―――. " 'Hello from Bertha' as a Source for *A Streetcar Named Desire.*" *Notes on Contemporary Literature* 27 (Jan. 1997): 6–7.

―――. " 'It's Only a Paper Moon': The Paper Ontologies in Tennessee Williams's *A Streetcar Named Desire.*" *Modern Drama* 40 (Winter 1997). 454–67.

―――. "The Japanese Premiere of *A Streetcar Named Desire.*" *Mississippi Quarterly* 48 (Fall 1995): 713–34.

―――. "On a Trolley to the Cinema: Ingmar Bergman and the First Swedish Production of *A Streetcar Named Desire.*" *South Carolina Review* 27, nos. 1 and 2 (Fall 1994/ Spring 1995): 277–86.

―――. "Our Lady of the Quarter: Blanche DuBois and the Feast of the Mater Dolorosa." *ANQ: A Quarterly Journal of Short Articles, Notes, and Reviews* 4 (Apr. 1991): 81–87.

―――. " 'Red Hot!' in *A Streetcar Named Desire.*" *Notes on Contemporary Literature* 19 (Sept. 1989): 6–8.

―――. "Reflections on/of *A Streetcar Named Desire.*" *Confronting Tennessee Williams's A Streetcar Named Desire: Essays in Critical Pluralism.* Ed. Philip C. Kolin. Westport, CT: Greenwood, 1993. 1–17.

―――. "*A Streetcar Named Desire*: A Playwrights' Forum." *Michigan Quarterly Review* 29 (Spring 1990): 173–203.

―――. "Tennessee Williams's *A Streetcar Named Desire* in Havanna: Modesto Centeno's Cuban *Streetcars*, 1948–1965." *South Atlantic Review* 60 (Nov. 1995): 91–110.

―――. "Why Stanley and His Friends Drink Jax Beer in Tennessee Williams's *A Streetcar Named Desire.*" *Notes on Contemporary Literature* 20 (Sept. 1990): 2–3.

―――. "Williams in Ebony: Black and Multi-Racial Productions of *A Streetcar Named Desire.*" *Black American Literature Forum* 25 (Spring 1991): 147–181.

Kolin, Philip C., and Sherry Shao. "The First Production of *A Streetcar Named Desire* in Mainland China." *Tennessee Williams Literary Journal* 2 (Winter 1990–91): 19–32.

Koprince, Susan. "Tennessee Williams's Unseen Characters." *Southern Quarterly* 33 (Fall 1994): 87–95.

Kroll, Jack. "Battle of New Orleans." *Newsweek* 7 May 1973: 109–10.

Krutch, Joseph Wood. *Modernism in Modern Drama.* Ithaca: Cornell UP, 1953.

Kunkle, Francis L. "Tennessee Williams and the Death of God." *Commonweal* 23 Feb. 1968: 614–17.

Lant, Kathleen Margaret. "A Streetcar Named Misogyny." *Violence in Drama.* Ed. James Redmond. Cambridge: Cambridge UP, 1991. 225–38.

Leavitt, Richard F., ed. *The World of Tennessee Williams.* New York: Putnam's, 1978.

Leonard, Gail. "*Belle Reprieve.*" *Theatre Journal* 43 (Oct. 1991): 386–88.

Leverich, Lyle. *Tenn: The Timeless World of Tennessee Williams.* Vol. 2 (forthcoming).

Lilly, Mark. *Gay Men's Literature in the Twentieth Century.* New York: Macmillan, 1993.

Londré, Felicia Hardison. "A *Streetcar* Running Fifty Years." *The Cambridge Companion to Tennessee Williams.* Ed. Matthew C. Roudané. Cambridge: Cambridge UP, 1977. 45–66.

―――. *Tennessee Williams.* New York: Ungar, 1979.

MacColl, Rene. "Laughter dans le *Tramway.*" *Atlantic Monthly* July 1950: 94–95.

McCarthy, Mary. *"Streetcar." Partisan Review* 25 (Mar. 1948): 357–60. Rpt. in *Theatre Chronicles, 1937–1962.* New York: Farrar, 1963. 131–35.

McCraw, Harry W. "Tennessee Williams, Film Music, Alex North: An Interview with Luigi Zaninelli." *Mississippi Quarterly* 48 (Fall 1995): 763–75.

Melman, Lindy. "A Captive Maid: Blanche DuBois in *A Streetcar Named Desire." Dutch Quarterly Review of Anglo-American Letters* 16 (1986): 125–44.

Miller, Jordan Y., ed. *Twentieth Century Interpretations of "A Streetcar Named Desire": A Collection of Critical Essays.* Englewood Cliffs, NJ: Prentice-Hall, 1971.

Mood, John J. "The Structure of *A Streetcar Named Desire." Ball State University Forum* 14 (Summer 1973): 9–10.

Mosely, Leonard. "And Miss Leigh—Magnificent!" *Daily Express* [London] 13 Oct. 1949: 2.

Murphy, Brenda. *Tennessee Williams and Elia Kazan: A Collaboration in the Theatre.* Cambridge: Cambridge UP, 1992.

Nelson, Benjamin. *Tennessee Williams: The Man and His Work.* New York: Obolensky, 1961.

O'Connor, Jacqueline. *Dramatizing Dementia: Madness in the Plays of Tennessee Williams.* Bowling Green, OH: Bowling Green State U Popular P, 1997.

O'Connor, John. "Williams's 'Streetcar,' Not Kazan's." *New York Times* 27 Oct. 1995: D22.

Pagan, Nicholas. *Rethinking Literary Biography: A Postmodern Approach to Tennessee Williams.* Rutherford, NJ: Fairleigh Dickinson UP, 1993.

Palmer, R. Barton. "Hollywood in Crisis: Tennessee Williams and the Evolution of the Adult Film." *The Cambridge Companion to Tennessee Williams.* Ed. Matthew C. Roudané. Cambridge: Cambridge UP, 1997. 204–31.

Pauly, Thomas. *An American Odyssey: Elia Kazan and American Culture.* Philadelphia: Temple UP, 1983.

Phillips, Gene D., S. J. "Blanche's Phantom Husband: Homosexuality on Stage and Screen." *Louisiana Literature* 14 (Fall 1997): 36–47.

———. *The Films of Tennessee Williams.* Philadelphia: Art Alliance, 1980.

———. "*A Streetcar Named Desire*: Play and Film." *Confronting Tennessee Williams's A Streetcar Named Desire: Essays in Critical Pluralism.* Ed. Philip C. Kolin. Westport, CT: Greenwood, 1993. 223–35.

Popkin, Henry. "The Plays of Tennessee Williams." *Tulane Drama Review* 4 (Spring 1960): 45–64.

Porter, Thomas E. *Myth and Modern American Drama.* Detroit: Wayne State UP, 1969.

Prenshaw, Peggy W. "The Paradoxical Southern World of Tennessee Williams." *Tennessee Williams: A Tribute.* Ed. Jac Tharpe. Jackson: UP of Mississippi, 1977. 5–29.

Quirino, Leonard. "The Cards Indicate a Voyage on *A Streetcar Named Desire." Tennessee Williams: A Tribute.* Ed. Jac Tharpe. Jackson: UP of Mississippi, 1977. 77–96.

Rader, Dotson. *Tennessee: Cry of the Heart.* Garden City, NY: Doubleday, 1985.

Rice, Robert. *Saturday Evening Post* 2 May 1958.

Rich, Frank. "Alec Baldwin Does Battle with Ghosts." *New York Times* Apr. 13, 1992: C1, C18.

Richards, David. "This *Streetcar* Doesn't Travel Far Enough." *New York Times* 19 Apr. 1992, sec. 2: 5.

Richardson, Thomas J. "The City of Day and the City of Night: New Orleans and the

Exotic Unreality of Tennessee Williams." *Tennessee Williams: A Tribute.* Ed. Jac Tharpe. Jackson: UP of Mississippi, 1977. 631–46.

Riddell, Joseph N. "*A Streetcar Named Desire*: Nietzsche Descending." *Modern Drama* 5 (Feb. 1963): 421–30.

Robinson, Marc. *The Other American Drama.* Cambridge: Cambridge UP, 1994.

Roderick, John M. "From 'Tarantula Arms' to 'Della Robbia Blue': The Tennessee Williams Tragicomic Transit Authority." *Tennessee Williams: A Tribute.* Ed. Jac Tharpe. Jackson: UP of Mississippi, 1977. 116–25.

Rosenberg, Howard. " 'Streetcar' Rides on Lange's Performance." *Los Angeles Times* 27 Oct. 1995: F1, F21.

Savran, David. *Communists, Cowboys, and Queers: The Politics of Masculinity in the Work of Arthur Miller and Tennessee Williams.* Minneapolis: U of Minnesota P, 1992.

Schlueter, June. "Imitating an Icon: John Erman's Remake of Tennessee Williams's *A Streetcar Named Desire.*" *Modern Drama* 28 (1985): 139–47.

———. " 'We've Had This Date with Each Other from the Beginning': Reading toward Closure in *A Streetcar Named Desire.*" *Confronting Tennessee Williams's A Streetcar Named Desire: Essays in Critical Pluralism.* Ed. Philip C. Kolin. Westport, CT: Greenwood, 1993. 71–82.

Schnathmeier, Susanne. "The Unity of Place in Elia Kazan's Film Version of '*A Streetcar Named Desire*' by Tennessee Williams: A Traditional Dramatic Category Seen from a Semiotic Point of View." *Kodikas/Code* 10 (1987): 83–93.

Schultz, Rick. "A *Streetcar* to Be Desired." *Mr. Showbiz Reviews.* Internet, http:// www.abcnews.com. 27 June 1997.

Schvey, Henry I. "Madonna at the Poker Night: Pictorial Elements in Tennessee Williams's *A Streetcar Named Desire.*" *From Cooper to Philip Roth: Essays on American Literature.* Ed. J. Bakker and D. R. M. Wilkinson. Amsterdam: Rodopi, 1980. 71–77.

Shaland, Irene. *Tennessee Williams on the Soviet Stage.* Lanham, MD: UP of America, 1987. 11–21.

Sievers, W. David. *Freud on Broadway: A History of Psychoanalysis and the American Drama.* New York: Hermitage, 1955. Excerpted in *Twentieth Century Interpretations of "A Streetcar Named Desire": A Collection of Critical Essays.* Ed. Jordan Y. Miller. Englewood Cliffs, NJ: Prentice-Hall, 1971. 90–95.

Skei, Hans. "The Reception and Reputation of Tennessee Williams in Norway." *Notes on Mississippi Writers* 17 (1985): 63–81.

Spector, Susan. "Alternative Visions of Blanche DuBois: Uta Hagen and Jessica Tandy in *A Streetcar Named Desire.*" *Modern Drama* 32 (1989): 545–61.

Spoto, Donald. *The Kindness of Strangers: The Life of Tennessee Williams.* Boston: Little, Brown, 1985.

Sullivan, Dan. " 'Streetcar' on, off the Track." *Los Angeles Times* 21 Mar. 1973, sec. 4: 1, 10.

Tharpe, Jac, ed. *Tennessee Williams: A Tribute.* Jackson: UP of Mississippi, 1977.

Thompson, Judith J. *Tennessee Williams' Plays: Memory, Myth, and Symbol.* New York: Lang, 1987.

Tischler, Nancy M. "Sanitizing the *Streetcar.*" *Louisiana Literature* 14 (Fall 1997): 48–56.

———. *Tennessee Williams: Rebellious Puritan.* New York: Citadel, 1961.

Trewin, J. C. "Plays in Performance." *Drama* 3.15 (Winter 1949): 7.

Turan, Kenneth. "Interview with Ann-Margret." *TV Guide* 3–9 Mar. 1984: 27–28, 31–34.

Van Antwerp, Margaret A., and Sally Johns, eds. *Tennessee Williams. Dictionary of Literary Biography: Documentary Series* 4. Detroit: Gale, 1984.

Vineberg, Steve. "*A Streetcar Named Desire.*" *Theatre Journal* 39 (May 1987): 235–36.

Vlasopolos, Anca. "Authorizing History: Victimization in *A Streetcar Named Desire.*" *Theatre Journal* 38 (Oct. 1986): 322–38.

Wardle, Irving. "New Trip on Old *Streetcar.*" *London Times* 15 Mar. 1974: 15D.

Watts, Richard, Jr. "*Streetcar Named Desire* Is Striking Drama." *New York Times* 4 Dec. 1947: 43.

Williams, Tennessee. *A Streetcar Named Desire*. New York: New Directions, 1947.

———. *A Streetcar Named Desire*. New York: Dramatists Play Service, 1947. Acting Edition.

———. *A Streetcar Named Desire*. London: John Lehmann, 1949.

———. *Where I Live*. New York: New Directions, 1978.

Wilson, Edwin. "A Streetcar Named Desire." *Wall Street Journal* 14 May 1973: 12.

Winchell, Mark. "The Myth Is the Message, or, Why *Streetcar* Keeps Running." *Confronting Tennessee Williams's A Streetcar Named Desire: Essays in Cultural Pluralism*. Ed. Philip C. Kolin. Westport, CT: Greenwood, 1993. 133–46.

Wolter, Jürgen. "The Cultural Context of *A Streetcar Named Desire* in Germany." *Confronting Tennessee Williams's A Streetcar Named Desire: Essays in Cultural Pluralism*. Ed. Philip C. Kolin. Westport, CT: Greenwood, 1993. 199–222.

Wright, William. *Lillian Hellman: The Image, the Woman*. New York: Simon and Schuster, 1986.

Yacowar, Maurice. *Tennessee Williams and Film*. New York: Ungar, 1977.

Young, B. A. "A Streetcar Named Desire." *Financial Times* [London] 15 Mar. 1974: 3C.

Summer and Smoke and The Eccentricities of a Nightingale

RICHARD E. KRAMER

BIOGRAPHICAL CONTEXT

Like most of Williams's writing, *Summer and Smoke* and *The Eccentricities of a Nightingale* contain elements of his life. The foundation of both plays is Edwina Williams's tales of her youth in Port Gibson and Natchez, Mississippi (E. Williams 160–78). In 1916, the Williamses were living with Edwina's parents, the Dakins, in Clarksdale, Mississippi, the town that became Glorious Hill (Leverich 54). Like Rev. Winemiller, Rev. Dakin was the Episcopal minister of the town, and like Alma, Williams grew up at the rectory. Dakin's father had been a small-town doctor like the Drs. Buchanan, and Rose Otte Dakin had taught piano and voice like Alma (Leverich 17, 20). Rosa Gonzales shares her first name with Williams's sister and grandmother, and Williams himself had a hot-tempered lover, Pancho Rodriguez y Gonzalez, in the 1940s (Sheehy 123).

Both Mrs. Winemiller and Alma manifest characteristics of Williams's sister and mother. The older woman is drawn from the later, clearly disturbed Rose, but Edwina Williams's depiction of her daughter's overreaction to illness echoes Alma's (21–22). Much of Alma is also drawn from Edwina Williams, the small-town minister's daughter with a streak of puritanism who had been called a nightingale, though Williams also insisted, "I'm Alma" (Spoto 346–47, 353). The egocentric, carousing hedonist of *Summer and Smoke*, John, is a portrait of Williams's father, who lost part of his ear in a fight over a card game (Leverich 191–92), while John is knifed in a drunken fight while gambling (act 1, scene 4).

BIBLIOGRAPHIC HISTORY

Both *Summer and Smoke* and *Eccentricities* derive from "The Yellow Bird," a story first published in 1947. Though they both differ in style and resolution from the story, the two plays are closely linked bibliographically if not chronologically. *Eccentricities* premiered in 1964, more than fifteen years after *Summer and Smoke*. The most salient differences between them are the elimination of several characters—chiefly the senior Dr. Buchanan, Nellie Ewell, and the Gonzaleses—and the addition of Mrs. Buchanan. There is also no longer a stabbing or shooting, and the Moon Lake Casino episode has been replaced with a visit to a cheap hotel. John is less amoral and tempestuous in *Eccentricities* than in *Summer and Smoke* and more controlled by his mother than his counterpart is influenced by his father; Alma is less proper and prim and more peculiar. Crandell documents editions and printings of these related plays (65–72; 233–37).

MAJOR CRITICAL APPROACHES

Themes

Summer and Smoke, like *The Eccentricities of a Nightingale*, shows conflicts between soul and body, with some critics even calling these works morality plays (Heilman 118; Griffin 96). Donahue sees them as an "allegory of good and evil" (39), reflecting Williams's Puritan/Cavalier heritage (191); Tischler asserts that the theme is "Puritanism in battle with Lawrencian sex" (152). Boxill points out that Williams's plays also deal with illusion versus reality and past versus present (5), noting that time is a constant theme (27). Debusscher similarly asserts that the original play's title "evokes . . . a world long past its apogee and now declining" (115–16). From his Freudian point of view, Sievers suggests that Alma's neurosis results from sexual repression and that she loses John because she becomes his "mother-image" (382). He also lists children contending with controlling parents and the repercussions of inhibited sexuality as other Freudian themes in Williams (449). Using Jung's theories, Spero interprets *Summer and Smoke* as a journey to self-knowledge. The would-be lovers are "opposites" in a conflict (18) that is not the spirit/flesh dichotomy but the struggle "to achieve a higher consciousness" (42–46; also Jackson, *Broken World* 65–66, 84).

Williams demonstrates that the two opposites, according to Thomas P. Adler, must integrate before either Alma or John can become whole beings. "The spiritual," Adler insists Williams is saying, "can only be reached via, in union with, the physical" (116).

Another common interpretation of Williams's writing, which he vehemently denied ("Let Me Hang It All Out"), is that his women are really men, engendering examinations of his "Albertine Strategy" (Tischler 213; Londré 106–07; Clum, "From *Summer and Smoke*" 46). Though in *Acting Gay*, Clum maintains that Williams disguises his gay men as straight women (150–51), he later posits that in *Summer and Smoke* and *Eccentricities* Williams is "exploding gender distinctions" ("From *Summer and Smoke*" 42, 36).

Characters

Alma has been seen as the southern gentlewoman, the Puritan, and an avatar of the soul. Though she espouses its ideals (Jackson, *Broken World* 139), the community distrusts and misunderstands her (Griffin 15; Bigsby 70; Donahue 226), the outsider reaching for "something beyond the earth" (Costello 111). John, who clearly represents the body, reality, and the present, is cast as a "radiant primitive" (Falk 93), a "male animal, brutal and coarse" (Donahue 229).

The fathers, according to the critics, are the representatives of the mainstream who victimize the outcasts. Rev. Winemiller represents the church; Dr. Buchanan, Sr., the establishment (Falk 92). The mothers, Sievers suggests, are the "heavies" (76); Mrs. Winemiller, for Londré, acts like a "perverse child" in *Summer and Smoke*, but in *Eccentricities* she becomes "a social liability" (97, 102). Mrs. Buchanan, domineering, disagreeable, and somewhat foolish (Falk 156–57), assumes Dr. Buchanan's function in *Eccentricities*.

The literary circle foreshadows Alma's destiny. These misfits are to art what Rev. Winemiller is to spirituality: travesties (Hayman xv–xvi) whose prissiness contrasts with John's brawling and gambling (Boxill 98). Nellie and Rosa, however, are natural women who instinctively know that sex is healthy (Falk 76). Donahue, in fact, calls Nellie the "healthy yea-sayer of the universe" (229), and Latins like Rosa represent "elemental" humanity to Williams (Gunn 208–09; Brandt 167).

Symbols

The central symbol in both plays is the stone angel (Eternity) that embodies the gulf between Alma and John (on stage, there is Eternity between their houses). At once upwardly oriented (an angel, its wings lifted) and earth-bound (crouching, facing the ground), it connects the world of the spirit (the rectory) and that of the body (the doctor's office), forming part of the body-soul-eternity triad of the plays (Bigsby 70), which Thomas P. Adler sees manifested in the set design, "an altarpiece-like triptych" (115). Griffin notes that the angel also symbolizes the two sides of Alma: cold stone and life-giving water (81). John's anatomy chart depicts the physical and represents science (Boxill 105), and the Cavalier's plume epitomizes freedom from society's restraints (Londré 98).

Fireworks, a recurring symbol of sexual climax (Griffin 84), imply illumination, expansiveness, and an upward "extratemporal" impulse (Boxill 104). The sky, heaven, and the stars are further imagery of loftiness and spirituality, "non-earthly symbols for the pure" (Costello 121). Though also phallic, the Gothic cathedral, a symbol of timelessness, and the church steeple exemplify man's higher aspirations (Nelson 127).

The nightingale signifies "ecstasy carrying one beyond the present" (de Vries) and is Williams's private code word for sexual climax (*Memoirs* 110, 193). Summer and winter echo the two aspects of Alma, fire and ice (Griffin 96), and the passage from one to the other accompanies Alma's passing from "bloom to . . . decay" (Boxill 99). Time, in Williams's epistemology, is "life's destroyer" ("Timeless World" 54), the human spirit the adversary of its passage (Rice M2). This, as Thomas P. Adler notes, is a recurring motif in Williams (114).

Plot

Williams called *Summer and Smoke* a "synthetic" drama. In his "plastic theatre," Williams places essentially realistic characters in an impressionist setting and permeates their reality with the aura of illusions (Boxill 23). The nonverbal in Williams is essential, distinguishing him as "a theater poet" rather than "a poet in the theater" (Boxill 25), and Falk reminds us that *Summer and Smoke* is a "tone poem" (62), though Jackson adds that Williams sculpts scenes (*Broken World* 97–98).

Summer and Smoke and *Eccentricities* are laid out episodically, and, as Brandt notes, the mise-en-scènes bring to the theatre "the fluidity and sense of simultaneity" of the movies (168–69). Boxill describes Williams's dramatic form as "lyric" and "exfoliative" rather than linear and narrative, remarking that the "real action of *Summer and Smoke* is . . . a continual farewell" (22, 100). Jacob H. Adler sees this structure as a series "of . . . approaches and withdrawals" (355), similar for Griffin to a "ritualistic dance" (83).

Following de Chirico and the surrealists, Jackson believes that Williams uses insanity and dream as organizing principles because they suggest "extremity in human circumstance" (*Broken World* 48). Jackson earlier remarked that Williams's distinctly non-Aristotelian form elevates the lyrical over the narrative and emotion over thought ("Problem of Form" 9).

MAJOR PROBLEMS *SUMMER AND SMOKE* AND *THE ECCENTRICITIES OF A NIGHTINGALE* POSE FOR CRITICS

Most critics condemn Williams for re-covering the ground in *Summer and Smoke* he covered in *The Glass Menagerie* and *A Streetcar Named Desire*. Nearly every review in 1948 found it less dynamic and powerful than *Streetcar* and less moving and magical than *Menagerie* (Gassner 353; Morehouse; Watts). Several critics remarked that both *Summer and Smoke* and *Eccentricities* are structured with short scenes that do not cohere into a whole drama (Bron[son]; "New Play in Manhattan" 83). The overall point is often deemed too obvious, with schematic characters representing superficial traits making a simplistic statement

Tischler 155; Nelson 126). The play is too symmetrical and the reversals too neat (Heilman 119–20); Williams, some charge, composed an elementary psychology lecture, not a play (Saurel). Both texts, critics complain, are larded with obvious symbols (Nathan; Brown 31) and are too pat (Falk 161; Tynan, *Curtains* 263–64; Cohn 65). Brooking, however, notes that though *Summer and Smoke* seems "talky and too full of obvious symbolism," an existentialist approach will resolve problems in both interpretation and staging (377, 379). Finally, for many critics, Williams's language is overblown and pseudopoetic (Bentley 75), though for David Mamet it was "dramatic poetry" (Griffin 14).

CHIEF PRODUCTIONS

The world premiere of *Summer and Smoke* was presented by Margo Jones's Theater '47 in Dallas on 8 July 1947. Atkinson professed that Williams had "drawn the characters with tenderness. The dramatic ideas are mature and honest. . . . The writing is perfect in lucidity and tone" (3). Because *A Streetcar Named Desire* opened in December, the Broadway transfer of *Summer and Smoke* to the Music Box Theater was delayed until 6 October 1948, when nearly every critic compared it to *Streetcar* and *The Glass Menagerie*. Though they praised Jo Mielziner's set and Margaret Phillips's performance, the production closed on 1 January 1949 after 100 performances. See a discussion of this production in Tischler, 159–63.

On 22 November 1951, the London premiere, directed by Peter Glenville, was called "a collection of stock melodramatic situations given unimportant characteristic twists" (Worsley 664). Kenneth Tynan, though, felt that it "contains . . . brilliant and evocative hothouse writing" ("Summer and Smoke" 772).

On 24 April 1952, off-Broadway was born when Circle in the Square restaged *Summer and Smoke*, starring Geraldine Page. Running for 356 performances, the revival was praised as a "memorable, first-rate production" (Hawkins 32), though George Freedley found José Quintero's direction "the town's slowest and most ponderous" (3). Two years later, Washington's Arena Stage produced a popular *Summer and Smoke* (9 February–21 March 1954) directed by Alan Schneider with George Grizzard and Frances Sternhagen (Mrs. Winemiller).

In July 1986, Christopher Reeve and Laila Robins portrayed the would-be lovers at the Williamstown (Massachusetts) Theater Festival, and two years later, Marshall Mason directed Reeve for the Center Theater Group, Los Angeles, opposite Christine Lahti (11 February–1 April 1988). Reeve did "what he does well enough, though rather woodenly" (Warfield 8), but Lahti, somewhat at odds with the usual interpretation, made Alma "a right-on woman" (Sullivan 1). Minneapolis's Guthrie Theater has announced a revival of *Summer and Smoke* for April and May 1999.

The Eccentricities of a Nightingale premiered with Edie Adams on 25 June 1964 at the Tappan Zee Playhouse in Nyack, New York. Local revivals were staged until after a Public Broadcasting Service telecast when a production of Buffalo's Studio Arena Theater starring Betsy Palmer and David Selby moved to Broadway's Morosco Theater on 23 November 1976. Evaluations ranged from "a pleasing, small play" (Gill 134) to "a pale outline of a play" whose "production was in *every* way substandard" (Simon 26), and the Broadway premiere closed on 12 December.

The late 1970s saw, among other revivals, an *Eccentricities* at BergenStage in Teaneck, New Jersey (5–28 October 1979), that included additional revisions by Williams. The playwright himself attended a "generally admirable" (T. Williams, "I Am Widely Regarded" 3) opening on 15 April 1977 at Key West's Greene Street Theater. The October 1967 British premiere of *Eccentricities* in Guildford, starring Sian Phillips, was deemed "more melodramatic, and less easy to accept" than *Summer and Smoke* (Hobson 29). The German premiere, at Düsseldorf's Kammerspiele on 15 November 1979, was called "sentimental disharmony" (Schaumann 11).

FILM AND TELEVISION VERSIONS

Paramount produced the film adaptation of *Summer and Smoke*, with a screenplay by James Poe and Meade Roberts, in 1961. Geraldine Page, nominated for an Academy Award, repeated her 1952 stage success as Alma opposite Laurence Harvey under the direction of Peter Glenville (director of the London stage production). Criticism was mixed, ranging from Bosley Crowther's "overcrowded, overcolored" (41) to Paul Beckley's "one of the better American films this year" (15).

On 23 January 1972, a television adaptation of *Summer and Smoke* was aired in the British Broadcasting Company's "Play of the Month" series. Never broadcast in the United States, the program starred David Hedison and Lee Remick, who was declared "magnificent"—"Seldom, indeed, can a playwright have been better served by his cast" (L. Buckley 15).

The Public Broadcasting Service's "Theater in America" presented *The Eccentricities of a Nightingale*, starring Blythe Danner and Frank Langella, for "Great Performances" on 16 June 1976. Williams himself pronounced it his "most successful" television adaptation (O'Connor 17).

Summer and Smoke was the only major Williams play to be set to music during his lifetime (except for the Valerie Bettis's *Streetcar* ballet). Composed by Lee Hoiby with a libretto by Lanford Wilson, the opera debuted on 19 June 1971 in a production by the St. Paul Opera Association. Critics characterized Hoiby's music as "poetic and lyrical, often haunting and very moving" (Ericson 16). Productions in New York (1972) and Chicago (1977 and 1980) followed, and on 23 June 1982, PBS broadcast the 1980 Chicago production.

CONCLUDING OVERVIEW

These two plays are rooted in psychoanalysis, the characters' and their creator's. Both John and his father are, in part, portraits of Williams's own father.
Shortly before C. C. Williams's death in 1957, Williams acknowledged, he
stopped hating him and began to understand, even love him ("Preface: The Man"
xiv; Boxill 14). This adjustment, Williams has confessed, resulted from treatment
by Lawrence Kubie, a Freudian psychoanalyst he began seeing in 1957 (Hayman
170). During the time of this treatment, Williams also began to become estranged
from his mother (Leverich 273), whom he had adored as a child just as he had
hated his father.

It seems clear that Kubie's influence on Williams's feelings for his parents is reflected in the shifts in character manifested in the reworking of *Summer and Smoke*
into *Eccentricities*. Though Williams may have begun the new play in 1951, he certainly continued to work on it during the years he underwent psychoanalysis, and
the completed script illustrates the newfound Freudian outlook. Williams said that
he wrote *Eccentricities* in 1951, but we know that he never finished a play in one
draft. *Summer and Smoke* was begun as early as 1944 but not completed until 1948,
and there is reason to assume that *Eccentricities* went through the same lengthy
process. Indeed, a 1961 typescript essentially identical to the final version suggests
that Williams worked on the play for at least a decade.

The fruits of Williams's psychoanalysis are reflected in the evolution of the
scripts. Among the differences between *Summer and Smoke* and *The Eccentricities
of a Nightingale*, possibly the most discussed are the changes Alma and John
undergo. Alma, it has been observed, evolves from hyperconventional and old-
fashioned but essentially normal to truly eccentric. John, on the other hand,
mellows from a rebellious, hedonistic egocentric to a decent, if somewhat dull,
young man. The other significant alteration is the replacement of John's father
in *Summer and Smoke* with his mother in *Eccentricities*. Rather than a cold and
distant father, John now has a dominating, controlling mother, the "heavy" that
Sievers points to as a Freudian figure. (It is also significant that Mrs. Winemiller
is transformed from a childlike personality into a potentially destructive one.
Compare also the preanalysis mother, Amanda Wingfield, with the postanalysis
Eccentricities mothers.) John himself is no longer the undisciplined savage that
was Williams's other image of his father. Together, *Summer and Smoke* and *The
Eccentricities of a Nightingale* are a study of a shifting parent-child relationship, a
depiction of William's own vacillating allegiance.

WORKS CITED

Adler, Jacob H. "The Rose and the Fox: Notes on Southern Drama." *South: Modern
      Southern Literature in Its Cultural Setting*. Ed. Louis D. Rubin, Jr., and Robert D.
      Jacobs. Garden City, NY: Doubleday, 1961. 347–75.

Adler, Thomas P. "Before the Fall—and After: *Summer and Smoke* and *The Night of the*

Iguana.'' *The Cambridge Companion to Tennessee Williams.* Ed. Matthew C. Roudané. New York: Cambridge University Press, 1997. 114–27.

Atkinson, Brooks. "Times Critic Hails 'Summer and Smoke.' " *New York Times* 10 Aug. 1947, sec. 1: 3.

Beckley, Paul V. " 'Summer and Smoke.' " *New York Herald Tribune* 17 Nov. 1961: 15.

Bentley, Eric. "Camino Unreal." *What Is Theatre?* New York: Atheneum, 1968. 74–78.

Bigsby, C. W. E. *A Critical Introduction to Twentieth-Century American Drama.* Vol. 2. Cambridge: Cambridge UP, 1984.

Bloom, Harold, ed. *Tennessee Williams.* New York: Chelsea, 1987.

Boxill, Roger. *Tennessee Williams.* New York: St. Martin's, 1987.

Brandt, George. "Cinematic Structure in the Work of Tennessee Williams." *American Theatre.* Ed. John Russell Brown and Bernard Harris. London: Arnold, 1967. 163–87.

Bron[son, Arthur]. "Summer and Smoke." *Variety* 13 Oct. 1948: 50.

Brooking, Jack. "Directing *Summer and Smoke*: An Existentialist Approach." *Modern Drama* 2 (Feb. 1960): 377–85.

Brown, John Mason. "People Versus Characters." *Saturday Review* 30 Oct. 1948: 31–33.

Buckley, Leonard. "Summer and Smoke: BBC 1." *Times* [London] 24 Jan. 1972: 15.

Buckley, Tom. "Tennessee Williams Survives." *Conversations with Tennessee Williams.* Ed. Albert J. Devlin. Jackson: UP of Mississippi, 1986. 161–83.

Clum, John M. *Acting Gay: Male Homosexuality in Modern Drama.* New York: Columbia UP, 1992.

———. "From *Summer and Smoke* to *Eccentricities of a Nightingale*: The Evolution of the Queer Alma." *Modern Drama* 39 (Spring 1996): 31–50.

Clurman, Harold. "Man with a Problem." *New Republic* 25 Oct. 1948: 25–26.

Cohn, Ruby. "The Garrulous Grotesques of Tennessee Williams." *Tennessee Williams.* Ed. Harold Bloom. New York: Chelsea, 1987. 55–70.

Costello, Donald P. "Tennessee Williams' Fugitive Kind." *Tennessee Williams: A Collection of Critical Essays.* Ed. Stephen S. Stanton. Englewood Cliffs, NJ: Prentice-Hall, 1977. 107–22.

Crandell, George W. *Tennessee Williams: A Descriptive Bibliography.* Pittsburgh: U of Pittsburgh P, 1995.

Crowther, Bosley. " 'Summer and Smoke.' " *New York Times* 17 Nov. 1961: 41.

Debusscher, Gilbert. " 'Minting Their Separate Wills': Tennessee Williams and Hart Crane." *Tennessee Williams.* Ed. Harold Bloom. New York: Chelsea, 1987. 113–30.

de Vries, Ad. *Dictionary of Symbols and Imagery.* Amsterdam: North-Holland, 1984. S.v. "nightingale."

Donahue, Francis. *The Dramatic World of Tennessee Williams.* New York: Ungar, 1964.

Ericson, Raymond. " 'Summer and Smoke' Bows as an Opera." *New York Times* 25 June 1971: 18.

Falk, Signi [Lenea]. *Tennessee Williams.* New York: Twayne, 1962.

Freedley, George. "Off Stage—and On." *Morning Telegraph* [New York] 23 July 1952: 3.

Gassner, John. "The Theater Arts." *Forum* 110 (Dec. 1948): 351–53.

Gill, Brendan. "Woebegone Beginners." *New Yorker* 6 Dec. 1976: 134–35.

Griffin, Alice. *Understanding Tennessee Williams.* Columbia: U of South Carolina P, 1995.

Gunn, Drewey Wayne. *American and British Writers in Mexico, 1556–1973.* Austin: U of Texas P, 1974.

Hawkins, William. "Tennessee's Play a Hit in Village." *New York World-Telegram and Sun* 7 May 1952: 32.

Hayman, Ronald. *Tennessee Williams: Everyone Else Is an Audience.* New Haven: Yale UP, 1993.

Heilman, Robert Bechtold. *The Iceman, the Arsonist, and the Troubled Agent: Tragedy and Melodrama on the Modern Stage.* Seattle: U of Washington P, 1973.

Hobson, Harold. "Pity for the Pitiless." *Sunday Times* [London] 15 Oct. 1967: 29.

Hoiby, Lee. *Summer and Smoke: Opera in Two Acts.* Vocal score. [New York]: Belwin-Mills, 1976.

Jackson, Esther M. "The Problem of Form in the Drama of Tennessee Williams." *College Language Association Journal* 4 (Sept. 1960): 8–21.

Jackson, Esther Merle. *The Broken World of Tennessee Williams.* Madison: U of Wisconsin P, 1965.

Leverich, Lyle. *Tom: The Unknown Tennessee Williams.* New York: Crown, 1995.

Londré, Felicia Hardison. *Tennessee Williams.* New York: Ungar, 1979.

Morehouse, Ward. "Fine Acting, Weak Play." *New York Sun* 7 Oct. 1948: 28.

Nathan, George Jean. "The Menagerie Still Rides on the Streetcar." *New York Journal-American* 18 Oct. 1948: 12.

Nelson, Benjamin. *Tennessee Williams: The Man and His Work.* New York: Obolensky, 1961.

"New Play in Manhattan." *Time* 18 Oct. 1948: 82–83.

O'Connor, John J. "Corporate Funding Is Paying Dividends on Public TV." *New York Times* 4 July 1976, sec. 2: 17–18.

Rice, Robert. "A Man Called Tennessee." *New York Post* 30 Apr. 1958: M2.

Saurel, Renée. "La guerre en guenilles: Eté et Fumées." *Les Lettres françaises* [Paris] 24 Dec. 1953: 10.

Schaumann, Lore. "Tennessee-Williams-Premiere in Düsseldorf: Gefühlvolle Mißtöne." *Rheinische Post* [Düsseldorf] 17 Feb. 1979: [11].

Sheehy, Helen. *Margo: The Life and Theatre of Margo Jones.* Dallas: Southern Methodist UP, 1989.

Sievers, W. David. *Freud on Broadway: A History of Psychoanalysis and the American Drama.* New York: Hermitage, 1955.

Simon, John. "Two From Williams' Menagerie." *New Leader* 3 Jan. 1977: 25–26.

Smith, Bruce. *Costly Performances: Tennessee Williams: The Last Stage.* New York: Paragon, 1990.

Spero, Richard Henry. "The Jungian World of Tennessee Williams." Diss. U of Wisconsin, 1970.

Spoto, Donald. *The Kindness of Strangers: The Life of Tennessee Williams.* Boston: Little, Brown, 1985.

Sullivan, Dan. "Stage Review: Lahti Plays With Fire in 'Smoke.' " *Los Angeles Times* 20 Feb. 1988, sec. 6: 1, 7.

Tischler, Nancy M. *Tennessee Williams: Rebellious Puritan.* New York: Citadel, 1961.

Tynan, Kenneth. *Curtains.* New York: Atheneum, 1961.

———. " 'Summer and Smoke.' " *Spectator* 187 (7 Dec. 1951): 772.

Warfield, Polly. "Summer and Smoke." *Drama-Logue* 25 Feb.–2 Mar. 1988: 8.

Watts, Richard, Jr. "A Rather Gloomy Report on 'Summer and Smoke.' " *New York Post* 7 Oct. 1948: 33.

Williams, Edwina, as told to Lucy Freeman. *Remember Me To Tom.* New York: Putnam's, 1963.

Williams, Tennessee. *The Eccentricities of a Nightingale.* Typescript, Billy Rose Theatre Collection. New York Public Library. 20 June 1961.

———. *The Eccentricities of a Nightingale.* New York: Dramatists Play Service, 1977.

———. *The Eccentricities of a Nightingale. The Theatre of Tennessee Williams.* Vol. 2. New York: New Directions, 1971. 1–111.

———. *The Eccentricities of a Nightingale and Summer and Smoke: Two Plays by Tennessee Williams.* New York: New Directions, 1964.

———. "I Am Widely Regarded as the Ghost of a Writer." *New York Times* 8 May 1977, sec. 2: 3, 20.

———. "Let Me Hang It All Out." *New York Times* 4 Mar. 1973, sec. 2: 1, 3.

———. *Memoirs.* Garden City, NY: Doubleday, 1975.

———. "Preface: The Man in the Overstuffed Chair." *Collected Stories.* New York: New Directions, 1985. vii–xvii.

———. *Summer and Smoke.* New York: Dramatists Play Service, 1950.

———. *Summer and Smoke. The Theatre of Tennessee Williams.* Vol. 2. New York: New Directions, 1971. 113–256.

———. *Tennessee Williams: Four Plays.* New York: New American Library, 1976.

———. "The Timeless World of a Play." *Where I Live: Selected Essays.* Ed. Christine R. Day and Bob Woods. New York: New Directions, 1978. 49–54.

———. "The Yellow Bird." *One Arm and Other Stories.* [New York]: New Directions, 1954. 199–211.

———. "The Yellow Bird." *Town and Country* June 1947: 40–41, 102–03.

Wilson, Lanford. *Summer and Smoke: Opera in Two Acts.* Libretto. [New York]: Belwin-Mills, 1972.

Worsley, T. C. "Period Charms." *New Statesman and Nation* 42 (8 Dec. 1951): 664.

The Rose Tattoo

LESLIE ATKINS DURHAM AND
JOHN GRONBECK-TEDESCO

BIOGRAPHICAL CONTEXT

In his *Memoirs*, Williams claimed that *The Rose Tattoo* "was my love-play to the world. It was permeated with the happy young love for Frankie [Merlo]," to whom the play was dedicated (162). Personal allusions run throughout the script. Like Rosario Delle Rose and Alvaro Mangiacavallo, Frank Merlo, Williams's lover, had been a truck driver. In fact, the name Mangiacavallo was derived from Merlo's nickname, the Little Horse. Hayman notes that while the inspiration for the play may have been Williams's trip to Italy with Merlo, the playwright actually finished one complete draft of the play around Christmas of 1950 "while he was living in Florida with Frank Merlo and the Reverend Dakin" (133). Lyle Leverich further notes Williams's failed affair with Kip Kiernan, who broke the author's heart much as Rosario broke Serafina's.

Dakin Williams and Shepherd Mead offer what is perhaps the most provocative biographical framework for the play. They see *The Rose Tattoo* and *The Roman Spring of Mrs. Stone* as examples of expatriate writing. Whereas in the case of the latter, the author attempts to bring his own regional sensibility to Italy, with the play he is doing the opposite, trying to bring Italy into his own milieu, the Gulf Coast (171). Leverich's second volume of the biography discusses *The Rose Tattoo* in depth.

BIBLIOGRAPHIC HISTORY

Crandell documents three American editions and one British edition (93–101). The first two American editions received two printings each, and the third, nine. The British edition received two printings. In an important essay, Parker discusses the various drafts and revisions of the play in detail. His work fills an important lacuna in research on *The Rose Tattoo* and further documents that Williams was a "compulsive writer and reviser" (279). Gunn catalogues foreign productions of Williams's play. The *Online* (formerly the *Ohio*) *Computer Library Center Catalogues* supplements his efforts. For a broad Internet resource that includes several kinds of research opportunities, see *Theater Resources on the 'Net* (http://www.theatre,central.com/), maintained by Andrew Q. Kraft (akraft@ theater-central.com).

MAJOR CRITICAL APPROACHES

Themes

In key interviews for *Vogue* and *Harper's Bazaar* (Williams, "Interview"), Williams pointed out what he deemed the controlling themes that informed *The Rose Tattoo*: close association between order and death, on the one hand, and passionate disorder and life, on the other. In the play, as indeed in Williams's life, the two extremes seem irreconcilable. In part, the play is Williams's profession of faith in "the Dionysian element in human life, its mystery, its beauty, its significance" (Williams, "Interview," 55; Londré *Tennessee*, 105). But the Dionysian does not reduce to mere sexuality. For Williams, it "is higher and more distilled than [sexuality]. Its purest form is probably manifested by children and birds in their rhapsodic moments of flight and play" (Williams, "Interview," *Vogue* 55).

Boxill exclaims that Williams's comedy exudes the "puckish spirit of sex" (135). Some critics identify the major conflict of the play as the opposition between puritanical constraint and passionate rebellion couched in terms of sexual expression; for example, Hayman, Ganz, and Weldon classify this rebellion as "Lawrentian" and link the play with the antipuritanical thematics of Ernest Hemingway and Gertrude Stein. Adding Proust to the influences on Williams thematics, Griffin sees the sexuality and passion not only as a revolutionary gesture but also as part of a major problem that the play never really resolves: the place of sexuality in the individual's relationship to the community. Bigsby broadens Williams's theme to "resilience of the human spirit, the undeniable power of the will to live and the primacy of the sexual impulse" (73).

Characters

Serafina

Serafina Delle Rose embodies the conflict between constraint and passion, yet readers often disagree in their evaluation of what Williams achieved in creating her. Starnes, Adler, Hayman, Falk, Tischler, and Cohn view Serafina as an emblem of the playwright's own moral perspectives. In what is perhaps the most benevolent reading of *The Rose Tattoo*, Adler situates Serafina in a highly moral light, arguing that she chooses to nurture love even at the expense of ordinary social norms. Her reward is the return of fertility and passion. Starnes similarly observes that Serafina and the other major characters are almost allegorical: "In loving another, Williams would have us see in *The Rose Tattoo*, man most nearly succeeds in conquering the ultimate enemy of all significance, time" (369). Hayman's view of Serafina is more mixed, seeing her central action as a "sexual awakening": "Like other Tennessee Williams characters who try to forget their own sexuality, Serafina has to undergo both punishment and conversion" (135). The punishment would appear to be the emotional stagnation that comes after the death of her first husband (Rosario). Tischler considers Serafina a well-developed character who, despite some tragic qualities, is generally a successful and upbeat comic creation (172–73). Falk offers a very different moral assessment, classifying Serafina as a "southern wench," a term that encompasses a number of Williams's female characters, including Serafina's daughter, Rosa; Maggie in *Cat on a Hot Tin Roof*; and Baby Doll McCorkle.

Mangiacavallo

Mangiacavallo is an imperfect copy of Rosario, with the face of a clown and a counterfeit tattoo identical to his predecessor's. Consequently, as Phillips notes, Mangiacavallo cannot be idealized by Serafina as Rosario was because the son of a village fool is simply too silly and funny looking. Yet he spurs Serafina's rebirth. Londré likewise sees Mangiacavallo not only as a parody of Rosario, but at the same time the very symbol of passion (*Tennessee Williams*, 106). He may be totally "wrong headed" in his attempts to ingratiate himself to Serafina, but he is also completely effective (1989, 30). If Serafina is heading for the "big double bed" (Falk 95), it is Mangiacavallo who is attempting to lead the way. At the opposite end of the moral scale, Starnes's sunny judgment of Serafina necessarily implicates Mangiacavallo, who is clearly the sort of "other" whom it is distinctly difficult to love. By the end of the play, these two mad lovers already have a great deal to forgive and forget.

Rosa and Jack

Rosa's passion and sexuality in her relationship with Jack, a sailor, sends shock waves to begin the seismic shift that eventually brings sexual desire and love back into Serafina's life. Londré notes the association between Rosa and Williams's sister Rose, to whom he often tried to pay tribute in his plays; for example, one of the playwright's memories was of his mother attempting to "squelch" Rose's use of vulgar language (*Williams: Life*, 23). Serafina likewise strives obsessively to suppress her teenage daughter's sexuality. Despite Serafina's suspicion, Jack is a decent young man, himself sexually uninitiated, who is more than a foil to Serafina's attempt to seal herself and her daughter off from desire. He represents an ideal value in which sexual passion (eros) and love (philos) merge, however uncertainly.

Rosario Delle Rose

Although Rosario never appears on stage, his "image is strongly evoked for the audience and . . . [his] presence is deeply felt" (Koprince 87). Serafina's fervid memory of Rosario creates a love triangle: Rosario is Mangiacavallo's major competitor for the affections of Serafina. Rosario's is also the absent presence that Serafina must eventually put behind her with the help of Mangiacavallo, who, in the end, competes successfully with Rosario by creating a new life in Serafina. According to Adler, Serafina's new pregnancy spiritualizes her relationship to Mangiacavallo with associations of redemption and resurrection ("The Search for God" 146).

Estelle, Flora, Bessie, and the Strega

Several of Serafina's neighbors, a kind of female chorus, exhibit the feminine dilemma in the search for "relationships with men" (Blackwell 100). Yet their judgments are ironic and poignant because the men in their own lives are markedly absent. These women are left alone to scold their children and tend their gardens. These minor characters engage in social ridicule; they are all the living dead, filled with denial and without prospects for the future. Williams intends these female characters to contrast with Serafina. The svelte and blonde Estelle Hohengarten, Rosario's mistress, is "the antithesis of plump, dark Serafina" (Londré 1979, 106). Bessie and Flora are two man-minded floozies who cheapen the role of sexuality, regarding it as part sport and part escape. Tischler summarizes the social judgment embodied by several of Williams's characters: "[T]o accept the role imposed by society is to die" (159).

Symbols

Critics agree that *The Rose Tattoo* is as resplendent with symbols as Serafina herself is with passion. Key symbols include the rose tattoo, Serafina's dress-shop dummy, the goat and other animals, and the highly evocative names. Thompson discusses the rose tattoo, the play's central image, as the crux of an entire web of associated images and themes: "the union of spirit and flesh," human love and female sexuality, "communion," the Blessed Virgin, and "wholeness" (53). Griffin identifies the dummy as a surrogate for Serafina. The bleating goat represents wild, unbridled passion for many critics. Estelle Hohengarten bears the most sexual name (hoe the garden), while Serafina suggests "fine nights" to Falk (67).

Plot

The Rose Tattoo has often been viewed from the mythic perspectives of the Cambridge School that inform Francis Fergusson's *The Idea of a Theater* (1949). Mythical structures help to explain the surface plot of the play. For example, Thompson sees the play as a struggle between the suffocating effects of the mythic past and liberation from that past. Cohn believes that Williams intended his play to be a "saturnalia, a joyous celebration of sex" (66), and Ridell speaks of the play's "satyr-like spiritualism" (13) that results from a rising action based on first the suppression and then the reemergence of erotic love. Jackson, too, grounds the action in mythic structures seen from a Nietzschean point of view. Equally convincing, Kolin argues that the play is structured by a "potpourri of comic forms" (" 'Sentiment and Humor' " 216): farce, slapstick humor, romantic comedy, folk comedy, and tragicomedy.

MAJOR PROBLEMS *THE ROSE TATTOO* POSES FOR CRITICS

Critical response to *The Rose Tattoo* has been mixed. Some readers find Serafina too overheated. Hirsch, for example, thinks that the play's Sicilian heroine is "high-strung and thick headed . . . one of the playwright's most obsessed characters" (41). Against Williams's claim that he had kept the play free of a neurotic female character, Hirsch charges that Serafina "is no less disturbed than any of Williams's earlier heroines" (41). Brantley expresses a more balanced opinion: a "self-deluding woman versus the man who is Id incarnate" (C11) recurs frequently in Williams's work. Other critics have found the symbolism excessive and verging on the ludicrous. Adler (*American Drama* 147) considers the symbolism in the play too overstated, while others have regarded it as markedly comic. Thompson sees it more constructively as a positive force in the script. Brown calls Williams's prolific use of flower imagery "a lot of downright foolishness" (22). Cohn complains that the play "suffers from too much concreteness, with obvious symbolic intention" (66).

CHIEF PRODUCTIONS

The Rose Tattoo premiered at the Erlanger Theatre in Chicago on 29 December 1950 and made its New York City debut at the Martin Beck Theatre on 3 February 1951, starring Maureen Stapleton and Eli Wallach. Williams feared that the theatre public would "only like from a writer what they've liked from him before" (Gilroy 2: 1).

Atkinson applauded the shift away from Williams's usual lyricism: "For those of us who were afraid that Mr. Williams had been imprisoned within a formula it is especially gratifying" ("At the Theatre" 19). But the reviewer from *Time* found the comic shift merely cosmetic and labeled the play "a Banana Truck Named Desire" ("New Play in Manhattan" 54). Reviewers inevitably compared the women who played Serafina, especially Stapleton, to Anna Magnani, whom Williams had wanted to play the role on Broadway. Even before the show opened in New York, Maureen Stapleton was competing with Magnani. Gilroy wrote that Williams "visualized his central character . . . in the impressive form of the actress Anna Magnani" (2: 1). Though the reviews were divided in opinion about the play, Stapleton fared well in virtually all of them (e.g., Atkinson, Chapman, Guernsey). By the time Stapleton, who won a Tony for her original portrayal, had returned to the stage for the New York revival of *Rose Tattoo* in 1966, Anna Magnani ironically had more clearly left her indelible mark on the role through the 1955 film version, in which her portrayal won an Oscar. Stapleton's reprise nonetheless satisfied the critics. Pointing out the comparison with Magnani, Kerr observed that "the comparison can be made with no discredit to either actress" ("A 'Rose' Flowers Anew" 2: 1).

Kolin rightly points out that the play has gained in reputation over time. Though *The Rose Tattoo* was produced only rarely by regional theatres in the 1950s and 1960s, it gained momentum through the 1970s. In the lead were the foremost actors in America, including Rita Moreno, Olympia Dukakis, and Cicely Tyson. In 1966, the critic for *America* ventured that the play would become "a durable and treasured . . . piece" of the American theatre (" 'Rose Tattoo' " 786). Sullivan was bolder in forecasting, "I suspect that critics, and more importantly audiences, of the future are going to be as taken with this play as with anything in the Williams canon" (36).

Revivals in the 1990s allowed critics to judge the play within the context of Williams's completed canon, prompting reviewers such as Christiansen to call it blithely "the happiest of all dramas by Tennessee Williams" (18). The Peter Hall Company staged a stunning revival in London in June 1991 with Julie Walters and Ken Storr, "a comic masterpiece" (Thorson 103). A 1995 revival at the Circle in the Square starred Mercedes Ruehl as a spirited and inventive Serafina (see the interview with Charlie Rose).

FILM AND TELEVISION VERSIONS

Responses to the 1955 film have been mixed. While Anna Magnani was credited with a masterly performance, the film as a whole has been judged as flawed. Although Phillips credits the lighting of cinematographer James Wong Howe with giving the proper symbolic resonance to each scene, he fears that the film ends up exoticizing Italians. Yacowar argues that Hal Kanter's screen adaptation of the text lacks the challenge to norms governing sex and passion, precisely the challenge that was so emphatically present in the play. More specifically, Yacowar points out that "the film subverts the original in two basic ways: it scales down the passion and it simplifies the seriocomic complexity of Williams's play" (25).

CONCLUDING OVERVIEW

The Rose Tattoo satirizes sexual relationships within the framework of the post–World War II period. In the decade following the war, the emphasis in America was on a return to a traditional social order and normalcy. Throughout the play, sexual desire and the daily good order needed to live a peaceful life oppose one another gruesomely. Serafina, for example, can have one or the other but not both. Self-expression and creative energy in *The Rose Tattoo* become explosive precisely because they have no place in the politics of normalcy. Without a place, the impulse toward personal freedom (symbolized by but not reducible to sexual love) can only run wild. For example, Serafina's daughter, Rosa, cannot free herself from her mother's repression without rage and defiance. For nearly half the play, Serafina stages her own combative confrontations with all who would question her ongoing, subservient relationship to the memory of her unfaithful husband, Rosario. Part of the comedy comes from the fact that desire, when it can exist only outside of and at odds with the repressive standards of a 1950s normalcy, is doomed to become comically self-indulgent, even trivialized. Appropriately, the play is full of burlesque routines filled with symbolic resonance. Characters, too filled with passion, bump into sewing dummies, copy one another's tattoos, fall, chase goats, and drop condoms.

Much of the confusion in America's decompression after the war is encoded into Williams's play through Serafina's complex predicament. A widow because of an underworld "war" she cannot quite comprehend, she is left to find her own way back into the world of daily routines that are impervious to her husband's death and her own self-loathing. In idealizing her fallen husband, she denies the forces of human continuity—sexual desire, love, human connection—and the result is a cataclysmic sexuality for her and her daughter. Rosa is a "good girl" only if she abides by her mother's view that the death of Rosario constituted some kind of end without a concomitant new beginning; in Serafina's view, to begin again is to deny the ideal love she believes she shared with her husband. Her daughter, too, is supposed to live in the same twilight between an end and a beginning.

Serafina bears a problematized relationship to the collision between the normal order and personal desire. She begins as both the victim and proponent of the suppression of life, yet she is eventually a rebel against that suppression. By reaching out passionately, she rejects a version of normalcy based on the cessation of desire and passion. By the end of the play, Serafina finds a new beginning in the recognition of her husband's infidelity and in her own attraction to Mangiacavallo, who himself is immersed in suffocating daily obligations to an insensitive array of family members. Mangiacavallo is a wage earner in the era of normalcy who can look forward only to the repetitive daily grind and the disdain of those who dislike truck drivers or Italians. Serafina brings him new love.

But what of the American postwar society that lies beyond Williams's fictional Italian community? For a victorious nation, it is difficult to put to rest sons, husbands, and brothers who must be remembered as heroes. New beginnings come hard to a nation that can reach closure with a war only through the oversimplified frameworks of victory and heroism.

WORKS CITED

Adler, Thomas P. *American Drama, 1940–1960: A Critical History.* New York: Twayne, 1994.

———. "The Search for God in the Plays of Tennessee Williams." *Tennessee Williams: A Collection of Critical Essays.* Ed. Stephen S. Stanton. Englewood Cliffs, NJ: Prentice-Hall, 1977. 138–48.

Atkinson, Brooks. "At the Theater." *New York Times* 5 Feb. 1951: 19.

———. " 'The Rose Tattoo': Tennessee Williams Sketches Life in a Sicilian Village on the Gulf." *New York Times* 11 Feb. 1951, sec. 2: 1.

———. "Tattooing—Tennessee Williams Has Made Several Changes in His Current Play." *New York Times* 3 June 1951, sec. 2: 1.

Beyer, William H. "The State of the Theatre: Hits and Misses." *School and Society* 73 (24 Mar. 1951): 181–83.

Bigsby, C. W. E. *A Critical Introduction to Twentieth-Century American Drama.* Vol. 2. Cambridge: Cambridge UP, 1984.

Blackwell, Louise. "Tennessee Williams and the Predicament of Women." *Tennessee Williams: A Collection of Critical Essays.* Ed. Stephen S. Stanton. Englewood Cliffs, NJ: Prentice-Hall, 1977. 100–106.

Boxill, Roger. *Tennessee Williams.* New York: St. Martin's, 1987.

Brantley, Ben. "Upbeat Williams for a Change." *New York Times* 1 May 1995: C11.

"The Brighter Side of Tennessee." *New Yorker* 10 Feb. 1951: 58–60.

Brown, John Mason. "Saying It with Flowers." *Saturday Review* 10 Mar. 1951: 22–24.

Campbell, Bob. " 'Rose Tattoo' in Full Bloom." *Newark, New Jersey, Star-Ledger* 15 Mar. 1988. *Newsbank: Performing Arts* (1988): fiche 71, grids G1–G2.

Cassidy, Claudia. " 'Rose Tattoo' a Stimulating Drama in Bud." *Chicago Tribune* 31 Dec. 1950: F1, F5.

Chapman, John. " 'Rose Tattoo' Affectionately Written and Admirably Staged." *New York Daily News* 5 Feb. 1951. Rpt. in *New York Theatre Critics' Reviews* 12 Feb. 1951: 365.

Christiansen, Richard. " 'The Rose Tattoo' Again Leaves Its Indelible Mark." *Chicago Tribune* 2 May 1995: 18.

Clurman, Harold. "Tennessee Williams' Rose." *New Republic* 19 Feb. 1951: 22.

———. "Theater." *Nation* 203 (7 Nov. 1966): 493.

Cohn, Ruby. "The Garrulous Grotesques of Tennessee Williams." *Tennessee Williams.* Ed. Harold Bloom. New York: Chelsea, 1987. 55–70.

Coleman, Robert. " 'Rose Tattoo' Is Thorny, Much Too Earthy." *New York Daily Mirror* 5 Feb. 1951. Rpt. in *New York Theatre Critics' Reviews* 12 Feb. 1951: 364.

Crandell, George W. *Tennessee Williams: A Descriptive Bibliography.* Pittsburgh: U of Pittsburgh P, 1995.

Croce, Arlene. "New-Old, Old-New, and New." *National Review* 24 Jan. 1967: 99.

Dean, Lynn. "Moreno a Prize in 'Rose.' " *Stamford, Connecticut, Advocate* 18 May 1977. *Newsbank: Performing Arts* (1977): fiche 38, grid C4.

Durham, Weldon B., ed. *American Theatre Companies, 1931–1986.* New York: Greenwood, 1989.

"Eros and the Widow." *Time* 18 Nov. 1966: 80.

Falk, Signi Lenea. *Tennessee Williams.* New York: Twayne, 1962.

Feingold, Michael. "Bedtime Stories." *Village Voice* 16 May 1995: 87.

Ganz, Arthur. "Tennessee Williams: A Desperate Morality." *Tennessee Williams: A Collection of Critical Essays.* Ed. Stephen S. Stanton. Englewood Cliffs, NJ: Prentice-Hall, 1977. 123–37.

Gilroy, Harry. "Mr. Williams Turns to Comedy." *New York Times* 28 Jan. 1951, sec. 2: 1, 3.

Green, Judith. " 'Rose Tattoo' in Bloom." *San Francisco Examiner* 29 Oct. 1996: B1.

Griffin, Alice. *Understanding Tennessee Williams.* Columbia: U of South Carolina P, 1995.

Guernsey, Otis L. "Williams Tops the Season." *New York Herald Tribune* 5 Feb. 1951. Rpt. in *New York Theatre Critics' Reviews* 12 Feb. 1951: 363–64.

Gunn, Drewey Wayne. *Tennessee Williams: A Bibliography.* 2nd ed. Metuchen, NJ: Scarecrow, 1991.

Gussow, Mel. "Cicely Tyson Stars in 'Rose Tattoo.' " *New York Times* 10 Aug 1979, sec. 3: 3.

———. "Rita Moreno Excels in 'Rose Tattoo.' " *New York Times* 9 May 1977: 27.

Haugen, Peter. "A Flawed 'Tattoo' Has Heart." *Sacramento Bee* 3 Nov. 1996: E6.

Hawkins, William. "Williams Goes Comic in 'Rose Tattoo.' " *New York World-Telegram* 5 Feb. 1951. Rpt. in *New York Theatre Critics' Reviews* 12 Feb. 1951: 366.

Hayman, Ronald. *Tennessee Williams: Everyone Else Is an Audience.* New Haven: Yale UP, 1993.

Hewes, Henry. "Theater—Off the Leash." *Saturday Review* 26 Nov. 1966: 60.

Hirsch, Foster. *A Portrait of the Artist: The Plays of Tennessee Williams.* Port Washington, NY: Kennikat, 1979.

Hurwitt, Robert. "Love Blooms at ACT." *San Francisco Examiner* 31 Oct. 1996: C1.

Jackson, Esther Merle. *The Broken World of Tennessee Williams.* Madison: U of Wisconsin P, 1965.

Jefferson, Margo. "Sunday View." *New York Times* 14 May 1995, sec. 2: 5.

Johnson, Malcolm L. "Moreno Enlivens 'Tattoo.' " *Hartford, Connecticut, Courant* 15 May 1977. *Newsbank: Performing Arts* (1977): fiche 38, grid C5.

Kelly, Martin P. " 'Rose Tattoo' Casting Flaw: Italian Widow." *Albany, New York, Times Union* 8 Aug. 1979. *Newsbank: Performing Arts* (1979): fiche 17, grid A6.

Kerr, Walter. "A 'Rose' Flowers Anew." *New York Times* 20 Nov. 1966 sec. 2: 1.

———. " 'The Rose Tattoo.' " *Commonweal* 53 (23 Feb. 1951): 492–94.

Kolin, Philip C., ed. *American Playwrights Since 1945: A Guide to Scholarship, Criticism, and Performance.* New York: Greenwood, 1989.

———. " 'Sentiment and Humor in Equal Measure': Comic Forms in *The Rose Tattoo.*" *Tennessee Williams: A Tribute.* Ed. Jac Tharpe. Jackson: UP of Mississippi, 1977. 214–31.

Koprince, Susan. "Tennessee Williams's Unseen Characters." *Southern Quarterly* 33.1 (1994): 87–95.

Leonard, William. "Ivanhoe Takes a Giant Step." *Chicago Tribune* 25 Sept. 1968, sec. 2: 6.

Leverich, Lyle. *Tenn: The Timeless World of Tennessee Williams.* Vol. 2 (forthcoming).

Londré, Felicia Hardison. *Tennessee Williams.* New York: Ungar, 1979.

———. *Tennessee Williams: Life, Work, and Criticism.* Fredericton, Canada: York, 1989.

Marshall, Margaret. "Drama." *Nation* 172 (17 Feb. 1951): 161–62.

McClain, John. "Play Isn't Worthy of the Fine Acting." *Journal American* 5 Feb. 1951. Rpt. in *New York Theatre Critics' Reviews* 12 Feb. 1951: 364.

"New Play in Manhattan." *Time* 12 Feb. 1951: 53–54.

"New Play—'The Rose Tattoo.' " *Newsweek* 12 Feb. 1951: 72.

Parker, Brian. "A Provisional Stemma for Drafts, Alternatives, and Revisions of Tennessee Williams's *The Rose Tattoo.*" *Modern Drama* 40, no. 2 (1997): 279–94.

Phillips, Gene D. *The Films of Tennessee Williams.* London: Associated U Presses, 1980.

Riddel, Joseph N. "A *Streetcar Named Desire*—Nietzsche Descending." *Tennessee Williams*. Ed. Harold Bloom. New York: Chelsea, 1987. 13–22.

Rose, Charlie. "Interview with Mercedes Ruehl." *Charlie Rose Show*. WNET, New York City, 15 June 1995.

" 'Rose Tattoo.' " *America* 10 Dec. 1966: 786.

" 'The Rose Tattoo.' " *Theatre Arts* 35 (April 1951): 16.

" 'Rose Tattoo.' " *Variety* 15 May 1995: 234.

" 'The Rose Tattoo'—Tennessee Williams' Controversial Comedy Is Ode to Earthy Living." *Life* 26 Feb. 1951: 80–84.

Salem, James. *A Guide to Critical Reviews: Part I: American Drama, 1909–1982*. 3rd ed. Metuchen, NJ: Scarecrow, 1984.

Spero, Bette. "Rose Tattoo Thrives with Troupe's Treatment." *Newark, New Jersey, Star-Ledger* 12 Oct. 1976. *Newsbank: Performing Arts* (1976): fiche 90, grid E6.

Starnes, Leland. "The Grotesque Children of *The Rose Tattoo*." *Modern Drama* 12.4 (1970): 357–69.

Stearns, David Patrick. "In Spring, Theater's Fancy Turns to Love." *USA Today* 9 May 1995: 8D.

Sullivan, Dan. " 'Minor Artist' in a Major Key." *New York Times* 21 Oct. 1966: 36.

Thompson, Judith J. *Tennessee Williams' Plays: Memory, Myth, and Symbol*. New York: Lang, 1987.

Thorson, James. '*The Rose Tattoo*.' *Studies in American Drama, 1945–Present* 8 (1993): 101–3.

Tischler, Nancy M. *Tennessee Williams: Rebellious Puritan*. New York: Citadel, 1961.

Watts, Richard. "Mr. Williams among the Sicilians." *New York Post* 5 Feb. 1951. Rpt. in *New York Theatre Critics' Reviews* 12 Feb. 1951: 366.

Weldon, Roberta F. "*Rose Tattoo*: A Modern Version of *The Scarlet Letter*." *Interpretations* 15.1 (Fall 1983): 70–77.

Williams, Dakin, and Shepherd Mead. *Tennessee Williams: An Intimate Biography*. New York: Arbor Press, 1983.

Williams, Tennessee. Interview. *Harper's Bazaar* Feb. 1955: 124.

———. Interview. *Vogue* 15 Mar. 1951: 96.

———. *Memoirs*. Garden City, NY: Doubleday, 1975.

Winn, Steven. "ACT's Indelible 'Tattoo.' " *San Francisco Chronicle* 1 Nov. 1996: C1.

Yacowar, Maurice. *Tennessee Williams and Film*. New York: Ungar, 1977.

Camino Real

JAMES FISHER

BIOGRAPHICAL CONTEXT

Perhaps Williams's most controversial drama, *Camino Real* presents lyrical glimpses of autobiography in the attitudes of its main character Kilroy. Williams's romanticized attitude toward life and the basic human desire for love, compassion, and personal freedom are acknowledged by most critics as being central in *Camino*, as they were in Williams's life. Falk was among the first to see autobiographical strands in its themes and characters (95), but biographies (Hayman 140–44; Spoto 185–88) only briefly stress that the Broadway premiere was a devastating failure. *Camino* is a phantasmagoric mix of Spanish folklore and traditional Christianity, both significant influences on Williams's life. Williams insisted that "the ability to feel tenderness" is essential. "The ability to love" is necessary so that we do not "become brutalized by the brutalizing experiences that we do encounter on the Camino Real" (Frost 35). In correspondence with Williams, Windham points to *Camino* as a critical transition play. Prior to it, Williams's works seem to be "self-dramatization," but after *Camino*, Windham adds, they become "self-justification" (321). Kazan regarded *Camino* as Williams's finest work, but noted that it offered a disturbing revelation of Williams's psyche and was "as private as a nightmare" (494). Leverich's two-volume biography surpasses all previous Williams biographies in providing an account of the play's origins, from the inspiration of William Saroyan's *Jim Dandy* to Williams's desire to write about Don Quixote's seriocomic idealistic quest (*Tom* 463–64; *Tenn*).

BIBLIOGRAPHIC HISTORY

In 1946, Williams wrote the one-act play "Ten Blocks on the Camino Real" and published it in *American Blues* in 1948. Williams and director Elia Kazan discussed expanding it after Kazan directed a scene at the Actors Studio. Williams completed a full-length version in January 1952 and simplified its title to *Camino Real*. Murphy's study of Williams's collaboration with Kazan provides a narrative of changes made from its one-act through its full-length versions, as well as for the play's publication by New Directions (especially 64–75). Essential reading, too, is Parker's meticulous chronicle of the variant surviving versions of *Camino* ("Developmental").

Brian Parker's "Documentary Sources for *Camino Real*," from the first volume of *The Tennessee Williams Annual Review* (1998), is a carefully constructed essay illuminating the various versions of the play. It is an accounting of surviving drafts that updates Parker's previous essay on the subject in *Modern Drama* (1996) and includes a previously unpublished Williams foreword to the one-act version from 1946 that describes the inspirational background for the play. Crandell usefully documents American and British editions of *Camino* (107–15).

MAJOR CRITICAL APPROACHES

Themes

Byron's memorable proclamation to "make voyages, attempt them" mirrors Williams's unique experiment with *Camino*, which Robinson believes exudes an "anguished benevolence" (59). Bigsby delineates similarities between *Camino* and *A Streetcar Named Desire*; both plays poetically bind "the lyric and the tragic impulse" (71). Despite initial critical and commercial failure, *Camino* was increasingly praised by fellow playwrights (Edward Albee, for example) and has received valuable attention from Bigsby, Londré, and Turner. Williams believed that *Camino*'s strength was its "representation in fantasy of the world as it is now" (Rice 66). Critics frequently profess, as Savran does, that Williams shatters "the conventions of domestic realism" (92–93), despite criticism from Atkinson ("First Night" 26), Bentley (30–31), Gibbs (69–70), and Nathan (88–89) condemning Williams's movement away from the poetic realism he had established in earlier plays. Falk and Murphy provide the most complete analyses, with Falk focusing on moral themes and Murphy crediting Kazan for his contributions.

Among the diverse themes critics propose are the destructive power of time (Coakley 232–36; Corrigan 155; Griffin 127–28), the exploitation of the romantic sensibility (Cless 43; Clurman 21–23; Gill 50; Miller 83–88), resurrection (Boxill 137–38), and the need for love despite its failure to redeem (Bigsby 77–80; Clurman 21–22). Others point to Williams's fascination with grotesque and brutal imagery and characters (Atkinson, "First Night" 26; Bigsby 78–82; Clurman 21–22), which they believe obscured the play's inherent hopefulness. Savran sees

Camino as a political incitement to "turn expression to action" (174) and, along with Fisher (21–22), emphasizes the significance of Williams's homosexuality, particularly as manifested in Baron de Charlus. Bigsby explicates the play as "absurdist" (78), although Williams denied this influence.

Critics identify equally diverse sources and inspirations: Dante (Falk 93), Chekhov (Coakley 233), Kafka (Gibbs 69), T. S. Eliot (Griffin 128–29; Isaac 32), Thornton Wilder (Cless 42; Falk 95; Hayes 52), D. H. Lawrence (Bigsby 76; Kroll 82), Sean O'Casey (Clurman 22), Bertolt Brecht (Cless 41–50), Eugene O'Neill (Miller 83), Samuel Beckett (Coakley 235), and the art of M. C. Escher (Miller 83). Falk sees Gutman as Williams's variation on Wilder's stage manager in *Our Town* (95). Nathan scathingly attacks the play as "a cold stew of Kaiser expressionism, Cocteau extravaganza, Wedekind sexual anarchy, Strindberg nightmare fancy, Stein aural theory, Sartre dead-end philosophy and Schönberg tonal technique" (88).

In *The Cambridge Companion to Tennessee Williams*, edited by Matthew C. Roudané, Jan Balakian describes *Camino Real* as an "allegory about the fifties" (67), a play from Williams's most "eclectic" (67) and fertile period as a dramatist. Balakian's thorough historical accounting of the play's genesis and initial production, as well as text analysis, provides one of the most useful sources currently available on *Camino Real*. In addressing "a profound existential despair" (76), Williams, according to Balakian, has created an "affirmative" (91) play about "reclaiming one's heart" (91).

Characters

Corrigan asserts that *Camino*'s characters are "wanderers, rootless, displaced persons" (160), a view echoed by other critics. Robinson sees Kilroy as the only character to achieve three-dimensionality (53), while Bigsby calls him a nonconforming romantic (79). Hayman presents Kilroy as Williams's alter ego and believes that he is imbued with Williams's "spark of anarchy in his spirit" (142). For Falk, Kilroy is a courageous "all-American" (97), while others (Nightingale; Peter) distinguish him as an icon of corrupted America. Criticizing the development of Williams's characters, Robinson describes Kilroy as "more a gesture than a character—an exclamation point of a human being" (53); Boxill's Kilroy is an innocent victim (136–37); Turner proclaims him a "chosen hero" (243) on a journey from idealism to reality. For an examination of *Camino*'s "romantic characters," see Coakley (234), Clurman (21–22), Miller (85–86), and Murphy (75–81). Griffin also discusses the one-dimensionality of the characters (133), while Robinson believes that Williams was not "temperamentally suited" (54) to writing iconic figures in a nonrealistic play. Nelson speaks for several critics (Atkinson, "First Night" 26; Crist 22; Hayman 142; Robinson 53–54) by describing the characters as "attitudes rather than individuals" (183). Isaac is more approving of *Camino* as "an index to the traumatized sensibility" (32). Bigsby discusses "the rhythm of human relationships" (78). He claims that Williams avoids moralizing—or, in this case, providing fully dimensional beings whose actions are realistically motivated.

Coakley usefully discerns three distinct character types in *Camino*: decadents (Marguerite, Casanova, and Baron de Charlus), outcasts (bums and drunks), and idealists (Don Quixote, Kilroy, and Byron). He insists that Williams gives each ample opportunity "to examine his problems in the arrested depths of the moment" (234–36).

Symbols

Camino's symbolic elements begin with its title, which means either "*royal* road" or "*real* road," an ambiguity fully intended by Williams, who believed that symbols were the "natural speech of drama" (Foreword to *Camino Real, The Theatre of Tennessee Williams*, 421). Some critics (Falk 93–98) believe that Williams used symbols in place of action—as a "radical simplification of complex issues" (Bigsby 74). Williams insisted that symbols were a way of "saying a thing more vividly and dramatically" (Hewes 25) and that he did not use them unless they clarified meaning. Wolf studies "communication patterns" such as the symbolic "aversion to light" (reality) experienced by characters in *Camino*, as well as in other Williams plays (252–76).

Plot

Camino lacks a traditional plot structure. Some critics (Bigsby 76–78; Boxill 136–37; Wolf 253) discuss this as a strength, while others (Atkinson, "First Night" 26; Bentley 30–31; Clurman 22; Falk 94; Robinson 53–54) consider it a weakness. Critical debate has also centered on the play's linear plot. Robinson claims that it "remains incompletely defined" (54), but others insist that Williams was ahead of his time in creating a new kind of dramatic structure. Bigsby compares *Camino* to the works of Samuel Beckett and Eugene Ionesco, whose plays, like *Camino*, exist "outside time" and "become no more than a series of overlaid fictions, a collage of inventions" (80).

MAJOR PROBLEMS *CAMINO REAL* POSES FOR CRITICS

Bentley and Robinson find that Williams jeopardized his work when he tried to expand its form to describe "big ideas" (Robinson 53). Conversely, Clurman (21–22) and Peter applaud *Camino*'s assault on significant issues. Bigsby finds the play "less than convincing" (81) dramatically, while Bloom refers to it as a disaster of "misplaced lyricism" (2). For Fisher (21) and Murphy (64–67), Williams's lyricism and *Camino* itself are misunderstood. Londré has recast the argument for those who believe that *Camino* is "one of Williams's most remarkable achievements" (490), yet fiercely opposing views exist over its quality and style. Challenged by recent critics is the generally accepted (though perhaps inaccurate) notion that *Camino* is a failure.

CHIEF PRODUCTIONS

The critical reception of *Camino*, which premiered on 19 March 1953, at the Martin Beck Theatre, was predominantly negative. Kerr established a harsh critical tone, condemning it as "the worst play yet written by the best playwright of his generation" (12). Hawkins disagreed, stating that "we all weep and wail for imagination and novelty in the theater" (28). Lewis (25) and Gassner (89) agreed with Hawkins, but others (Atkinson, "First Night" 26; Gibbs 69–70; Hayes 51–52; Nathan 88–89; "New Play" 63; "New Play in Manhattan" 46; Richardson 22) fell strictly in line with Kerr. Bentley dismissed Williams's efforts and claimed that it was "Kazan's presence we feel most strongly" (30). Murphy details the controversy over this issue, adding that Williams was well aware that Kazan had "encoded a great deal of the play's meaning in the language of the stage" (95–96).

Among the earliest European productions were three German stagings (Darmstadt, 1954; Bochum, 1955; and Hanover, 1959) described as "full of banalities" ("Bochum Stages *Camino Real*"). Similar response greeted the 8 April 1957 British premiere at London's Phoenix Theatre, directed by Peter Hall and featuring Denholm Elliott as Kilroy, which "left most of the British newspaper critics cold," although one described it as "vital and shot with poetry and wit" ("*Camino Real* in London" 41). A 1960 American revival directed by José Quintero at New York's Circle in the Square was called "a hodge-podge of symbolism" (Crist 22). Yet despite such negativity, the production ran for a respectable 89 performances.

A 1968 production at Los Angeles's Mark Taper Forum under the direction of Milton Katselas, featuring Victor Buono as Gutman and Earl Holliman as Kilroy, was well received. With cast changes, it inspired a major New York revival at the Vivian Beaumont Theatre that opened on 8 January 1970, with Al Pacino as Kilroy, Jessica Tandy as Marguerite, and Jean-Pierre Aumont as Casanova. Kroll felt that the play was "occluded by too much verbal and philosophic gumminess" (82), while Gill wondered how viewers could fail to find "something amusing or touching or frightening" in "the ample purple palace" (50) of Williams's drama. Clurman had referred to *Camino* as "immature" (21) in 1953, but by the 1970 production, he described Williams as an ambitious "dramatist of lost souls" (227).

The first major revival of *Camino* in decades was staged in June 1997 by the Royal Shakespeare Company, the first production of a Williams play by the RSC. Under the direction of Steven Pimlott, and featuring Peter Egan as Casanova and Susannah York as Marguerite, it continued *Camino*'s controversial critical history. Peter thought it "comprehensible to the point of banality," but Nightingale found that its "protest against prejudice and brutality" is a struggle that "resonates still." He also saw it as a metaphor for the United States: "Goons suppress those who dare breathe such subversive words as 'brother.' "

FILM AND TELEVISION VERSIONS

The sole film or television adaptation is an NET Playhouse presentation of the one-act version of *Camino* that aired on 7 October 1966. Griffin found this production superior to the original Broadway version (140), and while Gould called it "a little silly" (63), he nonetheless praised the performances of Albert Dekker as Gutman, Lotte Lenya as Esmeralda, and Martin Sheen as Kilroy.

CONCLUDING OVERVIEW

On a 1994 television documentary, Edward Albee stated that Williams's *oeuvre* is "an act of aggression against the status quo, against people's smugness" ("Tennessee Williams"). *Camino* certainly confirms such a view. It offers a surreal and harshly decadent world redeemed by the faint but necessary possibility of romanticism's triumph over reality. A romantic nature could be achieved, Williams argues, through the unleashing of compassion for others in our souls. As Casanova lyrically proclaims at the play's conclusion, "violets in the mountains can break the rocks if you believe in them and allow them to grow!" Even though grotesque and often horrifying images can obscure their subtle optimism for some, late Williams plays such as *Suddenly Last Summer, The Milk Train Doesn't Stop Here Anymore,* and *The Seven Descents of Myrtle* also offer equally grotesque characters and imagery, but do not provide the hope for survival of the poetic spirit that is at the heart of *Camino*. Early Williams masterpieces such as *The Glass Menagerie* and *A Streetcar Named Desire* present an ultimately gloomier view. Perhaps the difference between *Camino* and these plays, though, is Williams's celebration of *Camino*'s characters, all of whom gallantly face life's pain with spirits that may, at times, seem corrupt or broken, but are ultimately hopeful. They survive to overwhelm nightmarish experiences by looking life's mysteries squarely in the eye. *Camino*'s remarkable and fantastic world breathtakingly pleads, as Williams's Marguerite Gautier does, for freedom and self-awareness as the most desirable traits in the face of the frightening, unanswerable eternal questions we must all face. "What are we sure of?" Marguerite wonders, "Not even our existence."

Camino Real's plea for romanticism, for compassion, for acceptance of life's fellow sufferers, and for redemption from our failings and for salvation in a cruel and unfriendly world are messages for contemporary audiences, despite the fact that previous generations tended to turn away from such messages, in part because of *Camino*'s frankness. *Camino* is now increasingly regarded as a most rewarding and challenging play in Williams's canon, a forerunner of plays like Tony Kushner's epic *Angels in America*, which pushes past the constrictions of traditional dramatic realism to address questions of spiritually, love, and human understanding. Williams himself believed that *Camino* required the "vulgarity of performance" to be fully appreciated. Perhaps like the later plays of Eugene O'Neill, that other towering figure of American drama, *Camino*'s profound philosophical, theatrical, and human issues need the liberation of an inventive and deeply felt production to unlock their complex riches.

WORKS CITED

Albee, Edward. Interview. "Tennessee Williams: Orpheus of the American Stage." Film by Merrill Brockway. *American Masters*. PBS-TV. 1994.

Atkinson, Brooks. "*Camino Real*: New Play by Tennessee Williams Offers Personal Conception of Life Today." *New York Times* 29 Mar. 1953, sec. 2: 1.

———. "First Night at the Theatre: Tennessee Williams Writes a Comic Fantasy Entitled *Camino Real*." *New York Times* 20 Mar. 1953: 26.

Balakian, Jan. "*Camino Real*: Williams's Allegory about the Fifties." *The Cambridge Companion to Tennessee Williams*. Ed. Matthew C. Roudané. Cambridge: Cambridge UP, 1997. 67–94.

Bentley, Eric. "Essays of Elia." *New Republic* 30 Mar. 1953: 30–31.

Bigsby, C. W. E. *A Critical Introduction to Twentieth-Century American Drama*. Williams, Miller, Albee. Vol. 2. Cambridge: Cambridge UP, 1984.

Bloom, Harold, ed. *Tennessee Williams*. New York: Chelsea, 1987.

"Bochum Stages *Camino Real*." *New York Times* 21 Mar. 1955: 21.

Boxill, Roger. *Tennessee Williams*. London: Macmillan, 1987.

"*Camino Real* in London." *New York Times* 9 Apr. 1957: 41.

Cless, Downing. "Alienation and Contradiction in *Camino Real*: A Convergence of Williams and Brecht." *Theatre Journal* 35 (Mar. 1983): 41–50.

Clurman, Harold. *The Divine Pastime*. New York: Macmillan, 1974. 11–23.

Coakley, James. "Time and Tide on the *Camino Real*." *Tennessee Williams: A Tribute*. Ed. Jac Tharpe. Jackson: UP of Mississippi, 1977. 232–36.

Corrigan, M. A. "Memory, Dream, and Myth in the Plays of Tennessee Williams." *Renascence* 28 (Spring 1976): 155–67.

Crandell, George, ed. "*Camino Real* (1953)." *The Critical Response to Tennessee Williams*. Westport, CT: Greenwood, 1996. 107–17.

Crist, Judith. "Revival of *Camino Real* at St. Mark's Playhouse." *New York Herald Tribune* 17 May 1960: 22.

Falk, Signi Lenea. *Tennessee Williams*. New York: Twayne, 1962.

Fisher, James. " 'The Angels of Fructification': Tennessee Williams, Tony Kushner, and Images of Homosexuality on the American Stage." *Mississippi Quarterly* 49 (Winter 1995–96): 13–32.

Frost, David. "Will God Talk Back to a Playwright?" *The Americans*. New York: Stein and Day, 1970. 33–40.

Gassner, John. "Tennessee Williams, 1950–1960." *Theatre at the Crossroads*. New York: Holt, 1960. 77–91.

Gibbs, Wolcott. "Erewhon." *New Yorker* 28 Mar. 1953: 69–70.

Gill, Brendan. "The Boulevard of Broken Dreams." *New Yorker* 17 Jan. 1970: 50–52.

Gould, Jack. "TV: A Somber Premiere: Bitter Allegory by Tennessee Williams Is Presented by N.E.T. Playhouse." *New York Times* 8 Oct. 1966: 63.

Griffin, Alice. *Understanding Tennessee Williams*. Columbia: U of South Carolina P, 1995.

Hawkins, William. "Camino Real?—Just Enjoy It!" *New York World-Telegram* 20 Mar. 1953: 28.

Hayes, Richard. "The Stage." *Commonweal* 17 Apr. 1953: 51–52.

Hayman, Ronald. *Tennessee Williams: Everyone Else Is an Audience*. New Haven: Yale UP, 1993.

Hewes, Henry. "Tennessee Williams—Last of Our Solid Gold Bohemians." *Saturday Review* 28 Mar. 1953: 25–27.

Hirsch, Foster. *A Portrait of the Artist: The Plays of Tennessee Williams*. Port Washington, NY: Kennikat, 1979.

Isaac, Dan. "On Stage: Tennessee Williams's Dream World." *New Leader* 53 (19 Jan. 1970): 32–33.

Kazan, Elia. *A Life*. New York: Knopf, 1988.

Kerr, Walter F. "*Camino Real*." *New York Herald Tribune* 20 Mar. 1953: 12.

Kroll, Jack. "Road to Tennessee." *Newsweek* 19 Jan. 1970: 82.

Leverich, Lyle. *Tenn: The Timeless World of Tennessee Williams*. Vol. 2. (forthcoming).

———. *Tom: The Unknown Tennessee Williams*. New York: Crown, 1995.

Lewis, Theophilus. "*Camino Real*." *America* 89 (4 Apr. 1953): 25; (11 Apr. 1953): 59–60.

Londré, Felicia Hardison. "Tennessee Williams." *American Playwrights Since 1945*. Ed. Philip C. Kolin. Westport, CT: Greenwood, 1989. 488–517.

Malcolm, Donald. "Off Broadway." *New Yorker* 28 May 1960: 92, 94.

Miller, Jordan Y. "The Three Halves of Tennessee Williams's World." *Studies in the Literary Imagination* 21 (Fall 1988): 83–95.

Murphy, Brenda. *Tennessee Williams and Elia Kazan*. Cambridge: Cambridge UP, 1992.

Nathan, George Jean. "Theatre." *Theatre Arts* 37 (June 1953): 88–89.

Nelson, Benjamin. *Tennessee Williams: The Man and His Work*. New York: Obolensky, 1961.

"New Play." *Newsweek* 30 Mar. 1953: 63.

"New Play in Manhattan." *Time* 30 Mar. 1953: 46.

Nightingale, Benedict. "Looking Glass Menagerie." *London Times* 1 March 1997.

"One Heart Breaking." *Time* 19 Jan. 1970: 61.

Parker, Brian. "A Developmental Stemma for Drafts and Revisions of Tennessee Williams's *Camino Real*." *Modern Drama* 39 (Summer 1996): 331–41.

———. "Documentary Sources for *Camino Real*." *The Tennessee Williams Annual Review* 1 (1998): 41–51.

Peter, John. "Why Is the RSC Staging *Camino Real* at the Swan, Asks John Peter." *London Times* 9 Mar. 1997.

Rice, Vernon. "The Talking Tennessee Williams." *New York Post* 18 Mar. 1953: 66.

Richardson, Jack. "Innocence Restaged." *Commentary* Mar. 1970: 20, 22, 28.

Robinson, Marc. *The Other American Drama*. Cambridge: Cambridge UP, 1994.

Savran, David. *Communists, Cowboys, and Queers: The Politics of Masculinity in the Work of Arthur Miller and Tennessee Williams*. Minneapolis: U of Minnesota P, 1992.

Spoto, Donald. *The Kindness of Strangers: The Life of Tennessee Williams*. Boston: Little, Brown, 1985.

Turner, Diane E. "The Mythic Vision in Tennessee Williams' *Camino Real.*" *Tennessee Williams: A Tribute.* Ed. Jac Tharpe. Jackson: UP of Mississippi, 1977. 237–51.

White, Stephen. "A Few Unkind Words for Tennessee Williams, Based on Two-Thirds of His Latest Play." *Look* 5 May 1953: 17.

Williams, Tennessee. *American Blues.* New York: Dramatists Play Service, 1948.

———. *Camino Real.* New York: New Directions, 1953; New Directions, 1970.

———. "On the *Camino Real.*" *New York Times* 15 Mar. 1953: sec. 2: 1, 3.

———. *The Theatre of Tennessee Williams.* Vol. 2. New York: New Directions, 1971.

Windham, Donald, ed. *Tennessee Williams Letters to Donald Windham, 1940–1965.* New York: Penguin, 1980.

Wolf, Morris Philip. "Casanova's Portmanteau: *Camino Real* and Recurring Communication Patterns of Tennessee Williams." *Tennessee Williams: A Tribute.* Ed. Jac Tharpe. Jackson: UP of Mississippi, 1977. 252–76.

Cat on a Hot Tin Roof

GEORGE W. CRANDELL

BIOGRAPHICAL CONTEXT

Tennessee Williams typically draws upon multiple and various resources to create a dynamic cast of characters imbued with all the diversity and vitality of living people. The inspirations and models for the characters in *Cat on a Hot Tin Roof* include family members, personal acquaintances, a close friend, and strangers, as well as Tennessee Williams himself. Biographies by Nelson (3, 213–14) and Spoto (198) identify Williams's parents as the prototypes for Big Daddy and Big Mama, but more recent critical work by Hale (33–36), Tischler ("On Creating Cat" 9–16), Murphy (97–98), and Price (324–25), coupled with Leverich's definitive two-volume biography, supersedes these accounts.

Leverich, for example, identifies a personal acquaintance, Jordan Massee, Sr., whom Williams met in 1941, as a prototype for Big Daddy (*Tom* 417). The character of Brick Pollitt also shares similarities with people Williams knew. Leverich reports the belief that Brick is "a composite of Albert 'Brick' Gotcher and John Wesley Clark," childhood acquaintances of Williams from Clarksdale, Mississippi, the place that also inspired the setting of the play (55). Similarly, Hale identifies Jack "Bud" Pollitt as a probable acquaintance of Williams at the University of Missouri (where both were students in 1932) and a likely basis for his namesake, Brick Pollitt (35).

Among Williams's close friends, Maria St. Just figures prominently as a model for Maggie. As Williams explains, Maggie's "vitality" was "inspired by the volatile Russian spirit of Maria" (*Five* xiv). On the other hand, Tischler contends that while St. Just "enriched [Williams's] understanding of women," the original sources for Maggie actually predate his friendship with her ("On Creating Cat" 15). Leverich concurs, suggesting that a Mississippi woman "named Maggie . . . became the prototype for Margaret" (*Tom* 56).

Another source for characters in *Cat on a Hot Tin Roof* may have been a group of strangers known to Williams from a newspaper clipping that Murphy discovered tipped into an early script of the play. The clipping features "a photograph of G. D. Perry, his substantial wife, and their nine children, five of them big strapping boys with short necks" (97), strangers who obviously resemble Big Daddy, Big Mama, and the five "no-neck monsters" belonging to Mae and Gooper Pollitt (Williams, *Cat* 1).

The autobiographical parallels between playwright Williams and characters in his plays, obvious between Tom "Tennessee" Williams and Tom Wingfield in *The Glass Menagerie*, for example, are no less apparent in *Cat on a Hot Tin Roof*. Interpreting the play as "literary autobiography," Price sees Maggie and Brick as the "warring but married sides of Williams's psyche" (324–25), the precedent for which is Williams's own statement: "I draw every character out of my very multiple split personality" (quoted in Price 324).

The "mystery" of Brick Pollitt's sexual identity and Williams's ambiguous treatment of homosexuality in *Cat on a Hot Tin Roof* provide yet another connection with Williams's biography. Like Price, Clum calls attention to Williams's "sense of a split personality," but unlike Price, he believes that Williams succeeded in keeping separate "the homosexual artist from his work," such that homosexuality never emerges as an explicit subject in *Cat* (162). Instead, Clum argues, Williams employs "the language of indirection" (165), a strategy that, according to Savran, enables and empowers Williams: "By appropriating the language of convention . . . and by absenting the homosexual subject . . . another homosexual subject, Tennessee Williams, is allowed not only to speak, but virtually to reign over the commercial theatre of the 1940s and '50s" (72). All of the biographical sources, including documentary compilations by Van Antwerp and Johns and Leavitt, suggest that Williams's store of inspirations and models incubated for years, even decades, before reaching fruition, and then only in stages.

BIBLIOGRAPHIC HISTORY

In the spring of 1954, Tennessee Williams drafted *Cat on a Hot Tin Roof* by reworking the narrative and developing some of the characters from a short story he had completed in 1952, "Three Players of a Summer Game." Addressing the relationship of story to play, Reck characterizes the significant changes (145–47). Focusing more specifically on a single character, May attributes Brick's inactivity in the play to his activity and subsequent failure in the short story (281). Murphy details the development of characters between the pre-production and Broadway versions of the play (103–8).

The publication history of *Cat* reflects Williams's ceaseless process of revision and his own uncertainty about the relative success of the changes. The first edition, published by New Directions in 1955, includes two third acts, Williams's original version and the "Broadway version," also written by Williams but incorporating changes suggested by Elia Kazan (see "Chief Productions"). Significant differences appear in later editions of the play as well. The 1958 Dramatists Play Service edition, which "follows the production script almost word for word" (Murphy 117), deletes the "elephant story," withdrawn from the production following protests, and substitutes a passage about "mendacity." The 1975 New Directions edition incorporates 140 substantive changes that Williams made for the American Shakespeare Theatre production in 1974 (it includes both the elephant story and the mendacity passage, for example). Crandell documents the publication history (127–43).

CRITICAL APPROACHES

Themes

The critical debate about themes in *Cat on a Hot Tin Roof* typically centers on one of three topics. Williams describes the theme as "the mendacity that underlies the thinking and feeling of our affluent society" (quoted in Hagopian 270). By far the majority of critics, including, for example, Bigsby and Hethmon, cite "mendacity" as the theme or attempt to define it more precisely: Tynan, for instance, describes the theme as a conflict between truth and illusion, while Kolin explains it as a problem of communication. A second group of critics, illustrated by Nelson and Hurley, raise the issue of whether homosexuality is a theme, whereas a third group maintains that the theme is best described as a struggle between the affirmative powers of life and the destructive powers of death, as in Sacksteder and Dukore. Despite these apparent differences in viewpoint, the critics almost unanimously characterize the theme in terms of a moral crisis, a dilemma primarily for Brick, who must come to terms with mendacity, his sexual identity, and the prospect of death—his father's and his own.

Bigsby emphasizes the social implications of the mendacity theme, arguing that the characters who lie or who deceive themselves about the truth reflect the world at large (82). Hethmon agrees that Williams depicts "a society that is false, lying, hypocritical and mendacious" (96–97). Tynan considers "mendacity" the more general term for Williams's exploration of "the impact of truth on illusion" (204). For Kolin, "mendacity and misanthropy" represent "obstacles to communication" (74).

Critics who discuss the subject of homosexuality in *Cat* necessarily scrutinize Brick's relationship with Skipper, but Williams's ambiguous treatment of the subject ultimately leads critics to relate homosexuality to other themes. Nelson insists that Brick's fault is not homosexuality, but "idealizing his relationship with Skipper" (218). Similarly, Hurley argues that Brick's problem has nothing to do with sexual identity but concerns how someone who appreciates "individual difference" can function in "a society which refuses to accept such differences" (53). Twenty-five years after the first production of the play, Williams could argue that "Brick's sexual confusion is no longer the sensation it was, . . . so that the real theme of the play—the general mendacity of our society—is more clearly seen" (quoted in Phillips 137). Shackelford, on the other hand, argues that Williams achieves a more subversive aim, expressing through *Cat* "a plea for tolerance of the gay lifestyle" (105).

For a third group of critics, the play deals with Maggie's attempt, aided by Big Daddy, to rescue Brick from his condition of "moral paralysis," a kind of death in life (Williams, *Cat* 152). Thus, as Sacksteder argues, a major theme in *Cat* is "reconciliation to death and to life" (254). Hurley also observes an alliance between Maggie and Big Daddy, but to him it signals a conflict of values: Maggie's and Big Daddy's values are "social whereas Brick's are non- (but not necessarily anti-) social" (51). For each of these critics, as for Dukore, Maggie's ultimate triumph represents Williams's "affirmation of life against death" (98).

Viewing *Cat on a Hot Tin Roof* from a cultural perspective, Thomas Adler politicizes the play, suggesting that Brick exemplifies "the latent homosexual forced . . . to remain securely in the closet" (660). From a gay/lesbian perspective, Clum treats homophobic discourse in *Cat* as a demonstration of Williams's "split vision" (165); at the same time that Williams denies his homosexuality, he writes about it, using coded language. Although Winchell adopts a similar methodological approach, he suggests that because the play "doubt[s] the 'innocence' " of Brick's relationship with Skipper, *Cat* is "scandalous and ultimately subversive" (701). Savran likewise interprets the play as a "bold rejoinder to the violently homophobic discourses of the 1950s" (57).

Characters

Big Daddy

In both size and dramatic importance, Big Daddy Pollitt figures prominently in the history of criticism of *Cat on a Hot Tin Roof*. Descriptions of him typically emphasize his autonomy and strength of character. To Bigsby, Big Daddy is the "image of power, of materiality, of authority" (89), while to Inge, he is the "epitome of Southern masculine virility and assertiveness" (158). According to Tischler, the elder Pollitt is both "profane" and heroic, but nevertheless, "a magnificent portrait" (*Tennessee Williams* 200). To Bentley, he is "Williams' best male character" (29). Williams believes that he gave to Big Daddy a "crude eloquence of expression" that "no other character" in the canon possesses (*Memoirs* 168). Devlin likewise considers Big Daddy an "exemplar of a rather crude domestic order" (104).

Rosselli sees Big Daddy as the organizing figure around whom the action centers (284). Phillips similarly concludes that the other characters are depicted "largely in terms of their relationship to him" (136). On the other hand, Bigsby argues that Big Daddy and Maggie together constitute the "principal focuses of the play" (83). With Maggie's assistance, Big Daddy must figure out "how he can infuse his own personality into the prostrated spirit of his son" (Bigsby 89). Also commenting on Big Daddy's genealogical function, Savran shows how the patriarch serves as a "carrier of homosexuality," the intermediary in a line of descent extending from Jack Straw and Peter Ochello to Brick (64). Shackelford emphasizes how Big Daddy tolerates "homosexual love as understandable human behavior" (114). Other critics consider Big Daddy secondary in importance to Maggie. Sacksteder, for example, maintains that Big Daddy merely "mirrors various aspects of [Maggie's] capacity" as the "life-force" of the play (264).

In Williams's original version of *Cat*, Big Daddy exits at the end of act 2, never to return, but in the "Broadway version," he comes back in the third act. Chesler concludes that his reappearance "serves no dramatic purpose" (862), but Tischler disagrees: "Dramatically, it is an enormous loss to drop Big Daddy so early in the play" (*Tennessee Williams* 207–08). Commenting on the effect of Big Daddy's reestablished presence, Murphy argues that Williams transforms Big Daddy's rage into "wisdom and acceptance" (129). As a result, the play concludes more positively; instead of valorizing Maggie's "amoral life spirit," Williams inspires hope for new life, to which Big Daddy gives his blessing (Murphy 129).

Maggie

For Williams, *Cat on a Hot Tin Roof* is Maggie's play, "the story of a strong determined creature (Life! Maggie!)" who manipulates "a broken, irresolute man" (*Five* 112). Blackwelder likewise emphasizes Maggie's centrality. Not only is she named as the "cat" of the title, but her "cattiness" results in a "psychological victory" and "resolves the thematic tension of the play" (18). Hagopian similarly believes that the "substance" of *Cat* lies in "the triumph of Maggie's heterosexual vitality over the pathological, almost necrophilic, homosexual commitment of Brick to Skipper" (274).

As the life force of the play, Maggie's role is that of intermediary between extremes. According to Blackwelder, she plays a "linking role between the animal and the spiritual extremities of human existence which create the tensions of the play's main theme" (17). Kolin likewise views Maggie as a mediator, someone who "attempts to break down barriers" to communication (74). Savran, too, describes Maggie as a "mediator . . . between the living [Brick] and the dead [Skipper]" (69).

As a redemptive spirit, Maggie has various mythic, psychological, and literary analogues. Inge sees Maggie primarily as an "Agrarian spirit, devoted to fertility and regeneration" (161). Hethmon likens Maggie to Artemis, Aphrodite, and Phaedra; however, in Williams's newly created myth, "Phaedra's death-dealing lie to Theseus about Hippolytus becomes Maggie's life-giving lie to Big Daddy about Brick" (100). Kataria applies Toni Wolff's characterization of the feminine psyche (derived from Jung) to Maggie, noting a parallel between the Hetaira or "companion woman" and Maggie (46). In this role, Maggie's "primary commit-

ment is to the interpersonal relationship and psychic fulfillment of the man"
(46). Both Weimer (522–25) and Barrick (313–15) compare *Cat* with García
Lorca's *Yerma*, noting how Maggie resembles Yerma, particularly in her desire for
children, her personal integrity, and her fierce determination. Both contrast
Yerma's "frigidity" (Barrick 313) or repressed "sensuality" (Weimer 523) with
Maggie's impassioned sexuality.

Brick

Brick Pollitt is simultaneously the object of *Cat on a Hot Tin Roof* and its most
peripheral major player. May labels Brick the "ambiguous center for all the characters in *Cat*" whose primary function is as a "catalyst for the dramatic action"
(277). Hethmon also attests to Brick's importance, primarily because "[t]he central duplicity of the play is Brick's" (97). Other critics, however, insist that Brick's
character is "exaggerated way out of proportion to his real interest or attraction"
(Hivor 126). As Nelson observes, "To the extent that Brick is an object for
analysis . . . he loses dramatic power" (207).

Critical commentary about Brick typically investigates Brick's mysterious problem (whether caused by homosexuality or by fidelity to an ideal of friendship) or
evaluates Williams's revisions to Brick's character in the "Broadway version" of
the play, in which Brick is reconciled to Maggie. Kerr accuses Williams of evading
the issue of Brick's homosexuality (1), to which Williams replies, "Some mystery
should be left in the revelation of character in a play" (*Cat* 98–99). Tischler
sides with Williams: "This is no evasion on Williams's part. Brick simply can't
acknowledge the homosexual tendency within himself because he accepts the
world's judgment upon it" (*Tennessee Williams* 214). Shackelford similarly sees
Brick as a symbol of "an American society unwilling to confront the truth of
homosexuality" (116).

Other critics fault Brick for "idealizing his relationship with Skipper" (Nelson
218), a glorified bond that suggests both mythical and literary parallels. Hethmon
likens Brick to Hippolytus, who similarly "devoted himself exclusively to an ideal
way of life" (99). Citing Homer's *Iliad*, Hurd compares the relationship between
Achilles and Patroclus to "the equally ambiguous parallel relationship between
Brick and Skipper" (63). Brick's idealism functions primarily, however, as a conflict pitting him against both Maggie and Big Daddy, who, according to Hurley,
"refuse even to entertain the possibility of an ideal world" (55). Price also argues
for the contest dividing Brick, the representative of Idealism, and Maggie, the
opposing representative of Success (324). Likening Brick to Williams, Devlin
describes Brick as "an unforgiving mirror of Williams's artistic identity" (105).

When Williams reconciles Brick to Maggie in the third act of the Broadway
version, critics routinely object to the rapidity of Brick's "miraculous transformation" (Mansur 153). Funatsu remarks that "[s]uch a nihilist as Brick could not
in such a short time be changed so much" (38). Winchell likewise characterizes
the change as "insufficiently motivated" (712). Although Bigsby considers the
revision inexplicable (89), Pease suggests a possible explanation: Even though

Brick "compromises" his "fidelity" to Skipper's memory, he nevertheless obeys his father's "command to reform himself" (846). Price submits that Brick's change is part of a greater compromise, insisting that Williams sacrificed his artistic integrity for "artistic survival" (334).

Big Mama

Critics unfortunately devote scant attention to Big Mama except to note positively that she is "a beautiful, strong study in unfulfilled love" (Tischler, *Tennessee Williams* 201). In this role, she performs a function similar to that of Maggie, although, as Mayberry says, it is "a more distorted manifestation of the frustrated love theme treated in Maggie herself" (361). As Blackwelder suggests, Big Mama also resembles Big Daddy, specifically in age and size; however, because she lacks his "power of will," she follows rather than leads (15). Consequently, her role is secondary, rather than primary, in importance.

Minor Characters

Although Skipper never appears on stage, he must be considered an important, if minor, character in *Cat on a Hot Tin Roof* because he functions, as Ganz points out, as the "motivating figure" in the play (286). Accenting a similarity between Skipper and Allan Grey in *A Streetcar Named Desire*, Ganz notes, too, that the absent character is once again a "rejected homosexual" (286). Pointing also to the importance of Skipper and other "unseen characters" in Williams's plays, Koprince demonstrates that these characters help to "explain the fragile emotional states" of leading characters, such as Brick, and serve to initiate the play's "central conflicts" (92). Shackelford elevates Skipper to the status of a "central figure," representing Williams's attempt to depict "gay male subjectivity" (105). Reverend Tooker, along with Gooper, Mae, and their brood, may also be counted among Williams's minor characters, more specifically, his physical "grotesques" (Mayberry 360).

Symbols

The most prominent symbols in *Cat on a Hot Tin Roof* function to illuminate characters or the relationships among them. Blackwelder, for example, links the "cat" and heat of the title to Maggie and "the fiery passion of sex" (17). Kataria adds that the cat symbolizes not only the "sensual," but also "the mystery, jealousy, savagery, vindictiveness and guilefulness associated with the Feminine" (51), all of which apply in some measure to Maggie. Comparing *Cat* with García Lorca's *Yerma*, Barrick observes that both authors frequently mention heat, attributing to it "sexual significance" (314).

Brick's broken ankle and crutch also function symbolically to illuminate character. For Higgs, the fracture is a symbol of Brick's spiritual woundedness (141), while for Ganz, the injury is a sign that Brick's symbolic "castration . . . will not be permanent" (288). For Savran, Brick's ankle in a cast is "the visible sign of guilt and eroticism, anxiety and power, confinement and freedom, secrecy and disclosure," characteristics of the closeted homosexual (71). The crutch, like Brick's alcohol, is a symbol of Brick's weakness, his dependence upon "artificial supports," but it also represents "Big Daddy's strength," which, as Murphy points out, Big Daddy offers to Brick as a substitute (117).

Another important symbol, the bed, highlights the "central conflict" between Brick and Maggie and signifies their troubled marriage (Sacksteder 255). For Murphy, the bed represents "Maggie and Brick's failing marriage and the memory of Straw and Ochello," the homosexual couple who once occupied it (112). According to Clum, the bed symbolizes an "ideal relationship" that cannot be realized by the heterosexual couples in *Cat* (172).

Other symbols, such as the entertainment center and Brick's store of liquor, signify Brick's desire to "escape from reality" (Murphy 112). They also represent that which inhibits honest communication (Kolin 75–76). Mayberry and other critics agree that Gooper's family is a symbol of greed (361). Jacob Adler describes them as "the epitome of the crass and the personally weak, of sex uncontrolled" (43). The Pollitt plantation, a symbol of Big Daddy's "wealth and power," enlarges the dimensions of the struggle for the inheritance to epic proportions; Peterson, for instance, observes a parallel between the Pollitt estate and Lear's kingdom: "It is rejected by the favoured younger child and bitterly contested for by the less favored older one" (15).

Plot

Cat on a Hot Tin Roof departs from "the episodic structure of short emotional scenes" that characterized works such as *The Glass Menagerie* and *A Streetcar Named Desire* (Corrigan 394). Instead, Williams presents his audience with "three long introspective solos" (Tynan 204), subordinating plot to a series of "confessional monologues" (Corrigan 394). Some critics compare the structure of *Cat* to classical drama. Griffin, for example, points out that *Cat* "adheres to the classical unities" and "follows the pattern of a well-made play" (151). Inge also recognizes elements of classical tragedy in *Cat*: "Like the classical tragic figure, Brick has achieved success in the world through pride . . . and his tragic flaw lies in his inability to accept responsibility for his own downfall" (161). His "moment of recognition" comes "when he and his father exchange truths" (Inge 162).

Less certain about the play's affinities with tragedy, other critics identify the fight between rival sons for Big Daddy's estate as the play's central plot element. Hewes complains that the details of this plot are "never quite resolved" (33). Devlin notes how the domestic plot repeatedly emphasizes "the economic tenor of modern plantation life in the Delta" (103). Simon believes that this "inheritance story" weakens the drama because it is "the stuff of commercial theater" (94). Pointing to the mixture of modes in *Cat*, Hivor insightfully asks, "If the battle for inheritance be the core of the plot, how could we have anything but comedy?" (126). Falk (81–86), Griffin (145–52), Hagopian (269–70), and Londré (121–26) provide summary analyses of the plot.

PROBLEMS *CAT ON A HOT TIN ROOF* POSES FOR CRITICS

Williams's ambiguity regarding both the theme of the play and Brick's sexual identity continues to puzzle critics who debate what the play is really about. Not surprisingly, the focus of critical attention also shifts among various relationships. Is *Cat* primarily a story about a troubled marriage (Maggie and Brick), a possibly homosexual relationship (Brick and Skipper), a father and son's inability to communicate (Big Daddy and Brick), or a family squabble over an inheritance (Brick and Maggie versus Gooper and Mae)?

Of all the issues discussed, Williams's revisions to the third act of the play (see "Chief Productions") have prompted the most heated critical debate. Peterson compares and evaluates the differing versions. Sacksteder examines both texts and the subsequent film version as well. Murphy provides a comprehensive view of the production history, focusing on Williams, Kazan, and Mielziner in collaboration. Price and Griffin comment on the extent of Williams's complicity and responsibility for the various versions. Williams's summary view appears in his "Note of Explanation," published in *Cat on a Hot Tin Roof*. Kazan offers his reflections on the controversy in his autobiography (540–44). Major productions of the play featuring Williams's original third act (in London in 1988 and New York in 1990, for example) have initiated critical re-appraisals of the play.

Changing attitudes toward homosexuality have also led to re-evaluations of Brick's character and the role of Tennessee Williams as artist. Clum, for instance, examines Williams's use of homophobic discourse, while Savran explores *Cat on a Hot Tin Roof* as "a potentially revolutionary site of resistance" (72).

CHIEF PRODUCTIONS

Cat on a Hot Tin Roof proved to be one of Tennessee Williams's most popular and commercially successful plays and, at the same time, one of his most controversial. It premiered on Broadway on 24 March 1955 at the Morosco Theatre and closed after 694 performances, but not before winning the Drama Critics' Circle Award and the Pulitzer Prize. Early reviewers objected to "the play's crude language and its treatment of homosexuality" (Chesler 861), but most critics agreed with *Variety*'s assessment: "Despite its vulgarity, prolixity and opaqueness, it is undeniably engrossing" (Hobe 66). Directed by Elia Kazan, the original cast included Burl Ives (Big Daddy), Barbara Bel Geddes (Maggie), and Ben Gazzara (Brick). Jo Mielziner designed the set, as he did for *Streetcar* eight years earlier. Praise for the cast was almost uniformly positive.

Because of its objectionable language and subject matter, *Cat* inevitably sparked controversy, fueled by Williams's decision to publish, in the same volume (first in *Cat on a Hot Tin Roof*, New Directions, 1955), two versions of the play's third act: the original version (113–50) and the revised version as played on Broadway (153–97), written by Williams, but incorporating changes suggested by director Elia Kazan, separated by a "Note of Explanation" (151–52). Chesler concisely summarizes the significant changes in the Broadway version: "The three marked changes in this version are Big Daddy's return onstage . . . Brick's support of Maggie's lie about her being pregnant . . . and a more sympathetic portrayal of Maggie" (862). Williams claimed that he "embraced wholeheartedly" only the last of these ideas, the suggestion to soften Maggie's character (*Cat* 152). Williams's comments to the contrary, most critics hold Williams rather than Kazan responsible for the results. Pease, for example, argues that "Williams compromised his own vision of the play" (843) by acquiescing to Kazan's judgment. Price likewise contends that Williams violated his principles of artistic integrity in order to guarantee commercial success (334).

The fault line between playwright and director is evident in critical reviews of the first Broadway production. Observing a "failure of artistic control" in *Cat*, Zolotow blames the conflicting influences of Williams and Kazan (93). Although Murphy considered the result a "brilliant production," it was no longer "the tight, claustrophobic, classically structured family drama" that Williams originally wrote (126). Instead, it was a much less realistic production, distinctive in that characters addressed the audience directly (Murphy 126).

Critics demonstrate a strong preference for Williams's first version of the play. Hewes claims that the original "is truer to the spirit of Mr. Williams's great short story" (33); Mansur concludes that the first version, even "with its own peculiar faults, is preferable to the *Cat* in its Broadway version" (151). Many critics specifically objected to the "Pollyanna ending" of the revision (Huzzard 47), but Chesler, echoing the view of Leonard Quirino, writes that "neither ending of *Cat* satisfactorily concludes the play" (863). Critics, however, could not completely discount Kazan's positive influence and his contribution to the dramatic and commercial success of the play. Murphy credits Kazan with influencing Williams's conception of *Cat* such that Williams wrote two fundamentally different plays, the first more pleasing to Williams and the majority of critics, the second one more appealing to Kazan and to theatre audiences (129–30). Obviously preferring the Broadway version, Becker writes that successors to the collaboration of Williams, Kazan, and Mielziner "can only vary in the direction of inferiority" (269).

The first European production of *Cat on a Hot Tin Roof* opened in Malmö, Sweden, in the summer of 1955, directed by Ingmar Bergman with "bold dimensions and intensive compression in scenes between Max von Sydow (Brick) and Benkt-Åke Benktsson (Big Daddy)" (Sjögren 489). Tischler remarks that it received a "cool" critical reception, but "was a box-office success" (*Tennessee Williams* 212). Williams saw the production and complained that it was "done . . . badly" (without explanation), but also remarked that it was a "huge success" (*Five* 127). The French production of *Cat* opened in Paris at the Théâtre Antoine on 16 December 1956 and provoked unfavorable reaction. Falb reports that "the denunciation was even stronger and more vehement" than the negative response to *Streetcar*; nonetheless, *Cat* was successful, running for 192 performances (26). Gassner witnessed a "well-paced" amateur production in Dublin in 1962 (522).

In England in 1958, the Lord Chamberlain banned the public presentation of *Cat* because of its homosexual content. As a result, it opened to a private-club audience at the Comedy Theatre on 30 January 1958. Peter Hall directed Leo McKern (Big Daddy), Kim Stanley (Maggie), and Paul Massie (Brick). Although the players performed Williams's original third act, the critical response was no more positive than the New York reviews; for instance, an anonymous reviewer for the *London Times* objected to the play's sluggish pace and lamented that "we feel no concern for anybody's soul" ("*Cat*" 3).

Cat on a Hot Tin Roof was revived in 1974, first at the American Shakespeare Theatre in Stratford, Connecticut, and then at the ANTA Theatre in New York on 24 September 1974. Directed by Michael Kahn, the play starred Fred Gwynne (Big Daddy), Elizabeth Ashley (Maggie), and Keir Dullea (Brick). Unlike any previous production of *Cat*, the 1974 revival incorporated changes Williams made to the script combining elements from both the original and Broadway versions of the third act. In this version, Kauffmann notes, Big Daddy returns to tell an old joke, but, more importantly, "the happy ending has been tempered somewhat by keeping the couple out of bed and by adding a few final ambiguous lines from the original version" (16). As a result of the changes, "Big Daddy becomes rather more important than before" (Barnes 26). As in 1955, critics focused primarily on the problematic conclusion. Kauffmann, for example, echoed the sentiments of many: "No matter how you slice these versions, [the third act is] still a weak act" (16). Other critics comparing the 1974 revival and the original Broadway production noted that the language and subject matter of *Cat* were no longer shocking (Barnes 26). To some observers, Williams's treatment of homosexuality seemed dated (Kauffmann 16). Assessing the status of the play in 1974, Feingold wrote that *Cat on a Hot Tin Roof* was "the most awkwardly formed and indecisive of Williams's major works" (76).

The 1988 London revival, which opened on February 17 at the Lyttelton Theatre, was distinctive for "restor[ing] (most of) the original, less optimistic third act, retaining only the theatrical innovations of the first New York production" (Fender 164). Howard Davies was credited with directing a "superlative production" (Edwardes 29). Although Eric Porter, who played Big Daddy, was frequently singled out for praise, both Lindsay Duncan, as Maggie, and Ian Charleson, as Brick, gave "excellent performances" (Jameson 139).

Howard Davies, who directed the London production in 1988, also directed the New York revival at the Eugene O'Neill Theatre, which opened on 21 March 1990. The cast featured Charles Durning (Big Daddy), Kathleen Turner (Maggie), and Daniel Hugh Kelly (Brick). In this production, the cast performed Williams's original third act, prompting more than one critic to re-evaluate Williams's work. "The power of the present version suggests that Williams's first instincts about the play may have been right after all" (Wilson A6). Griffin reaches a similar conclusion: "It took thirty-five years to appreciate how much better Williams's original third act served the play in production" (167). On the other hand, Winer contends that the times changed more quickly than Williams's drama: "The '50s sexual tension now seems overripe; its hush-hush attitude toward cancer and scandal over childlessness seem almost quaint" (358). In short, Winer concludes, *Cat* "has not aged as gracefully as we may have hoped" (358).

FILM AND TELEVISION VERSIONS

Directed by Richard Brooks, the film version of *Cat on a Hot Tin Roof*, adapted by Brooks and James Poe, premiered on 6 August 1958, with Burl Ives reprising his Broadway Big Daddy. The film helped propel Paul Newman (Brick) and Elizabeth Taylor (Maggie) to "superstardom" (Huskins 310). Although Williams disliked the film because it lacked the "purity of the play" and because Elizabeth Taylor "was never [his] idea of Maggie the Cat" (quoted in Jennings 82), it was a great commercial success, grossing more than $10 million in the United States; it was also nominated for six Academy Awards (Phillips 152).

The most obvious and significant change apparent in the film version is that " 'immature dependence' has replaced any hint of homosexuality" (Ron 6). Donahue similarly concludes that the film addresses Brick's failure "to grow up, to face responsibility, and to act maturely" (77). As a result, Brick's actions become inexplicable. As Hartung explains, "Brick's hatred of his wife and his refusal to share her bed are almost without motivation" (637). For other critics, Brick's change at the end of the film is "even less convincing" than in the play (Kauffmann 21). Yacowar and Phillips comprehensively analyze the film.

The first television broadcast, aired by NBC on 6 December 1976, mirrored the 1974 version of the play performed at the American Shakespeare Festival Theatre. Laurence Olivier was Big Daddy, Natalie Wood played Maggie, and Robert Wagner was Brick. Phillips boldly asserts that while the television version is franker than the film, "the latter is still superior to the former since the trio of performances given by Paul Newman, Elizabeth Taylor, and Burl Ives remain the definitive interpretations" (154).

A second television production was broadcast by Showtime on 19 August 1984. The production featured Jessica Lange (Maggie), Rip Torn (Big Daddy), and Tommy Lee Jones (Brick). Critics generally agreed that it did not improve upon previous productions. The production was re-broadcast on PBS on 24 June 1985.

CONCLUDING OVERVIEW

Twice awarded the Pulitzer Prize for Drama (for *A Streetcar Named Desire* in 1948 and again for *Cat on a Hot Tin Roof* in 1955), Tennessee Williams always regarded *Cat* as the "best" of his major plays (*Memoirs* 234). For one reason, he was particularly proud of the fact that he had observed Aristotle's unities of time and place; for another, he was especially pleased with what he described as "the kingly magnitude" of Big Daddy (*Memoirs* 234). In an age when "no one can write tragedy out of contemporary life on the level of classical tragedy" (Atkinson 1), Williams succeeds at creating a modern tragedy befitting Ada Lou and Herbert L. Carson's definition of the genre: "Modern tragedy looks into the effects of social change, into the deceptions of the human heart, and portrays the ordinary tragedies that occur to ordinary people in an ever-changing world" (363). Emphasizing the tragic in contemporary problems such as mendacity, alcoholism, cancer, and death, *Cat on a Hot Tin Roof* compares with Eugene O'Neill's *Desire Under the Elms* and Arthur Miller's *Death of a Salesman* as a distinctive and significant work in the genre of modern domestic tragedy.

As much as *Cat on a Hot Tin Roof* is a modern work, it nevertheless shares with its classical antecedents a fundamental principle: "Man is not the master of his soul. The great decisions are made by forces beyond his control" (Atkinson 1). In *Cat* the superior forces against which the characters battle are biological, economic, psychological, and social. Big Daddy's destiny is determined by the cancer against which he battles for his life. Maggie competes against Gooper and Mae for an inheritance that promises economic security in a materialistic society indifferent to the needs of the unattractive poor. Brick struggles to define himself as either hetero- or homosexual. At the same time, Brick, the idealistic individual, wages war with a realistic American society.

Comparing the heroes of classical and modern tragedy, Atkinson suggests that modern protagonists lack the understanding to relate their personal experience to the workings of fate (1). In *Cat on a Hot Tin Roof*, Brick least of all understands the reasons why he drinks and why he prefers solitude to social interaction. In Williams's original version of the play, Big Daddy can do little more than rage against his impending death. In the Broadway version, he is granted "wisdom and acceptance," Murphy claims, but he succumbs nevertheless to death's superior power (129). Of the three main characters, Maggie is the only character "sufficiently enlightened," the one character with enough awareness to question the purpose of her existence (Atkinson 1). Maggie asks, "What is the victory of a cat on a hot tin roof?" (Williams, *Cat* 15). She suggests, in response, that to endure, to remain on the roof for as long as possible, is one kind of victory, but one that is not sufficient for her (Williams, *Cat* 15). Instead, she is propelled by strength of will beyond mere victory to triumph. In her determination, Maggie perhaps shares with William Faulkner the belief "that man will not merely endure: he will prevail" (Faulkner 4). Admittedly, Maggie's confidence and her faith in the future have no basis in fact, any more than her "pregnancy" has any basis in truth, but in a play in which "mendacity" is the central theme, in which rival versions of "truth" compete for supremacy (and, at the same time, vie for the sympathies of the audience), the conviction of faith can be as certain and as powerful as truth. Uncertain, it seems, of his own convictions, Williams presents his public with rival versions of *Cat on a Hot Tin Roof*. In the original version, Maggie endures. In the Broadway version, Maggie not only endures, she prevails.

WORKS CITED

Adler, Jacob H. "Tennessee Williams' South: The Culture and the Power." *Tennessee Williams: A Tribute*. Ed. Jac Tharpe. Jackson: UP of Mississippi, 1977. 30–52.

Adler, Thomas P. "Culture, Power, and the (En)gendering of Community: Tennessee Williams and Politics." *Mississippi Quarterly* 48 (1995): 649–65.

Atkinson, Brooks. "Tragedy to Scale." *New York Times* 1 Sept. 1957, sec. 2: 1.

Barnes, Clive. "New and Gripping *Cat* at the ANTA." *New York Times* 25 Sept. 1974: 26.

Barrick, Mac E. "Maggie the Cat—Tennessee Williams' Yerma." *American Notes and Queries Supplement*. Ed. John L. Cutler and Lawrence S. Thompson. Vol. 1. Studies in English and American Literature. Troy, NY: Whitston, 1978. 312–15.

Becker, William. "Reflections on Three New Plays." *Hudson Review* 8 (1955): 258–72.

Bentley, Eric. "Theatre." *New Republic* 11 Apr. 1955: 28–29.

Bigsby, C. W. E. *A Critical Introduction to Twentieth-Century American Drama*. Vol. 2. *Williams, Miller, Albee*. Cambridge: Cambridge UP, 1984.

Blackwelder, James Ray. "The Human Extremities of Emotion in *Cat on a Hot Tin Roof*." *Research Studies* 38 (1970): 13–21.

Carson, Ada Lou, and Herbert L. Carson. *Domestic Tragedy in English: Brief Survey*. Vol. 2. Poetic Drama and Poetic Theory 67. Salzburg: Institut für Anglistik und Amerikanistik, Universität Salzburg, 1982.

"*Cat on a Hot Tin Roof*, Mr. Tennessee Williams's Play at the Comedy Theatre." *London Times* 31 Jan. 1958: 3.

Chesler, S. Alan. "Tennessee Williams: Reassessment and Assessment." *Tennessee Williams: A Tribute*. Ed. Jac Tharpe. Jackson: UP of Mississippi, 1977. 848–80.

Clum, John M. " 'Something Cloudy, Something Clear': Homophobic Discourse in Tennessee Williams." *South Atlantic Quarterly* 88 (1989): 161–79.

Corrigan, Mary Ann. "Beyond Verisimilitude: Echoes of Expressionism in Williams' Plays." *Tennessee Williams: A Tribute*. Ed. Jac Tharpe. Jackson: UP of Mississippi, 1977. 375–412.

Crandell, George W. *Tennessee Williams: A Descriptive Bibliography*. Pittsburgh: U of Pittsburgh P, 1995.

Devlin, Albert J. "Writing in 'A Place of Stone': *Cat on a Hot Tin Roof*." *The Cambridge Companion to Tennessee Williams*. Ed. Matthew C. Roudané. Cambridge: Cambridge UP 1997.

Donahue, Francis. *The Dramatic World of Tennessee Williams*. New York: Ungar, 1964.

Dukore, Bernard F. "The Cat Has Nine Lives." *Tulane Drama Review* 8.1 (1963): 95–100.

Edwardes, Jane. "*Cat on a Hot Roof*." *Time Out* 10 Feb. 1988: 29.

Falb, Lewis W. *American Drama in Paris, 1945–1970: A Study of Its Critical Reception*. Chapel Hill: U of North Carolina P, 1973.

Falk, Signi. *Tennessee Williams*. 2nd ed. Boston: Twayne, 1978.

Faulkner, William. "William Faulkner's Speech of Acceptance upon the Award of the Nobel Prize for Literature." *The Faulkner Reader: Selections from the Works of William Faulkner*. New York: Modern Library, 1961. 3–4.

Feingold, Michael. "Cooling the Tin Roof." *Village Voice* 30 Oct. 1974: 76–77.

Fender, Stephen. "In Southern Climes." *Times Literary Supplement* 12–18 Feb. 1988: 164.

Funatsu, Tatsumi. "A Study of *Cat on a Hot Tin Roof.*" *Kyushu American Literature* 2 (1959): 33–39.

Ganz, Arthur. "The Desperate Morality of the Plays of Tennessee Williams." *American Scholar* 31 (1962): 278–94.

Gassner, John. *Dramatic Soundings: Evaluations and Retractions Culled from 30 Years of Dramatic Criticism.* Ed. Glenn Loney. New York: Crown, 1968.

Griffin, Alice. *Understanding Tennessee Williams.* Columbia: U of South Carolina P, 1995.

Hagopian, John V. "*Cat on a Hot Tin Roof.*" *Insight: Analyses of Modern British and American Drama.* Vol. 4. Ed. Hermann J. Weiand. Frankfurt: Hirschgraben, 1975. 269–75.

Hale, Allean. "How a Tiger Became The Cat." *Tennessee Williams Literary Journal* 2.1 (1990–91): 33–36.

Hartung, Philip T. "Through a Glass Darkly." *Commonweal* 26 Sept. 1958: 637–38.

Hethmon, Robert. "The Foul Rag-and-Bone Shop of the Heart." *Drama Critique* 8.3 (1965): 94–102.

Hewes, Henry. "A Streetcar Named Mendacity." *Saturday Review* 9 Apr. 1955: 32–33.

Higgs, Robert J. *Laurel and Thorn: The Athlete in American Literature.* Lexington: UP of Kentucky, 1981.

Hivor, Mary. "Theatre Letter." *Kenyon Review* 18 (1956): 125–26.

Hobe. "*Cat on a Hot Tin Roof.*" *Variety* 30 Mar. 1955: 66.

Hurd, Myles Raymond. "Cats and Catamites: Achilles, Patroclus, and Williams' *Cat on a Hot Tin Roof.*" *Notes on Mississippi Writers* 23 (1991): 63–65.

Hurley, Paul J. "Tennessee Williams: The Playwright as Social Critic." *Theatre Annual* 21 (1964): 40–56.

Huskins, D. Gail. *Magill's Survey of Cinema: English Language Films.* Ed. Frank N. Magill. 1st ser. Vol. 1. Englewood Cliffs, NJ: Salem, 1980. 308–11.

Huzzard, Jere. "Williams' *Cat on a Hot Tin Roof.*" *Explicator* 43.2 (1985): 46–47.

Inge, M. Thomas. "The South, Tragedy, and Comedy in Tennessee Williams's *Cat on a Hot Tin Roof.*" *The United States South: Regionalism and Identity.* Ed. Valeria Lerda and Tjebbe Westendorp. Rome: Bulzoni, 1991. 157–65.

Jameson, Sue. *London Broadcasting* 4 Feb. 1988. Rpt. in *London Theatre Record* 29 Jan.–11 Feb. 1988: 139.

Jennings, C. Robert. "Playboy Interview: Tennessee Williams." *Playboy* 20.4 (April 1973): 69+.

Kataria, Gulshan Rai. "A Hetaira of Tennessee Williams: Maggie." *Indian Journal of American Studies* 7.1 (1982): 45–55.

Kauffmann, Stanley. "Two Revivals." *New Republic* 19 Oct. 1974: 16+.

Kazan, Elia. *Elia Kazan: A Life.* New York: Knopf, 1988.

Kerr, Walter F. "A Secret Is Half-Told In Fountains of Words." *New York Herald Tribune* 3 Apr. 1955, sec. 4: 1.

Kolin, Philip C. "Obstacles to Communication in *Cat on a Hot Tin Roof.*" *Western Speech Communication* 39 (1975): 74–80.

Koprince, Susan. "Tennessee Williams's Unseen Characters." *Southern Quarterly* 33.1 (1994): 87–95.

Leavitt, Richard F., ed. *The World of Tennessee Williams.* New York: Putnam's, 1978.

Leverich, Lyle. *Tenn: The Timeless World of Tennessee Williams.* Vol. 2 (Forthcoming).

————. *Tom: The Unknown Tennessee Williams*. New York: Crown, 1995.

"London Sees *Cat*; Opinion Is Divided." *New York Times* 31 Jan. 1958: 24.

Londré, Felicia Hardison. *Tennessee Williams*. New York: Ungar, 1979.

Mansur, R. M. "The Two 'Cats' on the Tin Roof: A Study of Tennessee Williams's *Cat on a Hot Tin Roof." Journal of the Karnatak University: Humanities* [Dharwad, India] 14 (1970): 150–58.

May, Charles E. "Brick Pollitt as Homo Ludens: 'Three Players of a Summer Game' and *Cat on a Hot Tin Roof." Tennessee Williams: A Tribute*. Ed. Jac Tharpe. Jackson: UP of Mississippi, 1977. 277–91.

Mayberry, Susan Neal. "A Study of Illusion and the Grotesque in Tennessee Williams' *Cat on a Hot Tin Roof." Southern Studies* 22 (1983): 359–65.

Murphy, Brenda. *Tennessee Williams and Elia Kazan: A Collaboration in the Theatre*. Cambridge: Cambridge UP, 1992.

Nelson, Benjamin. *Tennessee Williams: The Man and His Work*. New York: Obolensky, 1961.

Pease, Donald. "Reflections on Moon Lake: The Presences of the Playwright." *Tennessee Williams: A Tribute*. Ed. Jac Tharpe. Jackson: UP of Mississippi, 1977. 829–47.

Peterson, William. "Williams, Kazan, and the Two Cats." *New Theatre Magazine* 7.3 (1967): 14–19.

Phillips, Gene D. *The Films of Tennessee Williams*. Philadelphia: Art Alliance, 1980.

Price, Marian. "*Cat on a Hot Tin Roof*: The Uneasy Marriage of Success and Idealism." *Modern Drama* 38 (1995): 324–35.

Reck, Tom S. "The Short Stories of Tennessee Williams: Nucleus for His Drama." *Tennessee Studies in Literature* 16 (1971): 141–54.

Ron. "*Cat on a Hot Tin Roof." Variety* 13 Aug. 1958: 6.

Rosselli, John. "A Moral Play." *Spectator* 196 (1956): 284.

Sacksteder, William. "The Three Cats: A Study in Dramatic Structure." *Drama Survey* 5.3 (1966–67): 252–66.

Savran, David. " 'By coming suddenly into a room that I thought was empty': Mapping the Closet with Tennessee Williams." *Studies in the Literary Imagination* 24.2 (1991): 57–74.

Shackelford, Dean. "The Truth That Must Be Told: Gay Subjectivity, Homophobia, and Social History in *Cat on a Hot Tin Roof." Tennessee Williams Annual Review* 1 (1998): 103–18.

Simon, John. "Oklahoma, Tennessee, and Beyond." *New York* 2 Apr. 1990: 93–94.

Sjögren, Henrik. "Malmö City Theatre." Trans. Carla Waal. *Theatre Companies of the World*. Ed. Colby H. Kullman and William C. Young. Vol. 1. New York: Greenwood, 1986. 487–91.

Spoto, Donald. *The Kindness of Strangers: The Life of Tennessee Williams*. Boston: Little, Brown, 1985.

Tischler, Nancy M. "On Creating Cat." *Tennessee Williams Literary Journal* 2.2 (1991–92): 9–16.

————. *Tennessee Williams: Rebellious Puritan*. New York: Citadel, 1961.

Tynan, Kenneth. *Curtains: Selections from the Drama Criticism and Related Writings*. New York: Atheneum, 1961.

Van Antwerp, Margaret A., and Sally Johns, eds. *Tennessee Williams*. Dictionary of Literary Biography Documentary Series 4. Detroit: Gale, 1984.

Weimer, Christopher Brian. "Journeys from Frustration to Empowerment: *Cat on a Hot*

Tin Roof and Its Debt to García Lorca's *Yerma.*" *Modern Drama* 35 (1992): 520–29.

Williams, Tennessee. *Cat on a Hot Tin Roof.* New York: New Directions, 1955.

———. *Five O'Clock Angel: Letters of Tennessee Williams to Maria St. Just, 1948–1982.* London: André Deutsch, 1991.

———. *Memoirs.* Garden City, NY: Doubleday, 1975.

Wilson, Edwin. "American Classics." *Wall Street Journal* 26 Mar. 1990: A6.

Winchell, Mark Royden. "Come Back to the Locker Room Ag'in, Brick Honey!" *Mississippi Quarterly* 48 (Fall 1995): 701–12.

Winer, Linda. "In 'Cat,' It's Kathleen's Show." *New York Newsday* 22 Mar. 1990. Rpt. in *New York Theatre Critics' Reviews* (1990): 358.

Yacowar, Maurice. *Tennessee Williams and Film.* New York: Ungar, 1977.

Zolotow, Maurice. "The Season on and off Broadway." *Theatre Arts* 39.6 (1955): 22–23, 93.

Suddenly Last Summer

MARILYN CLAIRE FORD

BIOGRAPHICAL CONTEXT

Tennessee Williams once confessed that *Suddenly Last Summer* was "the first work that reflected the emotional trauma" of his life ("Tennessee Williams" 287). Written at the nadir of his life, the play reflects Williams's experience in psychoanalysis with Dr. Lawrence Kubie, who sought to wean Williams not only of his artistic anxiety, but also of his homosexuality by urging him to forgo writing (Spoto 215, 219–20; Bruhm, "Blond Ambition" 99).

Suddenly Last Summer shows Williams's profound distrust of medical science by starkly contrasting the enormous power that society grants medicine with the severe limitations of medical technology. The potential lobotomy threatening Catharine echoes the fate of his beloved sister Rose, who remained permanently institutionalized after a bilateral lobotomy in 1943 (Leverich 480). In this "painfully autobiographical" play (Spoto 219), Williams exorcizes himself through the ritualistic murder of the perverse, pretentious poet Sebastian Venable by the indigent youths whom he exploited. Hayman concedes that the predatory "Sebastian resembles Williams closely" (175), but he insists that the play primarily indicts "the mother figure" (176), that Williams unfairly condemns his mother for authorizing Rose's lobotomy (172). Leverich details the synergism of personal and artistic pressures that propel *Suddenly Last Summer*.

BIBLIOGRAPHIC HISTORY

Two published versions of the play exist, showing significant variations in the dialogue between Violet Venable and Dr. Cukrowicz in scene 1 where she defines

Sebastian's religious experience in The Encantadas. According to Colanzi, Williams deleted each character's explanation of religious philosophy during the run of the first edition, printed in April 1958, and New Directions included these changes in the second printing of June/July 1959 (651). Thompson argues that Williams may have reworked Cukrowicz's role to create a more equivocal character, thus expressing the playwright's increasing disaffection with psychoanalysis and his disenchantment with medical science (126–32). Crandell documents major editions and printings (176–81).

CRITICAL APPROACHES

Themes

Niesen sees *Suddenly Last Summer* as Williams's "strongest statement concerning the artist's condition" (481). Adler considers *Suddenly Last Summer* as Williams's "nadir of hope" (45), but Thompson argues that the play evokes "an epic vision of the savagery" comprising Western civilization (111) by conflating mythology and hagiography to depict the struggle between good and evil in a Darwinian universe (99). Houston insists that the play betrays Williams's "religious apostasy": an impassive God creates, exploits, then destroys man. Hurley, on the other hand, argues that Williams does not endorse Sebastian's vision of an irredeemable universe, since he is a villain who sins by forfeiting his humanity and by seeing only "cruelty and vulgarity" in others. Sexual perversion is moral corruption, not a psychological abnormality; therefore, homosexuality and cannibalism become metaphors for Sebastian's spurning of humanity and his self-destruction (396).

Debusscher asserts that Williams's "ambiguous" hagiography contrasts "the grandeur of the past" with "the shabbiness of the present," but believes that the play endorses Sebastian's vision of a predatory universe: Williams portrays "scapegoat[s]" rather than debased saints ("Tennessee Williams' Lives" 156, 157). Thompson affirms that Williams "invert[s], pervert[s], and degrade[s]" the self-sacrifice implicit in the saint's martyrdom "to an act of retributive violence without redemptive significance," so Sebastian's cannibalization becomes "a sexual parody of the Eucharistic Feast" (103–04). Armato believes that St. Sebastian's exemplary life highlights the poet's perversity; therefore, Christianity triumphs over existentialism (562). Conversely, Satterfield believes that the play illustrates the ambiguity of existentialism: "Each man is free to decide what is good and what is not" (33). Ford, however, interprets the play as a "stark political drama" that parodies the sterile mythology of fascism through the "megalomania" of Violet Venable (19).

Hart Crane is both theme and submerged character. Debusscher, for example, deduces that Crane's life inspired the basic scenario for *Suddenly Last Summer* because the poet embodied the playwright's ideal of "the poet-wanderer" (" 'Minting' " 470). Gross insists that Crane's poetry pervades the play, creating a "Gothic melodrama" in which Williams "recast[s] Edmund Burke's concept of the Sublime . . . within a gay subjectivity" (229).

Analyzing Williams's allusions to Melville, Hurt concludes that *Suddenly Last Summer* depicts "the spiritual vacuum of the modern world which Melville foreshadowed" (400). Elaborating on Hurley's interpretation, Thompson stresses that white appalled Melville because its very "blankness" evoked universal vacuity, while Williams's white only camouflages darkness (108–10). Reppert argues that Melville's "Norfolk Isle and the Chola Widow" inspired Williams to create an "ambivalent" Catharine whose emotional instability illustrates "Melville's theme of the relativity of good and evil" (11).

Psychoanalytic readings of *Suddenly Last Summer* offer conflicting interpretations of the characters. For example, Satterfield translates Sebastian as the id, Violet as the superego, and Catharine as the embattled ego (32). For Dervin, however, Catharine embodies "the forbidden instinctual drives of the id"; Violet, "the rational, socially acceptable superego"; and Dr. Cukrowicz strives to reconcile the two (178). According to Thompson, Violet exults over her "emotionally incestuous" relationship with her son, but her obsession stymies his emotional, moral, and social development in the Oedipal stage, inflating his ego to outrageous proportions (114). Thompson interprets Catharine's predicament as "the ego's struggle for self-preservation," torn between Sebastian, the id, and Dr. Cukrowicz, the superego (124).

Many readings stress the homoerotic in *Suddenly Last Summer*. Significantly, St. Sebastian pierced to death with arrows encoded homoeroticism. Boxill contends that Sebastian suffered the "St. Sebastian syndrome," dying for his possessive paramour/creator (131). Thompson believes that Sebastian's homosexuality results from a "mutually exploitative" and "symbiotic" relationship that he shares with his mother (114, 116). Bruhm coins the phrase "blond ambition" to describe "the pathologized pairing of homosexuality and egomania" in *Suddenly Last Summer* ("Blond Ambition" 99). Bruhm believes that Williams indicts the "social structures that regulate homosexual behaviour," not homosexuality itself ("Blackmailed" 537). Because the McCarthy era equated homosexuality with sedition, Bruhm argues that Williams uses cannibalism as "a trope for the social anxiety surrounding homosexuality," depicting it as "a *mutually consumptive* bond between men" that collapses civilization with savagery ("Blackmailed" 533). According to Clum, Williams used the theme of "the beautiful male as sexual martyr" to show how people become "willing victims" to erotic passion (128, 132). Sebastian's martyrdom is thus "not divine justice, but divine economy" as death frees the homosexual from the pains of desire (133).

Bigsby avers that "art is at the heart of Sebastian's inhumanity" because Sebastian never places anything in perspective (101–02). Similarly, Hurley believes that Sebastian fails as an artist because he isolates himself from humanity and moral responsibility, and thus his moral perversion destroys him (401). Prenshaw argues that Sebastian's poetry merely distracted him from self-destruction (24).

Similarly, Nelson maintains that Sebastian only ordered the universe's "destructive chaos" superficially with his fastidious lifestyle and his laborious poetry (256).

Characters

Williams's characters continually perform various versions of themselves (and of their creator) to the rapacious world, and in the process they are continually being depleted.

Catharine

Catharine emerges as the leading character for many critics. Houston considers Catharine the "saint of truth" in the play who exposes Sebastian's "illusion of omnipotence" (152, 151). Van Laan claims that Catharine materializes as the play's central character when her narrative of Sebastian's death acquires the status of "vision" to become a "truth-embodying parable" (260). Catharine defeats Violet because she refuses to become an aggressor, using "story, parable, and vision—the products of a writer—to witness to the truth" (262). For Hurley, Catharine is the play's true poet because she defies authority to tell the truth and to exert her ability to love (399). O'Connor argues that Catharine's predicament resembles that of Blanche in *Streetcar*; society ostracizes both women as insane because they compel others to reassess the truth by discussing forbidden acts of sex and violence (64–67). Sofer believes that Catharine plays the role of "exploited ingenue" by using her sexuality as a "secret weapon" (343), while Gross likens Catharine to "the archetypal persecuted maiden of Gothic fiction," save that her commitment to speak the truth measures her personal integrity rather than her physical chastity (233–34). Catharine's story is sublime because it produces horror, remains unverifiable by factual evidence, overwhelms all attempts to suppress it, and sustains "the truth of artistic vision" (236). According to Dervin, Catharine overcomes Violet because the "trauma of her tragic [sexual] initiation" has left her "psychically mutilated," so she perceives "Sebastian's perversions without shock, denial, or disapproval" (174). Satterfield affiliates Catharine's name with the Aristotelian concept of catharsis and compares her to Catharine of Alexandria, the third-century virgin martyr who bested the imperial judges who attempted to make her recant her faith (30–31).

Sebastian

Sebastian, the play's "most complex allegorical character," is for Satterfield an Aristotelian tragic hero who, in striving to be more than human, ultimately reenacts Christ's passion (29–30). Gross finds Sebastian "a figure of unresolvable contradiction" because the audience cannot integrate Violet and Catharine's disparate accounts of his character into a coherent personality (239): Violet embodies Sebastian's artistic aspirations; Catharine exhibits his sexual desire (240); Violet celebrates Sebastian's mysticism; Catharine witnesses his mortality

(241). Because the audience has no means of verifying Catharine's story, Sebastian is Williams's "consummate self-consuming icon": "Williams writes a play without a subject, for an audience utterly excluded from the frame of representation posited by realism" (Sofer 347).

Thompson argues that Sebastian and Violet parody the myth of Attis and Cybele (118). Satterfield considers Sebastian's relationship with Violet "redolent of suppressed incest" (27); the hapless son succumbs to "his mother's culture, and it inverts, introverts, and perverts him" (29–30). Dervin believes that the frustrated artist retreats into a sadomasochistic homosexuality to protect himself from his despotic mother as well as to redirect his own aggressions away from her (175). Beyond doubt, Dervin continues, Sebastian sacrifices himself to avoid incest, so his grisly death is "the supreme and irrevocable act of castration" (176). Nelson concludes that Sebastian sacrifices himself in an act of purification when he realizes that his life, his poetry, has been a lie (258). Prenshaw, however, believes that Catharine's moral discrimination awakens Sebastian's conscience, and thus he "renounces his corruption in an act of self-sacrifice" (23).

Violet

Satterfield sees Violet as the "mother-bride-church" of the Christ-like Sebastian who will disseminate her son's work after he has sacrificed himself (30). For Gross, Violet represents aesthetic values and Catharine, ethical values (243). Niesen, however, labels Violet an "antiartist" who refuses to accept her mortality (479–80). Satterfield etymologizes Violet Venable's names to the play's themes: "Violet" conflates "vile," "violent," and "vie" to stress her domineering personality; Venable fuses "vendible," "venal," "venial," and "venerable" to stress her "authoritarian attitude" (29). For Thompson, Violet Venable's names evoke "venal," "venomous," and "Venus," while "venerable" echoes the family's surname to imply "the archetypal agelessness of their mutual savagery" (112–13). Ford describes Violet as an "outrageous dictator," a caricature of Mussolini and Hitler, who "bribes, bullies, and beguiles" all within her power (19).

Dr. Cukrowicz

Dr. Cukrowicz expresses the play's "controlling ambiguity": "the scientist who willingly suspends judgment . . . on moral as well as on scientific questions" (Satterfield 28, 29). "Cukrowicz" is the Polish word for "sugar": Satterfield considers the doctor's "caloric energy" to be inviting but dangerous (29), while Sofer labels the doctor "the fly in Violet Venable's web" (340). Gross believes that Williams felt "ambivalent" about this "pivotal non-character" who embodies "a spectral echo of the late Sebastian Venable" (237). Dervin also considers the doctor a reincarnation of Sebastian who, unlike the poet, manages to appease Violet, the mother figure, while responding to Catharine, the sister figure (178–79); Bruhm judges Cukrowicz "the erotic centre of the play" as "both the desiring Sebastian and the object of Sebastian's desire, a theatrical embodiment of the queerly split subject" ("Blond Ambition" 102).

Symbols

Major symbols in *Suddenly Last Summer* focus on Sebastian's vision of a vicious world of predators. Thompson avers that the play's ruthless Darwinian universe debases humanity, degrades love into homosexuality and incest, and compels everyone to portray "the dual role of victim and victimizer, predator and prey, engaged in a struggle for survival rather than salvation" (99). Thompson argues that Sebastian's primeval garden in the midst of the exclusive Garden District of New Orleans symbolizes the "Darwinian usurpation of the Biblical Eden" that draws striking parallels between "the primeval past and the ostensibly civilized present" (112). Many critics have assessed the importance of the Venus's-flytrap, the garden's centerpiece. For example, Sofer argues that this cloistered tropical plant symbolizes the pampered Sebastian and hints of "Nazi medical experiments" (337), while Thompson believes that the carnivorous plant represents Violet because a "seductive deadliness" lurks beneath the matriarch's "civilized veneer" (112). When Sebastian attempts to escape his stifling relationship with his mother, first by fleeing to a Buddhist monastery, then by appropriating Catharine as his traveling companion, he becomes as vulnerable as the hatchlings on The Encantadas. According to Satterfield, Sebastian becomes a "frightened sea turtle running in the wrong direction" as he stumbles into his fate at Cabeza de Lobo (28). Similarly, Thompson claims that the analogy of the devouring of the hatchlings with the murder of Sebastian debases the megalomaniac poet (103–04). Ford argues that the birds that annihilate the turtles mimic the tactics of the German Luftwaffe during the Spanish Civil War, while the hatchlings epitomize the "myopic champions of fascist appeasement" (21).

Plot

Two opposing narratives comprise *Suddenly Last Summer*: Violet Venable extols the memory of her son to Dr. Cukrowicz; then Catharine Holly debunks her aunt's eulogy. Van Laan divides the play into three distinct parts: Violet's "monologue" to Cukrowicz lauding her son's virtues; the introduction of Catharine and her family; and the confrontation between Catharine and Violet (257–60). According to Thompson, the play's protagonist romanticizes the past by mythicizing an "*idyllic* memory" (1). However, the narrative's exalted status is diminished by dramatizing it ironically or derisively, thus re-creating humanity's fall from grace (3). Williams deprives the character of mythic illusions (5), but softens this tragic vision to "an existential comedy of survival" (7). Each narrative focuses on Sebastian, but the play as a whole concentrates on Catharine, who is in danger of suffering the same fate as her cousin. Dr. Cukrowicz resolves the conflict of the two cousins in an "existentially ambiguous" way (100).

PROBLEMS *SUDDENLY LAST SUMMER* POSES FOR CRITICS

Some critics consider *Suddenly Last Summer* exclusively as a confessional drama in which Williams condemns his own sexual proclivities in the exploitive character of Sebastian Venable. The specter of Sebastian, ensconced in his sterile artistry, strips the poetic wanderer—usually a hallowed figure with Williams—of both purpose and dignity. Critics who equate Williams with the wretched poet believe that Williams sanctioned Sebastian's vision of a vicious, irredeemable universe. Haunted by his sister's wasted life and disgusted by his own dissipation, Williams "felt that he had abused the freedom of the creative life, and of life itself" (Spoto 219).

The play's ambiguity, the difficulty of discerning and affirming any sense of truth, troubles many critics and consequently has generated a variety of conflicting interpretations, especially those dealing with Sebastian. Critics who champion Sebastian as a fallen hero contend that he renounces his perversity by sacrificing himself in Cabeza de Lobo; critics who abhor Sebastian argue that his murder does not redeem his malignancy. How one perceives the spectral poet depends largely on whether one sympathizes with Catharine or with Violet. These women present antithetical versions of Sebastian, and both have hidden agendas: Catharine wishes to absolve herself of Sebastian's murder; Violet wishes to mythologize her son and to implicate Catharine in his death. Although the play's structure highlights Catharine's narrative, some critics consider the ending equivocal. The enigmatic Dr. Cukrowicz, often regarded as Sebastian's alter ego, seems for some readers to be an insidious arbitrator of Catharine's fate.

CHIEF PRODUCTIONS

Suddenly Last Summer premiered in New York on 7 January 1958 at the York Theatre, starring Hortense Alden as Violet Venable, Anne Meacham as Catharine Holly, and Robert Lansing as Dr. Cukrowicz, directed by Herbert Machiz. Although some critics disparaged the play's brutality, Brooks Atkinson praised Williams's "necromancy" as a "superb achievement" (23), and Wolcott Gibbs admired this "impressive" play as "genuinely shocking" (66). *Newsweek* applauded Williams's "shattering best" achievement ("Off-Broadway Triumphs" 84). The play's few revivals have received little critical attention. Williams himself exulted over the "vigorous" and "marvelous" Greene Street Theatre production in Key West in April 1976 in which William Prosser directed Roxana Stuart as Catharine, Janice White as Violet, and Jay Drury as Dr. Cukrowicz (Rev. of *Suddenly* 28).

International productions of *Suddenly Last Summer* have not been so favorably received. The play premiered in London in September 1958 at the Arts Theatre, starring Beatrix Lehmann as Violet Venable, Patricia Neal as Catharine Holly, and David Cameron as Dr. Cukrowicz. Although Machiz also directed this production, it was coldly received by British critics. Robert Robinson regarded *Suddenly Last Summer* as "primarily an anecdote, a melodrama" (407). Alan Brien castigated the play as a "pedagogic approach to pederasty" (quoted in McCann 122). An even more devastating reaction occurred when Tad Danielewski, director of the New York Repertory Company's 1961 production in Rio de Janeiro, was forced to cancel all performances because critics condemned the play as too violent and vulgar ("U.S. Stage Troupe" 18).

Jean Danet's Tréteaux de France first performed *Suddenly Last Summer* in regional theatres in France in the spring of 1965, then brought the production to Paris that winter. Although French critics generally attacked Williams's plays, especially the Jean Cocteau adaptation of *Streetcar* in 1949, *Suddenly Last Summer* fared better than earlier translations of the playwright's work because this adaptation captured the poetic quality of Williams's writing (Falb 27, 35). Londré notes that "the 1965 Paris production marked a turning point in French acceptance of Williams's 'strange, bewitching' dramatic world" (501).

FILM AND TELEVISION VERSIONS

Columbia produced the only screen version of *Suddenly, Last Summer* in 1959, directed by Joseph L. Mankiewicz and starring Elizabeth Taylor as Catharine Holly, Montgomery Clift as Dr. Cukrowicz, and Katharine Hepburn as Violet Venable. Taylor and Hepburn received Academy Award nominations for their performances. The film was a commercial and artistic success. Although Williams's name appears on the screenplay, Gore Vidal insists that he adapted *Suddenly* without the author's assistance, and almost all film scholars give him complete credit for the screenplay. The film significantly alters the play's tone and plot by romanticizing Dr. Cukrowicz as an unambiguous hero who selflessly devotes himself to healing. He falls in love with Catharine and saves her by resisting not only Violet's wiles, but also the pressures exerted on him by an older doctor who administers the financially strapped Lion's View.

CONCLUDING OVERVIEW

Violet Venable's own *Poem of Summer, 1936* perishes, fortuitously stillborn, as Williams satirizes the travesties of fascism. *Suddenly Last Summer*, a stark political drama replete with civilized and uncivilized ferocity, parodies fascism. Williams inverts and reconfigures the ideology's male chauvinism to caricature the arrogance of Mussolini and the fanaticism of Hitler through the megalomania of Violet Venable, a wealthy New Orleans widow determined to deify her only child, Sebastian, who was brutally murdered while vacationing in Spain, a highly symbolic location. The play begins approximately one year after the murder, in the late summer of 1936—coinciding, significantly, with the outbreak of the Spanish Civil War—when Violet attempts to suborn a young psychiatrist, Dr. Cukrowicz, into performing a lobotomy on her niece, Catharine Holly, the only witness to her son's grisly demise. Ostensibly the story of a desperate mother's attempt to protect her late son's reputation by stifling his bizarre murder, *Suddenly Last Summer* ultimately allegorizes Violet as an outrageous dictator shamelessly exploiting every means of acquiring power (Ford 19).

Violet embodies the Venus's-flytrap prized by her son: desperately flamboyant, superficially enticing, and ultimately insidious. This carnivorous plant flourishes in Sebastian's primeval garden only with vigilant care and will perish if neglected. Like the Venus's-flytrap, Violet must be pampered, medicated, and cloistered within her own hothouse in New Orleans's exclusive Garden District. Like the Venus's-flytrap, Violet will endure only a short season, although she clings desperately to life (Ford 19–20).

Williams's haunting title, *Suddenly Last Summer*, encodes the havoc wreaked by the launching of the Fascist war machine. Violet recounts how Sebastian was fascinated by birds slaughtering the defenseless hatchlings as they struggled instinctively toward the sea: the narrow beach teeming with turtles, the sky black with rapacious birds, The Encantadas enact the slaughter of battlefields. During the Spanish Civil War, the German Luftwaffe perfected the new art of aerial combat, which included the massive bombing of designated sites, and Violet recounts the disemboweling and devouring of the hatchlings with military precision: "the birds hovered and swooped to attack . . . diving down on the hatched sea turtles, turning them over to expose their soft undersides, tearing . . . and rending and eating their flesh." Sebastian, mesmerized by the massacre, estimates that "only a hundredth of one per cent" of the hatchlings survive (*Suddenly* 356). The Encantadas allegorize a primeval Guernica in which the helpless hatchlings symbolize the myopic champions of Fascist appeasement who insisted that civilized nations no longer wage war (Ford 21–22).

The enticing Dr. Cukrowicz favors the Nordic youths whom Sebastian found so alluring, save that his Slavic heritage would have disfranchised him in the Fascist regime. Violet attempts to suborn the doctor and exploit medical research to secure her Fascist mythology, but he resists becoming her minion. He refuses to compromise his profession, refuses to stoop to ruthlessness, and refuses to sanction barbarity. Cukrowicz, unlike Catharine's family, preserves his integrity by adhering to a code of ethics that transcends Violet's economic power and aristocratic privilege (Ford 22–23).

Like a Fascist demagogue, Violet Venable bribes, bullies, and beguiles all within her sphere of influence; she commands all of the blessings of civilization, but persists morally and spiritually as a savage. The unprecedented atrocities of the Spanish Civil War damn Violet's vision of her son's legend. On Violet's "withered bosom" (*Suddenly* 350)—that sterile, depleted cavity that once nurtured Sebastian—shines a diamond starfish pin. This primeval Star of David, this tawdry symbol of social Darwinism, ultimately targets her for annihilation (Ford 23).

WORKS CITED

Adler, Jacob H. "Tennessee Williams' South: The Culture and the Power." *Tennessee Williams: A Tribute*. Ed. Jac Tharpe. Jackson: UP of Mississippi, 1977. 30–52.

Armato, Philip M. "Tennessee Williams' Meditations of Life and Death in *Suddenly Last Summer, The Night of the Iguana*, and *The Milk Train Doesn't Stop Here Anymore*." *Tennessee Williams: A Tribute*. Ed. Jac Tharpe. Jackson: UP of Mississippi, 1977. 58–70.

Atkinson, Brooks. "Theatre: 2 by Tennessee." Rev. of *Garden District*, by Tennessee Williams. Premiere at York Theatre. *New York Times* 8 Jan. 1958: 23.

Bigsby, C. W. E. "Tennessee Williams." *A Critical Introduction to Twentieth-Century American Drama*. Vol. 2. Cambridge: Cambridge UP, 1984. 15–134.

Boxill, Roger. *Tennessee Williams*. New York: St. Martin's, 1987.

Bruhm, Steven. "Blackmailed by Sex: Tennessee Williams and the Economics of Desire." *Modern Drama* 34 (1991): 528–37.

———. "Blond Ambition: Tennessee Williams's Homographesis." *Essays in Theatre* 14 (1996): 97–105.

Clum, John M. "The Sacrificial Stud and the Fugitive Female in *Suddenly Last Summer, Orpheus Descending*, and *Sweet Bird of Youth*." *Cambridge Companion to Tennessee Williams*. Ed. Matthew C. Roudané. New York: Cambridge UP, 1977. 128–46.

Colanzi, Rita M. "Tennessee Williams's Revision of *Suddenly Last Summer*." *Journal of Modern Literature* 16 (1990): 651–52.

Crandell, George W. *Tennessee Williams: A Descriptive Bibliography*. Pittsburgh: U of Pittsburgh P, 1995.

Debusscher, Gilbert. " 'Minting Their Separate Wills': Tennessee Williams and Hart Crane." *Modern Drama* 26 (1983): 455–76.

———. "Tennessee Williams' Lives of the Saints: A Playwright's Obliquity." *Tennessee Williams: A Collection of Critical Essays*. Ed. Stephen S. Stanton. Englewood Cliffs, NJ: Prentice-Hall, 1977. 149–57. Rpt. of "Tennessee Williams as Hagiographer: An Aspect of Obliquity in Drama." *Revue des Langues Vivantes* 40 (1974): 449–56.

Dervin, Daniel A. "The Spook in the Rainforest: The Incestuous Structure of Tennessee Williams's Plays." *Psychocultural Review* 3 (1979): 153–83.

Falb, Lewis W. *American Drama in Paris, 1945–1970: A Study of Its Critical Reception*. Chapel Hill: U of North Carolina P, 1973.

Ford, Marilyn Claire. "Parodying Fascism: *Suddenly Last Summer* as Political Allegory." *Publications of the Mississippi Philological Association* (1997): 19–26.

Gibbs, Wolcott. "Oddities, Domestic and Imported." Rev. of *Garden District*, by Tennessee Williams. *New Yorker* 18 Jan. 1958: 66, 68.

Gross, Robert F. "Consuming Hart: Sublimity and Gay Poetics in *Suddenly Last Summer*." *Theatre Journal* 47 (1995): 229–51.

Hayman, Ronald. *Tennessee Williams: Everyone Else Is an Audience*. New Haven: Yale UP, 1993.

Houston, Neal B. "Meaning by Analogy in *Suddenly Last Summer*." *Notes on Modern American Literature* 4.4 (1980): Item 24.

————. "Meaning by Analogy in *Suddenly Last Summer.*" *RE:AL* 21 (1996): 150–52.

Hurley, Paul J. "*Suddenly Last Summer* as 'Morality Play.' " *Modern Drama* 8 (1966): 392–402.

Hurt, James R. "*Suddenly Last Summer*: Williams and Melville." *Modern Drama* 3 (1961): 396–400.

Leverich, Lyle. *Tom: The Unknown Tennessee Williams.* New York: Crown Publishers, 1995.

Londré, Felicia Hardison. "Tennessee Williams." *American Playwrights since 1945: A Guide to Scholarship, Criticism, and Performance.* Ed. Philip C. Kolin. New York: Greenwood, 1989. 488–517.

McCann, John S. *The Critical Reputation of Tennessee Williams: A Reference Guide.* Boston: Hall, 1983.

Nelson, Benjamin. *Tennessee Williams: The Man and His Work.* New York: Obolensky, 1961.

Niesen, George. "The Artist against the Reality in the Plays of Tennessee Williams." *Tennessee Williams: A Tribute.* Ed. Jac Tharpe. Jackson: UP of Mississippi, 1977. 463–93.

O'Connor, Jacqueline. *Dramatizing Dementia: Madness in the Plays of Tennessee Williams.* Bowling Green, OH: Bowling Green State Popular P, 1997.

"Off-Broadway Triumphs." Rev. of *Garden District*, by Tennessee Williams. *Newsweek* 20 Jan. 1958: 84.

Prenshaw, Peggy W. "The Paradoxical Southern World of Tennessee Williams." *Tennessee Williams: A Tribute.* Ed. Jac Tharpe. Jackson: UP of Mississippi, 1977. 5–29.

Reppert, Carol F. "*Suddenly Last Summer*: A Re-Evaluation of Catharine Holly in Light of Melville's Chola Widow." *Tennessee Williams Newsletter* 1.2 (1979): 8–11.

Robinson, Robert. "Here Be Cannibals." Rev. of *Suddenly Last Summer*, by Tennessee Williams. *New Statesman* 27 Sept. 1958: 407–08.

Satterfield, John. "Williams's *Suddenly Last Summer*: The Eye of the Needle." *Markham Review* 6 (1976): 27–33.

Sofer, Andrew. "Self-Consuming Artifacts: Power, Performance, and the Body in Tennessee Williams' *Suddenly Last Summer.*" *Modern Drama* 38 (1995): 336–47.

Spoto, Donald. *The Kindness of Strangers: The Life of Tennessee Williams.* Boston: Little, Brown, 1985.

Suddenly, Last Summer. Adapt. Gore Vidal. Dir. Joseph L. Mankiewicz. Perf. Elizabeth Taylor, Montgomery Clift, and Katharine Hepburn. 1959. Videocassette. RCA-Columbia, 1995.

Rev. of *Suddenly Last Summer*, by Tennessee Williams. *New York Times* 27 Apr. 1976: 28.

Thompson, Judith J. *Tennessee Williams' Plays: Memory, Myth, and Symbol.* New York: Peter Lang, 1987.

"U.S. Stage Troupe Is Blasted in Rio." *New York Times* 21 Aug. 1961: 18.

Van Laan, Thomas F. " 'Shut Up!' 'Be Quiet!' 'Hush!': Talk and Its Suppression in Three Plays by Tennessee Williams." *Comparative Drama* 22 (1988): 244–65.

Williams, Tennessee. *Suddenly Last Summer. The Theatre of Tennessee Williams.* Vol. 3. New York: New Directions, 1971. 345–423.

————. "Tennessee Williams." *Conversations with American Writers.* By Charles Ruas. New York: Alfred A. Knopf, 1985. 75–90. Rpt. in *Conversations with Tennessee Williams.* Ed. Albert J. Devlin. Jackson: UP of Mississippi, 1986. 284–95.

Sweet Bird of Youth

ROBERT BRAY

BIOGRAPHICAL CONTEXT

In 1948, when Tennessee Williams was thirty-seven, he began working on a one-act sketch called *The Enemy: Time* that would, as with so many of his short works, evolve into a familiar full-length play. This play (published in the March 1959 issue of *Theatre*), in keeping with so much of Williams's work, reflects elements of the author's personal life. As with *The Rose Tattoo*, *Sweet Bird*'s setting is on the Mississippi Gulf Coast, very close to Gulfport, where Williams's parents spent their honeymoon and "would often speak of Gulfport nostalgically" (Leverich 32). Williams, nicknamed "the Bird" by Gore Vidal, invests his play with referents to the darker side of his private life: drugs, alcohol abuse, and an affiliation with prostitutes were all part of the author's well-publicized indiscretions. As Clum observed: "Williams, no stranger to hiring MEN for sex, used the related (sometimes identical) figures of the male hustler in a number of works, particularly . . . 'Sweet Bird' " (141). In addition, Williams's own gradual excursion into middle age reverberates in Chance Wayne's obsession with recapturing his youth and also in Williams's looking toward the time when he, like the Princess, would lament the demise of a career. As Spoto notes, "Considered later, as part of Williams's complex late development, *Sweet Bird of Youth* might be regarded as the best example of an earnestness of continued confession" (231). Elsewhere the author confessed his obsession with flux, what Andrew Marvell called "Time's winged chariot hurrying near." For example, in "The Timeless World of a Play," Williams contends that human dignity is achieved only by "snatching the eternal out of human existence" (131). Of all Williams's plays dealing with mutability and its consequences for the human condition, *Sweet Bird* remains his most direct treatment of this motif.

BIBLIOGRAPHIC HISTORY

As with so many of Williams's plays, the number and variety of the *Sweet Bird* manuscripts testify to his inveterate reworking and expansion processes. Two articles by Gunn and Debusscher demonstrate the almost bewildering metamorphosis of *Sweet Bird*. Gunn has detected "three distinct sets of characters and themes" that "would one day be woven together" ("Troubled Flight" 27). *Sweet Bird* eventually emerged from "a varied assortment of one-act plays and sketches" that date back to 1949 (26–27). There are over 400 pages of manuscript "from this incubatory stage . . . often in a fragmented and confused state" (27). Sorting out these myriad drafts becomes a challenge for scholars because "Williams shuffled pages of dialogue from one version to another" and sometimes "discarded scripts" chaotically (27). According to a composite 135-page script and completion date, the first draft of the full-length play was created "in two weeks of intense writing" around 1956 (29), reworked again in 1958 and expanded to 475 pages, and then altered after consultations with Elia Kazan, which resulted in Williams's "original concept to be cheapened to an incredible extent" (32). Murphy details Williams's "resentment of Kazan's role in this complex relationship" (135) and notes that the director "took constant criticism for tampering with Williams's play" (160).

Debusscher also discovered a "fragment of eight unnumbered pages without title or date" (26) that also seems to adumbrate *Sweet Bird*. This scene, which takes place in a New Orleans hotel, "involves two characters, Mrs. Venable, presumably a prostitute, and Casky, a former sailor" (26). Enough similarities exist between these two characters and the later Princess and Chance to indicate that this was also a rough sketch of the play *Sweet Bird*. As Debusscher claims, "It is fascinating to watch Williams ascribe motivations to his characters, express feelings, adopt attitudes that can be shifted at will" (29). For information about the play's editions, printings, and forms, see George Crandell's descriptive bibliography (182–90).

MAJOR CRITICAL APPROACHES

Themes

As Londré maintains, "Williams's two most prominent themes" dominate the play: the corrupting effects of time and recapturing lost innocence (135). The futility of this quest inevitably leads to a sense of loss, another prominently recurring theme in Williams's drama. MacNicholas notes that "the interval between loss, or more specifically the *recognition* of loss, and subsequent recovery or its impossibility, is the typical focus of most of Williams's plays" (581). Niesen expands on this view of loss and finds that "indeed the entire play is one of destruction, castration, and impotence" (483). Reading *Sweet Bird* in light of existential "bad faith," or self-deception, Colanzi finds it ironic that "while Williams' travelers seek to retreat from their nothingness, they are always journeying forward" (453). Similarly, Robinson observes that Williams "allowed scenes to follow the course of sexual approach and retreat, the strategies with seduction" (31). Examining the relationship between Chance and the Princess, Herron thinks that *Sweet Bird* "reveals that Williams is still pursuing some of his favorite theories about sex and love, idealism and reality, loneliness and the need for friendship and communication" (370). In agreeing with Londré's findings, Herron also contends that the relationship between these two characters "helps to introduce a thematic motif—the ill effects of time . . . on the individual—which saves the play from total disunity" (371). Boxill sees the play's Easter setting, a period of time when "the blind rush of events" should be frozen out, as another of Williams's "ruined" celebrations (27).

Other critics, such as Bigsby, see Williams as portraying a dysfunctional society: "The collapse of values, ideals, relationships, social models, love, coherence, mental stability, hope, fiction, is at the heart of his concern" (*Critical Introduction* 104). For Bigsby, "Insanity and violence stand as appropriate images of moral anarchy," and in *Sweet Bird* Williams "was also responding to a cultural neurosis, a sense of lost values and high hopes, which he witnessed in America in the 1950s" (104). Bigsby and Thomas Adler astutely focus on the play's sociopolitical content to dispel any lingering notion that Williams was apolitical in his drama. Bigsby contends that "*Sweet Bird of Youth* is another indictment of Southern bigotry . . . blind to the hermetic and incestuous implications of its denial of history" (*Modern American Drama* 640). Adler similarly concludes that *Sweet Bird* is "where Williams most decisively portrays the pre–Civil Rights white South's peculiar blend of conservative Protestantism, capitalism, and racism" ("Culture" 658). Finally, along similar lines, King explores *Sweet Bird*'s southern history in terms of its "rituals and taboos" (629).

Characters

For many critics, *Sweet Bird* has few, if any, sympathetic characters. According to Falk, for example, Williams includes in *Sweet Bird* "an assembly of sorry characters" (155); for Jackson, Williams's characters "are linked together by their common worship of the 'god of success' " (148).

Chance

A number of readers emphasize mythic analogues with Chance. Hays identifies Chance with Adonis "by appearance, theme, setting, allusion, and music" (257). Thompson also thinks that Williams associates Chance with Adonis (136). Dukore sees striking parallels between Chance and Abelard, a twelfth-century cleric (631). Many critics point to Chance's moral bankruptcy and the inability of audiences and readers to be sympathetic to his predicaments. His narcissism, occupation as a gigolo, and lack of responsibility result in rather harsh critical assessments. Niesen finds Chance "an unsympathetic character" (482), and most agree with Williams himself, who thinks that Chance "went too far into his corruption" (Devlin 211). Bigsby contends that "his failure is that he has internalized the values of those he despises" (*Critical Introduction* 105). Chance, like Gatsby, wants "to win what the world denies him" (105). Though he is engulfed in self-pity at the play's conclusion, Chance's submission to his punishment—his castration—has elicited differing critical responses as to whether this constitutes an act of atonement. According to Hays, Chance "waits to have his guilt removed by surrendering himself to the violent treatment of others" (257). But Thompson contends that it is unclear whether Chance submits to death because of a desire to atone for his past faults (149). Some readers, like Herron, blame the circumstances of Chance's past, those beyond his control, for his moral lassitude. Despite his frantic attempt to recapture his lost youth, Chance is "still striving to outgrow the obscurity and poverty which shackled his youth" (370). A few critics also remain suspicious about Chance's "conversion" at the play's end. Hays acknowledges that this " 'religious' conversion is quite abrupt" and that "the change in Chance's character is sudden and inadequately prepared for by Williams" (257–58). Londré also questions Chance's motives and concludes that he offers little virtue for the audience (140). According to Clum, "Chance, figuratively, is the black-sheep brother of Brick Pollitt in *Cat*" (140) as well as the "gigolo" illustrating "the most fascinating case of the reversal of the sex/ gender system" (141).

The Princess

Alexandra del Lago shares many of Chance's unseemly flaws yet emerges with more dignity and with more forbearance from the critics. In Clum's view, Alexandra "is the core of the play, not Chance," since she expresses "the philosophy of adaptability and endurance that are the positive counter to the mutilation of Williams's martyrs" (144). She does use Chance as he uses her, and "the plight of each of these two lost seekers touches upon their attempts to find a solution in sex" (Herron 370). But she tries to forget her past through the "act of lovemaking" (371), even as both Chance and the Princess "believe in the inevitable nexus between success and sexual fulfillment" (Bigsby, *Critical Introduction* 105). Like Blanche, an aging Cleopatra (Kolin, "Cleopatra"), the Princess, with her fondness for younger men, also has definite links to Karen Stone, the protagonist in *The Roman Spring of Mrs. Stone*.

Despite her deficiencies, readers admire the Princess's tenacity and resilience. Tischler argues that Chance is no match for the Princess's "magnificence." A force clearly to be reckoned with, "She towers over the other characters in her rage and in her lust, sharing none of their pettiness or vengefulness" (498). Tischler believes that the Princess is a "tribute to the many heroic aging actresses" Williams saw, such as Laurette Taylor and Tallulah Bankhead, and thus she is a very believable character, "no simple archetype" (498).

Boss Finley

Finley, who has "heard the voice of God," represents virtually everything loathsome to his creator and certainly is "chiefly responsible for the prevalence of bigotry and chicanery in St. Cloud" (Herron 370). "A cross between Big Daddy . . . and Huey Long," Finley "gradually gains power over gullible constituents by skillful demagoguery in preaching hate and racism" (370). Finley, who "subordinates everything to his lust for power," is for Bigsby "the god envisaged by Sebastian Venable . . . a god whose consuming hatred for his creation leaves no space for life" (*Critical Introduction* 104–05). Elsewhere, Finley is compared with Jabe of *Orpheus Descending*, each with their "self-righteous 'truths' " (Shaland 41), and with Fitzgerald's Dr. T. J. Eckleberg, the "blind, indifferent God" of the " 'valley of ashes' " (Thompson 143). Thomas Adler, who echoes Bigsby, finds that Finley "casts himself as the anointed prophet of the Old Testament God of vengeance" ("Culture" 658), and King thinks that Finley "resembles to some degree both Robert Penn Warren's Willie Stark and Arkansas' segregationist governor, Orville [sic] Faubus" (635). Suggesting another parallel, Kolin maintains that Eugene O'Neill's Ephraim Cabot in *Desire under the Elms* "may have suggested or at least helped Williams shape the character of Thomas Boss Finley" ("Parallels" 23).

Heavenly

Like Gatsby's Daisy, Heavenly represents the "unattainable" for Chance (Hays 256). Chance's quest for Heavenly in St. Cloud suggests both the ethereal and the ephemeral. Thompson finds "that Williams used a symbolic home to characterize the dreams Chance hopes to fulfill by rejoining Heavenly—youth and stardom" (133–34). As Williams reworked his play, he deleted several of Heavenly's passages. As a result, he truncated her delineation, and she thus remains "a cardboard angel" (Thompson 141), functioning more as a symbol than as a convincing character.

The Heckler

Of the supporting characters, perhaps the shadowy, enigmatic Heckler emerges as the most interesting. Thomas Adler (*American Drama*) contends that "though only a minor character, the Heckler holds a privileged status as the audience's onstage representative," and so "the theatregoers share in his moral indignation . . . [and] experience outrage over his beating." Adler also finds that "like Chance, the Heckler, too, undergoes a kind of castration by being silenced and denied a voice" (158). According to Falk, the beating scene demands comparison with Val Xavier's punishment at the end of *Orpheus Descending* and Sebastian Venable's fate at the hands of cannibals in *Suddenly Last Summer* (159).

Symbols

As is the case with other Williams works, many readers believe that the playwright invests *Sweet Bird* with excessive symbols. Adler finds that one of "several deficiencies" in *Sweet Bird* is the "use of too-insistent symbolism," in which "Williams blends extensive classical, Christian, and archetypal imagery" with the "questionable universality" of Chance (*Modern American* 156). As in *Orpheus Descending*, the combination of "classical (the waxing and waning of the god Adonis, the sacred palm groves associated with fertility kings) and Christian (church bells, lilies, psalms, the 'alleluia chorus' of Passiontide and Easter)" (158) clash with and obfuscate rather than clarify and complement each other. Falk questions the idea of the Easter setting, contending that Williams was not a respecter of religions (160).

Of course, the names are also symbolic in this Williams play—too much so for some readers. Dukore asserts that "in most of his plays Williams uses names symbolically; sometimes he is subtle; usually he is blatant," and "in *Sweet Bird of Youth* itself the obvious symbolism of the names Heavenly and Chance" was chosen "to provide the play with mythic overtones" (632–33). However, Thompson finds that in providing these overtones, Williams also "demythicises" the main characters via their castration, either "literal or symbolic." Other secular symbols, such as the venereal disease (the impurity that ultimately categorizes Chance and Heavenly's relationship), the drugs and liquor, which connote dependency and corruption, and the Princess's bedroom, a place for refuge as well as sexual commodity, all help form a mosaic known as " 'the beanstalk country' [that] symbolizes the private worlds in which two derelicts become lost in their frantic search for fulfillment" (Herron 370).

Plot

The plot of *Sweet Bird* went through a variety of radical alterations before emerging in its most recognizable form. The final plot essentially focuses on two disparate stories somewhat awkwardly welded together: the saga of Chance and the Princess, and the story of Boss Finley. In the former, "The plight of each of these two lost seekers touches upon their attempts to find a solution in sex," and act 2 "pushes the personal and sexual plot of the initial plot into the background" so that "as the act moves forward, the second story, or social plot, accentuates the disjointed quality of the play" (Herron 370–72). Other commentary has focused on the play's structural pattern, which involves two "very different major memory-stories," Chance's and the Princess's (Thompson 133). In broad terms, Falk sees that "the first act sharply sets the mood and creates the general atmosphere of human decay," the second act "belongs mainly to Boss Finley," and in the third act, "Boss Finley has exited in favor of the Princess" (118–19). Clum identifies a structure "comprised of intersecting triangles: Chance, Heavenly, and Heavenly's Father, Boss Finley; but far more important, Chance, Heavenly, and

Alexandra del Lago" (140). Herron finds that "certain exaggerated effects [such as the political rally] change the focus of the action from the personal del Lago–Wayne liaison to a powerful materialistic spell binder" (372). Finally, Dukore suggests that Williams might have had other plots in mind when he was composing his play: "This story is strongly reminiscent of an older story, a very famous love story which also ends in castration: the tale of Heloise and Abelard" (631).

MAJOR PROBLEMS *SWEET BIRD OF YOUTH* POSES FOR CRITICS

Critics point to difficulties with the play's structure, its excessive symbolism, and Chance's concluding plea. Thompson, for example, thinks that "the romantic and mythical prototypes of the characters" are so at odds with their behavior in the play that they are turned into caricatures (135). Jacob Adler admits that "*Sweet Bird* can be exciting on the stage," but finds the excitement "largely spurious," the power "of mindless violence," and the culture "dissipated through fear and misuse," so that the people we are asked to take an interest in are monsters (46). As a result, when we are "asked to sympathize with fallen characters," "their sympathy is both undeserved and ungrantable" (48), and, as Bigsby adds, "a source of sentimentality" (*Critical Introduction* 106). MacNicholas faults the play's structure, contending that *Sweet Bird* "is weakened by the fragmentations of dramatic energy inherent in the protagonist's confusion" (584). Perhaps the play's myriad problems are due to the playwright's inability to let well enough alone, for, as Williams admitted, "*Sweet Bird* was in the works too long. . . . Sometimes I wish I had not tried to deal with so much" (Devlin 60).

CHIEF PRODUCTIONS

Sweet Bird of Youth premiered at Studio M Playhouse in Coral Gables, Florida, in 1956. The Broadway premiere took place in March 1959 at the Martin Beck Theatre in New York and ran for 383 performances. It starred Geraldine Page who, according to Coleman, gave "a compelling, bravura performance" as Alexandra, and Paul Newman who "was superb in a role that requires him to be almost constantly repugnant" (Aston). While some critics praised the play, Robert Brustein found it "disturbingly bad" (59); Harold Clurman wrote that "it interested me more as a phenomenon than as a play" in 1959 (281). Brooks Atkinson recoiled from a play that "ranges wide through the lower depths, touching on political violence, as well as diseases of the mind and body." John Gassner described the play's "power" in terms of both acting and script (122–23). For the most thorough discussion of the Kazan/Williams collaboration on this production, see Murphy (131–65).

Subsequent major productions ran in Hollywood, Buenos Aires, and Rio de Janeiro (all in 1961); Manchester, England (1964); Moscow and Brooklyn (1975); and London (1985). Of the Brooklyn Academy of Music's production,

Walter Kerr wrote, "Mr. Williams' play . . . seems richer and more complex today than it did when it was first produced" (5). Clive Barnes found that "the whole play is delicately cast and balanced" (53), and Harold Clurman asserted that "the best I can say for it at this point is that it has all the marks of a best-seller" in 1975 (700). Clurman's review is, therefore, an exception to Crandell's general observation that the 1975 production "enjoyed surprisingly positive reviews" (*Critical Response* xxxiv). Of the London Haymarket staging, Nightingale admitted that "exaggerated *Sweet Bird* may be, ill-constructed and worse it probably is, but it still bangs across a view of human nature that few will be able altogether to disown" (32). Writing of the same production, Mel Gussow found that "what is lacking in the London production are the elements of eloquence and amplitude" (16).

FILM AND TELEVISION VERSIONS

Richard Brooks both directed and wrote the screenplay for the 1962 film of *Sweet Bird*, starring Paul Newman as Chance and Geraldine Page as the Princess. Reviews were mixed; for example, Gill wrote that "the picture is even more unbelievable than the play" (148), while the reviewer for *Time* found it "a fast, smart, squalid melodrama" ("Putting on the Cat" 83). Most reviewers, such as Winsten and Crowther, faulted Brooks's substantial alteration to the play's ending.

The Gavin Lambert television adaptation (1989), with Mark Harmon as Chance and Elizabeth Taylor as the Princess, demonstrated greater fidelity to the script than Brooks's film, but some critics, such as *New York*'s John Leonard, attacked the television production for its miscasting, finding Taylor "silly instead of monstrous" and the adaptation "an embarrassment" (76).

CONCLUDING OVERVIEW

In virtually his entire corpus, Williams valorizes sex and its ancillary component, youthfulness, as commodities in the marketplace of the heart. For each major character in *Sweet Bird* (as well as most minor ones), sex is their raison d'être, their capital in which they deal to further their private agendas. In economizing sex, Williams vitiates American commercialism and poses interesting questions about the relationship between art, marketplace economics, and affairs of the heart.

Scene 1 of *Sweet Bird* establishes the sexual capital Chance and the Princess must both save and spend in order to achieve relative power in their sexual/ mercenary relationship. For the Princess, whose "interest always increases with satisfaction" (39), sex provides the therapeutic capital she requires to make it through the day. For Chance, who feebly denies being "on salary" (24), rendering services means being paid promptly, and he must ultimately resort to blackmail in order to shift the balance of power his way. Incidentally, a degree of dignity for Alexandra is reached only under two circumstances, and in both cases sex is omitted from the economy. One is in those moments when, sexually distanced, if not maternal, she reaches out to aid the hapless Chance by trying to force him toward self-realization. The second is when she confronts "the legend that I've outlived" (118) and determines, during the conversation with Sally Powers, that her success as a star does not totally depend on her youth or sex appeal. It seems entirely fair, therefore, to question Roulet's assumption that Chance and the Princess represent "two people who no longer are of any use to the world" (32). In scene 2, Chance, now paid off in traveler's checks, turns his attention to the pursuit of Heavenly, who represents for him the ultimate sexual commodity— purity (with selective memory typical of Williams's characters, he looks beyond her venereal infection), beauty, youth—the perfect sexual package that satisfies his ego and would seem to guarantee him material success with his costar.

In act 2, Boss Finley, a widower now "too old to cut the mustard" (68) with Miss Lucy, seems to sublimate his sexual desire with questionable admiration for his own daughter and uses her in his quest for political power—again, seeking political capital through her sexual appeal, holding up the "purity of our own blood" as an ideal threatened by the "blood pollution" (107) of African Americans. It is interesting, therefore, that Finley would codify his political platform by blatantly announcing Heavenly's sexual "purity," and it is, therefore, most incumbent that he silence the Heckler, who is bent on exposing her operation. In the "beanstalk country," the land of moral bankruptcy and sexual illusion, appearance bears little resemblance to reality.

Sweet Bird of Youth emerges as Williams's most damning indictment of venal consumption, his most direct assault on the sometimes twisted relationship between art (in this case the relative screen appeal of Chance and the Princess) and the marketplace, with its insatiable appetite for youth, sex, and beauty. Chance's waning sexual capital—both in terms of his potential screen appeal and self-concept—also comments on our society's/Williams's obsession with the commodity of desirability. If there is hope to be found in this cynical view, it is only in the Princess's renewed self-image and in the implication that, in spite of her age and reputation, she remains a viable attraction in the commercial/sexual marketplace.

WORKS CITED

Adler, Jacob. "Tennessee Williams' South: The Culture and the Power." *Tennessee Williams: A Tribute*. Ed. Jac Tharpe. Jackson: UP of Mississippi. 30–52.

Adler, Thomas P. *American Drama, 1940–1960: A Critical History*. New York: Twayne, 1994.

———. "Culture, Power, and the (En)gendering of Community: Tennessee Williams and Politics." *Mississippi Quarterly* 48 (Fall 1995): 649–65.

Aston, Frank. Rev. of *Sweet Bird of Youth*. *New York World-Telegram* 11 Mar. 1959: 30. Rpt. in *New York Theatre Critics' Reviews* 20 (1959): 348.

Atkinson, Brooks. Rev. of *Sweet Bird of Youth*. *New York Times* 11 Mar. 1959: 39. Rpt. in *New York Theatre Critics' Reviews* 20 (1959): 350.

Barnes, Clive. Rev. of *Sweet Bird of Youth*. *New York Times* 4 Dec. 1975: 53.

Bigsby, C. W. E. *A Critical Introduction to Twentieth-Century American Drama. Williams, Miller, Albee.* Vol. 2. Cambridge: Cambridge UP, 1984.

———. *Modern American Drama, 1945–1990.* Cambridge: Cambridge UP, 1992.

Boxill, Roger. *Tennessee Williams.* New York: St. Martin's, 1987.

Brustein, Robert. "Sweet Bird of Success." *Encounter* 12 (June 1959): 59–60.

Clum, John. "The Sacrificial Stud and the Fugitive Female in *Suddenly Last Summer, Orpheus Descending,* and *Sweet Bird of Youth.*" *The Cambridge Companion to Tennessee Williams.* Ed. Matthew C. Roudané. Cambridge: Cambridge UP, 1997. 128–46.

Clurman, Harold. Rev. of *Sweet Bird of Youth*. *Nation* 188 (Mar. 1959): 281.

———. Rev. of *Sweet Bird of Youth*. *Nation* 221 (Dec. 1975): 700.

Colanzi, Rita. "Caged Birds: Bad Faith in Tennessee Williams's Drama." *Modern Drama* 35 (1992): 451–65.

Coleman, Robert. Rev. of *Sweet Bird of Youth*. *New York Daily Mirror* 11 Mar. 1959: A 1. Rpt. in *New York Theatre Critics' Reviews* 20 (1959): 349.

Crandell, George, ed. *The Critical Response to Tennessee Williams.* Westport, CT: Greenwood, 1996.

———. *Tennessee Williams: A Descriptive Bibliography.* Pittsburgh: U of Pittsburgh P, 1995.

Crowther, Bosley. "Screen: 'Sweet Bird of Youth' Opens." *New York Times* 29 Mar. 1962: 28.

Debusscher, Gilbert. "And the Sailor Turned into a Princess: New Light on the Genesis of *Sweet Bird of Youth.*" *Studies in American Drama, 1945–Present* 1 (1986): 25–31.

Devlin, Albert J., ed. *Conversations with Tennessee Williams.* Jackson: UP of Mississippi, 1986.

Donahue, Francis. *The Dramatic World of Tennessee Williams.* New York: Ungar, 1964.

Dukore, Bernard F. "American Abelard: A Footnote to *Sweet Bird of Youth.*" *College English* 26 (May 1965): 630–34.

Falk, Signi Lenea. *Tennessee Williams.* New York: Twayne, 1962.

Gassner, John. Rev. of *Sweet Bird of Youth*. *Educational Theatre Journal* 11 (May 1959): 122–24.

Gill, Brendan. "Men in Trouble." *New Yorker* 7 Apr. 1962: 148–50.

Gunn, Drewey Wayne. *Tennessee Williams: A Bibliography.* 2nd ed. Metuchen, NJ: Scarecrow, 1991.

———. "The Troubled Flight of Tennessee Williams's *Sweet Bird*: From Manuscript through Published Texts." *Modern Drama* 24 (Mar. 1981): 26–35.

Gussow, Mel. Rev. of *Sweet Bird of Youth*. *New York Times* 1 Aug. 1985: sec. 3: 16.

Hays, Peter L. "Tennessee Williams' Use of Myth in *Sweet Bird of Youth.*" *Educational Theatre Journal* 18 (Oct. 1966): 255–58.

Herron, Ima Honaker. *The Small Town in American Drama.* Dallas: Southern Methodist UP, 1969.

Jackson, Esther Merle. *The Broken World of Tennessee Williams.* Madison: U of Wisconsin P, 1965.

Kerr, Walter. Rev. of *Sweet Bird of Youth*. *New York Times* 21 Dec. 1975: sec. 2: 5.

King, Kimball. "Tennessee Williams: A Southern Writer." *Mississippi Quarterly* 48 (Fall 1995): 627–47.

Kolin, Philip C. "Cleopatra of the Nile and Blanche DuBois of the French Quarter: *Antony and Cleopatra* and *A Streetcar Named Desire*." *Shakespeare Bulletin* 11 (Winter 1993): 25–27.

———. "Parallels between *Desire under the Elms* and *Sweet Bird of Youth*." *Eugene O'Neill Review* 13.2 (1989): 23–35.

Leonard, John. "For the Birds." *New York* 2 Oct. 1989: 76.

Leverich, Lyle. *Tom: The Unknown Tennessee Williams*. New York: Crown, 1995.

Londré, Felicia Hardison. *Tennessee Williams*. New York: Ungar, 1979.

MacNicholas, John. "Williams' Power of the Keys." *Tennessee Williams: A Tribute*. Ed. Jac Tharpe. Jackson: UP of Mississippi, 1977. 581–605.

Murphy, Brenda. *Tennessee Williams and Elia Kazan: A Collaboration in the Theatre*. Cambridge: Cambridge UP, 1992.

Niesen, George. "The Artist Against Reality in the Plays of Tennessee Williams." *Tennessee Williams: A Tribute*. Ed. Jac Tharpe. Jackson: UP of Mississippi, 1977. 463–93.

Nightingale, Benedict. Rev. of *Sweet Bird of Youth*. *New Statesman* 19 July 1985: 32.

"Putting on the Cat." *Time* (30 Mar. 1962): 83.

Robinson, Marc. *The Other American Drama*. Cambridge: Cambridge UP, 1994.

Roulet, William M. "*Sweet Bird of Youth*: Williams' Redemptive Ethic." *Cithara* 3 (1964): 31–36.

Shaland, Irene. *Tennessee Williams on the Soviet Stage*. Lanham, MD: UP of America, 1987.

Spoto, Donald. *The Kindness of Strangers: The Life of Tennessee Williams*. Boston: Little, Brown, 1985.

Thompson, Judith J. *Tennessee Williams' Plays: Memory, Myth, and Symbol*. New York: Lang, 1987.

Tischler, Nancy M. "A Gallery of Witches." *Tennessee Williams: A Tribute*. Ed. Jac Tharpe. Jackson: UP of Mississippi, 1977. 494–50.

———. *Sweet Bird of Youth*. New York: New Directions, 1975.

———. "The Timeless World of a Play." *Three by Tennessee*. New York: Signet, 1976. 129–33.

Winsten, Archer. " 'Sweet Bird of Youth' in Dual Bow." *New York Post* 29 Mar. 1962: 26.

The Night of the Iguana

GEORGE W. CRANDELL

BIOGRAPHICAL CONTEXT

Many Williams plays reflect both his experience of life and his ideas, but in *The Night of the Iguana*, Spoto contends, "the lineaments of [Williams's] inner life were transcended into something universal" (239). Williams's biographers recognize in both Hannah Jelkes and T. Lawrence Shannon autobiographical traces of the playwright. Falk, for example, views Hannah as a spokesperson for Williams (74). Leverich recognizes in Hannah "traces of [Williams's] personality," but adds that Hannah may also be "a projection of what might have become of Rose," Williams's lobotomized and institutionalized sister (376). Like Hannah, Shannon, too, functions to "express the author's sentiments, for example, in rejecting the Puritanical concept of God as a ferocious judge devoid of compassion" (Phillips 286). Falk also observes a similarity between Shannon's view of God and Williams's own (74). Although Canby sees Shannon as an autobiographical character, he contends that "he's only Williams as the playwright romantically read himself" (C18).

The Reverend Walter Dakin, Williams's long-lived grandfather, provides the principal basis for Nonno, although, as Spoto suggests, the aged figure of the "wandering poet" combines elements of both Reverend Dakin and Williams (239). Hayman adds that Williams's love for his maternal grandfather is "reflected in Hannah's tenderness toward the old poet" (183). In the character of Maxine, Hayman recognizes a woman named Zola, Williams's landlady in Hollywood in the early 1940s. Hayman also believes that "Maxine's husband . . . derives from Zola's husband" (182).

The setting of the play and some of its minor characters (the German tourists, for example) can be traced to Williams's experiences in Acapulco, Mexico, during the summer of 1940 (Leverich 377), described by Williams in "A Summer of Discovery." Documentary evidence related to the play appears in Van Antwerp and Johns and Leavitt.

BIBLIOGRAPHIC HISTORY

The Night of the Iguana derives from a short story with the same title written between April 1946 and February 1948 and published in the collection *One Arm and Other Stories*. Moorman contends that the story bears little resemblance to the later play (321), but as Donahue points out, "the iguana, Acapulco, and the female character [Edith Jelkes]" would later "serve as the nucleus for a new full-length play" (138). *Iguana* was first performed as a one-act play and later expanded (see "Chief Productions"). Spoto discusses the play's development (see 239, 243–48), while Matthews analyzes revisions in the manuscript record. An early version of *Iguana* was published in the February 1962 issue of *Esquire*, differing slightly from the New Directions text published in the same month. Williams again revised the text for the 1963 Dramatists Play Service edition. Crandell details the various editions and major changes among them (209–18).

CRITICAL APPROACHES

Themes

Jackson has called *The Night of the Iguana* a "morality" play (130). This classification suggests that the forces of good and evil, represented by Hannah and Maxine, respectively, battle for the soul of Reverend Shannon. Indeed, as various critics have noted, the central conflict of the play is "between the physical and spiritual in modern man" (Jacob Adler 61). In this struggle, Carpenter notes, Williams focuses on "the crippling power of repressed sexual desire" (1145). The notion that sex is both "disgusting and dangerous," Embrey also contends, is the subterranean "theme that haunts" *Iguana* (326). Shannon's moral struggle has also been characterized as a quest—more specifically, a "search for God" (Yacowar 105). As several critics point out, however, Shannon's spiritual quest leads not to God, but to acceptance of the human condition. For example, Thompson argues that "endurance is the theme of the play . . . not ascension to a higher world" but learning to live in and improve the real world the characters inhabit (153). Embrey agrees that Williams addresses the difference between "acceptance and endurance," acceptance being the "more positive notion" (334). Williams himself identifies the theme as "how to live beyond despair and still live" (quoted in Funke and Booth 72). The basic conflict has also been described as a struggle of "the real versus the fantastic" (Leon 93). Fleche highlights this " 'real/fantastic' " distinction to illustrate Williams's "obsessive" concern with the problems of representation, especially "the relation of 'art' to 'reality,' " and Williams's penchant for "tricks that call attention to the theatrical illusion" (1).

Other themes have been suggested by Carpenter—for example, the failure to communicate (1145)—and by Embrey, who points out that Hannah's "Japanese Kabuki robe" is a visual sign of "the East-West theme" (332). Hendrick contends, however, that "[t]he Oriental themes become hopelessly confused" (405). He focuses instead on the play's relationship to Christianity and, more specifically, to D. H. Lawrence's *The Man Who Died* (399).

Characters

Shannon

If the Reverend T. Lawrence Shannon is not, as Bigsby contends, "the play's central character" (65), he is its "fulcrum" (Phillips 282). The "contrary demands of flesh and spirit" compete for control of Shannon (Boxill 141). Unlike Blanche DuBois, however, Shannon "finds protection" (Hirsch 70). Shannon is thus unique, avoiding "the violent fate usually in store for Williams's heroes" by establishing "what promises to be a lasting sexual relationship with a mature woman" (Embrey 326). Jacob Adler sees Shannon's effort to remain with Maxine as "a positive gesture" (62), but other critics, Embrey, for example, contend that the change comes about too quickly (334).

Considering Shannon to be one of Williams's "most complex" characters (Canby C1), critics variously try to explain his problem. For Thomas Adler, Shannon's difficulty is a "crisis in faith" that "springs from his conception of . . . a vengeful God" (55). Embrey identifies his problem as a combination of "terrible guilt, fear of God, and an overpowering sex drive" (334). Shannon's own psychological explanation (guilt resulting from repression), Thompson argues, is validated by Freudian psychology (160).

Shannon's similarities to Christ have frequently been noted. Newlove sees Shannon as a "self-crucified" Christ figure (66). Similarly, Thompson writes that Shannon plays "the role of an ironic Christ" (164). Rogers likewise concludes that Shannon's "alleged similarity to Christ is . . . only a superficial pose, not a true conviction" (84).

Newlove documents some of the analogues suggested by T. Lawrence Shannon, including Thomas Lanier (Tennessee) Williams, D. H. Lawrence, T. E. Lawrence, and Ireland's River Shannon, "the river of death that the sufferer must cross in atonement" (66). Thompson likens Shannon to Saint Lawrence (164), while Moritz argues for similarities between Shannon and Oedipus (309).

Hannah

Courageous, dignified, and self-aware, Hannah Jelkes is unique: "a creation as large as Blanche ever was, a character of enormous appeal and stature" (Bolton 2). Compared with earlier Williams heroines, she is also, as Kerr recognizes, "an entirely new kind of woman" (3). Unlike some of her counterparts, Hannah "lives in neither the lost past nor the elusive future" (Boxill 142). Although she shares "the determination of Maggie and the final courage of Alma," Jacob Adler writes, "only Hannah displays absolute values retained in a relative world" (68). Hannah's "refined nature, sensitive reaction to a fellow sufferer, her unemotional acceptance of her fate, and her luminous presence," Donahue contends, "all qualify her for a preferential position among the theatrical portraits of Tennessee Williams" (148).

Hannah is most often viewed as "the strongest figure in the Williams spiritual pantheon" (Fedder 113). In a pitched battle between the spiritual and the physical, with Shannon's tortured soul in between, Hannah plays "the saint, to Maxine's whore" (Hirsch 68). Thompson agrees that Hannah represents "spiritual strength and goodness" (167). On the other hand, Carpenter sees Hannah as neither saint nor whore but as "the synthesis" of Maxine's uninhibited sexuality and Judith Fellowes's puritanical prudishness (1145).

As a spiritual savior, Hannah has been likened by Rogers to Christ (134), by Hendrick to Isis, who "offers Shannon spiritual love" (404), and by Thompson to the Jungian "Good Mother" (167). Thompson also notes Hannah's similarity to Mary, Beatrice, and Cordelia (168) as well as "the Chinese deity Kwan-Yin" and "the Hindu goddess, Tara" (172). In each of these likenesses, Hannah plays a "redemptive role as Shannon's spiritual mentor" (Thompson 167). In Hannah's relationship to Nonno, Moritz also sees a similarity to Antigone, who makes sacrifices for an aged man (306).

Maxine

Maxine Faulk is generally considered the earthy and physical counterpart to Hannah's ethereal and spiritual character. Leon, for example, characterizes her as "an earthy calculator" who carries "the 'realistic' level of Williams's drama" (89). Her aggressive physicality is often a source of comment. Jacob Adler notes that she is a "blatantly sexual being" (62), while Embrey catalogues the images that suggest her "animallike nature" (336). Shannon's acceptance of Maxine at the play's conclusion depends in part upon her metamorphosis from a "female version of Big Daddy Pollitt" to "a mellow Oriental goddess," a change Embrey finds unbelievable (337). Hendrick likens Maxine to "the Ur-Isis, the lusty Egyptian corn goddess" (401). Griffin notes her similarity to the temptress Eve (226). For Thompson, Maxine is the "Terrible Mother" (162).

Nonno (Jonathan Coffin)

Like Hannah, Nonno endures and accepts adversity with courage. Thompson likens the aged Jonathan Coffin to Tiresias, the blind prophet and androgyne (168). Armato sees Nonno as an "effective example of modern man's potential to accept death as gracefully as Socrates or St. Sebastian" (566). Moritz compares the "blind and aging" Nonno to "Oedipus and Antigone in Sophocles' *Oedipus at Colonus*" (305).

Symbols

While many critics contend that Williams depends "too much" on symbolism or that his symbols are "too obvious" (Tallmer 9), Jacob Adler believes that the iguana works effectively as a symbol (67). A number of critics, Griffin (229) and Embrey, for example, see a likeness between the "frantic iguana" and Shannon, who is also "at the end of his rope" (Embrey 326). McCarten suggests that the iguana "represents . . . everybody who can't make an adjustment to the world" (61), a sentiment echoed by Williams: "It stands for the human situation" (quoted in Peck 5).

The German family, considered extraneous by many critics, nevertheless functions "as a device by which Williams can magnify Shannon's personal war to a global one between nations" (Carpenter 1146). According to Embrey, the Nazis "epitomize the cruelty and violence of the Western world" (333).

Other symbols include the Costa Verde hotel, a "microcosm of the existential universe" (Thompson 154), and the cross around Shannon's neck, representing "a perverted system of religion" (Thomas Adler 56) as well as his "obsessive, self-destructive notions" (Embrey 331). Thompson considers the hammock an emblem of Christ's cross and Shannon's release from it "a dynamic symbol of his psychological rebirth" (165). Matthews mentions the storm as a symbol of "some overwhelming presence," while the "row of solitary cubicles" stands for "the mental isolation of the characters" (72).

Plot

Sorrell claims that The Night of the Iguana is "a masterpiece of a play without a plot" (21). Leon agrees that although "very little happens" in the play, Williams successfully creates a timeless world in which memory plays "a felicitous part in defining character, creating conflict, and determining the direction of the action" (96). Phillips groups Iguana with Williams's later works in which the playwright concerns himself "less and less with action and more and more with character analysis" (284). Hirsch likewise classifies Iguana as one of Williams's "confession dramas," plays organized not by a series of actions but by a "series of monologues" (70). Accordingly, Jacob Adler identifies the "center of the play" as "the series of dialogues between Hannah and Shannon" (62). Taubman similarly observes that "[t]he crux of the drama is in the struggle of Hannah and Shannon to slash the rope that tethers them to their grim, lonely destinies" (1).

Some critics contrast the plot in Iguana with the typical structure of romance. Observing how Shannon resists becoming "merely Maxine Faulk's lover," Brooks argues that "[t]he plot of The Night of the Iguana is the opposite of sexual union as a romantic triumph" (733). Thompson similarly sees the play's conclusion as ironically reversing romantic expectations (152). Boxill (139–44), Carpenter (1143–44), Donahue (140–48), Falk (69–75), and Griffin (217–36) provide summary analyses of the plot.

PROBLEMS *THE NIGHT OF THE IGUANA* POSES FOR CRITICS

For some critics, the lack of dramatic action in *Iguana* is problematic. Leon concludes that "it holds together better in an armchair than in front row center" (96). For others, the play lacks an organizing point of view. Comparing *Iguana* with other works by Williams, Embrey observes that there is "no one to point out that . . . the characters are confused, incorrect, or self-contradictory" (340).

Critics consider the resolution of the play even more problematic. Embrey complains that "[t]he optimistic conclusion" undermines the carefully drawn "psychological portrait" of Shannon (334). Thompson similarly sees Shannon's reconciliation to Maxine as troublesome, comparing it to Maggie's miraculous and therefore problematic transformation of Brick in *Cat on a Hot Tin Roof*; she nevertheless considers *Iguana*'s resolution effective because it conforms to a basic pattern of death and rebirth. (180).

CHIEF PRODUCTIONS

The Night of the Iguana evolved from a one-act play, first performed on 2 July 1959 at the Festival of Two Worlds in Spoleto, Italy, to a full-length Broadway production. Before opening in New York, the play underwent development in a series of productions, first at the Coconut Grove Playhouse in Miami in August 1960, then in Rochester, Detroit, Cleveland, and Chicago. During this time, Williams revised the play extensively.

Iguana first opened on Broadway on 28 December 1961 at the Royale Theatre, directed by Frank Corsaro. The "beautiful dignity and affecting gentleness" of Margaret Leighton's performance as Hannah won the immediate praise of many critics (Chapman 44). Patrick O'Neal (Shannon) joined Leighton, along with Bette Davis as Maxine (later replaced by Shelley Winters) and Alan Webb as Nonno. Although critical response to the play was mixed—Chapman ranked the play among Williams's "finest dramas" (44), while Simon accused Williams of "self-plagiarism and arbitrariness" (57)—it earned for Williams his fourth Drama Critics' Circle Award. For many critics, *Iguana* represented Williams's best effort since *Cat on a Hot Tin Roof* (Gilman 460).

The first London production of *Iguana*, directed by Philip Wiseman, also opened to mixed reviews, first at the Ashcroft Theatre in February, and then at the Savoy on 24 March 1965. Although the *Times* (London) praised Sian Phillips (Hannah), Mark Eden (Shannon), and Donald Eccles (Nonno) ("Landscape" 16), other reviewers echoed the diverse sentiments of American critics in 1962. Characterizing German productions of the play, Wolter observes how "German self-righteousness" is evidenced in "depoliticized and moderated" depictions of the Nazi tourists (15).

The first Broadway revival opened on 16 December 1976 at the Circle in the Square Theatre. Directed by Joseph Hardy, the production starred Dorothy

McGuire (Hannah), Richard Chamberlain (Shannon), and Sylvia Miles (Maxine). This production suffered by comparison with the original Broadway performance and the 1964 film. Critics generally agreed with Kerr that McGuire "plays the role with great charm and intelligence" but not as well as Margaret Leighton did in 1962 (3). Critics likewise compared Chamberlain unfavorably with Richard Burton's performance in the 1964 film. Kerr faulted Miles for her lack of range as Maxine, and Williams for the "underwritten role of the proprietress" (8). Comparing this production with the original, Clurman observed that "[t]he glamour and soiled lyricism that the play seemed initially to possess have faded" (28).

At a February 1981 production in Key West, Tennessee Williams praised Roxanna Stuart's performance as Hannah (Mitchner 21). Lisa McMillan played Maxine, and Douglas Stender appeared as Shannon, directed by William Prosser.

Revived again at the Circle in the Square Theatre on 26 June 1988, *Iguana* featured Maria Tucci (Hannah), Nicolas Surovy (Shannon), Jane Alexander (Maxine), and William Le Massena (Nonno) under the direction of Theodore Mann. Representing the majority view, Oliver credits Tucci with giving a "weak" production "whatever strength and focus it attains" (77).

Richard Eyre directed the London revival that opened on 6 February 1992 at the Lyttelton Theatre to generally favorable reviews. Unlike earlier productions, the 1992 British revival of *Iguana* was "the first major production . . . to fully realize its complex values" (Griffin 238). Alfred Molina (Shannon), Eileen Atkins (Hannah), and Frances Barber (Maxine) starred.

The 1996 production at New York's Criterion Center Stage Right enjoyed both positive reviews and the distinction of presenting Shannon as a "radically rethought" character, displaying all "the clichéd mannerisms of an insecurely closeted homosexual" (Canby C18). Robert Falls directed William Petersen (Shannon), Cherry Jones (Hannah), Marsha Mason (Maxine), and Lawrence McCauley (Nonno). Although Lyons praised Petersen as the "best Shannon I've seen" (A10), Canby dissented: "With Petersen playing only the [homosexual] subtext, there's a large emptiness at the heart of this production" (C18).

FILM AND TELEVISION VERSIONS

In 1964, MGM produced a film version of *Iguana* with a screenplay by Anthony Veiller and John Huston. Huston also directed the film, which featured Richard Burton (Shannon), Deborah Kerr (Hannah), Ava Gardner (Maxine), and Cyril Delevanti (Nonno). Grayson Hall received an Oscar nomination as Judith Fellows (Phillips 294). Yacowar considers the film "more positive" (106) than the play, while Griffin, on the other hand, concludes that the film "preserves a faithful if condensed version of the play" (238). Phillips offers a comprehensive analysis (280–98).

CONCLUDING OVERVIEW

The Night of the Iguana takes as its starting point a Nietzschean assertion, "God is dead" (*Portable* 447), and puts this hypothesis to the test. In Shannon's ensuing search for God, the uncertain minister collects "evidence," but only of God's "oblivious majesty" (Williams, *Night* 304–05). In the absence of convincing proof of God's existence, Shannon suffers from existential dread, a fear that the world is absurd and without meaning, a fear that beyond the grave lies absolute nothingness. In the midst of his spiritual crisis, the Christian minister is saved, ironically, not by Christ, but by Hannah Jelkes, a woman who resembles Nietzsche's personification of "art" in *The Birth of Tragedy*, a "saving sorceress, expert at healing" (60). Administering a potion of poppyseed tea, Hannah performs a function similar to that of art as described by Nietzsche: "She alone knows how to turn . . . nauseous thoughts about the horror or absurdity of existence into notions with which one can live" (*Birth* 60). In the figure of Hannah, we see illustrated an existential faith in the power of human beings to create meaning through art and to bring salvation to others by means of the healing power of art. Adding to the irony, the woman characterized as the "Thin-Standing-Up-Female Buddha" functions as a Christlike redeemer in a play that duplicates a Christian archetype (Williams, *Night* 346). As Sylvan Barnet notes, "The Christian pattern moves from weakness to strength, from death to life, from sin to bliss. Its form is therefore comic" (200). Likewise, the outline of *Iguana*, tracing the progression of Shannon's spiritual malaise until his miraculous recovery (including his return to health, to meaningful life, to some measure of happiness), has the shape and the restorative power of comedy. Affirming life over death, *Iguana* demonstrates "how to live with dignity after despair" (Williams, quoted in Peck 5). Acceptance of the human condition and courage in the face of despair are Williams's affirmative responses to the apparent meaninglessness of life.

WORKS CITED

Adler, Jacob H. "*Night of the Iguana*: A New Tennessee Williams?" *Ramparts* 1.3 (1962): 59–68.

Adler, Thomas P. "The Search for God in the Plays of Tennessee Williams." *Renascence* 26 (1973): 48–56.

Armato, Philip M. "Tennessee Williams' Meditations on Life and Death in *Suddenly Last Summer, The Night of the Iguana*, and *The Milk Train Doesn't Stop Here Anymore*." *Tennessee Williams: A Tribute*. Ed. Jac Tharpe. Jackson: UP of Mississippi, 1977. 558–70.

Barnet, Sylvan. "Some Limitations of a Christian Approach to Shakespeare." *Tragedy: Modern Essays in Criticism*. Ed. Laurence Michel and Richard B. Sewall. Westport, CT: Greenwood, 1978. 199–209.

Bigsby, C. W. E. *Modern American Drama, 1945–1990*. Cambridge: Cambridge UP, 1992.

Bolton, Whitney. "*Night of the Iguana* Eloquent, Moving." *New York Morning Telegraph* 30 Dec. 1961: 2.

Boxill, Roger. *Tennessee Williams*. London: Macmillan, 1987.

Brooks, Charles B. "Williams' Comedy." *Tennessee Williams: A Tribute*. Ed. Jac Tharpe. Jackson: UP of Mississippi, 1977. 720–35.

Canby, Vincent. "Tennessee Williams in Deep Complexity." *New York Times* 22 Mar. 1996: C1, C18.

Carpenter, David A. "*The Night of the Iguana*." *Masterplots II Drama Series*. Ed. Frank N. Magill. Pasadena, CA: Salem, 1990. 1143–47.

Chapman, John. "Williams Is at His Poetic, Moving Best with *Night of the Iguana*." *New York Daily News* 29 Dec. 1961: 44.

Clurman, Harold. "Theatre." *Nation* 8 Jan. 1977: 28–29.

Crandell, George W. *Tennessee Williams: A Descriptive Bibliography*. Pittsburgh: U of Pittsburgh P, 1995.

Donahue, Francis. *The Dramatic World of Tennessee Williams*. New York: Ungar, 1964.

Embrey, Glenn. "The Subterranean World of *The Night of the Iguana*." *Tennessee Williams: A Tribute*. Ed. Jac Tharpe. Jackson: UP of Mississippi, 1977. 325–40.

Falk, Signi. *Tennessee Williams*. 2nd ed. Boston: Twayne, 1978.

Fedder, Norman J. *The Influence of D. H. Lawrence on Tennessee Williams*. The Hague: Mouton, 1966.

Fleche, Anne. *Mimetic Disillusion: Eugene O'Neill, Tennessee Williams, and U.S. Dramatic Realism*. Tuscaloosa: U of Alabama P, 1997.

Funke, Lewis, and John E. Booth. "Williams on Williams." *Theatre Arts* 46.1 (1962): 16–19, 72–73.

Gilman, Richard. "Williams as Phoenix." *Commonweal* 26 Jan. 1962: 460–61.

Griffin, Alice. *Understanding Tennessee Williams*. Columbia: U of South Carolina P, 1995.

Hayman, Ronald. *Tennessee Williams: Everyone Else Is an Audience*. New Haven: Yale UP, 1993.

Hendrick, George. "Jesus and the Osiris-Isis Myth: Lawrence's *The Man Who Died* and Williams's *The Night of the Iguana*." *Anglia* 84 (1966): 398–406.

Hirsch, Foster. *A Portrait of the Artist: The Plays of Tennessee Williams*. Port Washington, NY: Kennikat, 1979.

Jackson, Esther Merle. *The Broken World of Tennessee Williams*. Madison: U of Wisconsin P, 1965.

Kerr, Walter. "Never Mind the Echoes, Listen to Williams." *New York Times* 19 Dec. 1976: 3, 8.

"Landscape of the Fallen." *Times* [London] 18 Feb. 1965: 16.

Leavitt, Richard F., ed. *The World of Tennessee Williams*. New York: Putnam's, 1978.

Leon, Ferdinand. "Time, Fantasy, and Reality in *Night of the Iguana*." *Modern Drama* 11 (1968): 87–96.

Leverich, Lyle. *Tom: The Unknown Tennessee Williams*. New York: Crown, 1995.

Lyons, Donald. "Lost Souls." *Wall Street Journal* 22 Mar. 1996: A10.

Matthews, Kevin. "The Evolution of *The Night of the Iguana*: Three Symbols in the Manuscript Record." *Library Chronicle of the University of Texas* 25.2 (1994): 67–89.

McCarten, John. "Lonely, Loquacious, and Doomed." *New Yorker* 13 Jan. 1962: 61–62.

Mitchner, Robert W. "*The Night of the Iguana*." *Tennessee Williams Review* 3.1 (1981): 19–21.

Moorman, Charles. "*The Night of the Iguana*: A Long Introduction, a General Essay, and

No Explication at All." *Tennessee Williams: A Tribute*. Ed. Jac Tharpe. Jackson: UP of Mississippi, 1977. 318–24.

Moritz, Helen E. "Apparent Sophoclean Echoes in Tennessee Williams's *Night of the Iguana*." *Classical and Modern Literature* 5 (1985): 305–14.

Newlove, Donald. "A Dream of Tennessee Williams." *Esquire* Nov. 1969: 172+.

Nietzsche, Friedrich. *The Birth of Tragedy and The Case of Wagner*. Trans. Walter Kaufmann. New York: Vintage Books, 1967.

———. *The Portable Nietzsche*. Trans. Walter Kaufmann. New York: Viking, 1954.

Oliver, Edith. "Son et Lumière." *New Yorker* 11 July 1988: 77.

Peck, Seymour. "Williams and 'The Iguana.' " *New York Times* 24 Dec. 1961, sec. 2: 5.

Phillips, Gene D. *The Films of Tennessee Williams*. Philadelphia: Art Alliance, 1980.

Rogers, Ingrid. *Tennessee Williams: A Moralist's Answers to the Perils of Life*. Frankfurt: Lang, 1976.

Simon, John. "*The Night of the Iguana*." *Theatre Arts* 46 (1962): 57.

Sorrell, Walter. "The New Tennessee Williams." *Cresset* Mar. 1962: 21.

Spoto, Donald. *The Kindness of Strangers: The Life of Tennessee Williams*. Boston: Little, Brown, 1985.

Tallmer, Jerry. "The Lizard's Skin." *Village Voice* 4 Jan. 1962: 9–10.

Taubman, Howard. "Williams and Ratigan Offer New Styles." *New York Times* 7 Jan. 1962, sec. 2: 1.

Thompson, Judith J. *Tennessee Williams' Plays: Memory, Myth, and Symbol*. New York: Lang, 1987.

Van Antwerp, Margaret A., and Sally Johns, eds. *Tennessee Williams*. Dictionary of Literary Biography Documentary Series 4. Detroit: Gale, 1984.

Williams, Tennessee. *The Night of the Iguana*. *The Theatre of Tennessee Williams*. Vol. 4. New York: New Directions, 1971. 247–376.

———. "A Summer of Discovery." *Where I Live: Selected Essays by Tennessee Williams*. Ed. Christine R. Day and Bob Woods. New York: New Directions, 1978. 137–47.

Wolter, Jurgen C. "Tennessee Williams in Germany." *Tennessee Williams Literary Journal* 3.2 (1995): 13–20.

Yacowar, Maurice. *Tennessee Williams and Film*. New York: Ungar, 1977.

The Milk Train Doesn't Stop Here Anymore

FRANCESCA OGLESBY HITCHCOCK

BIOGRAPHICAL CONTEXT

From 1953, when he began work on the short story "Man Bring This up Road," until 1980, when he continued to work on *Goforth*, Tennessee Williams labored over *The Milk Train Doesn't Stop Here Anymore*, calling this "rewriting" of *Milk Train* "the most frustrating experience" he had ever undergone (Reed 196). Always disappointed in what he saw as critics' overly harsh treatment of this "*emotionally* autobiographical" play (Rader 287), Williams admitted that *Milk Train* "reflected . . . the deepening shadows of [his] life as man and artist" (*Memoirs* 188) during the early 1960s, a decade in which he ended his fourteen-year relationship with Frank Merlo, endured a devastating loneliness after Merlo's death from lung cancer in 1963, and indulged an increasingly dangerous dependence on drugs and alcohol.

Leavitt (133–34), Spoto (283–90), Rader (167–69), and Leverich note the connections among *Milk Train*'s creation, its production history, and Williams's personal life, as Williams himself does in his *Memoirs* (192–201), where he intersperses his recollections about *Milk Train* with his memories of Frank Merlo. While *Milk Train*'s Flora Goforth—dying of cancer, injecting herself nightly with morphine, screaming her memoirs over a loudspeaker, and consuming drugs and liquor—reflects both her creator and his longtime companion, it is Flora who gives voice to Williams's own despair and loneliness and "expresses [Williams's] 'interior world' more directly than any character in his work" (Spoto 289). This expression, although less direct, extends to Chris Flanders as well.

During the 1960s Williams's dependence on alcohol, amphetamines, and barbiturates exacerbated his emotional fragility and compounded his lifelong fear of illness and dying. "Death," according to Williams, "doesn't like crowds. It comes to you when you're alone" (Rader 340–41). As the Angel of Death, then, Chris provides rich, dying old women like Flora Goforth what Williams himself most needed: a companion during the night so death would not find him unattended. Williams feared not just physical death, however, but the "death" of his creative powers as well; thus the plight of Chris Flanders (and of his predecessor Jimmy Dobyne), a burnt-out poet who had "coasted on his early celebrity all through the forties" (Williams, "Man Bring" 369) symbolizes Williams's own fear of artistic failure and foreshadows what many critics would declare about Williams from the 1960s onward: that he "coasted on" the success he achieved in the 1940s and 1950s.

BIBLIOGRAPHIC HISTORY

The plot of *Milk Train* grew out of the short story "Man Bring This up Road." Inspired by Williams's belief that he had "contracted a deadly fever" (Spoto 211), written in Italy in 1953, and published in 1959 in *Mademoiselle*, "Man Bring This up Road" focuses on the plight of Jimmy Dobyne, a thirty-four-year-old failed and starving one-book poet, and his unfortunate confrontation with Flora Goforth, a harpylike siren in the guise of a seventy-two-year-old art patron, who lures young men to her sea-cliff villa on Italy's Divina Costiera.

Although Williams periodically worked on *Milk Train* for almost twenty years, there are only three published versions of the play: (*a*) the earliest version, a composite of the 1962 Spoleto and the 1963 New York performances, published as excerpts in *The Best Plays of 1962–1963*; (*b*) the 1964 standard full-length American version, revised—with Author's Notes, a Prologue, and the addition of two Kabuki-style stage assistants—for the 1964 Broadway production; and (*c*) a revision of the American edition, published only in England, also in 1964. Although this edition contains numerous variants, such as minor modifications to dialogue and stage directions, and an additional sixteen-line passage in scene 5 (62), their effect on the play is minimal. Crandell's bibliography provides detailed information on versions and changes (221–30).

MAJOR CRITICAL APPROACHES

Themes

Milk Train focuses on many of the same philosophical and metaphysical themes that generated favorable critical attention in Williams's major works of the 1940s and 1950s. Scheick argues that *Milk Train* reflects the desperate need of its characters to reconcile "the dichotomy of flesh and spirit" (763) through human intercourse, that is, through conversation and sex. For these characters, talk and touch are "religious, even sacramental" (Scheick 772) and the means of transcending the self. This transcendence manifests itself in what Chris Flanders calls the need for "somebody or something to mean God" to each person (*Milk Train* 113). Searching for God in others through acts of human intercourse in hopes of defeating time and death establishes *Milk Train*, according to Adler, as a Williamsian morality play, "a modern 'Death of Everywoman'" (144). Similarly, Armato contends that *Milk Train* offers Williams's "meditation" on life and death; while "love, charity, [and] compassion" are possible in our "harsh universe" (570), death should be embraced as "a revolt against a tyrannical existence" (568).

Characters

Both Chris Flanders and Flora Goforth are recurring Williams character types. Chris is one of Williams's fugitive kind (Costello 113), a wanderer (Ganz 134), who, rather than rescuing older women through the redemptive power of sexual intercourse, appears instead as a celibate, "itinerant poet-priest" (Thompson 190) to guide the dying toward an Oriental-like acceptance of death's inevitability. Presley, however, argues against Chris as a beneficent savior and instead sees him as a selfish and egocentric character whose real mission is to speed along "his own psychological satisfaction" (578). Casper points out that although Chris serves "at best as custodian of the deathwatch," it is actually Flora who "keeps the play alive" through "her rage, her refusal to be less than she was or ever to cease" (749). Tischler and McBride portray Flora's will to survive much less positively, labeling her as one of Williams's "witches," a "gorgon lady," an archetypal image of the "Terrible Mother" (Tischler 497), whose inability to accept the "grimness" of her present "reality" forces an illusionary escape into a "pretense" of her "past" (McBride 342).

Symbols

While critics readily apprehend the symbolism inherent in Flora's name ("Flora," Williams's ubiquitous flower imagery; "Goforth," his motto, *"En avant!"*) and in her possessions (the golden griffin banner and pink "cupid" bed, symbolic, respectively, of wealth and sexuality), many attribute greater symbolic significance to Chris Flanders. Readers almost unanimously support Gilbert Debusscher's detailed analysis of Chris as a "modern version" of St. Christopher ("Tennessee Williams' Lives" 154); theater critics, however, initially seemed to view Chris as a Christ figure. Although a few critics briefly comment on the symbolic significance of Chris's mobile, "The Earth Is a Wheel in a Great Big Gambling Casino," Armato explains the mobile's function "as a preamble to all that Chris will say about life and death" (567).

Plot

While *Milk Train*'s plot, discussed by such authors as Falk (123–26) and Londré (172–77), remains essentially the same as in "Man Bring This up Road," the play's unconventional narrative structure and its excessive poetic philosophizing have generated predominantly negative criticism. For instance, instead of achieving a "Brechtian detachment," as Hirsch argues (72), Weales insists that the play is "hampered by the bogus Kabuki framework in which stage assistants set the scene and offer explanations where none are needed" (65). Furthermore, most critics notice the "collapse" of Williams's language, which in *Milk Train* "devolv[ed] into a pseudo-poetic rhetoric, a kind of baroque prose" (Bigsby 110).

MAJOR PROBLEMS *THE MILK TRAIN DOESN'T STOP HERE ANYMORE* POSES FOR CRITICS

Critics view *Milk Train* as a minor work that marks a decline from Williams's major critical and commercial successes. Consequently, *Milk Train* is frequently discussed as a part of such chapters as "The Deteriorating Artist" (Falk) and "Portraits of the Playwright as Failure" (Hirsch) or those focusing on Williams as "an artist with the misfortune to outlive his talent" (Berkowitz 161). Although Williams's "disconnected and unmanageable" poetic diction (Berkowitz 164), inappropriate combination of characters and theme (Hirsch 73), and "remoteness from his audience" (Bigsby 110) negatively affected the play's critical reception, most readers attribute *Milk Train*'s failure to its intensely autobiographical nature. Apparently, "the more autobiographical" his work, "the more [Williams] lost the fine artistic discipline and control that mark the major plays" (Griffin 8), and the less accepting audiences were of Williams's personal life overcoming his plays (Falk 127). Unfortunately, *Milk Train* has engendered little critical dialogue, aside from the rewarding readings by Armato, Debusscher, and McBride.

CHIEF PRODUCTIONS

Milk Train was first produced at the Festival of Two Worlds in Spoleto, Italy, on 11 July 1962. Although Williams, sitting in the balcony and "sipping scotch," "gleefully" relished "the repugnance of his new creation" ("Milk-Run" 40), and the mostly American audience "gave the play a cordial reception" ("Tennessee Williams' Work" 19), the "guarded but ominous" critical response hinted that the play was "silly" (West 211), "willfully obscure," and not "a complete success" ("Spoleto Gets" 4).

Milk Train's first Broadway production opened on 16 January 1963 during a newspaper strike that Williams believed kept the play from receiving "the sort of controversy in the press" necessary for its success (" 'Milk Train' Gets" 32). Although not published in the daily papers, the predominantly negative reviews seem to agree with Kerr's "disappointment over" the "surprisingly uncertain, drained, [and] out of breath" *Milk Train* (392) that had "stopped far short of its destination" (McClain 393). *Milk Train* closed after 69 performances.

After David Merrick's "unprecedented offer to re-present" *Milk Train* for the next Broadway season (Phillips 300), Williams revised the play for its second New York production on 1 January 1964. Called "a grotesque hybrid of a play" (Nadel 397), the revised *Milk Train* was regarded as "weaker, more discursive, and less dramatic" than the previous Broadway production ("Second Mrs. Goforth" 52). Not at all impressed with the addition of Kabuki-style stage assistants, critics were especially appalled by the bad acting of Tallulah Bankhead, who could have been "no more wrong as heroine" of the play than "Jack Benny in a wig" ("Tallulah and Tennessee" 70), and Tab Hunter, who lunged "about like a wounded antelope on snowshoes" (Nadel 398). *Milk Train* closed after only 4 performances. With additional revisions, *Milk Train* premiered in San Francisco on 23 July 1965. In a production viewed as "a remarkable scoop for an amateur company" of a previously "unjustly belittled piece" (Wardle 16), *Milk Train* premiered in London in the fall of 1968. It opened in Paris on 3 February 1971 in an adaptation by Michel Arnaud. Revisions were under way in 1979–80 to stage *Goforth* in Vienna, a production that never took place.

Although the twenty-fifth-year revival of *Milk Train* in New York on 4 November 1987 received some negative reviews, most critics responded enthusiastically, calling this version "the least stylized and most realistic" of the productions to that time (Beaufort 26). By combining the "first Broadway text" with "touches from . . . other versions," director Kevin Conway "wisely downplay[ed] the religious allegory that bothered critics in the past" (Wallach 98).

FILM AND TELEVISION VERSIONS

Boom!, Williams's film adaptation of *Milk Train*, opened in May 1968 to generally unfavorable reviews, in spite of the public's interest in the private lives of its stars, Elizabeth Taylor and Richard Burton. Joseph Losey's five-million-dollar production of *Boom!*, a "fuzzy unconsummated work" with "no real confrontation or dramatic progression" (Canby 56), was "[r]egarded as one of the biggest bombs in Hollywood history" (Nash and Ross 262). Williams's friend and fellow playwright William Inge attributed *Boom!*'s failure to its producers, who had "changed," "destroyed," and "understood nothing" of Williams's "flawless film script" (quoted in Steen 106).

CONCLUDING OVERVIEW

In *Milk Train*, Williams continues to explore the theme—the search for the androgynous ideal—that had preoccupied him since his first nationally published short story, "The Vengeance of Nitocris" (Hitchcock 595–608). He transfers to the majority of his characters his own need to return to a time when he was one-half of a psychologically reciprocal relationship, when he felt a sense of completion, of interconnectedness, with his sister Rose when they were children. Through his characters, Williams conveys humankind's longing to alleviate alienation and fragmentation and to return to the primordial wholeness of the first androgynes, Adam and Eve. According to Williams, he had never actually created any of his characters, except for Leona in *Small Craft Warnings*, with a totally integrated personality (Gaines 216). Significantly, throughout his career, Williams pursued the androgynous ideal by trying to reconcile the fragmented personalities of characters whom he considered to be "ambiguous" (Funke and Booth 98).

Since his characters represent broken halves, Williams pairs them so that they achieve, or at least attempt to find, completion or wholeness in their relationship with the "other." Most frequently, this search for fulfillment manifests itself in sexual intercourse. Unfortunately, however, for a majority of these characters, interconnectedness through sexual involvement leads neither to completion nor to reunion, rebirth, or regeneration, but rather to physical destruction and mental disintegration. Punished for their sexual desires, Williams's characters are raped, castrated, blowtorched, cannibalized, mutilated, murdered, or driven to madness. In *Milk Train*, however, as he had done earlier with *Night of the Iguana*'s virginal Hannah Jelkes, Williams sends a celibate, "saintly" messenger—Chris Flanders—to preach the efficacy of a nonsexual reconciliation of opposites as a means of achieving the androgynous ideal. As a symbolic St. Christophoros, who spiritually carries Christ, Chris recognizes his own fragmentation, describing it as a "panicky" feeling of alienation and "lostness"; in order to feel "sheltered" and "protected" (*Milk Train* 75), that is, to achieve a momentary alleviation of this alienation, Chris must care for some "other," providing such "others" as Flora with what they lack. Thus, unable to alleviate her own vague sense of fragmentation, Flora requires the ministrations of Chris—the Angel of Death—who appears to her as the "ascetic 'reincarnation'" (Thompson 190) of her beloved fourth husband Alex. By refusing to fulfill her sexual demands, by removing the rings from her fingers before she dies, Chris divests Flora of carnality and materialism, her strongest ties to the physical world, and thereby provides the spiritual purity necessary for her encounter with death, and possibly the final step, according to Williams, toward the androgynous ideal (Fayard 212).

WORKS CITED

Adler, Thomas P. "The Search for God in the Plays of Tennessee Williams." *Renascence* 26 (Autumn 1973): 48–56. Rpt. in *Tennessee Williams: A Collection of Critical Essays*. Ed. Stephen S. Stanton. Englewood Cliffs, NJ: Prentice-Hall, 1977. 138–48.

Armato, Philip. "Tennessee Williams' Meditations on Life and Death in *Suddenly Last Summer, The Night of the Iguana*, and *The Milk Train Doesn't Stop Here Anymore*." *Tennessee Williams: A Tribute*. Ed. Jac Tharpe. Jackson: UP of Mississippi, 1977. 558–70.

Beaufort, John. "Well-acted Revival of 'Milk Train.' " *Christian Science Monitor* 27 Nov. 1987: 26.

Berkowitz, Gerald M. *American Drama of the Twentieth Century.* New York: Longman, 1992.

Bigsby, C. W. E. *A Critical Introduction to Twentieth-Century American Drama. Williams, Miller, Albee.* Vol. 2. Cambridge: Cambridge UP, 1984.

Canby, Vincent. Rev. of *Boom!*, by Tennessee Williams. *New York Times* 27 May 1968, late ed.: 56.

Casper, Leonard. "Triangles of Transaction in Tennessee Williams." *Tennessee Williams: A Tribute.* Ed. Jac Tharpe. Jackson: UP of Mississippi, 1977. 736–52.

Costello, Donald P. "Tennessee Williams' Fugitive Kind." *Modern Drama* 15 (May 1972): 26–43. Rpt. in *Tennessee Williams: A Collection of Critical Essays.* Ed. Stephen S. Stanton. Englewood Cliffs, NJ: Prentice-Hall, 1977. 107–22.

Crandell, George W. *Tennessee Williams: A Descriptive Bibliography.* Pittsburgh: U of Pittsburgh P, 1995.

Debusscher, Gilbert. "French Stowaways on an American Milk Train: Williams, Cocteau, and Peyrefitte." *Modern Drama* 25 (1982): 399–408.

———. "Tennessee Williams' Lives of the Saints: A Playwright's Obliquity." *Tennessee Williams: A Collection of Critical Essays.* Ed. Stephen S. Stanton. Englewood Cliffs, NJ: Prentice-Hall, 1977. 149–57. Rpt. of "Tennessee Williams as Hagiographer: An Aspect of Obliquity in Drama." *Revue des Langues Vivantes* 40 (1974): 449–56.

Falk, Signi Lenea. *Tennessee Williams.* New York: Twayne, 1962.

Fayard, Jeanne. "Meeting with Tennessee Williams." *Tennessee Williams.* Paris: Editions Seghers, 1972. 130–35. Rpt in *Conversations with Tennessee Williams.* Ed. Albert J. Devlin. Jackson: UP of Mississippi, 1986. 208–12.

Funke, Lewis, and John E. Booth. "Williams on Williams." *Theatre Arts* (Jan. 1962): 16–19, 72–73. Rpt. in *Conversations with Tennessee Williams.* Ed. Albert J. Devlin. Jackson: UP of Mississippi, 1986. 97–106.

Gaines, Jim. "A Talk about Life and Style with Tennessee Williams." *Saturday Review* 29 Apr. 1972: 25–29. Rpt. in *Conversations with Tennessee Williams.* Ed. Albert J. Devlin. Jackson: UP of Mississippi, 1986. 213–23.

Ganz, Arthur. "Tennessee Williams: A Desperate Morality." *Tennessee Williams: A Collection of Critical Essays.* Ed. Stephen S. Stanton. Englewood Cliffs, NJ: Prentice-Hall, 1977. 123–37.

Griffin, Alice. *Understanding Tennessee Williams.* Columbia: U of South Carolina P, 1995.

Hirsch, Foster. *A Portrait of the Artist: The Plays of Tennessee Williams.* Port Washington, NY: Kennikat, 1979.

Hitchcock, Francesca. "Tennessee Williams's 'Vengeance of Nitocris': The Keynote to Future Works." *Mississippi Quarterly* 48 (Fall 1995): 595–608.

Kerr, Walter. *New York Theatre Critics' Reviews* 24: 392–93.

Leavitt, Richard F., ed. *The World of Tennessee Williams.* New York: Putnam's, 1978.

Leverich, Lyle. *Tenn: The Timeless World of Tennessee Williams.* Vol. 2 (forthcoming).

Londré, Felicia Hardison. *Tennessee Williams.* New York: Ungar, 1979.

McBride, Mary. "Prisoners of Illusion: Surrealistic Escape in *The Milk Train Doesn't Stop Here Anymore.*" *Tennessee Williams: A Tribute.* Ed. Jac Tharpe. Jackson: UP of Mississippi, 1977. 341–48.

McClain, John. *New York Theatre Critics' Reviews* 24: 393.

"Milk-Run." *Time* 20 July 1962: 40.

" 'Milk Train' Gets a Second Chance." *New York Times* 18 Sept. 1963, late ed.: 32.

Nadel, Norman. " 'Milk Train' Never Gets Rolling." *New York World Telegram* 2 Jan. 1964: 18. Rpt. in *New York Theatre Critics' Reviews* 25: 397–98.

Nash, Jay Robert, and Stanley Ralph Ross, eds. *The Motion Picture Guide: 1927–1983.* Vol. 1. A–B. Chicago: Cinebooks, 1985.

Phillips, Gene D. *The Films of Tennessee Williams.* Philadelphia: Art Alliance, 1980.

Presley, Delma Eugene. "Little Acts of Grace." *Tennessee Williams: A Tribute.* Ed. Jac Tharpe. Jackson: UP of Mississippi, 1977. 571–80.

Rader, Dotson. *Tennessee: Cry of the Heart.* Garden City, NY: Doubleday, 1985.

Reed, Rex. "Tennessee Williams Turns Sixty." *Esquire* Sept. 1971: 105–08, 216–23. Rpt. in *Conversations with Tennessee Williams.* Ed. Albert J. Devlin. Jackson: UP of Mississippi, 1986. 184–207.

Scheick, William. " 'An Intercourse Not Well Designed': Talk and Touch in the Plays of Tennessee Williams." *Tennessee Williams: A Tribute.* Ed. Jac Tharpe. Jackson: UP of Mississippi, 1977. 763–73.

"The Second Mrs. Goforth." *Time* 10 Jan. 1964: 52.

"Spoleto Gets a New Play from Tennessee Williams." *London Times* 14 July 1962: 4.

Spoto, Donald. *The Kindness of Strangers: The Life of Tennessee Williams.* Boston: Little, Brown, 1985.

Steen, Mike. *A Look at Tennessee Williams.* New York: Hawthorn, 1969.

"Tallulah and Tennessee." *Newsweek* 13 Jan. 1964: 70.

"Tennessee Williams' Work Has Premiere at Spoleto." *New York Times* 12 July 1962, late ed.: 19.

Thompson, Judith J. *Tennessee Williams' Plays: Memory, Myth, and Symbol.* New York: Lang, 1987.

Tischler, Nancy. "A Gallery of Witches." *Tennessee Williams: A Tribute.* Ed. Jac Tharpe. Jackson: UP of Mississippi, 1977. 494–509.

Wallach, Allan. "Williams' 'Milk Train' Still Doesn't Stop." *New York Newsday* 23 Nov. 1987. Rpt. in *New York Theatre Critics' Reviews* 48: 98.

Wardle, Irving. "Amateurs Do Well by Tennessee Williams." *London Times* 2 Dec. 1968: 16.

Weales, Gerald. "Tennessee Williams' Achievement in the Sixties." *The Jumping-Off Place: American Drama in the 1960s.* New York: Macmillan, 1969. 3–14. Rpt. in *Tennessee Williams: A Collection of Critical Essays.* Ed. Stephen S. Stanton. Englewood Cliffs, NJ: Prentice-Hall, 1977. 61–70.

West, Anthony. "One Milk Train, One Scandal." *Show* 3.4 (Apr. 1963): 40–41. Rpt. in *The Critical Response to Tennessee Williams.* Ed. George W. Crandell. Westport, CT: Greenwood Press, 1996. 211–14.

Williams, Tennessee. "Man Bring This up Road." *Tennessee Williams: Collected Stories.* New York: Ballantine, 1989. 366–77.

———. *Memoirs.* Garden City, NY: Doubleday, 1975.

———. *The Milk Train Doesn't Stop Here Anymore. The Best Plays of 1962–1963.* Ed. Henry Hewes. New York: Dodd, Mead, 1963. 151–69.

———. *The Milk Train Doesn't Stop Here Anymore. The Theatre of Tennessee Williams.* Vol. 5. New York: New Directions, 1990. 1–120.

———. *The Milk Train Doesn't Stop Here Anymore: A Play.* London: Secker and Warburg, 1964.

Kingdom of Earth/The Seven Descents of Myrtle

PHILIP C. KOLIN

BIOGRAPHICAL CONTEXT

Williams's biography runs throughout *Kingdom of Earth*. The play is set in his boyhood South of the Mississippi Delta, in the mythical Two River County, the same location as that of the heavily biographical *Orpheus Descending* and *Baby Doll*. *Kingdom* is steeped in Williams's southern Gothicism with its mythos of violence and absurdity. The rivalry of the two brothers—the "mixed-breed" Chicken and his white sibling Lot—may have its roots in the struggle between Williams and his brother Dakin. Bigsby, however, finds that a "high camp" figure like Lot more closely reflected Williams's "self parody, a kind of paranoia" (65). Lot was a watershed character in Williams's creative life, even providing the playwright with an exorcism of sorts. Mike Steen recounts that "Tennessee told me that when he has Lot die, he is killing off all the wispy, willowy women he has written about, that he wasn't going to write that kind of woman anymore."

The production of *Kingdom of Earth* dates from the late 1960s, "a period of personal and artistic debacle" for Williams (Bigsby 65). During the 1960s, Williams was strung out on drugs, and so it is no wonder that plays like *Kingdom* were "often brutal, apocalyptic, and death-centered" (Bigsby 65). According to Londré, the sense of survival stems from Williams's "health problems in the mid-1960s" (180). Nor did the critics help Williams's mental health. In an interview with C. Robert Jennings, the playwright lamented: "Reviews can be devastating to me. A barrage of bad reviews contributed enormously to my demoralization. The plays weren't that bad—*Slapstick Comedy* and *Kingdom of Earth*" (quoted in Devlin 235). Celebrating Williams's revolutionary spirit in *Kingdom of Earth*,

Kolin maintains that the play offers his attack on the Vietnam War and the "ravages of colonization" (143). Kolin concludes that *"Kingdom's* social message in 1968 was prophetic" (159), showing the American theatre that Williams was a playwright with a carefully articulated political agenda. The second volume of Leverich's biography also gives much commentary on the play.

BIBLIOGRAPHIC HISTORY

Gunn (64) provides a concise publication history, while Crandell (*Tennessee Williams* 254–58) documents the editions and printings of *Kingdom*. Like most of Williams's works, *Kingdom of Earth* boasts a complex evolution; Williams repeatedly visited his "dramatic storehouse" (*Memoirs*) in writing the play. The idea first came to him in Mexico in the early 1940s when he wrote a short story, the germ of which dealt with the Lot/Chicken relationship. The story was subsequently revised and published in Williams's collections of stories *Hard Candy* (1954) and *The Knightly Quest* (1968). He later transformed the short story into a one-act play published in the February 1967 issue of *Esquire*. By March 1968, he had expanded the one-act play into the seven-scene script of *The Seven Descents of Myrtle* that had a lamentably short run on Broadway. By October 1968, when New Directions published the play, Williams had made still more (though slight) changes and retitled it *Kingdom of Earth*. Kolin observes, however, "It's significant that Williams changed Chicken's racial identity from a Cherokee Indian in the short story 'Kingdom of Earth' (1954) that preceded the play *Kingdom of Earth* (1968) to a 'mixed breed' " (143). Derounian discusses Williams's "expansion of material from one genre to another" (150), claiming that "our approval of Chicken in the short story is very different from our view of him in the play" (153). Williams again revised the play and published a considerably shorter version of *Kingdom* in 1976.

MAJOR CRITICAL APPROACHES

Themes

Critics have inevitably compared *Kingdom of Earth* to Williams's earlier plays, especially *Streetcar*, to arrive at Williams's purpose, his message. Mirko Tuma expressed a highly representative response to *Kingdom* in his review of the McCarter Theater production of the play in March 1975: "Williams writes almost exclusively about the disintegration of southern gentility and about aesthetics and grace being raped by the brutal forces of man's modern quest." According to this view, Chicken ravishes the world of art and culture. But there are other critical variations on this theme. Thompson, for example, separates the world of *Streetcar* from the far more pessimistic existence in *Kingdom*: "Those who survive in 'the kingdom of earth' are the strong, the sexual and the pragmatic," though *Kingdom* valorizes "naturalistic existence—no matter how corrupt"—instead of mourning lost romantic hopes (193). For Adler, even the sex act itself, heralded in *Streetcar*, has descended into corruption in *Kingdom*: "The sexuality seems bitter and cynical, devoid of any positive value, almost a puritan disgust for the body and over-reaction against what had perhaps before (in Williams's plays) been a too tolerant attitude toward fleshly acts as a saving grace" ("Two Plays" 6). According to Kalson, *Kingdom of Earth* is "an extended dramatic metaphor for the act of fellatio which becomes . . . a metaphor for any brutal, degrading, sterile relationship between a man and a woman" (92).

As with other Williams's plays, critics have been fond of identifying polarities in *Kingdom*. Londré, for example, claims that *Kingdom* presents a "dichotomy of flesh and spirit" (178). According to Phillips, "The play is a confrontation between aspects of the human psyche" in which Lot's "cold rationalism" is up against Chicken's destructive sexuality and "brutality" (351–52). Exploring *Kingdom* from the vantage point of postcolonial discourse, Kolin finds that "the focal point of the script . . . challenges race ideology by destabilizing the 'either/or' economy of colonialism and demoralizes such mythologies upon which racial stereotypes are grounded" (144).

Characters

Clive Barnes took the occasion of *Kingdom*'s premiere to fault Williams for his characters: "Time was when Tennessee Williams wrote plays; nowadays he seems to prefer to write characters" (54). Responding to this assessment, Marc Robinson usefully pointed out, "For Williams there could have been no higher praise; this was precisely his prime virtue" (33). Though Chicken, Lot, and Myrtle in *Kingdom* are certainly not Williams's most significant characters, they do reflect his ability to create memorable individuals whose lives challenge conventionality. Derounian claims that *Kingdom* is an "absurd parody of three favorite Williams types: the determined desperate Southern woman; the poetic artist; and the carnal man-as-beast" (154).

Chicken

Unquestionably, Chicken Ravenstock, Lot's half brother, is the main character in *Kingdom*. Kolin reminds readers that Chicken is the only person of color in the Williams canon to play a leading (major) role. By his own admission, Chicken is a "woods colt," "someone with colored blood." His "very different" mother had some black blood, while he and Lot had the same white father.

Many critics have found little to praise in Chicken. His vulgarity, coarseness, and blatant sexuality—he has Myrtle fellate him on stage—have earned him critical contempt. He has been branded as "the other," the "misfit," and the "outsider." Kalson castigates him as "subhuman" (92); Nelsen calls him "single-minded, ape-like" (77); and Derounian attacks him for being "grotesque and mindless" (156). For Phillips, Chicken represents "primeval animality" (351). Admitting that he "ultimately assumes the role of ironic savior" by saving Myrtle from the floodwaters, Thompson nonetheless concludes that he is the "vulgar, phallic Chicken" (193).

For most critics, Chicken's stature has been minimized through the taint of parody. According to Kalson, Chicken is a parody of the Lawrentian hero whom Williams once admired (91). Phillips claims that Chicken is "a muddled hybrid like Stanley Kowalski" (353). Extending the comparison, Adler believes that "Chicken seems to be Stanley Kowalski taken to extremes" (*American Drama* 165). Moving away from comparisons within the Williams canon, Clinton dismisses Chicken as a perverse parody of Orpheus, claiming that his cowardice, stupidity, and "overwhelming desire to possess" make him "no less abhorrent than death itself" (32).

The most laudatory reading of Chicken comes from Kolin, who tries to rehabilitate the character in the context of Williams's perceived anticolonialism: "A man of color, freed from the ravages of an oppressive legal and social order, Chicken can now enter freely into building a more diverse and healthy society" (159). Kolin further affirms that "Chicken's sexual victory should be seen in light of the ideological struggle of a decadent empire versus a healthy emergent nation" symbolized by Chicken (159).

Myrtle

Myrtle Kain (whose symbolic name Phillips glosses as Cain; Myrtilus, "the legendary Greek involved . . . in the curse on the house of Pelops"; and Aphrodite [353]) has been divergently interpreted by the critics. A floozy whom Lot sees on a television show, Myrtle becomes his instrument in a revengeful plan to swindle Chicken out of his inheritance. Most critics have focused on three areas of Myrtle's character: her maternity, her role as wife both to Lot and to Chicken, and her sexuality. Londré praises her as "vulgar, but warm, generous, and funny" (174) and maintains that Myrtle wed Lot because of "maternal instinct" (179). Thompson approves of her "instinct for self-preservation" (201); Boxill claims that she is "the faded belle less the malleable wife" (153). The most favorable view of Myrtle comes from Kolin, who hails her role as wife and mother to future Ravenstocks through Chicken. "Paradoxically the whore for Chicken will become the new Eve" (160) who will be responsible for a new empowered race of men of color owning and governing the land.

Perhaps the action in the play most frequently commented on is Myrtle performing fellatio on Chicken in the kitchen of his mother's house. Many critics view it as unnatural, revolting, or suspicious. Seeing her as Chicken's "victim" and as someone who "will feel at home in her new freak show environment" (90), Kalson claims that "the sex act between Myrtle and Chicken climaxes the play and signifies her complete capitulation to him . . . itself a further sign of Chicken's incompleteness as a man" (91). Similarly, Derounian asserts that "as representative of the white race Myrtle has been enslaved and humbled by a representative of the black race. . . . By performing fellatio, they parody the regenerative aspect of sexual intercourse" (155). She concludes that Myrtle is "morally weak" (154). For Kolin, the "so-called perverse act between Myrtle and Chicken takes on almost a religious quality" (158).

Lot

Unlike the divided critical response to Chicken and Myrtle, Lot is repeatedly denounced as an unsympathetic character for a sundry host of sins. A tubercular transvestite, Lot dresses as his own mother and holds court in her parlor. Beyond doubt, Williams incorporated some O'Neillian mother fixation from *Desire Under the Elms*. Lot is unscrupulous with his older brother Chicken, trying to swindle him and lying to accomplish the deed. Phillips and Thompson find Lot as culpable, though, as Chicken. For example, Thompson vilifies him as "selfish, sexless, and fully as depraved in his own way as Chicken." For Thompson, Lot "parodies Blanche DuBois," and his own death "devaluates her romantic tragedy" (194). Lot's association with and febrile appreciation of the world of art have been severely censured by the critics. Londré dismisses him as "effete" (178), while Kalson even more strongly attacks Chicken's half brother: "Lot with the soul of an artist has no chance to survive, but unlike the artist-figures of earlier Williams plays, he is only the parody of impotent aestheticism" (91). Derounian agrees: "In death, Lot suggests a final parody of the artist, who also dedicates his life to recreation of the past" (155).

Lot has fared no better in interpretations of *Kingdom* that examine the play in light of social criticism. A Russian critic, K. Komissarzhevsky, who reviewed the Moscow premiere of *Kingdom*, summarized much that has been written about Lot's sins against society: "Why is Lot dying? . . . Because of tuberculosis or because of the metastases of his greed and racial hatred? Lot does not have to demonstrate his physical sickness but to overcome it. Only then will his diseased attitude be revealed; the refined prince turns into an ordinary racist" (quoted in Shaland 78–79). Kolin likewise brands Lot as a "spoiled aristocrat" (154), a "decadent Prospero" (153), the embodiment of the dominant white power structure dedicated to oppressing any person of color.

Symbols

Like other works of Williams, *Kingdom of Earth* is rich in religious and sexual symbolism. Boxill, Falk, Hirsch, Londré, and Thompson discuss the wide range of these symbols in *Kingdom*. Thompson explicates the biblical allusions that are the underpinning for both character and location: Noah and the Flood; Lot's disobedient wife; inheriting the kingdom (193–95). Perhaps the most significant—and largest—symbol is the dilapidated farmhouse itself with its dimly lit kitchen—Chicken's domain (Kolin)—and Lot's mother's "parlour" with its chandelier and chairs. According to Boxill, the house is "the lost place of refuge or gentility" (153), a "metaphor of alienation" (26). For Kalson, the house, with its symbolic stairway to the bedrooms upstairs, is a site for sexual perversion. For Kolin, the house represents the decadent and imminently fatal world of colonizing aristocrats. Bigsby offers the gestalt: "Williams' places are elaborations of the metaphors they enclose" (44).

Water symbolism abounds in *Kingdom* as well. The rising floodwaters as a result of the storm variously signal death or rebirth to the critics. "The water symbolism emphasizes Chicken's association with elemental nature" for Phillips (352), while Kalson attempts to incorporate Myrtle's act of fellatio into the water symbolism of the play.

The land itself—the inheritance over which the brothers struggle and war— is also filled with symbolic overtones. Kalson judges it a "wasteland" (90), but for Kolin the land becomes a new world washed clean after the flood, a community ready to be populated by the new breed of Chicken and Myrtle.

Plot

Williams called *Kingdom* a "funny melodrama" (*Memoirs* 40), characterizing the plot of the play in response to an inhospitable reception in the critical forum. Thompson more generously concludes that *Kingdom* is a "comic revision of *Streetcar*'s predominant tragic mode" (195). Kalson also characterizes the play as a "curious comedy" (90). Like *Streetcar*, *Kingdom* uses the familiar love triangle to generate conflict (Boxill; Kalson). Boxill maintains that the action of *Kingdom* is like that of *Streetcar*. In this three-character play, "the widow of the dead homosexual is possessed carnally by her ape-like brother-in-law," as in *Streetcar* (153). For Adler, *Kingdom* "reworks the body/soul tension explored in *Summer and Smoke*" (*American Drama* 165).

MAJOR PROBLEMS *KINGDOM OF EARTH* AND *THE SEVEN DESCENTS OF MYRTLE* POSE FOR CRITICS

Opinion about *Kingdom* is sharply divided. Phillips sees it as a "work of great imaginative power and compelling intensity" (349), while Kalson and Derounian, for example, stamp *Kingdom* as an artistic failure. Beyond question, the biggest problem for critics with *Kingdom* is seeing it as a parody, an impoverished attempt by Williams to reclaim his fame. Bitterly, Howell quipped, "The Old Pretender has brought us a play that is in nearly every respect a parody and travesty of his great works of the past." Simon likewise pronounced that *Kingdom of Earth* was "stale self-plagiarism, self-parody, all self-flagellation" (208). Similarly, Vosburgh bristled, "No parodist could write up a more wicked send-up of Tennessee Williams than did Williams himself in *Kingdom of Earth*" (356).

Chicken's status is still another problematic issue—is he a beast or a savior, a sexual deviant or the progenitor of a new race of men and women of color freed from the bonds of colonialism (Kolin)? Derounian claims that he is "anti-heroic, anti-poetic" (152). Another point of contention for the critics has to do with the ending of *Kingdom*. For Kalson, the ending offers only "seeming optimism," a "falsification" of any sexual hope engendered in Chicken and Myrtle;

it is Williams's "bleakest vision to date" (90). Kolin, on the other hand, sees the ending as an affirmation of a new and decolonized future. Finally, Cohn complains that "insistence on symbols weakens the dramatic drive of several Williams plays [including] . . . *Kingdom of Earth*" (128–29). And according to Derounian, Williams "subjugates his characters to theme" so that they "are incapable of spontaneous and convincing . . . action" (156).

CHIEF PRODUCTIONS

The Seven Descents of Myrtle premiered on 27 March 1968 at the Ethel Barrymore Theatre in New York, but ran for only 29 performances, until 20 April. José Quintero directed Harry Guardino as Chicken, Estelle Parsons as Myrtle, and Brian Bedford as Lot. Williams told Dotson Rader that Quintero was drinking so heavily that Estelle Parsons said that she could not take directions from him, "which nearly led producer David Merrick to close the show before it began" (quoted in Devlin 336). Longtime Williams scenographer Jo Mielziner designed the sets. The reviewers were ungenerous. Typical was Walter Kerr's assessment that the script was "unfinished . . . unrealized"; the staging was faulty, the acting awkward, and the direction missing. "We are forced to filter a graphic performance through an earache" was Kerr's reaction to Parsons. Guardino's Chicken also came in for critical censure, not least because a white man was playing one of color. Gill faulted attempts to make the first white Chicken look black: "Guardino has his skin implausibly darkened by something that looks like Man Tan." Cooke complained that Guardino "seems somewhat too articulate and too much in command of his grammar for an uneducated outcast" (315).

A significant production of *Kingdom* was staged at Princeton's McCarter Theater from 6 March to 16 March 1975, directed by Garland Wright. This was the first time an actor of color was cast as Chicken. David Pendleton, who appeared in such daytime television series as *Edge of Night, The Doctors*, and *Guiding Light*, marvelously represented Chicken's liminal status. Pendleton garnered much praise for his work: his performance was hailed as "superb" and "terrifying." Sympathetically, Jean Ogden recognized that "Chicken's mean and tough. He's been fighting being black and a bastard all his life," an observation made even more poignant thanks to Pendleton's acting.

Few critics appreciated Williams's social message, however. One who did was Fred Porter, who wrote, "*Kingdom* is a picture of the anti-massar caste system still prevalent in the deep South in 1960." Critics attacked Williams. Coleen Zirnite bristled: "His message or purpose is nebulous. It is almost as if the author lost his way, forgot where he was going and groped for the nearest exit." Linda Holt castigated Chicken as Lot's "bestial half brother" and then added, "There's a scruffy Neanderthalism about him that's quite fetching, and a mercurial sense of humor." According to Ernest Albrecht, Chicken was the dreaded fulfillment of Blanche's admonition to Stella: "Myrtle must turn back (to the apes as it were) and cast her lot with the brother, Chicken, which suggests a variation on the animal imagery." In 1991, the Boston Post Road Stage cast Hispanic actor Ramiro Carrillo as Chicken and gave the character a Mexican, instead of black, mother.

There were three important British productions of *Kingdom*—the New Vic, Bristol, 1978; the Hampstead Theatre, London, 1984; and the Redgrave, Farnham, 1991. Chicken was played by white actors. Peter Postlethwaite's Chicken in the British premiere at the New Vic was criticized for portraying Chicken as "hyper-sensitive to a suspicion of coloured blood that has kept him out of society" (Young).

Overall, the critics of the London *Kingdom* echoed those in New York in giving the play mixed to unfavorable reviews. Giles Gordon called Lot's half brother a "brutish, embittered Stanley Kowalski–esque quadroon." Actor Stephen Rea fared slightly better in the critics' eyes than the character he played in the 1984 production, though Rea's "glowering hulk" made the act of sex even more "brutal" for Francis King. But Milton Shulman caustically jabbed, "Stephen Rea seems at times to be doing an imitation of Jimmy Cagney as he bullies and threatens the other two" (355). Shaland documents the Soviet premiere of *Kingdom*.

FILM AND TELEVISION VERSIONS

Williams's friend and verbal sparring partner Gore Vidal wrote the screenplay of *Kingdom*—*Last of the Mobile Hot Shots*—which was directed by Sidney Lumet. It starred Robert Hooks, a black actor, as Chicken; Lynn Redgrave as Myrtle; and James Coburn as Job (Lot). Vidal altered Williams's script substantially.

CONCLUDING OVERVIEW

Williams was the perpetual champion of the marginalized, the Other, the fugitive from the codes of conventionality, just as he himself was. He reveled in publicizing the unconventional and promoted a revolutionary agenda that would enfranchise those who had the most to suffer in an oppressive patriarchy. Among the various marginalized groups to which Williams owed an emotional alliance were black Americans. Williams once proclaimed, "I always thought I was black" (Rasky 10). He cherished his black maid Ossie, who helped rear him; he recalled scores of black songs and expressions incorporated into the early plays and *Sweet Bird of Youth*; and when he was at the University of Iowa, Williams played the role of a black preacher in Thomas Pawley's (a black student at Iowa when Williams was there) drama *Ku Klux*, staged at a university workshop in 1938 (Pawley 67).

A vibrant black presence infuses the Williams canon, even though there is not always an easy mingling of the races. But that is essentially the sociopolitical point Williams repeatedly stressed from "Big Black: A Mississippi Idyll," his early short story about a black worker eroticized for a white audience, to Lance, the black ice skater in Williams's late novel *Moise and the World of Reason*. Williams even recruits traditionally white characters such as Stanley Kowalski into a black ethos (Crandell, "Misrepresentation"), and is always on the side of the oppressed, the marginalized.

When he wrote about Chicken Ravenstock, Williams seized the glorious opportunity to display the oppression of a bigoted, hegemonic white world in the way Lot treats his brother, but he also took the daring and self-congratulatory risk of openly and freely having the black man, the historical victim, the hunted fugitive, win the day, and perhaps the epoch. Rather than being a parody of earlier Williams characters or even a self-parody, Chicken Ravenstock is Williams's emancipatory voice, the sign and symbol of the enfranchisement that had rightfully come to blacks in the South and, by extension, to Tennessee Williams himself. Race, politics, and sex were the three sides of Williams's eternal triangle.

WORKS CITED

Adler, Thomas P. *American Drama, 1940–1960: A Critical History*. New York: Twayne, 1994.

———. "Two Plays for Puritans." *Tennessee Williams Newsletter* 1.1 (Spring 1979): 5–7.

Albrecht, Ernest. "Williams Digs More Bones of Old Glories." *Home News* [New Brunswick, NJ] 7 Mar. 1975.

Barnes, Clive. "Theater: Williams Drama." *New York Times* 28 Mar. 1968: 54. Rpt. in *New York Theatre Critics' Reviews* 29 (1968): 313.

Bigsby, C. W. E. *Modern American Drama, 1945–1990*. Cambridge: Cambridge UP, 1992.

Boxill, Roger. *Tennessee Williams*. New York: St. Martin's, 1987.

Clinton, Craig D. "Tennessee Williams's *Kingdom of Earth*: The Orpheus Myth Revisited." *Theatre Annual* 33 (1977): 25–37.

Cohn, Ruby. *Dialogue in American Drama*. Bloomington: Indiana UP, 1971.

Cooke, Richard F. "Chicken on a Cold Wet Roof." *Wall Street Journal* 29 Mar. 1968: 16. Rpt. in *New York Theatre Critics' Reviews* 29 (1968): 315.

Crandell, George W. "Misrepresentation and Miscegenation: Reading the Racialized Discourse of Tennessee Williams's *A Streetcar Named Desire*." *Modern Drama* 40 (1997): 337–46.

———. *Tennessee Williams: A Descriptive Bibliography*. Pittsburgh: U of Pittsburgh P, 1995.

Derounian, Kathryn Zabelle. " 'The Kingdom of Earth' and *Kingdom of Earth (The Seven Descents of Myrtle)*: Tennessee Williams' Parody." *University of Mississippi Studies in English* 4 (1983): 150–58.

Devlin, Albert J., ed. *Conversations with Tennessee Williams*. Jackson: UP of Mississippi, 1986.

Falk, Signi Lenea. *Tennessee Williams*. New York: Twayne, 1962.

Gill, Brendan. Rev. of *The Seven Descents of Myrtle*. *New Yorker* 6 Apr. 1968: 109–10.

Gordon, Giles. "Creatures Great and Small." *Spectator* 5 May 1984: 28–29. Rpt. in *London Theatre Record* 4 (1984): 356.

Gunn, Drewey Wayne. *Tennessee Williams: A Bibliography*. 2nd ed. Metuchen, NJ: Scarecrow, 1991.

Hirsch, Foster. "Sexual Imagery in Tennessee Williams' *Kingdom of Earth*." *Notes on Contemporary Literature* 1.2 (1971): 10–13.

Holt, Linda. "Little Good in 'Kingdom.' " *The Trentonian* [NJ] 11 Mar. 1975.

Howell, Chauncey. *"Kingdom of Earth." Women's Wear Daily* 28 Mar. 1968. Rpt. in *New York Theatre Critics' Reviews* 29 (1968): 316.

Kalson, Albert E. "Tennessee Williams' *Kingdom of Earth*: A Sterile Promontory." *Drama and Theatre* [Purdue U] 8 (Winter 1969–70): 90–93.

Kerr, Walter. "The Name of the Game Is Blame." *New York Times* 7 Apr. 1968, sec. 2: 1, 3.

King, Francis. *"Kingdom." London Sunday Telegraph* 6 May 1984. Rpt. in *London Theatre Record* 4 (1984): 350, 355.

Kolin, Philip C. "Sleeping with Caliban: The Politics of Race in Tennessee Williams's *Kingdom of Earth." Studies in American Drama, 1945–Present* 8.2 (Spring 1993): 140–62.

Leverich, Lyle. *Tenn: The Timeless World of Tennessee Williams.* Forthcoming.

Londré, Felícia Hardison. *Tennessee Williams.* New York: Ungar, 1979.

Nelsen, Don. "Myrtle's Last Descent." *New York Daily News* 15 July 1977: 77.

Ogden, Jean. "Tennessee Williams Revival: Chicken on a Cold Wet Roof." *Somerset Messenger Gazette* [Somersville, NJ] 13 Mar. 1975.

Pawley, Thomas. "Experimental Theatre Seminar; or, The Basic Training of Tennessee Williams: A Memoir." *Iowa Review* 19 (Winter 1989): 65–76.

Phillips, Jerrold A. *"Kingdom of Earth*: Some Approaches." *Tennessee Williams: A Tribute.* Ed. Jac Tharpe. Jackson: UP of Mississippi, 1977. 349–53.

Porter, Fred. "Theatre: Town and Country: *Kingdom of Earth." Store News* [Dunellen, NJ] 12 Mar. 1975.

Rader, Dotson. *Tennessee: Cry of the Heart.* Garden City, NY: Doubleday, 1985.

Rasky, Harry. *Tennessee Williams: A Portrait in Laughter and Lamentation.* New York: Dodd, Mead, 1986.

Robinson, Marc. *The Other American Drama.* Baltimore: Johns Hopkins UP, 1994.

Shaland, Irene. *Tennessee Williams on the Soviet Stage.* Lanham, MD: UP of America, 1987.

Shulman, Milton. "Kingdom of Earth." *London Standard* 2 May 1984. Rpt. in *London Theatre Record* 4 (1984): 355.

Simon, John. *"Kingdom." Commonweal* 88 (3 May 1968): 208–9.

Steen, Mike. *A Look at Tennessee Williams.* New York: Hawthorn, 1969.

Thompson, Judith J. *Tennessee Williams' Plays: Memory, Myth, and Symbol.* New York: Lang, 1987.

Tuma, Mirko. "Williams Revision Opens at McCarter." *News Tribune* [Woodbridge, NJ] 4 Mar. 1975.

Vosburgh, Dick. Rev. *Punch* 9 May 1984. Rpt. in *London Theatre Record* 4 (1984): 356.

Williams, Tennessee. *Kingdom of Earth. Theatre of Tennessee Williams.* Vol. 5. New York: New Directions, 1976.

———. *Kingdom of Earth. Esquire* 67 (Feb. 1967): 98–100, 132, 134.

———. *Memoirs.* Garden City, NY: Doubleday, 1975.

Young, B. A. "Kingdom of Earth." *Financial Times* 23 Feb. 1978.

Zirnite, Colleen. "Tennessee Williams Rewrite: Poor Play with a Good Cast." *The Democrat* [Flemington, NJ] 11 Mar. 1975.

The Two-Character Play and Out Cry

LANELLE DANIEL

BIOGRAPHICAL CONTEXT

When Tennessee Williams was in San Francisco in 1976 to attend rehearsals of the critically doomed *This Is*, he met director and later biographer Lyle Leverich to discuss *The Two-Character Play* and a tandem production with *The Glass Menagerie*. During the process of choosing the actors, Williams described *The Two-Character Play* as "the most difficult he had ever written, 'the interior landscape of the most terrible period of my life' " (Leverich xix). He later claimed that for him this play represented a catharsis dealing with his dark period, specifically the 1960s when he was so terribly depressed because it seemed that his life had come apart (Funke 27). According to Novick, "Williams is wrestling with his demons as desperately as Eugene O'Neill used to do" (58).

In some ways, *The Two-Character Play* seems a frail precursor of *The Glass Menagerie*, but it is not—it was written much later. It has even been seen as a sequel (Parker 523). However, as Wilson points out, the brother and sister could be Williams himself, two entities being one whole, or "they could be autobiographical in another way: Williams has a sister who has been institutionalized for many years and of whom he has taken great care" (24). Certainly, Clare and Felice reflect aspects of Williams's life. The brother and sister in the play are the offspring of wildly dysfunctional parents, a flamboyant father and a prudish mother, much like Williams's parents, Cornelius Coffin Williams and Edwina Dakin Williams. Parker and Leverich have intensely scrutinized Williams's family background, his relationship to his sister, his affinity for androgynous young men, and his plunge into a plethora of substance abuses. Parker cogently points out that *Two-Character Play* reveals "the two central and interlocked experiences of [Williams's] life: his ambiguous, near-incestuous love for his schizophrenic sister, Rose; and his compulsive need for theatre as personal escape and therapy" (521).

The Two-Character Play is also a product of Williams's later life. The 1960s were clearly a period of substance abuse and psychiatric therapy for the talented writer, and he ultimately wound up in the violent ward of the Friggins Division of Barnes Hospital for a time (Gillen 229). George Niesen asserts that the play is "Williams's most intellectually realistic statement concerning the artist's untenable and isolated position in modern culture" (488). All of these attributes are reflected in *The Two-Character Play*. Stamper concludes, "The play is blatantly confessional and therapeutic" (355).

Williams himself expounded on his writing of the time by saying in his *Memoirs*, "I am doing a different thing which is altogether my own, not influenced at all by other playwrights at home or abroad or by other schools of theater. My thing is what it always was: to express my world and my experience of it in whatever form seems suitable to the material" (xvii). Apparently he succeeded in this goal, for, as Devlin remarks, "What Tennessee Williams knew, or hoped to learn, in writing *The Two-Character Play* confounds any paradigmatic view of his distinguished life in letters. . . . [It is] the inner story of Williams's career: his constant struggle to renew the artistic motive amid nearly overwhelming personal and professional adversity" (8). No wonder that in Williams's own assessment *The Two-Character Play* was the "big one . . . a major work" (*Memoirs* 129).

BIBLIOGRAPHIC HISTORY

The Two-Character Play has "at least four versions" (Stamper 354). It premiered in 1967 and was first published in 1969 in a limited edition by New Directions. Obviously, though, Williams had been working on the script for some time, since there are references to it as early as 1959. Even after the premiere, Williams continued to tinker with the play, and it appeared revised in 1973 as *Out Cry* and again was published by New Directions. There was also a 1971 unpublished version of *Out Cry*. Finally, it was published in a third version in 1979 with its original title. Crandell (263–65) and Gunn provide specific bibliographic details.

MAJOR CRITICAL APPROACHES

Themes

Virtually every consideration of *The Two-Character Play* is based on its overt psychological implications as well as its obvious relationship to *The Glass Menagerie*, perhaps considered its prototype. According to Londré, Williams wanted to issue "a personal statement about the artist in society" (185). Her analysis of the play, including glossing the names, is precise and thorough. Parker raises the specter of psychic individuation (the self-consciousness's struggle to reconcile with its sense of separate selves) as the explanation of the play and of Williams. Stamper also picks up the theme of psychic individuation, explaining that *The Two-Character Play* is important (although not good) because it denotes Williams's shift to a more personal and less sympathetic referent for his work (360). "By focusing on himself . . . [and using] . . . drama as personal therapy, he has lost the mythic, public spectacle necessary for all great drama" (Stamper 361). Dramatizing his psychosis, Williams revealed new levels of meaning—not always seen or appreciated by the critics—in his work. According to Clurman, "The theme is fear" (380), he further points out that a moral impasse is at the root of this fear as well as the sense of being cut off from the world that makes living impossible. The difficult task is identifying exactly where the fear originates. Part of it is the isolation; part, for Clurman and other critics, is a dread of confinement. O'Connor analyzes the role madness plays in presenting and containing the artist in society (89) and with the "issue of language and madness" (68–70).

Characters

Devlin links Clare and Felice to Pirandellian characters and concedes that Felice herself may have "spoken for Tennessee Williams" on theatre (15). Marc Robinson points out that the most memorable Williams characters stand out from their plays "like lighthouses in stormy weather" (33). But, he warns, "Williams's people can't be other than what they are, and that's what is so troubling" (33). O'Connor argues that "Williams takes considerable care to present Felice and Clare as equals, not opposites" (95), admitting, though, that Clare has "greater skill as an actor" while Felice assumes power in his "role as the playwright" (94). In essence, then, whether Felice and Clare are representatives of Williams's life or whether they are artistic metaphors, they are still "Williams's people" existing in a shadowy, claustrophobic setting that denies them life. O'Connor and Parker offer the most sustained discussion of character.

Symbols

Stamper identifies "two chief symbols of exhaustion and regeneration within the inner play [as] the faded rose on the carpet and the sunflowers surrounding the house" (359). Kahn labels *Out Cry* Williams's "least realistic and most symbolic setting" (41). He also points out how the symbols in the play change with the revisions from one version to another. The "huge dark statue upstage, a work of great power and darkly subjective meaning" suggesting things "anguished and perverse" of *Out Cry* becomes a papier-mâché statue of a giant with a "sinister look" in *The Two-Character Play*. For Kahn, the statue of the giant seems a specific ogre in a nightmare, not a contextual symbol of potential, emerging clarity, as first written (42). Felice and Clare are strong symbols themselves in the 1973 production, as noted by Julius Novick, emphasizing that the play is evidently a metaphor for Williams's current and long-standing sorrows, "with Clare representing his impulse to collapse under the strain, and Felice standing for his determination to go on" (58). O'Connor sees them signifying "the collective madness of the modern world" (91).

Plot

Director George Keathley informed a reviewer that *The Two-Character Play* was "a play-within-a-play, involving a brother and sister who play the parts of actors. The brother is also a playwright" ("New Williams Play" L33). But his play constantly breaks down on stage because of the actors' fears of outside threats (Gillen 228). They are trapped in their broken play with its bits of missing props and scenery and the audience that has left. "As Felice and Clare are trapped within the theater, . . . so the playwright, too, is trapped within himself, never knowing if the reality that he perceives is ever understood by anyone" (Gillen 229). Parker recognizes that "implicit in the very structure . . . is a connection between sex and art whose common denominator is a recognition and fear of solipsism—of consciousness turned in on itself" (520). Stamper maintains that the play "dramatizes a confrontation with the unconscious" (358). Devlin claims that "the dual structure of *Six Characters in Search of an Author* provided Williams with a vehicle for restaging his quintessential drama" (14). Despite the critical distaste for *The Two-Character Play*, Londré calls it a major work, going so far as to suggest that it needed time—perhaps even the seventeen-year gestation period required before *Camino Real* became popular (192). O'Connor relates "the inner play" and "outer frame" to the lives of the characters (90–91).

MAJOR PROBLEMS *OUT CRY* AND *THE TWO-CHARACTER PLAY* POSE FOR CRITICS

Speaking for many critics, Novick emphasized that *The Two-Character Play* had "its crippling faults," not the least of which were an absence of humor and being "both over-explicit and vague" at the same time. Ultimately, for the critics, Williams could not maintain the better parts of the play. Just as the audience tentatively accepts his theatrical metaphor and enters his created world, Williams nevertheless loses his objectivity and crosses the line from artistic statement to personal disclosure (Wilson 30). In the end, the audience is trapped in and with the ineffectual characters who cannot move in any direction. Everyone leaves the play unnourished, fearful, and slightly paranoid. As Novick says, "The play is not short enough or concentrated enough or unified enough to make its consistency of emotion a virtue" (58). Stanley Kauffmann dwells on *The Two-Character Play*'s likeness to Pirandello's work and then castigates the play, the director, and the actors, as well as the author: "I suppose that Williams has earned the right to have everything he writes produced . . . but he is trying this right severely" (170). O'Connor discusses the problem of seeing the ending as "optimistic" (97–99).

CHIEF PRODUCTIONS

The 1967 version of *The Two-Character Play* had its world premiere at the Hampstead Theatre in London in December 1967, with Peter Wyngarde and Mary Ure, directed by James Rosse-Evans. In July 1971, it was revised and presented at the Ivanhoe Theatre as *Out Cry*, with George Keathley directing Donald Madden and Eileen Merlie in this version. In 1973, *Out Cry*, revised again, with Michael York and Cara Duff-MacCormick, directed by Peter Glenville, with a set designed by Jo Mielziner, was scorched by Brendan Gill: "It is an exercise in dramatic composition but not a play . . . directed in the most shameless fancy-campy fashion" (104). Novick complained, too, although Glenville was in sympathy with Williams's "Romantic extravagance," he failed to capture the "horror" in the play. Longtime Williams scenographer Jo Mielziner designed sets most critics found too realistic. There was a brief New York production in 1974 in which Laura Zucker directed the Thirteenth Street Repertory Company. This version was considerably altered—the brother and sister remained, but were much younger than before. It still was a study in fear (Funke 27).

Under the title of *The Two-Character Play*, the work was offered in an August 1975 production at the Quaigh Theater in New York, directed by Bill Lentsch. Van Gelder noted, "It is not an entertainment . . . it is a play for players—a darkly passionate salute to the heroism of performers" (16). Robert Stattel played Felice, and Mayellen Flynn took the part of Clare. In his director's notes for a 1976 San Francisco production of *The Two-Character Play*, Jay Leo Colt mused, "It is writing for posterity by the mature artist" (8). In March 1995, the Theatre Marigny presented *The Two-Character Play* in New Orleans with Linda Westbrook and William Heard, who directed as well as acted, though he was judged "notably awkward in his performance" (Dodds).

FILM AND TELEVISION VERSIONS

No film or television version has been made of *Out Cry* or *The Two-Character Play*.

CONCLUDING OVERVIEW

Perhaps best considered as one play, *The Two-Character Play* and *Out Cry* is/are saturated with archetypes bringing the characters' fear and incompleteness hauntingly before and into the reader/viewer. Before the play is over, the astrological walls, the untended garden, the spectral nature of the dark theatre, and the tension between brother and sister all cohere into a claustrophobic blanket that drops over the audience, pushing theatre, audience, and even the cast onto the brink of artistic suffocation. There is no release, no catharsis waiting. Closure is impossible. Felice and Clare are trapped in the play, trapped in their existential angst, fearful of leaving their house, apprehensive of a future synonymous with the void. Their inability to move in any direction leaves the audience frozen also—immersed in frustration, lost in the futility of it all. It is easy to understand why Wilson labeled *The Two-Character Play* "a writer's cry of desolation . . . difficult to grasp and . . . difficult to endure" (30).

The torture the characters suffer is most painfully evident in one of the symbols of Williams's later works—cold isolation. This psychic climate envelops the "existential nightmare" of Williams's *The Chalky White Substance* (Kolin). Clare and Felice are alone; they are cold. The ubiquitous cold gradually renders Clare and Felice incapable of positive action. Every aspect of their lives—physical, emotional, and spiritual—is draped in cold. They try to lose the physical coldness of their environment by losing themselves in their craft, but that is only a temporary palliative. There is no audience to give warmth to their craft; their fellow troupe members have long disappeared, leaving only a note testifying to the siblings' insanity. Wrapped in a paralyzing fear that chills the soul, they cannot leave their physical environment either by walking out the door or by embracing death. Like Hamlet, they fear the undiscovered country beyond their realm far more than they fear their immediate misery, though their stage history is far less pronounced. Their play-within-a-play, unlike Hamlet's, brings no one to a turning point. Since Felice and Clare, light and brightness, are so overtly expressions of Williams's own divided psyche, it is obvious that the fear and coldness they as one individual experience emanates from the suffering depths of Williams's own soul, reflective no doubt of his self-doubts in his stoned decade of the 1960s.

Yet Clare and Felice have each other. Paradoxically, then, the situation is both stark and intimate simultaneously. Like their creator, their motto is *En Avant!*, however Sisyphian it becomes in *The Two-Character Play*. Their inability to kill either themselves or each other is an integral factor for continuance in the psychic/sexual connection that energized Williams's own work.

WORKS CITED

Adler, Thomas P. "The Dialogue of Incompletion: Language in Tennessee Williams's Later Plays." *Quarterly Journal of Speech* 61 (Feb. 1975): 48–58.

Boxill, Roger. *Tennessee Williams*. New York: St. Martin's, 1987.

Clurman, Harold. "Theatre." *Nation* 216 (19 Mar. 1973): 380.

Colt, Jay Leo. "Dancing in Red Hot Shoes." *Tennessee Williams Review* 3.2 (1982): 6–8.

Crandell, George. *Tennessee Williams: A Descriptive Bibliography*. Pittsburgh: U of Pittsburgh P, 1995.

Devlin, Albert J. "The Later Career of Tennessee Williams." *Tennessee Williams Literary Journal* 1.2 (Winter 1989–90): 7–17.

Dodds, Richard. "Late Play by Williams is Given a Hearing." *Times Picayune* 21 Mar. 1997: LAG24 .

Funke, Lewis. "Tennessee's 'Cry.'" *New York Times* 3 Dec. 1972, sec. 2: 1, 27.

Gill, Brendan. *"Out Cry." New Yorker* 10 Mar. 1973: 104.

Gillen, Francis. "Horror Shows, Inside and Outside My Skull: Theater and Life in Tennessee Williams's *Two-Character Play." Forms of the Fantastic: Selected Essays from the Third International Conference on the Fantastic in Literature and Film.* Ed. Jan Hokenson and Howard D. Pearce. New York: Greenwood, 1986. 227–31.

Gunn, Drewey Wayne. *Tennessee Williams: A Bibliography.* 2nd ed. Metuchen, NJ: Scarecrow, 1991.

Kahn, Sy M. "Listening to *Out Cry*: Bird of Paradox in a Gilded Cage." *New Essays on American Drama.* Ed. Gilbert Debusscher and Henry I. Schevy. Amsterdam: Rodopi, 1989. 41–62.

Kauffmann, Stanley. *Persons of the Drama: Theater Criticism and Comment.* New York: Harper and Row, 1976. 168–71.

Kolin, Philip C. "The Existential Nightmare in Tennessee Williams's *The Chalky White Substance." Notes on Contemporary Literature* 23 (Jan. 1993): 8–11.

Leverich, Lyle. *Tom: The Unknown Tennessee Williams.* New York: Crown, 1995.

Londré, Felicia Hardison. *Tennessee Williams.* New York: Ungar, 1979.

"New Williams Play Due to Open July 8." *New York Times* 10 Mar. 1971: L33.

Niesen, George. "The Artist Against Reality in the Plays of Tennessee Williams." *Tennessee Williams: A Tribute.* Ed. Jac Tharpe. Jackson: UP of Mississippi, 1977. 463–93.

Novick, Julius. *"Out Cry (Two-Character Play)* (1973)." *Village Voice* 8 Mar. 1973: 58.

O'Connor, Jacqueline. *Dramatizing Dementia: Madness in the Plays of Tennessee Williams.* Bowling Green, OH: Bowling Green State U Popular P, 1997.

Pagan, Nicholas O. "Tennessee Williams' Out Cry in the *Two-Character Play." Notes on Mississippi Writers* 24.2 (1992): 67–79.

Parker, R. B. "The Circle Closed: A Psychological Reading of *The Glass Menagerie* and *The Two-Character Play." Modern Drama* 28.4 (1985): 517–34.

Robinson, Marc. *The Other American Drama.* Baltimore: Johns Hopkins UP, 1994.

Stamper, Rexford. *"The Two-Character Play*: Psychic Individuation." *Tennessee Williams: A Tribute.* Ed. Jac Tharpe. Jackson: UP of Mississippi, 1977. 354–61.

Van Gelder, Lawrence. "Stage: Williams's '2 Character Play.'" *New York Times* 22 Aug. 1975: 16.

Williams, Tennessee. *Memoirs.* Garden City, NY: Doubleday, 1975.

———. *Out Cry.* New York: New Directions, 1973.

———. *The Two-Character Play.* New York: New Directions, 1969.

"Williams Drama Baffles Critics." *New York Times* 13 Dec. 1967: 54.

Wilson, Edwin. "A Writer's Cry of Desolation." *Wall Street Journal* 6 Mar. 1973: 30.

Small Craft Warnings, Vieux Carré, and A Lovely Sunday for Creve Coeur

MARK W. ROCHA

BIOGRAPHICAL CONTEXT

The second volume of Leverich's biography provides biographical commentary on *Small Craft Warnings* (1972), *Vieux Carré* (1978), and *A Lovely Sunday for Creve Coeur* (1979). Leverich knew Williams well and was interested in his post-*Iguana* work, producing *The Two-Character Play* in San Francisco in 1976. Leverich's concise assessment of Williams and his work during the 1970s is a helpful starting point: "Trying to move from what he saw as his 'operas' to his 'chamber pieces,' Tom, the poet, was attempting to divorce himself from Tennessee, the playwright. And so he wrote plays that clearly reflected his own tensions and those of the times he was living" (*Tom* xxiii). Other biographies of Williams cursorily dismiss these plays, which too often have been viewed as the failures of Williams's wilderness years after his reputation had suffered and he had begun to seem a "period piece" to many critics and scholars (Gunn xi), though Griffin reminds us that "the only popular success that Williams enjoyed after *Iguana* was *Small Craft Warnings*" (154). See also Kakutani's interview.

It is crucial not to see these three plays of the 1970s as forming a "period" in either the life or work of Williams. As Free insists, "to allegorize Doc in *Small Craft Warnings* [the role Williams himself took in the 1975 production] . . . as a description of Williams's sense of his own alienation from contemporary theater [is] . . . too easy to have much value" (816). *Small Craft Warnings*, *Vieux Carré*, and *A Lovely Sunday for Creve Coeur* are as different from each other as they are alike in being all creations of the time after the playwright's "lost decade" of the 1960s that brought the death of longtime partner Frank Merlo and a creative dry spell owing to drug abuse. These three plays can, however, be connected to a time in Williams's career that can be termed "post": post-Broadway (the end of serious drama on Broadway) and post-Stonewall (the beginning of the gay liberation movement marked by riots in Greenwich Village, June 1969).

Small Craft Warnings is especially significant since it represents a coming out in several senses. The 1972 production of *Small Craft Warnings*, which opened off-Broadway at the New Theatre, was the occasion of Williams's first and only professional appearance upon the stage in the role of Doc. *Small Craft Warnings*'s importance may ultimately be as an emblem of Williams's almost ferocious desire to put himself back on public display and to announce himself as a new man and a new artist, going so far as holding post-performance chats with the audience (Leavitt 154). Such an appearance was a plaintive attempt by Williams to re-possess his own personality from the media and speak directly with his audience. Robinson concludes, "A gallant move, surely, a testimony to his commitment to art, but also pathetic, one exposure too many" (57). Williams was exploiting his own media-created celebrity to sell tickets.

Williams repeatedly observed that a playwright's persona was inevitably the "organic" source of a play (*Small Craft Warnings* 5). Perhaps the most organic (and biographical) aspect of *Small Craft Warnings* is that it is the first Williams play to refer explicitly to a character as "gay." Whether one sides with John Clum, who sees Williams's treatment of homosexuality as stereotypical and homophobic (162), or with David Savran, who argues that Williams effectively destabilizes mid-century notions of masculinity and femininity (80), the essential biographical fact is that Williams wrote these three late plays out of the closet.

The last years of Williams's life may be characterized as an experiment to reinvent himself as a work-in-progress against the calcified notions of a "Williams play" and Williams himself. Bigsby suggests that the late work, while flawed, shows signs of a recovery and a return from exile: "His death . . . denied us the opportunity of seeing Williams wrestle with his own demons [like O'Neill]" (124). In other words, it might be possible to avoid reading Williams's last plays as a decline. Gussow employed the metaphor of the "cameo" for Williams's last plays, enabling us to view them as an image of Williams's profile.

BIBLIOGRAPHIC HISTORY

Crandell's 1995 bibliography offers the essential bibliographic information on editions and printings of these three plays. *Small Craft Warnings*, begun as the short story "Confessional," was first published as a play in 1969 in *Dragon Country* and was then dramatized and produced as a play of the same title in Bar Harbor, Maine, in July 1971. Williams expanded it into *Small Craft Warnings*, which was then published by New Directions in 1972. The appendix to this first edition, entitled *Small Craft Warnings*: Genesis and Evolution," addresses the evolution of the manuscript of this play. According to a letter to Williams' agent Bill

Barnes on 10 May 1972, the revisions included extensive changes to the beginning of the play and the building up of the character of Doc, the role Williams would soon play on stage (79–81).

Vieux Carré began as the early one-act "The Lady of Larkspur Lotion," first published in *The Best One-Act Plays of 1941* and later produced in Paris in July 1949, and uses the same setting and landlady as in the short story "The Angel of the Alcove," the play's source. The first act of the first unpublished version of *Vieux Carré* was titled "The Angel in the Alcove," and the second act was entitled "I Never Get Dressed until after Dark on Sundays." When the play closed after 5 performances in New York, Williams made further revisions for a production in England in 1978, the text of which was published by New Directions in 1979.

The screenplay from which *Creve Coeur*, the original title of the play, was adapted—*All Gaul Is Divided*—was written sometime in the late 1950s but laid aside until Williams returned to it around 1975 or 1976 in San Francisco. In a 1979 interview Williams remarked, "It was a long one-act [three years ago]. Maybe it should have remained that way" (quoted in Bilowit 308).

MAJOR CRITICAL APPROACHES

Themes

Almost all of the criticism of Williams's post-*Iguana* plays has compared these later works to the earlier ones, and, regrettably, has summarily dismissed them as inferior, a "collapse" (Falk 153). Few studies of any length extensively treat *Small Craft Warnings*, *Vieux Carré*, and *Creve Coeur*. In their brief surveys of the plays, Bigsby and Londré (*Tennessee Williams*) note how the plays rehearse the familiar Williams problem of how one strives for human connection despite inhumane circumstances. Free isolates two key themes: an old Williams one, "dulling repetition" (818), and a "new note of boredom and weariness with life" (819). Most reviewers have also unfavorably noted the plays' more explicit, indeed, scatological, treatment of sexuality, and especially homosexuality. Critics unanimously panned Williams's "obsession with social degeneracy" (Smith F3).

On the other hand, Savran regards the later plays as the product of "a writer who called himself a revolutionary and meant it, a playwright who produced a new and radical theater that challenged and undermined the Cold World order" (ix). While Savran does not see these late plays as consistently brilliant, he does counter the "policing" of the Williams *oeuvre* that tends to close off discussion at *Night of the Iguana*: "Vividly, the post-*Iguana* plays document both Williams's keen response to the social and political crises of a tumultuous era and his restless experimentation, his almost systematic attempt to push style, dramatic form, and language to their limits" (132).

Characters

In *Small Craft Warnings*, *Vieux Carré*, and *Creve Coeur*, an assortment of characters lead lives of quiet desperation that result from "the compromises forced on the individual by a life which refuses to satisfy a desperate longing for human contact, or to fulfill the aspirations of those who long for a dream but exist in harsh reality" (Bigsby 122). For MacNicholas, the characters in *Small Craft Warnings* form a family, yet "their family is not so much a death trap as the other families in the Williams canon . . . but [a family] supported by the kindness of strangers [and] portrayed with extraordinary sympathy" (603). Chief among the characters in *Small Craft Warnings* are the two women Leona Dawson and Violet. Of Leona, a beautician who pays her own way, Williams claimed that she was his "first wholly triumphant character" (quoted in Londré, *Tennessee Williams* 182). According to Boxill, "Leona's courageous willingness to endure . . . [allies] her with Hannah Jelkes as an inversion of the defeated wanderer" (156). Hall honors Leona for her "maternal life force" (684). Leona clashes directly with her "double," the weary and broken Violet, who is described as "if she is a fetus trying to leave the womb" (Hall 684). As the play ends, both women realize their immediate desires, yet they will remain as small craft to be continually buffeted by conditions. Doc is the jaundiced doctor who has lost his medical license and continues to practice in the shadows of trailer parks. Hewes observes that Doc is "haunted" by medicine's diminishing the "mystery" of "birth and death."

The rest of the denizens of Monk's bar are familiar types of the American "saloon play." The exception is the explicitly gay character Quentin, a tired writer of blue movies, who befriends Bobby, a young drifter from Iowa. This is the first Williams play to include a clearly announced homosexual character (Jones). Of interest, too, is an important offstage character, an oft-used device in these late plays. Leona is haunted by her young gay brother who died of pernicious anemia (*Small Craft Warnings* 32–33).

Vieux Carré and *Creve Coeur* differ from *Small Craft Warnings* in that the former are memory plays that, like *Menagerie* from the opposite end of Williams's career, are both set in the late 1930s. The focus of *Vieux Carré* is the deliberately allegorical character of the Writer—Williams himself—who discovers, if not accepts, his homosexuality and also discovers that his principal subject is loneliness. For Boxill, he is the characteristic Williams wanderer (157–58). The other tenants of the boarding house include Nightingale, a gay artist dying of tuberculosis, and Jane, a woman from New York dying of loneliness, whom Boxill labels a "faded belle" who is "a Northern variant of the fallen Southern gentlewoman" (158). The conventional Williams "Kowalski" type is also present in the person of Tye, a barker at a strip joint who overpowers and controls Jane with his sexuality. In his overt homophobia, Tye bears considerable resemblance to the character of Bill in *Small Craft Warnings* who lives off of Leona. Comparing the characters of *Vieux Carré* with those of *Summer and Smoke*, Robinson concludes that the former play "render[s] this contrast between sex and death so starkly that the characters seem caught in nothing more mysterious than a diagram" (54).

In *Creve Coeur*, Williams situates his characters in an apartment house in St. Louis where one encounters Dorothea, a schoolteacher whose hopes of marrying well have been betrayed by the offstage male character Ralph Ellis, who seduced her while pretending to marry another. Dorothea personifies what happens to a dream deferred. Boxill links her with Blanche DuBois and Alma Winemiller in being haunted by an idealized sexual partner from the past while being defeated by a current and questionable lover (159). The other women characters—Bodey the stolid German and Helena, an art-history teacher at the school where Dorothea teaches civics—represent opposite poles in a triangulated relationship in which both compete for possession of Dorothea.

Symbols

All three of these plays offer symbolic titles and locations. *Small Craft Warnings*, referring to weather advisories, is appropriate for Doc, who runs a "refuge" for damaged "human vessels" (*Small Craft* 15). Griffin also notes that the title refers "symbolically to the collection of drifters and misfits" who gather at Monk's bar (9). *Vieux Carré*, the old French Quarter where Williams's boardinghouse at 722 Toulouse Street was located, symbolically resonates as a shadowy and intoxicating world inhabited by artists and others who are "dispossessed and misbegotten" (Leverich, *Tom* 278). In *A Lovely Sunday for Creve Coeur*, Bodey tries to persuade Dorothea to join her and Buddy for a picnic at Creve Coeur Lake in St. Louis, a city amusement park frequented by the working class. Creve Coeur ("broken heart") functions as a floating signifier throughout the play, since to Bodey it is heaven, yet for Dorothea it is at first a trap to avoid and finally an inevitable (and painful) destination.

These three plays are profuse with other symbols, some of which are Williams's trademarks and some of which are new, as the critics have pointed out. In *Small Craft Warnings* and *Creve Coeur*, flowers are identifying symbols for women characters. Violet in *Small Craft Warnings* is not only allegorically named but is compared by Leona to a water lily floating temporarily on the surface. Bodey in *Creve Coeur* wears a tiger lily to cover her hearing aid, an act that suggests how much identity is a matter of self-conscious theatrical presentation. Bodey's handicap also symbolizes Williams's prevalent use of handicap or disease to paint the world as a ward of narcotized patients. Along the same lines, Dorothea suffers from depression and anxiety that require frequent doses of mebaral. In *Vieux Carré*, Jane is suffering from a "blood thing" that is eased by marijuana, Nightingale is dying of tuberculosis that he denies, and the Writer has a cataract he cannot afford to treat.

Stairs and the phallus also function as major symbols in these plays. The stairs in these three plays symbolize obstacles and separations in a dense vertical civilization. *Small Craft Warnings* ends with Monk optimistically climbing the stairs to join Violet. In *Vieux Carré*, the stairs virtually become a character upon which everyone comments as they climb. In *Creve Coeur*, the stairs take on the role of an offstage character as the upstairs neighbor Mrs. Gluck's only wish is not to be put out of Bodey's apartment and made to "go up" alone. Williams deliberately presents the male phallus itself as a means of highlighting and then decentering masculine sexual identity and power in these late works. Both Bill McCorkle in *Small Craft Warnings* and Tye McCool in *Vieux Carré* explicitly refer to their own erections as the source of their identity and power while simultaneously Leona and Jane deconstruct the phallus by denying these men. Symbolically, masculinity is not so much an overbearing source as it is a problematized space for human sexuality.

Plot

Creve Coeur, the most conventionally plotted of the three plays, shows the conflict between Bodey and Helena for possession of Dorothea. Helena is described as a "predatory bird," and anyone would cheer her comeuppance at the hands of Bodey. But at the same time one is unable to cheer Bodey's victory since the picnic at Creve Coeur signifies differently to Dorothea. In *Small Craft Warnings*, the action is not linear but shifts from character to character as they make their entrances and exits. The play is loosely framed by Leona's coming to the bar and then departing to set out north to make a new life. Upon this thread are strung beads of the subplots: Violet's conflict with Leona over Bill and Monk's eventual rescue of Violet for just one night; Doc's disastrous house call to deliver a baby that resulted in a stillbirth and the death of the mother; Quentin's failed attempt to keep his young pickup, Bobby, with him. When Monk permits Violet to stay the night at the play's end, it will be but a momentary stay against the endemic loneliness and debilitation.

Since *Vieux Carré* is a "memory play," the action is framed within the narration to the audience of the twenty-eight-year-old Writer. The play is about a young man's leap into his future upon discovering himself as an artist and as a gay man. The ultimate discovery for the Writer as witness is the understanding of his position as essentially paradoxical, both within the experience as an earnest participant and at the same time standing outside it as a "shameless spy."

MAJOR PROBLEMS *SMALL CRAFT WARNINGS, VIEUX CARRÉ,* AND *A LOVELY SUNDAY FOR CREVE COEUR* POSE FOR CRITICS

The major problem these plays pose for critics concerns their relationship as obviously "inferior" work when compared to Williams's great earlier successes. Much critical commentary can be succinctly stated as follows: these plays offer the usual Williams themes and characters without the usual Williams poetry.

Dorff, for example, demonstrates that useful readings of these three plays and others have been made virtually impossible by the existence of what the critical establishment holds in mind as a "Williams play," a construction Williams himself helped to create. Free, however, maintains that "*Small Craft Warnings* like *Out Cry* are failures of dramatizations rather than failures of theme. . . . Their problem is not that they are autobiographical or that they . . . repeat Williams's other work but that they are inadequate expressions of whatever is in the playwright's imagination" (817).

Williams's death has not made successes of *Small Craft Warnings*, *Vieux Carré*, and *A Lovely Sunday for Creve Coeur*, nor are they ever likely to be. But there is also little doubt that the three plays have risen in the general estimation of critics and directors alike as these individuals lurch their way past Williams's biography and toward the plays themselves. One may view this as fitting poetic justice that compensates for the often merciless treatment Williams received for his late work. A case in point was the Russian poet Yevgeny Yevtushenko, who remarked to Williams that *Small Craft Warnings* contained only 30 percent of his talent. Williams replied coolly that he was happy to hear he still possessed so much of his creativity (Stearns 1D).

A prerequisite for reappraisal of Williams's late work, therefore, must be a willingness to discard the narrative model of achievement and decline out of which Williams's biography has been fashioned. This model of reading Williams's last plays has driven some critics to anger at Williams for failing them; for example, in reviewing the first production of *Small Craft Warnings*, Gottfried declared, "It is one more stumble in the tragic collapse of one of the finest playwrights in theater history" (273).

CHIEF PRODUCTIONS

The production histories of *Small Craft Warnings*, *Vieux Carré*, and *A Lovely Sunday for Creve Coeur* entail a premiere encountering "mixed" reviews followed by a long a period of quiescence now coming to an end thanks to adventurous and welcoming repertory productions around the world. *Small Craft Warnings* opened on 2 April 1972 at the Truck and Warehouse Theater in New York (now the New York Theater Workshop), directed by Richard Altman. The *New York Daily News* termed it a "pretty sorry play" (Watt), a characteristic response that prompted Williams to throw himself into efforts to rewrite and restage the play elsewhere. Though praising the "quixotic figure" of the young homosexual Williams, Hewes concluded that *Small Craft Warnings* was "less a play than it is a series of personal self-revelations offered by seven of the play's nine characters" (22). On 6 June 1972, the production moved to the New Theater in New York. Running a total of 200 performances, *Small Craft Warnings* was a commercial if not critical success. A review of a 1984 production of *Small Craft Warnings* in Lindenhurst, Long Island, a year after Williams's death, called it "embarrassing and tedious" (Frank 15); more recent productions seem to have encountered more varying responses, with some appreciation. A 1994 production at the Library Theatre in Manchester, England, received praise for Leona's "aching poignancy" and identified the play as an "oratorio" that "displays [Williams's] distinctive verbal excitement" ("A Rarely Performed Play" 23). Interestingly, though, another review of the same production was titled "Williams at His Worst" (Bassett). Two years later in Chicago, the 1996 production at the Steppenwolf Theater "received a fascinating full-force production" that was "highly recommended" (Weiss 23), perhaps foreshadowing promise.

The Broadway opening of *Vieux Carré* at the St. James Theatre on 11 May 1977 met with ruinous notices, and the play closed after only 5 performances. Arthur Allan Seidelman directed, and the cast included Sylvia Sidney in the role of the boardinghouse landlady, Mrs. Wire. The following year the play was turned over to the director Keith Hack, who presented it at the Playhouse Theatre in Nottingham on 16 May 1978 and then at the Piccadilly Theatre in London on 9 August 1978. *Vieux Carré* received no greater approbation in England than in the United States. The WPA Theater in New York staged a production during April 1984. In 1995 the Nottingham Theatre in England revived this play that it had first presented seventeen years earlier, which caused Kate Bassett of the *Times* (London) to label it as "distinctly weird," a comment that one might take as both praise and pan. Reviewing the 1997 production of *Vieux Carré* at the New Heights Theater in Houston, Evans claimed that the play was Williams at his best and saw it as "the strongest and most confident of his later plays," which was "distinguished by poetic dialogue and deep understanding of the human heart." This particular production also experimented with the "useful device" of presenting Writer as two characters, one middle-aged man who spoke the narration and one young man who acted out the scenes from the past.

Creve Coeur premiered on 1 June 1978 at the Spoleto Festival in Charleston, South Carolina, in a production at the Dock Street Theater directed by Keith Hack. The first two productions of *A Lovely Sunday for Creve Coeur* starred Shirley Knight in the role of Dorothea. (As an interesting aside, Williams once said that Maureen Stapleton read for the part of Bodey and implied that she backed out because Knight's role had all the "goodies" [Bilowit 315].) The play and Knight's performance were praised as a highlight of the festival, and the production was transferred to New York the following winter, opening at the Hudson Guild Theater on 17 January 1979, again with Knight starring and Hack directing. The response from the New York critics was respectful though annoyed, and the play closed after 36 performances. Identifying Williams's theme through his characters, Weales observed, "Both Bodey's blowzy cheerfulness and Helena's thin-lipped bitchiness (she has most of the good lines) are forms of desperation" (147). Except for a three-week stint in London in 1986 (Gunn 74) and a 1987 performance in Malvern, Pennsylvania (Londré, "Tennessee Williams" 504–05), *Creve Coeur* has received little attention despite Williams's assertion (or perhaps because of it) that the play is "almost a different genre" (Bilowit 316).

FILM AND TELEVISION VERSIONS

There have been to date no films of these three plays.

CONCLUDING OVERVIEW

As Savran and Dorff point out, these plays exhibit a conscious theatricalism, vital to Williams's radical poetics. By steadfastly refusing to compare Williams to himself, readers can open their eyes to how an unknown and unknowable Williams is signifying upon himself and his earlier work, to borrow Henry Louis Gates's term. In these three late plays, Williams becomes the trickster who comments upon, and even parodies, his earlier plays. His signifying is most clearly reflected in two standard character types that he relied upon previously and that appear again in these three late plays: the southern belle waiting upon the gentleman caller, like Dorothea in *Creve Coeur*, and the brute macho, like Tye McCool in *Vieux Carré*. When the gentleman caller fails to arrive for Dorothea and Helena tries to puncture her pathetic hope as her "Southern belle complex," Amanda in *Menagerie* at once comes to mind. Similarly, when in *Vieux Carré* Tye rapes Jane shortly after her own gentleman caller fails to arrive, shades of Stanley Kowalski appear.

But these are character comparisons with a difference, especially since in these two instances Williams is signifying upon two characters so indelible they have achieved iconic status in the American imagination. Amanda and Stanley are "called out" by Williams, to use the language of signifying, in the personas of Dorothea and Tye. This parodic act honors the original while it tears it down, clearing a space from and for which a new Williams could emerge and create. The late plays should be seen as a deliberate effort by Williams to move himself and the "Williams play" out of the way in order to continue to write. In personal terms this was a radical act, a dangerous venture for a playwright of Williams's stature. But it is precisely Williams's willingness to take the risk that makes these late plays politically radical by calling into question the "hegemonic notions of gender, sexuality and political praxis that have prevailed in the United States since World War II" (Savran x).

Seeing the late plays in this way deepens one's understanding of the ubiquitous and conscious theatricality at work in them. *Small Craft Warnings*, *Vieux Carré*, and *A Lovely Sunday for Creve Coeur* are at their cores metadramas, plays whose essential subject is the making of plays and that are therefore marked by a conscious self-referentiality. The most overt example of such self-referentiality, of course, is Writer in *Vieux Carré*, who at one point is typing a play and halts suddenly when he is displeased at what he has written, commenting, "*Exposition! Shit!*" (69). Bodey's preparation of the picnic in *Creve Coeur* and Leona's orchestration of her departure in *Small Craft Warnings* are represented in decidedly theatrical terms to underscore how these characters are striving to "direct" their own plays. At one point in *Creve Coeur*, Bodey criticizes Dorothea for the covert way she carries on with Ralph Ellis, going so far as to say, "I never trusted pretending." It is at this point that Dorothea seizes upon the tiger lily that hides Bodey's hearing aid, exposing Bodey as a pretender herself. This metadramatic moment effectively implicates everyone as an actor. Bodey's comment that she never trusted pretending might serve well as the thematic statement of these late plays as well as Williams's own self-fashioned epitaph. The late plays offer the opportunity to experience the paradox that while art is a "lie" not to be trusted, it is all we ever have to trust.

WORKS CITED

Barnes, Clive. "*Vieux Carré* by Williams Is Haunting." *New York Times* 12 May 1977: C22. Rpt. in *New York Theatre Critics' Reviews* 38 (1977): 244.

Bassett, Kate. "A Revival of Distinctly Weird Play by Tennessee Williams." *London Times* 23 May 1995.

———. "Williams at His Worst." *London Times* 29 Sept. 1994

Bigsby, C. W. E. *A Critical Introduction to Twentieth-Century American Drama. Williams, Miller, Albee.* Vol. 2. Cambridge: Cambridge UP, 1984.

Bilowit, Ira J. "Roundtable: Tennessee Williams, Craig Anderson, and T. E. Kalem Talk about *Creve Coeur*." *Conversations with Tennessee Williams.* Ed. Albert J. Devlin. Jackson: UP of Mississippi, 1986. 308–17.

Boxill, Roger. *Tennessee Williams.* New York: St. Martin's, 1987.

Clum, John. *Acting Gay: Male Homosexuality in Modern Drama.* New York: Columbia, 1992.

Cohn, Ruby. "Late Tennessee Williams." *Modern Drama* 27 (Sept. 1984): 336–44.

Crandell, George W. *Tennessee Williams: A Descriptive Bibliography.* Pittsburgh: U of Pittsburgh P, 1995.

Devlin, Albert J., ed. *Conversations with Tennessee Williams.* Jackson: UP of Mississippi, 1986.

Dorff, Linda. "Disfigured Stages: The Late Plays of Tennessee Williams, 1958–1983." Diss. New York U, 1997.

Evans, Everett. "*Vieux Carré* Is Tennessee Williams at His Best." *Houston Chronicle* 15 Mar. 1997.

Falk, Signi Lenea. *Tennessee Williams.* 2nd ed. Boston: Twayne, 1978.

Frank, Leah D. "Small Craft Warnings Becalmed." *New York Times* 29 Jan. 1984, II-LI: 15.

Free, William S. "Williams in the Seventies: Directions and Discontents." *Tennessee Williams: A Tribute.* Ed. Jac Tharpe. Jackson: UP of Mississippi, 1977. 815–28.

Gales, Henry Louis. *The Signifying Monkey: A Theory of Afro-American Literary Criticism.* New York: Oxford UP, 1989.

Gottfried, Martin. "Small Craft Warnings." *Women's Wear Daily* 4 Apr. 1972. Rpt. in *New York Theatre Critics' Reviews* 33 (1972): 273.

Griffin, Alice. *Understanding Tennessee Williams.* Columbia: U of South Carolina P, 1995.

Gunn, Drewey Wayne. *Tennessee Williams: A Bibliography.* 2nd ed. Metuchen, NJ: Scarecrow, 1991.

Gussow, Mel. "*Vieux Carré* by Tennessee Williams Is Revisited." *New York Times* 5 Apr. 1983, sec. 3: 13.

Hall, Joan Wylie. "The Stork and the Reaper, the Madonna and the Stud: Procreation and Mothering in Tennessee Williams's Plays." *Mississippi Quarterly* 48 (Fall 1995): 677–700.

Hewes, Henry. "The Deathday Party." *Saturday Review* 22 Apr. 1972: 22–24.

Jones, Robert Emmet. "Sexual Roles in the Works of Tennessee Williams." *Tennessee Williams: A Tribute*. Ed. Jac Tharpe. Jackson: UP of Mississippi, 1977. 545–57.

Kakutani, Michiko. "Tennessee Williams: 'I Keep Writing, Sometimes I Am Pleased.' " *New York Times* 13 Aug. 1981: C17.

Leavitt, Richard F., ed. *The World of Tennessee Williams*. New York: Putnam's, 1978.

Leverich, Lyle. *Tenn: The Timeless World of Tennessee Williams*. Vol. 2. (forthcoming).

———. *Tom: The Unknown Tennessee Williams*. New York: Crown, 1995.

Londré, Felicia Hardison. *Tennessee Williams*. New York: Ungar, 1979.

———. "Tennessee Williams." *American Playwrights since 1945: A Guide to Scholarship, Criticism, and Performance*. Ed. Philip C. Kolin. Westport, CT: Greenwood, 1989. 488–517.

MacNicholas, John. "Williams' Power of the Keys." *Tennessee Williams: A Tribute*. Ed. Jac Tharpe. Jackson: UP of Mississippi, 1977. 581–605.

"A Rarely Performed Play by Tennessee Williams." *Independent* [London], 29 Sept. 1994, "Arts": 23.

Robinson, Marc. *The Other American Drama*. Cambridge: Cambridge UP, 1994.

Savran, David. *Communists, Cowboys, and Queers: The Politics of Masculinity in the Work of Arthur Miller and Tennessee Williams*. Minneapolis: U of Minnesota P, 1992.

Smith, Marc Chalon. "*Small Craft Warnings*: Characters Set Adrift." *Los Angeles Times* 19 Mar. 1991: F3.

Spoto, Donald. *The Kindness of Strangers: The Life of Tennessee Williams*. Boston: Little, Brown, 1985.

Stearns, David Patrick. "Tennessee Williams' True Legacy Revealed: Works Headed to Stage, Print." *USA Today* 4 Sept. 1996, "Life": 1D.

Watt, Douglass. "New Play by Williams Opens." *New York Daily News* 3 Apr. 1972. Rpt. in *New York Theatre Critics' Reviews* 38 (1972): 271.

Weales, Gerald. "*A Lovely Sunday for Creve Coeur*." *Commonweal* 106 (16 Mar. 1979): 146–47.

Weiss, Hedy. "*Small Craft Warnings*." *Chicago Sun-Times* 29 Dec. 1996, "Year in Review": 23.

Williams, Tennessee. *All Gaul Is Divided* (screenplay). *Stopped Rocking and Other Screenplays*. New York: New Directions, 1984.

———. "The Angel in the Alcove" (short story). *One Arm and Other Stories*. New York: New Directions, 1948. 135–49.

———. *Dragon Country*. New York: New Directions, 1969.

———. *A Lovely Sunday for Creve Coeur*. New York: New Directions, 1980.

———. *Small Craft Warnings*. New York: New Directions, 1972.

———. *Vieux Carré*. New York: New Directions, 1979.

The Red Devil Battery Sign

COLBY H. KULLMAN

BIOGRAPHICAL CONTEXT

Interviewed during the filming of rehearsals for *The Red Devil Battery Sign*'s premiere in Boston, Anthony Quinn said that Tennessee Williams "has given a summation of his life in this play" (Hayman 224). Signs of the times—allusions to the assassination of John F. Kennedy and the Vietnam War; young people rebelling, National Guard troops "maintaining order," and CIA/FBI "crewcuts" ever watching; the corporate giants of the world and their operatives dominating America—are omnipresent throughout *Red Devil*. Adler calls attention to Williams's personal opposition to the "atrocity" of Vietnam in 1971 when he "actually spoke at an anti-war rally in New York's Cathedral of St. John the Divine" (*American Drama* 179). Williams himself explained to Lothar Schmidt-Mühlisch that his own personal crisis surfaced in the play: "It was the contradiction between two sides of my nature: between gentleness and violence, between tenderness and harshness" (297). According to Williams, at the center of *Red Devil* is "the relationship of people to each other, the need to escape from loneliness . . . [in] its social and political dimensions" (298).

Sometimes the allusions are even more specific. Discussing the 1996 WPA Theater production of *Red Devil*, Dan Isaac points out that according to Williams, Woman Downtown was modeled after Martha Mitchell, sequestered in a downtown Washington hotel during the Watergate hearings for fear that she was getting ready to "spill the beans" (Isaac 6). Williams aptly recalled with interviewer Cecil Brown that Dorothy Kilgallen "died very mysteriously" (252) before her interview with Jack Ruby was published. Williams's personal neuroses, his depression, his paranoia, and his self-destruction are all present in the fibre and fabric of *Red Devil*.

Describing his play as "a passionate love story which happens to coincide with the assassination of John F. Kennedy," Williams explained that *Red Devil* is set in Dallas and "also deals with the progression of moral decay in today's society" ("New Williams Play" L40). In an interview with Charles Raus, Williams further observed that all of his plays have a social conscience, and that *The Red Devil Battery Sign* deals with "the moral decay of America, which really began with the Korean War." Proclaiming that Americans were "the death merchants of the world," he asserted that America went to Vietnam "so two hundred billion dollars worth of equipment could be destroyed" and repurchased from arms dealers (Raus 292). Considering himself a political writer, Williams saw the flow of history toward social upheaval, a theme vividly underscored in *Red Devil* and considered in critical essays by Adler ("Culture" 649–65) and Kolin (140–62).

BIBLIOGRAPHIC HISTORY

Williams's inspiration for *The Red Devil Battery Sign* orginated with a not-so-short story he began in 1946, finished in 1965, and published in 1966 called "The Knightly Quest." Instead of the military-industrial complex and its operatives seeking bureaucratic power control over the world, in "The Knightly Quest" Williams presents "the Center" ("them") and "the Project" (a "mysterious weapon of destruction"). Williams creates plainclothes detectives called "Pee Cees" instead of *The Red Devil Battery Sign*'s crewcuts and the "Laughing Boy Drive-In" with its "neon portrait" in place of the corporation's grinning devil sign. Meanwhile, just below the euphemistically structured corporate utopia, worlds ripe with social unrest and revolution flame into violence, rape, and murder.

As with many of his plays, Tennessee Williams revised and rewrote *Red Devil*. After a disastrous premiere at Boston's Shubert Theatre in 1975, he reworked it for the 1976 production at Vienna's English Theatre and the 1977 Roundhouse revival in London. By the time *Red Devil* arrived at the Vancouver Playhouse in 1980, it had been trimmed by at least another 20 percent. On 14 October 1980, Williams wrote to Maria St. Just that director, Roger Hodgman, was most helpful and that *Red Devil* was "now as tight as a fist, cut to eighty pages," far less cumbersome than it had been when the play was performed in England (*Five O'clock Angel* 381–82). Crandell documents the two most readily available editions of *Red Devil* (377–79, 409).

CRITICAL APPROACHES

Themes

The world of *The Red Devil Battery Sign* is well known to Tennessee Williams's audiences, for it is another broken world where money talks, where joy lies slain and hopes are never fulfilled, where civilization has lost its battle with barbarism. King says to his daughter, who has returned home pregnant, unmarried, and looking like a tramp, "Things have slipped from control! Money, Battery Money!" Woman Downtown knows that money talks. Only when civilization disintegrates and savagery rules does money give up its power. Adler observes that in *Red Devil* Williams is dealing with "not just destruction of art or illusion, . . . but of Western culture and civilization itself" (*American Drama* 178).

Amidst a catch-22, Big Brother, Red Devil Battery atmosphere of culprits as victims and victims as culprits, the redemptive power of love makes a brief appearance. As Adler explains, here again is "the need for the human heart to respond with compassion to the outcry of the other" (179). Adler further asserts that *Red Devil* deals with two relationships, "a central one between King del Ray and the Woman Downtown and a quite subsidiary but simultaneous one" involving King's daughter, La Niña, and McCabe, in which "sexuality is humanizing, life restoring, and regenerative, in short, an 'act of God' " (178). King del Ray, Woman Downtown, Perla, La Niña, and McCabe—each one needs something human to enter into his or her life, but the redemptive powers of love prove fleeting and powerless.

Love versus destruction, order versus chaos, culprits versus victims, gentleness versus violence, tenderness versus harshness, humans versus robots, illusion versus reality, the material versus the spiritual, death versus life—the ironic dualities of existence found throughout the world of Williams explode onto the landscape of *Red Devil* bureaucratic power control, a world of catch-22 rationality and irrationality, a world where an omnipotent "Big Brother" Red Devil sneers at the bestial sounds of the revolution. Kullman explores "Big Daddyism" in the realistic-surrealistic atmosphere of *Red Devil* and underscores Woman Downtown's knowledge that "corporate power structures protect their secret investments by aiding and abetting sympathetically corrupt regimes" who practice "genocide for profits undeclared" (673–74).

In *Red Devil*, Williams's sense of decline and fall, loss and decay, and disorder and chaos turn into an ever-darkening landscape of cosmic evil, a vision of Dante's Inferno, complete with fiery explosions, hellhounds, and grinning red devils. Kahn describes the play as "a grim parable of the contemporary world divided into two sets of menacing images: the slick power conspiracies, with the red devil sign as cosmic symbol of hex and hell, and the alternate savagery of fugitive street gangs shaped into a menacing counterforce" (369). Placing Williams among "infernalists and forgers of modern myth," Beate Hein Bennett sets *Red Devil* in the tradition of Dante's Inferno, "an immense prison where individual souls were subjected to systematized . . . torment," an "irreversible rigidification of evil and suffering" (437).

In light of the WPA Theater's 1996 production of *The Red Devil Battery Sign*, Grosch, who focuses on the theme of memory, claims that Elizabeth Ashley's Woman Downtown is another of Williams's "Sisters on the Brink," a haunted, irrational woman bedeviled by "the memory of industry's betrayal of humanity in its search for profits." Possessing the knowledge of a cover-up and unable to do anything about it, "words escape her" and "ideas slip from her grasp" as she becomes increasingly unhinged, no longer able to remember the meaning of civilization (120–21).

Choosing to call *The Red Devil Battery Sign* a "mytho-political" play, Schlatter connects Williams's grotesque Dallas dystopia with "the wasted landscapes of Sam Shepard, whose plays evoke a mythical America in which the primal forces of the nation's psyche—love, sex, death, dreams, and power—rise up and take exotic or grotesque human shape" (94). As the action of the play moves "inexorably from the plain of realism toward a deepening condition of collective dementia and expressionistic nightmare" (94), Williams evokes a "Kafkaesque political present" (99). Rather than being "a unified dramaturgical whole," *The Red Devil Battery Sign* is for Schlatter "a complex network of motifs woven around" the play's central idea of "the political worth of a free, independent, public voice" (101).

Characters

Woman Downtown

By birth, education, and marriage, Woman Downtown is a privileged member of society who has been watched and controlled throughout her life. Her guardians have been many: the black bead–clinking guardian tutor of her childhood, the "teachers" of the Institute for Rebirth (a private school for retarded children), the guards behind the estate walls of her husband's hacienda, the electroshock therapists of Paradise Meadows Nursing Home, and now the crewcuts and the manager of the Yellow Rose Hotel. No matter that she is the great southern statesman's daughter or the wife of the president of the Red Devil Battery Corporation, for she is also the imprisoned victim of "the evil of super-organizational power" (Kahn 366). She searches for love, honesty, something human, and the ultimate Truth, threatening to expose the conspiracy of the Red Devil Battery Corporation to a congressional committee in Washington, D.C. When her guardian is murdered and her lover is done in by a brain tumor, she descends into the Dallas wasteland, joining Wolf and the denizens of the Hollow as "Sister of Wolf," "Mother of all."

Hayman suggests that Woman Downtown is merely a weak character who is "yet another reincarnation of the faded Southern belle" (221). Bennett notices that she does possess the traits of other familiar Williams heroines ("she is haunted and persecuted by a brutal society, she has experienced alcoholism and madness, and she is aging"), yet she clearly transcends these characteristics, by "uniting the young people who take her as their Madonna while they cry out for a holocaust" (436). Her namelessness and transfiguration raise her above comparison to the half-crazed, rebellious aristocrat Carol Cutrere of *Orpheus Descending*, and her larger-than-life image strengthens rather than weakens her character.

She is compared to "a secularized Joan of Arc" (Kahn 364), a "secular goddess-mother who will lead . . . fallen humanity" (Kahn 368). Kahn claims that whether the Woman Downtown is savior, terrorist leader, or avenger, she is the antidote to corporate guile and greed and consequently becomes a source of strength for the rebellious gangs dwelling in the wasteland on the outskirts of Dallas (368).

King

Starting as a Mexican street musician, King gradually comes close to achieving the American Dream when his mariachi band "King's Men" begins to get bookings at the best clubs in America. When a brain tumor "flowers" in his head, he loses his kingdom, submitting to a humiliating dependence on his wife. Only his love for Woman Downtown gives meaning once again to his broken life. Kahn discusses King's realm and the various ways he is deposed as father, husband, and lover (367).

Symbols

Bigsby asserts that Williams's sets do much more than "provide the context for action," for they are "charged with a symbolic function, from the enclosing space of *The Glass Menagerie*" to the "urban wasteland of *The Red Devil Battery Sign*" (*Modern American Drama* 36). With its explosions and flares, defiant outcries and wolf calls, Bigsby explains, the inferno of the Hollow draws us into "a world being given over to man turned ravaging beast" (*Critical Introduction* 110).

The major symbol of the play is the battery sign itself. With its international business and political connections, the Red Devil Battery military-industrial complex is bent on world domination, and its symbolic sign represents the evil nature of such power conspiracies. While Kelly thinks that "the voltage in the symbolism wouldn't light a penlight" (25), Kahn suggests that the red sign is a "bloody and vicious hex upon mankind" (365). The flashing neon sign's phantasmagoric, nightmarish dimension is emphasized by Hayman, who explains that Williams's "paranoid hysteria derived largely from his use of drugs, especially Seconal, which was often called 'red devil' " (221). Spoto thinks that the symbol's connection with a dangerous drug reinforces ideas associating "desire with danger, the personal with the public" (347).

Alcohol, music, roses, fresh linen, silk gowns, and clean air cover the harsh realities of brain tumors, physical violence, and broken relationships as well as the demonic struggle for control between the Red Devil Battery "order" and the Hollow wasteland "chaos." King and Woman Downtown escape to lovemaking in the penthouse bedroom of the Yellow Rose Hotel, which is ironically just as much a prison as a retreat. Kahn explains that because of the loss of values, collapse of high hopes, and decay of innocence, "the tension which holds the present and the past apart has gone." However barbaric it may be, Wolf's revolutionary outcry proves an "alternative" to a cruel, mechanistic world (364).

Plot

Williams felt that *Red Devil* was "the best thing" he'd "written in a long time" (Brown 274), and he compared it with his greatest works: *Streetcar*, *The Glass Menagerie*, and *Camino Real*. Hayman suggests that the characters and the plot are "too weak to bear such a heavy load" (221); Levin asserts that *Red Devil* is "a dark and haunting and coherent play, as strong as anything he has written except his very best" (37); and Blake indicates that "Mr. Williams has written too much for one play—and too diffusely for clear comprehension" (9). When the plot changes in the final scene from realism to surrealism, Kahn points out that some critics are provoked by the "purely metaphoric theatricality" of the play (368). Others readers, like Elwood, argue that Williams "need not be restricted to one mode of writing" and that he does not have to decide "between psychological and political motivations in the play" as long as he makes clear to us that "we may not and cannot retreat from social reality to a world of feeling" (116). Although Blake argues the need for a "tauter construction," he feels that "even as it stands the corruption of society emerges strongly as the theme, underlined by those ever-present howling wolves ready to tear society to pieces" (9).

PROBLEMS *THE RED DEVIL BATTERY SIGN* POSES FOR CRITICS

Red Devil's chief problem for the critics is its crude ending, in which Woman Downtown leaves her penthouse apartment and Red Devil Battery tormentors to join Wolf and the revolutionary youths of the Hollow. She too quickly transforms herself into a surreal matriarch as realism turns into expressionism.

CHIEF PRODUCTIONS

Red Devil's has had five noteworthy professional productions to date. Opening at Boston's Shubert Theatre on 18 June 1975 and running less than two weeks until 28 June, the initial production of *Red Devil* was slated for a five-week engagement at Washington's National Theatre before moving on to a 12 August premiere at Broadway's Broadhurst Theatre. Directed by Edwin Sherin and starring Anthony Quinn (King) and Claire Bloom (Woman Downtown), the production was ripe with promise. Quinn received outstanding reviews, while some thought Bloom unsuited to the vulgar part of Woman Downtown. Kelly found the play "dreadful" and "utterly raucous," with "lurking pomposity" in its "ever darkening vision" (25), while Norton considered it in need of rewriting as it "teeters and totters eerily between true tragedy and mawkish melodrama" (14). Coproducer David Merrick closed the play in Boston. As Dakin Williams and Shepherd Mead point out, the closing was unjustified because the audiences were big (318). Williams was devastated by all the theatrical brouhaha.

Seven months later, *Red Devil* opened at the English Theatre in Vienna on 17 January 1976, with Williams convinced, according to Kahn, that in Vienna his play would not be "ruined by the technicians" and that Europeans "love artists better and forgive them for being sometimes less than good" (363). Having revised the play considerably, Williams was pleased by director Franz Schafranek and actors Keith Baxter (King), Ruth Brinkmann (Woman Downtown), and Maria Britneva (Perla). Elwood found the play to be "important," although "it needs judicious cutting," and proclaimed that "Williams's latest vision, however apocalyptic, must not be ignored" (117). *Variety* critic "Curt" praised Williams's dialogue for its "pungency," pronounced *Red Devil* a "financially rewarding hit," and thought that the tiny English Theatre's employment of abstract slides as its scenic setting gave "a sense of depth" to the production (90).

On 8 June 1977, a new version of the Vienna production arrived at London's Roundhouse, only to move on to London's Phoenix Theatre from 7 to 23 July 1977. Directed now by Keith Baxter and David Leland, this production retained Keith Baxter (King) and Maria Britneva (Perla) while adding to the cast Estelle Kohler (Woman Downtown). Wardle called attention to the fact that in this production the author's "personal obsessions are now expanding into the public domain" (13); Blake praised the strength of the play's main theme of "the corruption of society" (9); and Radin responded to the production's "three hours of confusion" by observing that "Williams is now shifting responsibility for human happiness from the individual to society" (26). Suspecting that "Mr. Williams has imbibed more of Watergate than is good for his sense and stability," Nightingale found the text to be a "woozy, scattered, deeply paranoid melodrama" with a "tendency to collapse into cliche" (3). Watt explained that although *Red Devil* needed work, there was glory enough to merit it in "this superb production—so wonderfully staged, acted and designed" (L7).

The Vancouver Playhouse's production of *Red Devil* ran from 18 October until 15 November 1980. With Roger Hodgman directing, this "premiere" starred Richard Donat (King) and Diane D'Aquila (Woman Downtown). In an eloquent program note, Williams admitted that *Red Devil* was "melodrama, not classically-pure tragedy." Noting that general critical response to the play was "respectful," Page did not like the work and resented the idea that Williams felt that he was doing Vancouver and the Playhouse a favor by permitting his play to be produced (95).

The 13 November to 1 December 1996 WPA production of *Red Devil* addressed the problem of too diffuse a plot by focusing on and intensifying the relationship between King and Woman Downtown. In order to do this, the mariachis, La Niña, and her boyfriend, McCabe, were omitted from Williams's 1988 text (see Isaac 5, 34). Directed by Michael Wilson, this production featured Elizabeth Ashley (Woman Downtown), James Victor (King), and Annette Cardona (Perla). Ashley compared the play to "a gunshot, very stark and expressionistic" (Lipton 16); and Wilson argues that "Williams with 'Red Devil' did for the '60s and '70s what Tony Kushner's 'Angels in America' did for the '80s" (Isaac 34). See also Schlatter's discussion of this production.

FILM AND TELEVISION VERSIONS

In 1976, the Encyclopedia Britannica Educational Corporation worked with Signet Producers to film a twenty-nine-minute color introduction to Tennessee Williams's *Red Devil Battery Sign*. Called *Tennessee Williams: Theatre in Process*, this film records the history of the first production from initial readings to more formal rehearsals to opening night in Boston. Viewers watch playwright Tennessee Williams, director Edwin Sherin, and actors Anthony Quinn (King del Rey), Claire Bloom (Woman Downtown), Katy Jurado (Perla), Annette Cardona (La Niña), and Stephen McHattie (McCabe) as they work through William's text, define the characters, and polish the dialogue, sharpening the play for the opening as well as the hoped-for New York premiere.

CONCLUDING OVERVIEW

"Thought Control"; "Big Brother Is Watching You"; "Who Controls the Past Controls the Future" and "Who Controls the Present Controls the Past"; "War Is Peace"; "Freedom Is Slavery"; and "Ignorance Is Strength": The catchwords, slogans, and maxims of George Orwell's *1984* (1949) and the illogical chaos of Joseph Heller's *Catch-22* (1955 and 1961) supply a context for understanding the political, personal, and artistic implications of bureaucratic power control in Tennessee Williams's *Red Devil*. Orwell, Heller, and Williams are soulmates in attacking the tyranny and bullyism of mind-controlling corporate structures and the concept of an omnipotent Big Brother who watches everyone constantly as he commands attention and obedience to his will.

"Privilege" does not necessarily mean that one is immune to the totalitarian tactics of power conspiracies. Born into and married off to the power elite, Woman Downtown, the great statesman's daughter, should have it all, yet her fate has been a life of indoctrination into subservience, training to be nonhuman, and learning to smile a smile that masks emotion and thought. Her keepers have been many: first, ruled by the black bead–clinking guardian tutor; then bullied during a stretch at a private school for distressed children euphemistically called the Institute for Rebirth; next, locked up behind the estate walls of her husband's hacienda, where she played hostess to Red Devil Battery Monsters; more recently, subjected to a stretch of electroshock therapy at Paradise Meadows Nursing Home; and, now, imprisoned in the Yellow Rose Hotel with "crewcuts" for guards.

When Woman Downtown's godfather, Judge Collister, tries to help her, he is murdered. She knows how corporate power structures protect their secret investments by aiding and abetting sympathetically corrupt regimes. The privileged lifestyle disgusts Woman Downtown as much as playing hostess to Red Devil Battery Monsters, so she opts for revolutionary counterattack when she joins forces with Wolf to lead the rebellious denizens of the Hollow. Big Brother is valiantly challenged by Sister of Wolf.

WORKS CITED

Adler, Thomas P. *American Drama, 1940–1960: A Critical History*. New York: Twayne, 1994.

———. "Culture, Power, and the (En)gendering of Community: Tennessee Williams and Politics." *Mississippi Quarterly* 48.4 (Fall 1995): 649–65.

Bennett, Beate Hein. "Williams and European Drama: Infernalists and Forgers of Modern Myths." *Tennessee Williams: A Tribute*. Ed. Jac Tharpe. Jackson: UP of Mississippi, 1977. 429–59.

Bigsby, C. W. E. *A Critical Introduction to Twentieth-Century American Drama*. Vol. 2. *Tennessee Williams, Arthur Miller, Edward Albee*. Cambridge: Cambridge UP, 1984.

———. *Modern American Drama, 1945–1990*. Cambridge: Cambridge UP, 1992.

Blake, Douglas. " 'The Red Devil Battery Sign' at the Round House." *Stage and Television Today* 16 June 1977: 9.

Brown, Cecil. "Interview with Tennessee Williams." *Conversations with Tennessee Williams*. Ed. Albert J. Devlin. Jackson: UP of Mississippi, 1986. 251–83.

Crandell, George W. *Tennessee Williams: A Descriptive Bibliography*. Pittsburgh: U of Pittsburgh P, 1995.

"Curt." " 'Red Devil Battery Sign,' Vienna, Jan. 31." *Variety* 3 Mar. 1976: 90.

Elwood, William R. "*The Red Devil Battery Sign* by Tennessee Williams." *Educational Theatre Journal* 30.1 (March 1978): 116–17.

Grosch, Robert J. "Memory as Theme and Production Value in Tennessee Williams's *The Red Devil Battery Sign*." *The Tennessee Williams Annual Review* 1 (1998): 119–24.

Gunn, Drewey Wayne. *Tennessee Williams: A Bibliography*. 2nd ed. Metuchen, NJ: Scarecrow, 1991.

Hayman, Ronald. *Tennessee Williams: Everyone Else Is an Audience*. New Haven: Yale UP, 1993.

Isaac, Dan. "A 'Sign' from Tennessee: WPA Mounts Williams' 'Red Devil.' " *Backstage* 8 Nov. 1996: 5, 34.

Kahn, Sy. "*The Red Devil Battery Sign*: Williams' Götterdämmerung in Vienna." *Tennessee Williams: A Tribute*. Ed. Jac Tharpe. Jackson: UP of Mississippi, 1977. 362–71.

Kelly, Kevin. "Red Devil Battery Sign." *Boston Globe* 19 June 1975: 25.

Kolin, Philip C. "Sleeping with Caliban: The Politics of Race in Tennessee Williams's *Kingdom of Earth*." *Studies in American Drama, 1945–Present* 8.2 (1993): 140–62.

Kullman, Colby H. "Rule by Power: 'Big Daddyism' in the World of Tennessee Williams's Plays." *Mississippi Quarterly* 48.4 (Fall 1995): 667–76.

Levin, Bernard. "*Red Devil Battery*." *Sunday Times* (London) 12 June 1977: 37.

Lipton, Brian Scott. "The Miracle Worker [Elizabeth Ashley]." *Encore* Nov. 1996: 16, 18, 44.

"New Williams Play Set for Aug. 12." *New York Times* 12 May 1975: L40.

Nightingale, Benedict. "That's History." *New Statesman* 17 June 1977: 3.

Norton, Elliot. *Boston Herald American* 19 June 1975: 14.

Page, Malcolm. "Tennessee Williams in Vancouver." *Canadian Theatre Review* 33 (Winter 1982): 92–95.

Radin, Victoria. "Wolf-howls at the Door." *London Observer* 12 June 1977: 26.

Raus, Charles. "Tennessee Williams." *Conversations with Tennessee Williams*. Ed. Albert J. Devlin. Jackson: UP of Mississippi, 1986. 284–95.

Schlatter, James. "*Red Devil Battery Sign*: An Approach to a Mytho-Political Theatre." *The Tennessee Williams Annual Review* 1 (1998): 93–101.

Schmidt-Mühlisch, Lothar. "Life Is a Black Joke." *Conversations with Tennessee Williams*. Ed. Albert J. Devlin. Jackson: UP of Mississippi, 1986. 296–98.

Sherin, Edwin, dir. *Tennessee Williams: Theatre in Progress*. With Claire Bloom and Anthony Quinn. Signet Producers, 1976.

Spoto, Donald. *The Kindness of Strangers: The Life of Tennessee Williams*. New York: Ballantine, 1986.

Wardle, Irving. "Public Nightmare in Dallas." *Times* [London] 9 June 1997: 13.

Watt, Douglas. "There It Was: The Play." *New York Sunday News* 21 Aug. 1977: L7.

Williams, Dakin, and Shepherd Mead. *Tennessee Williams: An Intimate Biography*. New York: Arbor, 1983.

Williams, Tennessee. *Five O'Clock Angel: Letters of Tennessee Williams to Maria St. Just, 1948–1982*. New York: Alfred A. Knopf, 1990.

———. "The Knightly Quest." *Tennessee Williams: Collected Stories*. New York: Ballantine, 1986. 421–83.

———. *Memoirs*. New York: Doubleday, 1975.

———. *The Red Devil Battery Sign*. New York: New Directions, 1988.

———. *The Red Devil Battery Sign*. *The Theatre of Tennessee Williams*. Vol. 8. New York: New Directions, 1992. 281–378.

Wilson, Earl. "Comeback Ends in Boston for Tennessee Williams." *New York Post* 25 June 1975: 56.

Period of Adjustment: High Point over a Cavern: A Serious Comedy

CASSIE CARTER

BIOGRAPHICAL CONTEXT

In 1957, with *Sweet Bird of Youth* ready for rehearsals on Broadway, Tennessee Williams decided to try his hand at comedy. "I would like to write a happy play for a while," he quipped, "maybe some day I will suddenly become hilarious" (Donahue 121). Resolving to cease writing "black plays" and focus instead on "the kinder aspects of life" (quoted in Wenning 96), he began composing *Period of Adjustment*. Working on *Period* concurrently with *Suddenly Last Summer* and *Something Unspoken* and through the production of *Garden District* in January 1958 (Dakin Williams and Mead 216), he was still revising *Period* when he began *The Night of the Iguana* in 1959 (Donahue 138).

Period reflects an "increasingly sure moral position" in Williams's later work (Jackson 158), exemplifying his movement toward a new attitude of acceptance and resignation toward the human condition (Weales 62). Williams remarked that he had learned to "stop taking a problem as if it affected the future of the world" (Gassner 53). Even so, during the stock production in Miami, Williams quickly recognized that the play was not the lighthearted comedy he had thought it was: "I realized it was about as dark as *Orpheus Descending*" (Funke and Booth 16).

BIBLIOGRAPHIC HISTORY

Period of Adjustment first appeared in print in the December 1960 issue of *Esquire* magazine; it was soon published in the United States by New Directions and in England by Secker and Warburg. Crandell describes these and subsequent reprintings (191–99; 397–98; 405–06; 416) as well as translations (579–621); Gunn's bibliography also records translations and editions (99–103; 365–96).

As with other Williams scripts, the acting version of *Period* differs from the reading version. Williams revised and edited through each printing of the script, refining the dialogue and action of the plot (Gunn 99); by the time the play was published, the revision process was mostly complete. The setting changed from "Memphis" in the first New Directions printing to "Dixon," a town near Memphis, in the second (Crandell 194). Williams also added brief stage directions (Crandell 198, 199), and the subtitle evolved from "High Point Is Built on a Cavern" to "High Point over a Cavern" (Gunn 99–100). Both titles articulate "the Williams world in which men live tentatively, in an unending period of adjustment, over an abyss that is more than simply social" (Weales 62).

MAJOR CRITICAL APPROACHES

Themes

A reviewer of the Miami production of *Period of Adjustment* aptly observed, "Williams repaired no cracking masonry in his familiar dramatic neighborhood, but at least he slapped on a coat of whitewash" ("Tennessee Laughter" 54). The characters' dilemmas are standard in Williams's work, although "[n]ot a single person was raped, castrated, lynched, committed or even eaten" (Dakin Williams and Mead 22). *Period* departs noticeably from Williams's more violent themes, centering its attack on the suburban status quo (Weales 62). At worst, the play implies that the sexually bedeviled residents of High Point are average Americans (Falk 187; Clurman 443–44). At best, *Period of Adjustment* overflows with "warmth and wisdom and hilarious good humor," presenting an "uncomplicated attitude toward the relationship between boys and girls" (McClain 177).

Many critics have found *Period* trite. McCarten, for example, states, "His big message, when it is finally delivered, conceivably after being delayed in Vienna, advises us that we ought to be tender in human relations, and that husbands and wives should show tolerance for each other's weaknesses" (93). Further, redemption seems to be reduced to a matter of the characters being compatible bedfellows (Falk 141). Some critics, however, believe that shallowness is an important theme in the play. Williams's point is precisely that no one has changed when the final curtain falls, Goldfarb argues (316). Likewise, Stanton asserts, "The ominous cracking sound of the house settling an inch further into the cavern at the end . . . and the funeral coach the honeymooners use for a car belie the successful adjustments they seem to have made, the 'high point' they have reached" (8).

Characters

In a favorite Williams binary setup, *Period* centers on two couples: the Bateses have been married for five years, the Haversticks one day, and both couples are facing crises. *Period*'s lead character, Ralph Bates, is a thirty-seven-year-old "degenerating dreamer" suffering a middle-age crisis. Too weak to make a real escape, he lives in the past and escapes into fantasy (Goldfarb 311). Falk notes that the characters' and author's descriptions and intentions do not always mesh. For example, Ralph believes that he could transform "a buck-toothed bride" into a beauty queen (138). Ralph's army buddy, George Haverstick, likewise presents a facade that contradicts his behavior: he views women as either whores or iron-clad virgins in order to hide his fear of women. In effect, he is a "frustrated Stanley Kowalski" whose "brutality masks his fear of impotence" (Falk 139). George pretends to see sex as conquest, but his macho sex talk is just talk (Falk 139; Goldfarb 312). Ganz proposes that George "has rejected his homosexual nature or at least pretended to a virility he does not possess" (126).

Meanwhile, both wives have repressed their sexuality until marriage and have been expected to adjust their sexuality according to the needs of their husbands. Isabel Haverstick has been overprotected and now finds "herself in the grips of a bestial male." Although sexually inexperienced, Isabel is not frigid; rather, her strong sexual desires have been repressed in defending her virginity (Goldfarb 313). Dorothea Bates, on the other hand, is one of many Williams women who subordinate themselves to men (Blackwell 103). Suffering "psychological frigidity" at the time of her marriage, she has developed a sex drive her husband cannot always satisfy, and the fact that her parents bribed Ralph to marry her makes the problem worse.

Dorothea's parents, the McGillicuddys, are the intrusive outsiders blocking the resolution of differences. The McGillicuddys are caricatures Williams refers to as "the Moneybags." Representing materialism and greed (Falk 141; see also Brooks 726), they view even their daughter as property. Kolin argues that, in this respect, the black maid, Susie, "functions as Dorothea's surrogate, analogously suffering the abuse visited on the white woman by her parents" (10).

Symbols

Typical of Williams's strong sense of place, *Period*'s primary symbols are Ralph Bates's home in the suburb of High Point and the cavern it is sinking into. Dakin Williams and Shepherd Mead note that Williams "got the idea" for the Bates house "from one of Edwina's houses in Clayton, which was built over an underground cavern" (236; E. Williams 204). The Bates house embodies the play's central theme of "individuals sinking into quagmires along with their homes," the trap of middle-class existence, and superficial relationships built on questionable grounds. The Haversticks' honeymoon car, a funeral limousine, reflects Williams's view of such relationships, and the blaring television at the start of the play emphasizes the ersatz state of middle-class existence (Goldfarb 314–15). Williams softens the problem in the image of the neurological ward where George and Isabel meet, suggesting that the world is a hospital where all humans are trying to adjust to their assigned social roles (Donahue 133).

Plot

Period's sitcom plot introduces a rivalry between the sexes complicated by meddling in-laws, with the Bateses and Haversticks falling happily into bed by the time the curtain falls. Critics have generally found *Period*'s plot slow-moving, bogged down by background details, and well-written but with excessive dialogue and not enough action. As Pryce-Jones observes, "The comedy is kept afloat entirely on conversation. . . . But it is motionless conversation" (59). Reviewers have often stated that the play's message is not worth the time spent developing it.

MAJOR PROBLEMS *PERIOD OF ADJUSTMENT* POSES FOR CRITICS

While criticism since the Broadway production presents the play as a sardonic critique of middle-class America, the initial critical consensus was that the play was shallow and below par for Williams. Aston remarked, "If 'Period of Adjustment' were Tennessee Williams's first play I would say he showed great promise. As it is, he has paused to do little more than exhibit an aptitude for sentence tossing." In essence, many critics felt that *Period* lacked substance and subtlety. Simon found the solutions offered by *Period* too simple to be believable; even worse, he complained that the main theme of the play "is announced repeatedly with a subtlety that I can only call cymbalism" (84). Brustein went so far as to question the authorship of *Period*, declaring, "The play is so tedious, aimless, repetitive, and imitative—so utterly lacking in style, grace, or imaginativeness—that I have a sneaking suspicion it is really the work of an impostor" (117). An unresolved problem broached by the play's earliest critics was the sexually explicit dialogue in the third act, which Falk describes as "the kind of dialogue that prompted the late George Jean Nathan to call [Williams] the 'genital-man' of the contemporary theater" (141).

CHIEF PRODUCTIONS

Codirected by Williams and Owen Phillips, *Period of Adjustment* opened on 29 December 1958 in Miami at the Coconut Grove Playhouse, starring James Daly as Ralph, Barbara Baxley as Isabel, Robert Webber as George, and Martine Bartlett as Dorothea. Williams initially wanted to direct the play alone, but he conceded, "I can't direct my way out of a paper bag" (quoted in Donahue 123). Elia Kazan had been expected to direct the Broadway production, but when he opted out in favor of directing *Splendor in the Grass*, George Roy Hill took the directorial reins. The play went into rehearsal with Rosemary Murphy taking the role of Dorothea (Arnott 46; Falk 125–26); it opened at the Helen Hayes Theatre on 10 November 1960. *Period of Adjustment* received mainly positive but tepid reviews, with critics generally viewing it, in John Chapman's words, as "an affectionate and rather charming little domestic comedy" (176). Reviewers consistently admired the talent of the actors and Williams's technical proficiency, particularly his mastery of dialogue, and favorably commented on the new, upbeat direction in Williams's work.

In September 1961, Val May directed the first British production at Bristol's Theatre Royal, with Harry H. Corbett starring as Ralph, John Franklyn Robbins as George, Elizabeth Shepherd as Isabel, and Rhoda Lewis as Dorothea. A second production at the Royal Court Theatre in London, directed by Roger Graef, featured Bernard Braden as Ralph, Neill McGallum as George, Collin Wincox as Isabel, and Betty McDowall as Dorothea. This production moved to the Wyndham Theatre in July 1962 (Arnott 46). The play was also staged in Hamburg, Germany, in January 1962 (Gunn 381), and in Athens, Greece, in October 1963 (383).

FILM AND TELEVISION VERSIONS

George Roy Hill also directed a film adaptation released by Metro-Goldwyn-Mayer in 1962. Isobel Lennart's screenplay centers on Isabel (Jane Fonda), re-arranging the narrative to focus on the Haversticks' honeymoon disaster, which is presented at the start of the film. Ralph Bates (Tony Franciosa) is reduced to a secondary character, the war buddy of Isabel's husband George (Jim Hutton). Lois Nettleton played Dorothea. For critical reactions to the film, see representative reviews by Comerford, Crowther, and Whitehall.

CONCLUDING OVERVIEW

Much like the television sitcom genre it emulates, *Period* offers a peek into middle-class American life, and by presenting middle-class life as the audience expects it to be, the play exposes gender ideologies governing life in contemporary America. To Ralph and George, masculinity is an absolute that has been corrupted by female influence and modernity. As Ralph puts it, referring to his sissy son, "you got to be what your physical sex is or correct it in Denmark" (*Period* 52). Unfortunately, the men's masculine ideal exists only in television westerns and science fiction. Their wives and bourgeois existence quell their desires, having other ideals for them to fulfill.

Isabel dreams of marrying a man of sensitivity and feeling who is willing to die for her (26–28), but her husband wants to be John Wayne. George wants to be a western hero, but the best he can hope for is to raise longhorns for television westerns. Likewise, Ralph dreams of being a sexual superman inseminating the universe; he would like to "colonize and fertilize, to be the Adam on a—star in a different *galaxy*." In contrast to his fantasy, however, Ralph finds himself imprisoned in a stucco cottage (73), working a dead-end job at his father-in-law's dairy, and married to an ugly woman who demands sex so often that he feels "guilty" when he can't perform (76).

The frustration Ralph and George feel surfaces as brutality directed against their wives. Dorothea represents everything Ralph believes he has sacrificed, so he expresses his attempt to love her by having her nose surgically altered and her front teeth extracted (107). Ralph's only means of fulfilling his masculine ideal is to remodel Dorothea into an object he can desire. George, on the other hand, transfers his fear of impotence onto his wife. Unwilling to admit his ineptness at playing Clint Eastwood in the bedroom, he blames Isabel for seducing him in the hospital (58), convincing himself that she is the kind of woman who would "cut it off" if she could (83).

The battle between the sexes is indeed treacherous in *Period of Adjustment*, especially when the requirements of masculinity transform women into Charybdis and Scylla on either side of the passage.

WORKS CITED

Arnott, Catherine M., comp. *Tennessee Williams on File*. London: Methuen, 1985.

Aston, Frank. "Williams Play at the Hayes." *New York World-Telegram* 11 Nov. 1960. Rpt. in *New York Theatre Critics' Reviews* 21.28 (1960): 177.

Blackwell, Louise. "Tennessee Williams and the Predicament of Women." *Tennessee Williams: A Collection of Critical Essays*. Ed. Stephen S. Stanton. Englewood Cliffs, NJ: Prentice-Hall, 1977. 100–06.

Brooks, Charles B. "Williams' Comedy." *Tennessee Williams: A Tribute*. Ed. Jac Thorpe. Jackson: UP of Mississippi, 1977. 720–35.

Brustein, Robert. "Disputed Authorship: *Period of Adjustment* by Tennessee Williams." *Seasons of Discontent: Dramatic Opinions, 1959–1965*. New York: Simon and Schuster, 1965. 117–19.

Chapman, John. "Williams' 'Period of Adjustment' Is an Affectionate Little Comedy." *New York Daily News* 11 Nov. 1960: 60. Rpt. in *New York Theatre Critics' Reviews* 21.28 (1960): 176.

Comerford, Adelaide. *Films in Review* 8 (Dec. 1962): 627.

Clurman, Harold. Rev. of *Period of Adjustment. Nation* 3 Dec. 1960: 443–44.

Crandell, George W. *Tennessee Williams: A Descriptive Bibliography*. Pittsburgh: U of Pittsburgh P, 1995.

Crowther, Bosley. *New York Times* 1 Nov. 1962: 34.

Donahue, Francis. *The Dramatic World of Tennessee Williams*. New York: Ungar, 1964.

Falk, Signi Lenea. *Tennessee Williams*. New York: Twayne, 1962.

Funke, Lewis, and John E. Booth. "Williams on Williams." *Theatre Arts* (Jan. 1962): 16–19, 72–73.

Ganz, Arthur. "Tennessee Williams: A Desperate Morality." *American Scholar* 31 (Spring 1962): 278–94. Rpt. in *Tennessee Williams: A Collection of Critical Essays*. Ed. Stephen S. Stanton. Englewood Cliffs, NJ: Prentice-Hall, 1977. 123–37.

Gassner, John. "Broadway in Review." *Educational Theatre Journal* 13 (Mar. 1961): 51–53.

Goldfarb, Alvin. "*Period of Adjustment* and the New Tennessee Williams." *Tennessee Williams: A Tribute*. Ed. Jac Tharpe. Jackson: UP of Mississippi, 1977. 310–17.

Gunn, Drewey Wayne. *Tennessee Williams: A Bibliography*. 2nd ed. Metuchen, NJ: Scarecrow, 1991.

Jackson, Esther Merle. *The Broken World of Tennessee Williams*. Madison: U of Wisconsin
    P, 1965.
Kolin, Philip C. "The Function of Susie in Tennessee Williams's *Period of Adjustment*."
    Notes on Contemporary Literature 25.3 (May 1995): 10–11.
MacNicholas, John. "Williams' Power of the Keys." *Tennessee Williams: A Tribute*. Ed. Jac
    Tharpe. Jackson: UP of Mississippi, 1977. 581–605.
McCarten, John. "Tennessee Tries a Tender Pitch." *New Yorker* 19 Nov. 1960: 93–94.
McClain, John. "Tennessee at His Best." *New York Journal-American* 11 Nov. 1960: 11.
    Rpt. in *New York Theatre Critics' Reviews* 21.28 (1960): 177.
Nelson, Benjamin. *Tennessee Williams: The Man and His Work*. New York: Obolensky,
    1961.
Period of Adjustment. Dir. George Roy Hill. MGM, 1962. MGM Home Video, 1992.
Pryce-Jones, Alan. "Alan Pryce-Jones at the Theatre." *Theatre Arts* (Jan. 1961): 57–58.
Simon, John. "Theatre Chronicle." *Hudson Review* 14 (Spring 1961): 83–92.
Smith, Bruce. *Costly Performances: Tennessee Williams: The Last Stage*. New York: Paragon,
    1990.
Stanton, Stephen S., ed. *Tennessee Williams: A Collection of Critical Essays*. Englewood
    Cliffs, NJ: Prentice-Hall, 1977.
"Tennessee Laughter." *Time* 12 Jan. 1959: 54–56.
Weales, Gerald. "Tennessee Williams in the Sixties." *Tennessee Williams: A Collection of
    Critical Essays*. Ed. Stephen S. Stanton. Englewood Cliffs, NJ: Prentice-Hall, 1977.
    61–70.
Wenning, T. H. "Unbeastly Williams." *Newsweek* 27 June 1960: 96.
Whitehall, Richard. *Films and Filming* (Mar. 1963): 38.
Williams, Dakin, and Shepherd Mead. *Tennessee Williams: An Intimate Biography*. New
    York: Arbor, 1983.
Williams, Edwina Dakin, as told to Lucy Freeman. *Remember Me to Tom*. New York:
    Putnam's, 1963.
Williams, Tennessee. *Period of Adjustment: High Point over a Cavern: A Serious Comedy*.
    New York: New Directions, 1960.
———. *Period of Adjustment (or High Point Is Built on a Cavern: A Serious Comedy)*. *Esquire*
    54 (Dec. 1960): 210–76.
———. *Period of Adjustment: High Point over a Cavern: A Serious Comedy*. London: Secker
    & Warburg, 1961.
———. "Prelude to a Comedy." *New York Times* 6 Nov. 1960, sec. 2: 1, 3.

I Rise in Flame, Cried the Phoenix

CATHY HENDERSON

BIOGRAPHICAL CONTEXT

Dakin Williams and Shepherd Mead record Williams's decision to write a poetic and symbolic drama about D. H. Lawrence's dying days, claiming that Williams did not give a second thought to whether or not the one-act play had a chance of being produced. They point out that this was the only one of Williams's plays that his mother would not read because she believed Lawrence's novels to be dirty books (95).

Spoto establishes the essential facts of Williams's attraction to Lawrence's life and work. He traces the influence of Lawrence on Williams's early poetry and prose and marks its progression through *Battle of Angels* (1940) and its numerous reworkings, *I Rise in Flame, Cried the Phoenix* (1941), *The Purification* (1941), *You Touched Me* (1942), and finally, late in Williams's career, *Kingdom of Earth* (1968). However, he views Williams's concern with Lawrence as being predominantly obsessive, sentimental, and detrimental to the development of inspired drama (271).

Hayman offers details about the actual order of the play's composition, stating that Williams "began at the end" (63), writing first the scene of Lawrence's death. Williams envisioned a full-length play about Lawrence's life but, discouraged by his agent, never got beyond writing the one-act play. Years later, Williams voiced his regret to Cecil Brown, saying that he could have made "a wonderful play out of D. H. Lawrence's life" but wrote *Battle of Angels* instead (279).

Leverich, in the first volume of his biography of Williams, attaches more importance to the lifelong influence of Lawrence on Williams and better establishes

the lineage and constructive effect of Lawrence on the artistic development of
Williams as a playwright and as a person. He posits that the young Williams
might first have heard of Lawrence's views on sensuality and spirituality in consequence of the publicity surrounding Lawrence's death in March 1930 (114),
and that Lawrence's embrace of beauty and sexuality was manifest in the character of Esther in the earliest known play written by Williams, *Beauty Is the Word*
(1930). Further, Leverich believes that Williams's deepening absorption with
Lawrence's philosophy throughout the 1930s culminated in the transformation
of the person, Thomas Lanier Williams, into the playwright, Tennessee Williams.
Adopting a new persona was a way for Williams to release the artist he felt was
imprisoned within himself.

Leverich clearly points out that Williams conceived the idea of writing a play
about Lawrence's life in America after reading the Aldous Huxley edition of
Lawrence's letters in the summer of 1939. Williams wrote of his plans to his
agent, Audrey Wood, and to Lawrence's widow, Frieda, and traveled to Taos in
the fall of 1939 (314). There he met Dorothy Brett, Frieda Lawrence, and others
of Lawrence's acquaintance. Ganz (283), Tischler (*Tennessee Williams* 121), and
Leverich (321) call attention to Williams's poem "Cried the Fox," which was
written in Taos and dedicated to Lawrence. It depicts him as a fugitive creature
returning insistently and fatally to places and people who failed to be enlightened
by his message (Leverich 321).

Leverich usefully points to parallels between Lawrence's and Williams's early
lives—poor health, rejecting fathers, possessive mothers, and chaste first love
affairs—as further reasons for Williams's attraction to Lawrence (322). Williams
adopted Lawrence's conviction that sexuality was dual, the male and female
components variously seeking to dominate. The idea found voice in Williams's
first mature play effort, *Battle of Angels* (1940), which Williams dedicated to
Lawrence, but which was a critical failure.

BIBLIOGRAPHIC HISTORY

Leverich cites a 29 July 1939 Williams letter to Frieda Lawrence and a 30 July
1939 letter to Audrey Wood as containing the earliest expressions of his intentions to write a play based on Lawrence's experiences in America (313). Nelson,
without citing a source, puts the date "as early as 1934" (82).

Surviving manuscripts of the play (housed at the Harry Ransom Humanities
Research Center at the University of Texas at Austin) are grouped into three
distinct draft versions of the play, but because none of them are dated, it is
difficult to establish a firm chronology or hierarchy among them. In all versions
of the play, D. H. and Frieda Lawrence are constant characters who are paired
off against one or more foils. In one version, Williams introduces a French peas-
ant couple and their newly married son and daughter-in-law as sounding boards
for Lawrence. Another version of the play, which contains strong comedic elements, features an American spinster who makes a pilgrimage to Lawrence's

deathbed in order to sort out her emotions about a man she once met on a San Francisco ferry. Lawrence engages her in a long psychoanalytical session. At its conclusion, the woman's memory becomes unblocked and she acknowledges her love for the stranger on the boat and rushes back to San Francisco to find him. The drafts of the play most closely resembling its final form all feature Bertha (Dorothy Brett) as the third voice. A young wounded soldier (who speaks with a southern drawl) figures in a two-page draft of a fourth, fragmentary version of the play.

New Directions published a limited edition of the play in 1951 with a preface (composed in 1941) by Williams and a note by Frieda Lawrence. An acting edition was published the same year by Dramatists Play Service without the note by Frieda Lawrence and with a different ending. In the New Directions text, Lawrence's resolve to die alone weakens, and he calls out for Frieda, who rushes to him. In the acting version, Frieda, as she promised, restrains herself and Bertha from physically comforting Lawrence in his death throes. Crandell describes these editions and their substantive differences in more detail (*Tennessee Williams* 102–06). Gunn provides a synopsis of reprintings of the original and revised editions dating from 1952 to 1981 (62).

CRITICAL APPROACHES

Few critics pay attention to this play at all. When they do, it is viewed variously as a "tribute" (Londré 160), valuable for the light it sheds on Williams's "thought and experience" (Nelson 82), but distorting in its interpretation of Lawrence's views (Fedder 49), a fact Ganz admits but considers "irrelevant" in trying to understand Williams's own work. For Ganz, this play is important because it is evidence that Williams from early in his career saw himself as a disciple of "the great writer who 'celebrates the body' " (280).

Themes

Frieda Lawrence, in her introductory note to the limited edition of the play, stated the play's theme to be "the eternal antagonism and attraction between man and woman" (8). Falk's view of the central theme is more one-sided. She identifies it simply as antagonism toward women (42). Fedder restores the balance, identifying the theme as the duality of male and female natures and the often antagonistic relationship between the sexes, but he considers Williams's development of the theme to be "chaotic and distorted" since it is unclear whether Williams is praising or mocking Lawrence (50). In contrast, Nelson argues that to think that Williams is in perfect accord with the extreme expressions that he has his character vocalize is to misinterpret the playwright's ability to applaud Lawrence's monumental ideas while skewering his more "tangent obsessions," such as an insistence on female subservience (85).

Not surprisingly, Williams also explores the Lawrentian theme of the dichotomy between the spirit and the flesh, but Nelson puzzles over Williams's treatment of the sexual relationship in this play. If Williams wished most to celebrate and emulate Lawrence as a writer who liberates humanity from social prudery, Nelson observes, then it is "curious" that Williams has Lawrence consistently equate the sex act with destruction and treats so ambivalently the conflict in Lawrence's and Frieda's relationship (neither ever wins his or her arguments hands down). Nelson sees these points of view as coming directly from Williams's own life, not from his reading of Lawrence (86). Boxill cites Williams's focus in this play on Lawrence's death, rather than on his life, as further evidence that Williams's greatest dramatic themes were "decay" and "decline" (59).

Tied to the broader Lawrence-inspired theme of resistance to puritanism and prudery is the issue of censorship, unquestionably a major concern in this play, stated directly in Williams's preface and illustrated in the play by the failure of members of a ladies' club to get the authorities to burn Lawrence's paintings. In Williams's own life, his mother was a censorship threat because she disapproved of his reading Lawrence's novels (Leverich 330). Hayman points out that Williams was so fearful of Miss Edwina's censure that he instructed Audrey Wood, should he die unexpectedly, not to release any of his manuscripts to his parents, whom he feared would destroy his work in a misguided attempt to preserve his reputation (78).

Characters

Lawrence

The dying Lawrence, as described by Williams, is a man who, in an effort to control his fury, sits motionless with hands "that gripped the terrible stuff of life," a "tiger . . . trapped but not destroyed" (5). In the dialogue, however, Lawrence comes across as a bitter, irascible, stubborn, vain, willful, abusive, chauvinistic man. Critics either see "glimpses of Lawrence's phoenix spirit and poetic pain" (Barnes 31) or find his behavior repugnant, "no matter what it is attributed to" (Hughes 45). Fedder considers the depiction of Lawrence to be "uncomplimentary" and invalid (47). He faults Williams for accepting superficial and received opinion about Lawrence's character and refutes Williams's interpretation of Lawrence by quoting extensively from the edition of Lawrence letters Williams is known to have read (49–52). Nelson accepts the contradictory nature of Williams's depiction of Lawrence: the "liberator" of sex from prudery who is also "terrified" of its power in the hands of women; the artist and creator of works he hopes will immortalize him and the man who seeks to die alone yet fears the possibility (83).

Frieda

In the play, only through Frieda's eyes and voice is Lawrence seen in any kind of sympathetic light. She responds to his ravings "with patience and even mild amusement" (Nelson 85) and is the lightning rod through which his rage and disappointment are defused. She both challenges and cajoles him. In short, she "copes" (Nelson 85). Ultimately, it is Frieda who is portrayed as the most accurate interpreter of Lawrence's psyche. Ganz (278) points out that Williams has her recite the key line that reveals Williams's take on the true meaning of Lawrence, that "in all his work he celebrates the body." Frieda is the person who best understands how to mediate Lawrence's contradictions and who, as Nelson points out, "knows him better than he knows himself" (83). Barnes, however, characterizes her as "abrasive" (31).

Bertha

The character Bertha represents the real-life Dorothy Brett. Bertha is introduced as a messenger with no news. She has been sent, ostensibly, to report on the reception of Lawrence's paintings at an exhibition in London, but, in fact, Frieda has already read and Lawrence has intuited the nature of the reviews. Bertha, described by Williams in a character note to the acting edition as "a small, sprightly person . . . with a quick voice and eyes of a child" (12), stands in sharp contrast to Frieda, "a large, handsome woman of fifty, rather like a Valkyrie" (5). Bertha, Nelson argues, is unable to recognize Lawrence as mortal and therefore cannot imagine his death. In consequence, by denying Lawrence's mortality, by idolizing him as a prophet, she "cannot truly comprehend what he is prophesying" (84). She and Frieda quarrel about Lawrence's nature. Frieda defends his physicality and mortality in challenge to Bertha's view of Lawrence as an indestructible spirit, a god. This dialogue, Londré points out, functions to contrast Bertha's "spiritual" relationship with Lawrence against Frieda's physical one (161).

Symbols

Animism drives the symbolic content of this play. The overt symbol of Lawrence as a phoenix in a nest of flames is conveyed in the title and is reinforced by the property list's call for a silk banner embroidered with this image. Lawrence is also likened variously to a trapped tiger, a fox, and, by Frieda, to a snake, converting the rays of the sun into "venom" that he spews back at her. For Lawrence, the sun is an "old bitch" and "stingy *haus-frau*" to whom he looks for strength and good humor, but who leaves him begging and helpless. But each evening at sunset he remarks bitterly of the setting sun as the "young blond god" of day being seduced by the "harlot of darkness" who will sap his strength and consume him, only to see him escape the next morning and bring light again. Lawrence views himself as the prophet of this light escaping from darkness, life emerging from death. With this speech, Tischler argues, Lawrence's relationship with Frieda becomes "symbolically transformed into the cosmic" (*Tennessee Williams* 120). Nelson asserts that if there is any truth to these kind of outbursts on Lawrence's part, then Williams has made Frieda a symbol of "suffocating . . .

destructive woman" (87), but thinks that this situation is softened tremendously
by Lawrence's concluding need for her "tenderness and understanding" (87).

Frieda and Bertha are, respectively, symbols for the body and the soul, a contrast, Tischler points out, that emphasizes Williams's admiration for Lawrence's
"metaphysical veneration of the physical" (*Tennessee Williams* 120) over the
spiritual. Other symbols are ones of "crucifixion, human sacrifice, and the battle
between light and dark in the universe" (Tischler, *Tennessee Williams* 120; Falk
42).

The smothering effects of civilization on Lawrence are depicted as a battle
between "the little old maid in myself" whose life has "only come out in books"
(T. Williams, *I Rise*, Acting ed. 8) and the "savage" capable of "some kind of
violent action" (8) he hoped to convert himself into in the southwestern desert.
Lawrence himself in this play is a symbol for freedom from puritanism and the
enemy "of all petty feminine restrictions and demands, the old, primitive, independent male principle" (Tischler, "Distorted Mirror" 400).

Plot

The plot of this one-act play is exceedingly simple. Living in a cabin in the
Alpes-Maritimes in France, Lawrence is dying of tuberculosis. His wife Frieda is
trying to keep him calm, yet she also stands prepared to help him die as he wishes
to, "proud and alone" (Nelson 82). In the midst of a barrage of recriminations
exchanged "like screeching cats" (Nelson 83) between Lawrence and Frieda,
Bertha (Dorothy Brett) arrives with unhappy news about the public's reception
of a London exhibition of Lawrence's paintings. This final failure to "communicate the driving force of his life," even through another artistic medium, is
what Tischler believes finally kills Lawrence (*Tennessee Williams* 119).

Hewes noted that the plot, rather than following the literal facts of Lawrence's
last days, was an attempt "to fashion the poetic truth of Lawrence's spirit" as it
might have been revealed at the moment of death ("Tenstrikes" 23). Nelson
sees Bertha's dialogue with Frieda as anticipating "almost verbatim" conversations between Alma Winemiller and John Buchanan in *Summer and Smoke* (84).

PROBLEMS *I RISE IN FLAME, CRIED THE PHOENIX* POSES FOR CRITICS

Crandell points out that of the minor short plays by Williams that were performed in the 1950s, *I Rise in Flame, Cried the Phoenix* was praised most consistently. Tallmer called it "an exquisite fragment" (7), and Hewes was lavish in
his praise, calling it at season's end "Off Broadway's finest new play" ("Off Broadway" 50). Though Calta found it "interesting," he felt that the work was too
short to be of any worth as a theatrical piece (30), a criticism echoed by Donahue
(178). Like Fedder (47), Londré believes that Williams's portrait of Lawrence as
a man who both feared and wanted to master women was essentially unsym-

pathetic (161). Ganz declares it "an indifferent and undramatic one-acter," but asserts that it nevertheless is key to understanding all the rest of Williams's works because it identifies Lawrence as Williams's literary parent, the "father who will give him what he needs . . . a rationale for the sexual obsessions" that dominate his work (278).

CHIEF PRODUCTIONS

The play opened (along with Georges Arnaud's *Sweet Confession*) at the Theatre de Lys on 14 April 1959 as part of the New York Chapter of ANTA's Matinee Theatre Series under the direction of Tom Brennan. Alfred Ryder, as D. H. Lawrence, won an off-Broadway award for the most outstanding male performance of the season, playing the part, Tallmer reported, "with a fascinating sprung rhythm all his own" (7). Tallmer was equally taken with Viveca Lindfors's portrayal of Frieda Lawrence, calling the performance honest, "passionate and aching" (7). Hewes characterized the performances of Nan Martin as Bertha (Dorothy Brett) and Lindfors as being a "waltz of celibacy" played against a "visceral symphony" ("Tenstrikes" 23).

Hewes's review makes it clear that the sentimental ending was used in this premiere performance, but no critic has commented on how the piece might have played differently if Williams had retained in production the ending as originally published. Nevertheless, Hewes felt the play to be Williams's "purest piece of dramatic writing" ("Tenstrikes" 23) and puzzled over why Williams waited ten years to stage it. Tallmer expressed his wish that some way be found to bring "this beautiful brief effort" to a larger audience (7). The play premiered in London on 2 April 1971 at the Basement Theatre.

It is evident from unpublished correspondence to Audrey Wood (housed at the Harry Ransom Humanities Research Center at the University of Texas at Austin) that an operatic version of the play by Thomas J. Flannigan, Jr., was composed in 1959, but it was not performed until 7 February 1980 at the Golden Fleece in New York, with John Jellison as Lawrence, Lucille Sullam as Frieda, and Sally Ann Sward as Bertha. Hughes felt the opera "hard to like" because of the "unattractive" depiction of Lawrence's behavior and the "hostile personality at its core" (45).

FILM AND TELEVISION VERSIONS

A television dramatization of the play was broadcast on PBS Television's "Play of the Week" series on 6 February 1961 under the collective title *Four by Tennessee*. (The other three plays were *Hello from Bertha*, *The Lady of Larkspur Lotion*, and *The Purification*.) Alfred Ryder repeated his performance as Lawrence and Jo Van Fleet played Frieda. Shanley declared *I Rise* the best of the quartet, "a sympathetic and sometimes moving tribute," but felt the program overall to be of interest only to Williams devotees in the way the plays foreshadowed "greater achievements" since these particular selections were flawed by primitive form, pretentiousness, and the lack of a "coherent point of view." Williams himself narrated the program, and Shanley declared his comments "refreshing" because they were neither "condescending nor apologetic" (67).

CONCLUDING OVERVIEW

This "violent drama" (Nelson 82) was Williams's most overt and intense expression of homage to Lawrence, whose influence found repeated voice in Williams's mature work (especially A *Streetcar Named Desire*, *Orpheus Descending*, and *Kingdom of Earth*) and in the way Williams tried to live his own life. As Casper concludes, *I Rise* is essentially "about the pride and pleasure of being one person, alone and intact" (751). In his *Memoirs*, Williams acknowledges D. H. Lawrence as one of his idols (94) and "a highly *simpatico* figure" (41), but ranks him beneath Chekhov in order of influence. In a conversation with Jim Gaines, Williams pointed out that Lawrence had not influenced his writing per se but that he identified with his "intense view of life" (Brown 277) and that he and Lawrence were both trying to communicate a belief in the beauty and purity of "sensual life" (Gaines 28). Williams told Dotson Rader that he admired Lawrence "for his spirit . . . his understanding of sexuality, of life in general" (153). Leverich concludes that although Hart Crane ultimately eclipsed both Lawrence and Chekhov as the "true touchstone" (592) of literary influence on Williams, reading Lawrence and meeting Lawrence's Taos-based disciples early in his career helped Williams identify and fuse the opposing sides of his artistic nature. One aspect of this opposition is a disfiguring violence found in many of Williams's plays that stems from his inability to reconcile his belief that man's natural instincts should be trusted absolutely with his strong moral sense of sin. In consequence, Williams punishes the characters he most wants to pardon, but in order to punish them at all, he must do so with "ferocious violence" (Ganz 294), a violence that characterizes critics' perceptions of *I Rise*. When Williams can control this "self-lacerating" need to praise and punish simultaneously, he regains the "clarity and force" of his "moral vision," and his strength as a playwright reemerges (Ganz 278), making him a unique force in the world of theatre.

WORKS CITED

Arnott, Catherine, comp. *Tennessee Williams on File*. London: Methuen, 1985.

Barnes, Clive. "Stage: Williams Night." *New York Times* 9 Apr. 1976: 31.

Boxill, Roger. *Tennessee Williams*. New York: St. Martin's, 1987.

Brown, Cecil. "Interview with Tennessee Williams/1974." *Partisan Review* 45 (1978): 276–305.

Calta, Louis. "Play by Williams on ANTA Double Bill." *New York Times* 15 Apr. 1959: 30.

Casper, Leonard. "Triangles of Transaction in Tennessee Williams." *Tennessee Williams: A Tribute.* Ed. Jac Tharpe. Jackson: UP of Mississippi, 1977.

Crandell, George W., ed. *The Critical Response to Tennessee Williams.* Westport, CT: Greenwood, 1996.

———. *Tennessee Williams: A Descriptive Bibliography.* Pittsburgh: U of Pittsburgh P, 1995.

Donahue, Francis. *The Dramatic World of Tennessee Williams.* New York: Ungar, 1964.

Falk, Signi Lenea. *Tennessee Williams.* Rev. ed. Boston: Twayne, 1978.

Fedder, Norman J. *The Influence of D. H. Lawrence on Tennessee Williams.* The Hague: Mouton, 1966.

Gaines, Jim. "A Talk about Life and Style with Tennessee Williams." *Saturday Review* 29 Apr. 1972: 25–29.

Ganz, Arthur. "The Desperate Morality of the Plays of Tennessee Williams." *American Scholar* (Spring 1962): 278–94.

Gunn, Drewey Wayne. *Tennessee Williams: A Bibliography.* 2nd ed. Metuchen, NJ: Scarecrow, 1991.

Hayman, Ronald. *Tennessee Williams; Everyone Else Is an Audience.* New Haven: Yale UP, 1993.

Hewes, Henry. "Off Broadway." *The Best Plays of 1958–1959.* New York: Dodd, Mead, 1959: 50.

———. "Tenstrikes." *Saturday Review* 15 Apr. 1959: 23.

Hughes, Allen. *New York Times* 9 Feb. 1980: 45.

Leverich, Lyle. *Tom: The Unknown Tennessee Williams.* New York: Crown, 1995.

Londré, Felicia Hardison. *Tennessee Williams.* New York: Ungar, 1979.

Nelson, Benjamin. *Tennessee Williams: His Life and Work.* London: Owen, 1961.

Rader, Dotson. "The Art of Theatre V: Tennessee Williams. *Paris Review* 81 (Fall 1981): 145–85.

Shanley, John P. Rev. of *Four by Tennessee. New York Times* 7 Feb. 1961: 67.

Spoto, Donald. *The Kindness of Strangers: The Life of Tennessee Williams.* Boston: Little, Brown, 1985.

Tallmer, Jerry. "ANTA Matinee." *Village Voice* 22 Apr. 1959: 7.

Tischler, Nancy M. "The Distorted Mirror: Tennessee Williams' Self-Portraits." *Mississippi Quarterly* 25.4 (1972): 389–403.

———. *Tennessee Williams: Rebellious Puritan.* New York: Citadel, 1961.

Williams, Dakin, and Shepherd Mead. *Tennessee Williams: An Intimate Biography.* New York: Arbor, 1983.

Williams, Tennessee. "Cried the Fox." *In the Winter of Cities.* New York: New Directions, 1956. 16.

———. *Memoirs.* Garden City, NY: Doubleday, 1975.

———. *I Rise in Flame, Cried the Phoenix.* Acting ed. New York: Dramatists Play Service, 1952.

———. *I Rise in Flame, Cried the Phoenix.* Limited edition. Norfolk, CT: New Directions, 1952.

———. *I Rise in Flame, Cried the Phoenix.* New World Writing: First Mentor Selection. New York: New American Library, 1952. 46–67.

Tennessee Williams's Fiction

JÜRGEN C. WOLTER

BIOGRAPHICAL CONTEXT

Tennessee Williams's obvious urge to publicize his personal dilemmas shows not only in his *Memoirs* and the novel *Moise and the World of Reason*, which has been called a "fictional counterpart to the *Memoirs*" (Savran 154) and an "apologia pro vita sua" (Sklepowich 538), but in all of his writings, and particularly in his fiction. For Gore Vidal, the stories are "the true memoir of Tennessee Williams" (xx). Biographers (e.g., Leverich, Spoto) explain the authorial self-reflexiveness of his works and demonstrate that some stories are lightly veiled autobiographies. For example, Spoto introduces *The Roman Spring of Mrs. Stone* as a fictionalized journal of Williams's life in the late 1940s (156, 167). For Donahue, the stories are important for their autobiographical contents because they "help us to understand the playwright and his family better" (179).

Since fiction allows space for undramatic reflections and digressions and since the breaking of taboos can be much more radical in a text that is written for the private closet of the individual reader than in a script for the "public theatre," a story can be a more spontaneous reaction to and a less palliative expression of a writer's momentary and momentous problems than a play. Therefore, Williams's stories less frequently use what Hyman calls "the Albertine strategy" of disguising homosexual relations as heterosexual. As Savran (83) points out, in his fiction Williams could be much more candidly confessional about the central experience of his life, his homosexuality. Clum was among the first to draw attention to the difference in the treatment of homosexuality in Williams's "private" and "public" art. In reading "Hard Candy," Clum shows that this difference relates to Williams's "dual vision," which is highly conscious of the general split between the "public persona" and the private human being (165–68). Since they are less evasive, that is, more directly autobiographical than his plays, his stories seem to offer a more direct approach to the way Williams thought and worked (Grande 118). Nonetheless, even his stories use oblique discourse that, as Clum shows, testifies to Williams's homophobia. Similarly, in the most perceptive study of "The Mysteries of the Joy Rio" to date, Savran argues that this early text (1941), long before Williams was prepared to come out publicly (1970), reflects the playwright's homophobia in those years (see also Sklepowich 534).

Even though Williams's homosexuality was the paramount autobiographical impulse, other experiences influenced his fiction. His intimate relationship with his sister prompted what Vannatta (73) calls the "Rose trilogy" ("Portrait of a Girl in Glass," "The Resemblance between a Violin Case and a Coffin," and "Completed"; for an analysis of the sister figure in Williams's work, see Clayton). Williams's ties to northwest Mississippi clearly informed the spiritual space of his Two River County; in her detailed reconstruction of Williams's equivalent of Faulkner's Yoknapatawpha, Leahy draws on twenty works, including the stories "The Kingdom of Earth" and "Twenty-Seven Wagons Full of Cotton." Another story very much rooted in Williams's experiences in the South is "Big Black: A Mississippi Idyll," which, as Kolin ("Tennessee Williams's 'Big Black' ") has demonstrated, reflects Williams's keen interest in the social and racial problems of the early 1930s; Kolin also suggests that in the story Williams reacted to the Scottsboro case and, possibly, the movie *King Kong*. Williams's experiences in New Orleans surface in some stories in *One Arm*; Richardson argues that the city's duality (City of Day, the American, commercial, and residential world; City of Night, the Latin, exotic world of the French Quarter) served as an informing image for Williams's fiction. For Tischler (*Tennessee Williams: Rebellious Puritan* 87), New Orleans gave Williams an "obsession for the pariah theme." His trips abroad also influenced his fiction: his sojourn in Rome, for example, inspired *The Roman Spring of Mrs. Stone*.

The shock of World War II also left its traces in Williams's fiction. Spoto, for example, points out that Williams began "Desire and the Black Masseur" at the height of World War II, which, he suggests, may account for the "celebration of pain and the mute inevitability of self-sacrifice" in the story (123). From the 1960s on, Williams seems to have adopted the absurdists' existentialist point of view in that after *The Night of the Iguana* (1962) his work is dominated by an absurd world, a world without reason. This is most clearly demonstrated by *Moise and the World of Reason*, which gives a description of the absurd universe; according to Jackson, the title of this novel can only be read as irony (65).

BIBLIOGRAPHIC HISTORY

Tennessee Williams's creativity in the field of fiction was unflagging for over fifty years and was at least as continuous, though by far not as successful, as his achievements as a playwright. Apart from two poems, his first published work was the short story "A Great Tale Told at Katrina's Party" (October 1924; Crandell, *Tennessee Williams* 477–78; Leverich, *Tom* 65; Kolin discusses "Isolated," November 1924, as Williams's first published extant story [" 'Isolated' "]). During his last years, Williams was still working on nondramatic fiction: *It Happened the Day the Sun Rose* was published in 1981, and the projected novel *The Bag People* (Arnott 69) was announced for 1982, but never published. During his lifetime, he wrote over fifty short stories, some of which appeared first in such periodicals as *Antaeus, Esquire,* and *Playboy*. Most of them were collected in four anthologies: *One Arm and Other Stories* (1949); *Hard Candy: A Book of Stories* (1954); *The Knightly Quest: A Novella and Four Short Stories* (1967); and *Eight Mortal Ladies Possessed: A Book of Stories* (1974). In addition, Williams published two novels: *The Roman Spring of Mrs. Stone* (1950) and *Moise and the World of Reason* (1975). Crandell meticulously describes all of these publications (*Tennessee Williams* 73–92, 116–23, 200–04, 238–45, 286–301, 353–54, 362–70). Crandell's notes show that there are only a very few changes in subsequent editions of some stories (77–78, 89, 91–92, 293).

Apparently, Williams's attitude toward his fiction was completely different from that toward his plays. If he ever went back to a published story, it was never with the objective to revise it as a story, but to use its dramatic potential and turn it into a play. This difference in attitude may be due to the fact that the "text" behind most of his (more immediately autobiographical) fiction was his life experience, which could not be changed, whereas the texts behind his major plays were other texts (stories and one-act plays), which as more detached fictional constructs could be reconstructed. There are only two exceptions: "Hard Candy" is a rewriting of "The Mysteries of the Joy Rio" (for a comparison, see Summers 145–50), and "The Important Thing" reads like an "updated version" (Vannatta 44) of "The Field of Blue Children." Tischler ("Romantic Textures" 155) sees Williams's urge to constantly revise/rewrite his works as an expression of "the true romantic spirit."

Most critics have commented on the relationship between the stories and their stage versions, and many think that the stories are only "notable for the manner in which they serve as companion pieces to his larger dramatic works" (Nelson 165; Weales 15; Tischler, *Tennessee Williams,* 1969, 10–11). Since the stories may add to our understanding of the plays, as Goodfarb concludes, some critics have presented more substantial analyses of the prototype stories and the dramatic revisions: for "Portrait of a Girl in Glass" and *The Glass Menagerie,* see Beaurline and Cohn (98–102); for "Three Players of a Summer Game" and *Cat on a Hot Tin Roof,* see Cohn (111–12) and May; for "The Kingdom of Earth" and *Kingdom of Earth,* see Derounian; for "The Night of the Iguana" and for "The Malediction" and "The Strangest Kind of Romance," see Draya ("Fiction" 649–51). In what is still the most valuable study of the relationship between Williams's fiction and drama, Reck defines three ways in which Williams uses his stories in his plays: the transfer of a single line or element out of its context; the repetition of a particular theme, but with different characters and situations; and the direct transposition with similar characters and events, and sometimes even dialogue. That allusions and repetitions may serve the purpose of parody has been demonstrated by Derounian in her comparison of the story "The Kingdom of Earth" and its stage version.

The comparative studies foreground definite continuities in Williams's work, irrespective of the genre he used. Vannatta finds much of Williams's later fiction prefigured in his early story "The Vengeance of Nitocris" (6–7). Similarly, Kolin ("'No Masterpiece Has Been Overlooked'") not only outlines the genesis of "Big Black: A Mississippi Idyll" at the University of Missouri, but also shows that this early story already features many elements that were to become typical of Williams's later works. Vannatta traces the development of the short fiction from the apprenticeship years (1928–1940) through maturity (1941–1952) to decline (1953–1983). Crandell, however, is doubtful about such a pattern of progression (Rev. 91). Vannatta's book is supplemented by an important selection from Williams's own remarks about his writing, *Where I Live*.

MAJOR CRITICAL APPROACHES

Themes

In the only book-length study of Williams's short fiction to date, Vannatta identifies themes identical with the ones on which Williams focuses in his plays, such as "the power and destructiveness of passion" (20), "the fate of the fugitive in a harsh world" (42), and the need for love. Other critics supplement Vannatta's catalog: Nelson adds "loss" (174) and Draya "the passage of time" ("Fiction" 661) as central themes.

Williams used the "privacy" of the genre of fiction for a more straightforward elaboration of his major theme, the destructiveness of desire, than he could ever achieve or dare on the stage. Generally, "Desire and the Black Masseur" has been seen as a typical example of Williams's concept of personal and universal guilt in an imperfect, fragmented world and of the corresponding desire for at-one-ment through violence. Blades finds the story essential for an understanding of "the self-hatred and violent self-destruction found throughout Williams' works" (101), while Presley regards it as "the earliest and clearest example" of Williams's "grotesque vision" (43). Rogers reads the violence in this and other stories and plays as an indication of their characters' refusal to accept their hopeless existence in an absurd world (81–82). For Ganz, the violence is rather a form of ritual punishment for the key crime in Williams's moral world, the crime of the rejection of sexuality/life (111). Hurley ("Tennessee Williams" 107–13) sees the relationship between guilt and punishment in the story from the social-psychological perspective of David Riesman's *Individualism Reconsidered* (1954) with its claim that Americans have a desire to belong and to be accepted; however, identification and conformity with other members of society is never fully achieved and causes guilt that is expiated by self-punishment as self-sacrifice. Thus it is not the story that is "horrifying and repugnant," it is rather our world (112). Schubert explains Burns's desire for self-annihilation as due to the social situation in the United States of the 1940s as analyzed by Vance Packard (*The Status Seekers*, 1959) and David Riesman (*The Lonely Crowd*, 1950); he regards the story as an apocalyptic vision, as a prophetic warning about the potential violence of race relations in the United States, and as a foreshadowing of the threat of "Black Power" in the 1960s. Savran studies "Desire and the Black Masseur," "Big Black: A Mississippi Idyll," and "Rubio y Morena" in light of the relationship between differences in ethnicity or race and the intensity of desire: "the greater the difference in skin color, the more violent the sexual encounter." There is also a correlation between desire and speech: the fiercer the desire, the greater the vocal inarticulateness of the character, whose only means of expression left is the "pen(is)" (125–26). The idea of the inexpressibility of desire is taken up in Williams's late work, for example, in *Moise* (156).

The focus on sexuality in many of Williams's works suggests a kinship with D. H. Lawrence, which Fedder purports to analyze (see 27–46 for the fiction). He contrasts Lawrence's dexterity with Williams's "inept" writing (43). A more appreciative and appropriate study of Williams's treatment of sexuality and desire has been undertaken from the perspective of gay studies. Sklepowich was the first to discuss thoroughly homosexuality in Williams's fiction, arguing that what has been decried as grotesque, decadent, and neurotic in Williams's fiction can only be understood as the manifestation of a "homosexual sensibility"; his survey of the fiction from *One Arm* to *Moise* demonstrates that Williams's treatment of homosexuality changed from "a mystical to a more social perspective, . . . from the mythic to the real" (526–27). More elaborate studies of Williams as a homosexual writer have been presented by Summers and Savran. Summers focuses on the gay fictions in *One Arm* and *Hard Candy* and reads them as explorations of "universal themes of loneliness and isolation" (154). Savran argues against the widely accepted transvestite reading of Williams's fiction (a reading that is based on Hyman's theory of the "Albertine strategy") because it completely disregards the "complexly gendered network" (117) that Williams weaves and Savran, using *The Roman Spring of Mrs. Stone* as an example, unravels (115–18).

Whereas most early criticism of Williams's fiction focused on his interest in the dilemmas of the individual (Tischler, *Tennessee Williams: Rebellious Puritan*, for example, finds most of his work "free" of "social content" 39), more recent critics raise social and political issues in the canon. America is a constant theme in Williams's fiction, with Two River County as a fictional representation of contemporary America (Blades 25). Summers points out that the stories "document the cruelty and oppression suffered by gay people in mid-century America" (155), and he detects a strong undercurrent of social protest against a repressive and hypocritical society in "The Mysteries of the Joy Rio" (146–47). Savran locates "revolutionary potential" in the "fractured discourse" of *Moise and the World of Reason* (166). Hurley ("Tennessee Williams" 33–43) argues that

The Roman Spring of Mrs. Stone castigates the rugged individualism and perversion of values in America. Gérard, on the other hand, thinks that the destructive materialism that Williams condemns in the novel pertains "to man in general, not to America alone" (152–53). Falk sees Mrs. Stone as an epitome of "the corruption of her time" (146), while Tischler (*Tennessee Williams: Rebellious Puritan* 177) reads the novel as "a study of Anglo-Saxon decadence" (see also Nelson 149–54). The function of the artist in society is defined in Williams's story "The Poet," which Hurley ("Tennessee Williams" 159–67) analyzes as Williams's fictional manifesto on his concept of art and which Tischler ("Romantic Textures" 147) reads as the artistic creed of a "natural romantic."

A central issue has been whether Williams's worldview is optimistic or pessimistic. Disagreeing with critics who see Williams as a pessimistic writer of existentialist despair, Grande sees a metaphysical optimism behind the moral hell of the stories. For Rogers, Williams's view is more optimistic than that of the absurdists because his characters "still search and respond" (82).

Characters

The biographies (e.g., Leverich, Spoto) draw attention to the fact that many relatives and friends became models for characters in Williams's stories. In the process of fictionalization, their individual personalities were transformed to types. Draya points out that Williams, in his plays and his stories, used the same character types, such as "the earthy middle-aged woman," "the handsome . . . young man," and the repressed and fearful "outcast" ("Fiction" 653–54), but he concedes that "most of Williams's characters . . . are more complex" (655). Despite the similarities between the stories and the plays, there seems to be a significant difference: Most of Williams's short stories are dominated by male characters, whereas in the plays the women (Amanda, Laura, Blanche, Maggie, Alma) are the most memorable figures. This may be due to the generic differences outlined earlier: the stories are more "private," and therefore Williams could take the risk of being less oblique here about personal matters.

Vannatta is also an indispensable guide to Williams's representative, almost allegorical stock characters, such as the "sensitive artist, the fugitive, the vulnerable soul" (22), and "the Rose archetype" (74). Peden groups the stories in *One Arm* and *Hard Candy* into unsensational stories with nonexceptional characters and grotesque or Gothic "fantasies" about pathological outcasts and derelicts ("Mad Pilgrimage" 248). Dersnah investigates the Gothicism of Williams's characters (37–50). Blades (163–68) finds the "dominating female" and Boxill "the faded belle" as character types in Williams's fiction (31, 33). Ramaswamy's impressionistic study sees Williams's "typical" characters as "frustrated and incomplete," daydreamers who "are miserable when they are not indulging in their peculiar form of 'escape' like films or alcoholism" (277). Rogers (81–82) draws a much more positive picture of Williams's characters: they are never paralyzed by despair, but struggle on, although sometimes extremely violently. Reconstructing the mythic geography of Two River County, Leahy maps a spiritual space inhabited by "children of the earth," "corruptors of the earth," and "spirits of the wild."

Williams's black males in "Big Black: A Mississippi Idyll" and "Desire and the Black Masseur" frustrate critics because these characterizations seem to coincide with the racist stereotype (see, e.g., Hurley, "Williams' 'Desire' " 55). Kolin ("Tennessee Williams's 'Big Black' "), however, argues that the portrayal of Big Black is "compassionate and sophisticated" and surpasses the stereotype (11), while Savran (126–27) elaborates on the contradiction between Williams's "antiracist" notions and the way his work "objectifies and exoticizes the dark Other."

Symbols

Critics have frequently commented on Williams's use of religious symbols in his fiction, especially in "Desire and the Black Masseur" and "One Arm." Draya ("Frightened Heart" 49–51) and Dersnah (47–50) elaborate on Williams's Christian metaphors and imagery in "Desire," while Summers shows that by reducing the symbolic to the literal, Williams here parodies "theological doctrines" and "conventional religious symbolism," especially Christian communion (138–39). Similarly, Boxill (130) reads the title of "Desire and the Black Masseur" as a pun on Black Mass. The religious imagery and allusions in "One Arm" suggest for Summers a form of counterreligion to Christianity, an unchristian belief in the possibility of "salvation and resurrection" during life on earth through "sexual sharing" (137).

Other symbols have also found perceptive analyses: Vowles studies the images of liquid and water as symbols of homosexuality in Williams's works, using "The Field of Blue Children," "The Malediction," and *The Roman Spring of Mrs. Stone* as major examples. Falk and Gérard explicate the recurring vulture image in *The Roman Spring of Mrs. Stone* (Falk 146–47; Gérard 148–51), while Dersnah elucidates the Gothic imagery of "Desire and the Black Masseur" (37–50).

Some stories have recently been read as complex metaphors. Of particular interest here is Savran's excellent analysis of the description of the derelict movie theatre in "The Mysteries of the Joy Rio," which he reads as a metaphor for Williams's use of the dramatic tradition in general: "recolonizing an old-fashioned theater and turning it into an enigmatic, if slightly queer, site of resistance" (78). In his metaphoric reading of *Moise and the World of Reason*, Savran comments on the symmetry of pen and penis, of textuality and sexuality as a constant feature in Williams's work (156–57). May suggests that the meaning of Brick's enigmatic detachment in *Cat on a Hot Tin Roof* can best be approached (if not explained) by an analysis of the metaphor of game in "Three Players of a Summer Game"; he comments on the clash between the "ideal game of art" and "the real game of existential reality" (286).

Plot

Short stories in general and Williams's fictions in particular present a limited number of situations and instead focus on the development of character. Boxill (22–23, 69, 145) suggests that this typical characteristic of the genre might have influenced Williams's drama, that is, that the episodic, basically undramatic structure of many of Williams's plays might result from their genesis as stories. Reck's study of the metamorphosis from story to play comes to an interesting conclusion: when Williams "is most certain about the fiction . . . the chances are better that the resulting play will be successful" (153). Reck even suggests that the failure of Williams's plays of the 1960s may be due to the fact that these plays did not develop from prose tryouts.

MAJOR PROBLEMS THE FICTION POSES FOR CRITICS

Two major problems confront critics of the fiction. First, they have to accept homosexuality as a serious and genuine expression of humanity. Studies by Sklepowich, Clum, Summers, and Savran are among the most insightful on Williams's fiction. Savran's interpretation of "Hard Candy," for example, concludes that the text might be read as a metanarrative that polyvocally presents different ways of reading and thus provides a "guide . . . to the way that homosexuality . . . is coded and decoded" in a Williams text (113–14).

Second, critics have had trouble accepting the stories as works of art in their own right. Of particular interest are Vannatta's comments on Williams's experiments with elements of narrative technique, such as narrative voice, point of view, and dialogue.

CONCLUDING OVERVIEW

No standard history of the contemporary American novel mentions Williams as a novelist, and if studies of the American short story draw attention to his stories, they prefer the early ones. Even Williams specialists are undecided about the quality of his fiction. Their reactions are as mixed as those of one of the first reviewers of *The Roman Spring of Mrs. Stone*, who "liked the manner more than the substance; I admired and was repelled" (Alpert 19). The situation has hardly changed over the years and can still be characterized by the image Peden used in his 1955 review of *One Arm and Other Stories*: Williams's stories are "like a dead mackerel in the moonlight . . . that shines and stinks" ("Broken Apollos" 11). Such emotional reactions are perhaps inevitable with a writer who in his fiction (and life) was just as passionate in his responses. However, despite the critical disparagement of his fiction and the much more enthusiastic reception of the plays, Williams, surprisingly enough, never gave up fiction for drama. Even in the years of his greatest international success as a playwright, he did not desert the genre in which he had started his literary career; he even considered his "best writing to be in his short stories and one-act plays" (Gaines 217). His criteria for assessing the quality of a piece of art seem to have been as off-center/ex-centric as his life, and his fiction with its foregrounding of a homosexual sensibility and concern for the Other may also have been too unconventionally ex-centric for mainstream critics, who therefore found it impossible to give it appropriate, let alone sympathetic, attention.

Critics still have not really fathomed Williams's concept of writing as an autobiographically expressionist art: what did it mean to Williams to fix(ate) unresolved personal dilemmas in a linear, monovocal text on silent paper and then dissolve this text into polyvocal events, into voices and roles for acting? Why did he in many cases choose the narrative genre first and only later, sometimes many years later, turn these monologues into dramatic polylogues? Critics may not have found answers to these questions because they have not taken his fiction seriously enough. If they really want to understand Tennessee Williams's creative genius, its oscillation between writing and acting, text and role, "pencil and penis" (Savran 156), they cannot continue to ignore a large part of his work. Furthermore, Williams's stories and plays, in which he uses the same themes, characters, and images, provide excellent material for studies in the field of narratology and genre definition; critics have wrongly let themselves be obsessed by some of his plays and repelled by most of his fiction, just as they seem to have been obsessed by his biography, but repelled by his life.

Critics may have decried Williams's fiction as repulsive because they noticed, but could not appreciate, its revolutionary potential. Many of Williams's fictions are unconventional not only in their themes, but also in their narrative technique. In some cases, his experiments with the intrusive narrator and the first-person perspective are remarkable, for example, when the narrator is used as a persona, a mask in the sense of the ancient drama. Occasionally Williams takes off this mask, the persona becomes transparent, and then the narrator turns into the writer's substitute and mouthpiece.

Williams's "revolution" as regards both his unconventional themes and his experimental narrative technique is personally motivated and must be seen in the context of his ideology of love, which, in his fiction, is often expressed by images of (homo)sexual violence and longing. This ideology, however, is subversive only in that it attacks a world gripped by a cold war that mainstream society wages on the Other.

WORKS CITED

Alpert, Hollis. "Sex Fringed with Horror." *Saturday Review* 30 Sept. 1950: 18–19.

Arnott, Catherine M., comp. *Tennessee Williams on File.* London: Methuen, 1985.

Beaurline, Lester A. "*The Glass Menagerie:* From Story to Play." *Modern Drama* 8 (Sept. 1965): 142–49.

Blades, Larry Thomas. "Williams, Miller, and Albee: A Comparative Study." Diss. St. Louis U, 1971.

Boxill, Roger. *Tennessee Williams*. London: Macmillan, 1987.

Clayton, John Strother. "The Sister Figure in the Works of Tennessee Williams." *Carolina Quarterly* 11 (Summer 1960): 47–60.

Clum, John M. " 'Something Cloudy, Something Clear': Homophobic Discourse in Tennessee Williams." *South Atlantic Quarterly* 88 (Winter 1989): 161–79.

Cohn, Ruby. *Dialogue in American Drama*. Bloomington: Indiana UP, 1971.

Crandell, George W. Rev. of *Tennessee Williams: A Study of the Short Fiction*, by Dennis Vannatta. *Southern Humanities Review* 24 (1990): 90–92.

———. *Tennessee Williams: A Descriptive Bibliography*. Pittsburgh: U of Pittsburgh P, 1995.

Derounian, Kathryn Zabelle. " 'The Kingdom of Earth' and *Kingdom of Earth* (*The Seven Descents of Myrtle*): Tennessee Williams' Parody." *University of Mississippi Studies in English* 4 (1983): 150–58.

Dersnah, James Louis. "The Gothic World of Tennessee Williams." Diss. U of Wisconsin, 1984.

Donahue, Francis. *The Dramatic World of Tennessee Williams*. New York: Ungar, 1964.

Draya, Ren. "The Fiction of Tennessee Williams." *Tennessee Williams: A Tribute*. Ed. Jac Tharpe. Jackson: UP of Mississippi, 1977. 647–62.

———. "The Frightened Heart: A Study of Character and Theme in the Fiction, Poetry, Short Plays, and Recent Drama of Tennessee Williams." Diss. U of Colorado, 1977.

Falk, Signi Lenea. *Tennessee Williams*. New Haven, CT: College and University P, 1961.

Fedder, Norman J. *The Influence of D. H. Lawrence on Tennessee Williams*. The Hague: Mouton, 1966.

Gaines, Jim. "A Talk about Life and Style with Tennessee Williams." *Conversations with Tennessee Williams*. Ed. Albert J. Devlin. Jackson: UP of Mississippi, 1986. 213–23.

Ganz, Arthur. *Realms of the Self: Variations on a Theme in Modern Drama*. New York: New York UP, 1980.

Gérard, Albert. "The Eagle and the Star: Symbolic Motifs in *The Roman Spring of Mrs. Stone*." *English Studies* 36 (Aug. 1955): 145–53.

Goodfarb, Rowena Davis. "Heroic Gestures: Five Short Stories as Sources for the Plays of Tennessee Williams." Diss. Fordham U, 1988.

Grande, Luke M. "Metaphysics of Alienation in Tennessee Williams' Short Stories." *Drama Critique* 4.1 (Nov. 1961): 118–22.

Hurley, Paul J. "Tennessee Williams: Critic of American Society." Diss. Duke U, 1962.

———. "Williams' 'Desire and the Black Masseur': An Analysis." *Studies in Short Fiction* 2 (Fall 1964): 51–55.

Hyman, Stanley Edgar. "Some Notes on the Albertine Strategy." *Hudson Review* 6 (Autumn 1953): 416–22.

———. "Some Trends in the Novel." *College English* 20 (Oct. 1958): 2–9.

Jackson, Esther Merle. "Tennessee Williams: Poetic Consciousness in Crisis." *Tennessee Williams: A Tribute*. Ed. Jac Tharpe. Jackson: UP of Mississippi, 1977. 53–72.

Kolin, Philip C. " 'Isolated': Tennessee Williams's First Extant Published Short Story." *Tennessee Williams Literary Review* 1 (1998): 33–40.

———. " 'No Masterpiece Has Been Overlooked': The Early Reception and Significance of Tennessee Williams's 'Big Black: A Mississippi Idyll.' " *American Notes and Queries* 8 (Fall 1995): 27–35.

————. "Tennessee Williams's 'Big Black: A Mississippi Idyll' and Race Relations, 1932." *REAL* 20.2 (1995): 8–12.

Leahy, Sharon Lewis. "Tennessee Williams's Two River County: From the Kingdom of Earth to the Kingdom of Heaven." Diss. U of Notre Dame, 1993.

Leverich, Lyle. *Tenn: The Timeless World of Tennessee Williams.* (forthcoming).

————. *Tom: The Unknown Tennessee Williams.* London: Hodder, 1995.

May, Charles E. "Brick Pollitt as Homo Ludens: 'Three Players of a Summer Game' and *Cat on a Hot Tin Roof*." *Tennessee Williams: A Tribute.* Ed. Jac Tharpe. Jackson: UP of Mississippi, 1977. 277–91.

Nelson, Benjamin. *Tennessee Williams: His Life and Work.* London: Owen, 1961.

Peden, William. "Broken Apollos and Blasted Dreams." *Saturday Review* 8 Jan. 1955: 11–12.

————. "Mad Pilgrimage: The Short Stories of Tennessee Williams." *Studies in Short Fiction* 1 (Summer 1964): 243–50.

Presley, Delma Eugene. "The Moral Function of Distortion in Southern Grotesque." *South Atlantic Bulletin* 37 (Spring 1973): 37–46.

Ramaswamy, S. "The Short Stories of Tennessee Williams." *Indian Studies in American Fiction.* Ed. Madhukar K. Naih. Delhi: Macmilllan India, 1974. 263–85.

Reck, Tom S. "The Short Stories of Tennessee Williams: Nucleus for His Drama." *Tennessee Studies in Literature* 16 (1971): 141–54.

Richardson, Thomas J. "The City of Day and the City of Night: New Orleans and the Exotic Unreality of Tennessee Williams." *Tennessee Williams: A Tribute.* Ed. Jac Tharpe. Jackson: UP of Mississippi, 1977. 631–46.

Rogers, Ingrid. *Tennessee Williams: A Moralist's Answer to the Perils of Life.* Frankfurt: Lang, 1976.

Savran, David. *Communists, Cowboys and Queers: The Politics of Masculinity in the Work of Arthur Miller and Tennessee Williams.* Minneapolis: U of Minnesota P, 1992.

Schubert, Karl. "Tennessee Williams, 'Desire and the Black Masseur.' " *Die amerikanische Short Story der Gegenwart.* Ed. Peter Freese. Berlin: Schmidt, 1976. 119–28.

Sklepowich, Edward A. "In Pursuit of the Lyric Quarry: The Image of the Homosexual in Tennessee Williams' Prose Fiction." *Tennessee Williams: A Tribute.* Ed. Jac Tharpe Jackson: UP of Mississippi, 1977. 525–44.

Spoto, Donald. *The Kindness of Strangers: The Life of Tennessee Williams.* Boston: Little, Brown, 1985.

Summers, Claude J. *Gay Fictions: Wilde to Stonewall: Studies in a Male Homosexual Literary Tradition.* New York: Continuum, 1990.

Tischler, Nancy M. "Romantic Textures in Tennessee Williams's Plays and Short Stories." *The Cambridge Companion to Tennessee Williams.* Ed. Matthew C. Roudane. Cambridge: Cambridge UP, 1997. 147–66.

————. *Tennessee Williams.* Austin, TX: Steck-Vaughn, 1969.

————. *Tennessee Williams: Rebellious Puritan.* New York: Citadel, 1961.

Vannatta, Dennis. *Tennessee Williams: A Study of the Short Fiction.* Boston: Twayne, 1988.

Vidal, Gore. Introduction. *Collected Stories.* By Tennessee Williams. New York: New Directions, 1985. xix–xxv.

Vowles, Richard B. "Tennessee Williams: The World of His Imagery." *Tulane Drama Review* 3.2 (Dec. 1958): 51–56.

Weales, Gerald. *Tennessee Williams.* Minneapolis: U of Minnesota P, 1965.

Williams, Tennessee. *Collected Stories.* New York: New Directions, 1985.

————. *Eight Mortal Ladies Possessed*. New York: New Directions, 1974.

————. *Hard Candy: A Book of Stories*. New York: New Directions, 1954.

————. *It Happened the Day the Sun Rose*. Los Angeles: Sylvester and Orphanos, 1981.

————. *The Knightly Quest: A Novella and Four Short Stories*. New York: New Directions, 1967.

————. *Moise and the World of Reason*. New York: Simon and Schuster, 1975.

————. *One Arm and Other Stories*. New York: New Directions, 1949.

————. *The Roman Spring of Mrs. Stone*. New York: New Directions, 1950.

————. *Where I Live*. New York: New Directions, 1978.

Tennessee Williams's Poetry

PATRICIA GRIERSON

BIOGRAPHICAL CONTEXT

Poetry was as important as drama in the life of Tennessee Williams. He began writing poetry early in life, and by the time he was in his teens, he had published one of his poems in the Ben Blewett Junior High School *Annual* (Leverich; Kolin " 'Isolated' " 34). He transformed his poetry into dramatic event, or perhaps it was the other way around. In any case, Williams produced a major effort in poetry approximately every twenty years of his life. From 1924 to 1926, he wrote poems for his high-school paper, the *Junior Life* (Kolin " 'Isolated' " 34), and a college magazine (Kolin " 'No Masterpiece' ") and won a prize in the Mahon poetry contest at the University of Missouri. In November 1925, while he was only fourteen years old, his Thanksgiving poem was published, and in January 1926, "Old Things" followed and an entire page was devoted to a poem, "Demon Smoke" (Hale 615). By the time he was twenty-five, Williams published a poem in the distinguished *Poetry* magazine. Hale insists that these early years were very important in the development of Williams's sense of himself as a poet and as a writer (615). Early influences on Williams's poetry include the College Poetry Society and the Mummers while he attended the University of Missouri, Washington University, and the University of Iowa and are well documented by Hale (618–19). Williams's most formative poems were written during this period. "In 1944, James Laughlin—who would become Williams's longtime editor at New Directions—chose twenty-seven of Williams's poems . . . for inclusion in the third series of *Five Young American Poets*" (Adler, "Williams's Poetry" 63).

Many of Williams's poems later appeared in *In the Winter of Cities* (1954) or *Androgyne, Mon Amour* (1977). A span of approximately twenty years appears between each of these efforts, almost as if Williams's poetic vision is being used for rest stops, for the recharging of his overall dramatic imagination, or even for a scheduled break from the intensity, a passion that probably began with his intense admiration for the poetry of Hart Crane. Crane became Williams's poet hero, as the epigraph to *A Streetcar Named Desire*, paying homage to his poetic imagination in Williams's life, attests. The epigraph, from Crane's "The Broken Tower," introduces Blanche as a person who has found herself in "a broken world." Adler explores the connection between Crane's verses and Williams's literary vision (*Streetcar* 80–81). Crane's influence on Williams is succinctly evaluated in Bloom's "Introduction": "Williams truly had one precursor only. Hart Crane, the greatest of our lyrical poets" (2). Yet Tischler argues that "the life and work of Vachel Lindsay . . . live on in the poetry and plays of Tennessee Williams" ("Vagabond Poet" 78). Familiar with Edgar Lee Masters's biography, Williams found in Lindsay "a persona for his own cultivated image as a vagabond poet and even injected this persona into a planned ghostplay on Lindsay" (76). However, Williams, after *Battle of Angels*, had "outgrown" Lindsay and "moved on to a more mature" artist hero—D. H. Lawrence (78).

Drawing heavily on Williams's biography, Tischler (*Rebellious Puritan*) views Williams as a Romantic artist/poet. Leverich discusses Williams's early poetic efforts in light of life documents in his monumental biography. Other important scholarship has examined Tennessee William's life as it relates to his poetry (see the interviews in Devlin, the works of Edwina Dakin Williams and Spoto; and of course Williams's own autobiography, *Memoirs*). Adler ("Williams's Poetry") Holditch, and Taylor explore the poetry in light of the plays and the reciprocal influence they had on Williams.

BIBLIOGRAPHIC HISTORY

Although Williams published only two books of poetry, *In the Winter of Cities* and *Androgyne, Mon Amour*, many of the poems in these two volumes had appeared earlier in published form with other titles and in different forms. For example, previously published poems in *In the Winter of Cities* were "Blue Mountain Ballads," "The Christmas of Guadalajara," and poems that had appeared in *Five Young American Poets, Harper's Bazaar, Mademoiselle, New Directions, Panorama, Partisan Review, Semi-colon,* and *Voices*. Poems in *Androgyne* had earlier appeared in *Ambit, Evergreen Review, Five Young American Poets* (3rd series, 1944), *New Directions in Prose and Poetry,* and *Prairie Schooner.* "Crepe-de-Chine," for example, first appeared in the *New Yorker.* "A Liturgy of Roses" had previously been published in the *Chicago Review* before being reprinted in *Androgyne*. See Crandell for complete bibliographic citations (144–50; 321–25).

CRITICAL APPROACHES

Themes

The various thematic concerns that Williams covers in his plays also find expression in his poems. Adler ("Williams's Poetry"), Woods, Taylor, and Ower are especially helpful in this area. Williams's central theme—demon time— weaves in and out of his verses as often as does loneliness, redemption from the fall, and other themes. Roger Boxill identifies several of these dominant themes: "Time is always . . . the destroyer, never the healer" (28) and "life succumbs to death, youth to age, the yearning spirit to the waning flesh . . . even the energy of art to . . . 'declivity' " (28).

Williams's own emerging sexuality and the necessity of "outright rebellion" to free the adolescent from female dominance—a prominent idea in the poems— is covered well in Ower (616–17). Ower stresses the interdependence of Williams's homosexuality and his fixation on the mother (622). Ower also discusses what he calls the "two poles of Williams's sensibility manifested in his range and variety as a poet" (609). In addition, he compares Williams's poetry to Blake's and Yeats's and the relationship of the mind's response to a given influence that exists prior to any artistic expression, and that can spring from the poet's own life. Falk also focuses on how the author's psychology manifests itself in his works. Williams's *Where I Live: Selected Essays* especially (1–14) is required reading on understanding the poet-playwright's main ideas.

Savran demonstrates how elements of the "perverse" manifest themselves in the poems (83). Similarly, Hirsch calls Williams "our national poet of the perverse." Fedder is a good source for a discussion of Williams's use of perversion and sexual abnormality. He assesses the value systems of Williams and D. H. Lawrence, stressing the here and now, feelings, the senses over logic, and the material world as possibly significant in the casting of thematic concerns for the poems. Fedder examines differences as well as similarities in themes found in the poems of the two writers.

Adler identifies the central theme of "humankind's fallenness" and subdivides it into three individual categories: first, those stigmatized by society through no fault of their own; second, those who have failed another and have lost a belief in their own self-worth; and third, those who experience intimations of mortality and must somehow cope with them ("Tennessee Williams's Poetry" 67–72). The "fallen" of these three types populate the poems: "Poem for Paul" lists outsiders who will later flesh out his plays (70); Nonno's poem in *The Night of the Iguana* shows how fear springs from a recognition of "decay and death" and must be dealt with as a permanent fixture of life (67). This fear surfaces again in "Wolf Hour," which relates the Swedish "Hour of the Wolf" as that period during the night during which more people die from heart attacks than at any other time. Williams always hears time's winged chariot drawing near.

The fall from grace in Eden is another key theme running through Williams's works, especially the poems. The "fallen spirit's imprisonment" is linked to the enveloping feminine. Ower relates Williams's poem "The Soft City" on the creation in the mother's womb to this "partial loss of form," claiming that such "incarnation" is "the very essence of its intellectual nature" (614).

In yet another thematic category, Clurman, discussing Williams's attempt to reconcile body and soul, elaborates on the isolated individuals—the outcasts and despised. Ower alludes to the "fear" of the "awakening soul," of the freeing of mind from matter, "the power of heaven which potentially . . . is a little frightening" (617). He adds that "outright rebellion [as far as Williams is concerned] is necessary to free the adolescent from female dominance" (617). In "The Soft City," Everyman creeps into his wife's womb in the shape of a bird that Ower identifies with the husband and his bird form with divine spirit, while the feminine he associates with dead matter (617).

Falk explicates the theme of the "comparable intensity of religions and sexual passion" in "A Separate Poem," "Across the Space," and "San Sebastiano." In "Jack-O-Lantern's Weather," an expansion of the earlier "The Marvelous Children," Williams himself claims that losing the person one loves the most is his chief concern (Foreword to *Sweet Bird of Youth*).

In "Old Men with Sticks," Taylor contrasts the lifelessness with images of organic vitality, especially with the passion of youth (621). Ower also examines "Death Is High," "The Siege," and "Recuerdo," all from *In the Winter of Cities*, and explores Williams's development into a "comprehensive vision of human existence, his Platonic conception of its paradoxical and fundamentally tragic nature" (621). Clurman explores the conflict of body and soul that is integral to Williams's work.

Characters

Often the major "characters" of Williams's poems are not the clear-cut, recognizable people who inhabit the plays. They are the third-person pronouns that can be any or all of us, as in "Crepe-de-Chine" or "An Immense Black Man" or "Stones Are Thrown," or they can be animals, abstracts, or insects. "The plight of the fugitive caught in an aggressive, conventional society," as Falk describes the poet in Williams's poem "Cried the Fox," becomes the other estranged, isolated voice from his poems. Many of these "characters" are strange creatures molded into an almost schizophrenic beauty by their oddness. Having a carnival-like quality, they are the things the unconscious mind would describe were it conscious.

Some readily identifiable characters in the poems are angels, animals, circus performers, inanimate objects, abstractions, and a host of others. The "you" of "A Liturgy of Roses" is almost certainly his sister, Rose, who, in 1943, suffered a prefrontal lobotomy, an event that played a profound role in Williams's life. Rose also appears in other poems, such as "Recuerdo." A circus setting often shapes characters. The Williams-child-poet joins the "circus" and revels in the liminal world. His "Big Top" sequence of poems is full of con men and women, a "conjurer's trick," a gypsy, a haunted house, spooks, and apparitions in *In the Winter of Cities*. Williams created such a nightmarish world in *Camino Real* and pushed the carnavalesque to absurd proportions in *The Gnädiges Fräulein*. Sometimes the child follows the circus to meet bizarre people, characters that people a surreal landscape out of which dreams are made, dreams somehow unfinished in their recollection. Williams is aware of their presence, as he is aware of the animals that personify this childlike playfulness in the poet—Miss Puma and Miss Monkey in "Miss Puma, Miss Who?" in *Androgyne, Mon Amour*.

Persona, then, becomes vitally important in Williams's poetry. Taylor comments on "The Angels of Fructification" as a "fable narrated in the third person so that the 'speaker' of the poem all but disappears. He is there only by permission" (627). Taylor goes on to say that characters "become vivid as allegorical personifications . . . caricatures rather than characters" (628). In "Cinder Hill," Mathilda takes on the larger role of prostitute or fallen woman (*Androgyne*). In "Miss Puma, Miss Who?" from the same volume, the animals deliver the fable, humorously; there is even a reference in the poem to Williams's play *Suddenly Last Summer* when the persona refers to Miss Puma as "à la Sebastian" because she cannibalizes that with which she has just had sex. In "Everyman," the persona becomes part of the action in the poem merely by being an onlooker. The events in the "story" so overwhelm the presence of the "I" of the poem as to cause him (her) to fade out almost completely (*In The Winter* 57). In "Cried the Fox" from the same volume, the fox is the "I" of the poem.

In keeping with his theme of man's fall from grace, which dominates William's poems as it does the plays, many of the central characters of his poems are inscribed in the Judeo-Christian tradition. From *In the Winter*, for example, there are "The Angels of Fructification," "The Christmas of Guadalajara," "Heavenly Grass," "Her Head on the Pillow," and "San Sebastiano de Sodoma." In *Androgyne*, "The Couple" and "A Mendicant Order" constantly remind the reader of the good-evil, god-human aspect of the Williams universe.

Taylor makes a case for the persona of "Orpheus"—the "you" of the poem—as that of the fugitive poet who "seldom escapes and, if he does, is condemned to the role of the poète maudit" (627). Other favorite characters include blacks and the mother figure, both of whom play prominent roles in Williams's depiction of women and the feminine (627–28). Ower claims that in "Recuerdo, Part II" from *In the Winter*, "a terrible power is manifested . . . [through] the poet's black nurse, who perhaps suggests the 'earth mother' " (617). In "Dark Arm, Hanging over the Edge of Infinity," the persona warns the reader and the "Negro" that the hour of the wolf of fear may be near.

Tischler refers to many of Williams's characters as representing "the mood and people of Bourbon Street" (*Rebellious Puritan* 60). They are "rootless people with eccentric beauty" (61), yet nowhere in the plays is this "eccentricity" more obvious than in the androgynous persona, Williams's heroic ideal, from whom

Androgyne, Mon Amour takes its title and who appears in several poems in this volume.

Incorporated into the plays, the poems often serve as representative icons of the characters' problems. In *The Night of the Iguana*, for instance, Nonno's poems come to represent his life, as indeed they did for Williams. In *Something Cloudy, Something Clear*, the autobiographical character August, cites a revealing poem he had composed at a very early age asking God to end his life before it had a chance to become jaded.

Symbols

Tennessee Williams, like all other poets, occupies seminal symbols, those that he uses repeatedly and for definite purposes. His iterative symbols include fire, ice, birds and animals, roses, water, dreamers, and religious and sexual references. Freudian and Catholic allusions dominate his verse. Ower believes that Williams is following in the Romantic visionary tradition by using "myth and symbol, intuition and imagination, to chart the recesses of man's soul and of the universe" (609), and he further cites religious/spiritual images that are sexually energized in the poems. Williams tends to "invest human sexuality with a broader philosophical and spiritual significance" (611). Ower links Williams, therefore, with "the neoplatonizing bent of the English Romantic poetry" (612–13). Similarly, Taylor expertly explicates "The Siege" from *In the Winter* and claims that the poet develops a metaphysical conceit out of the person's blood, which goes voyaging "in search of one unknown before but recognized on sight" (629). Adler observes that Williams "sacramentalizes the physical," pointing out that "the tongue of the beloved" in "Iron Is the Winter" is denominated as "holy bread" ("Tennessee Williams's Poetry" 64). Ower also explores the "religious symbology" Williams uses to portray love in "San Sebastiano De Sodoma" (613–14). Taylor also provides a fruitful analysis of the forces of light or spirit against the face of darkness. Williams also uses other key symbols—candles, Everyman, the womb, colors—that have religious overtones. Jackson concentrates on Williams's poetic techniques and how they contribute to the development of a new form in his plays, while John Fritscher looks at Williams's use of the sacred in the plays and poems.

Much Freudian psychology lies within the poems in the form of sexual allusions, situations, and conflicts. Ower suggests that in "Lady Anemone," in which a "blade" and a "scabbard" are used, Williams is metaphorizing intercourse and the conflict between the sexes (610). The image of the phallus is also crucial to the symbolic world of "Recuerdo." According to Ower, the images of the violets, the violent electrical storm, the washing machine, and others all point out that Williams links his "two magnified phallic symbols with terror and destruction." In "Old Men with Sticks," Ower finds symbols of the inversion of the three images of metal, winter cold, and a frozen, empty space (621).

Plot

"Coherent sense cannot be made of Williams' poetry except through patterns of symbolism" (Ower 612). These "patterns of symbolism" become the "plot" of Williams's poems, narratives without actually telling a linear story. Edwina Dakin Williams's motherly remembrances (*Remember Me to Tom*) about her son's life give clues to the poet's need for a different kind of canvas, one necessarily without the rigid structure of plot. Exhaustion with the dramatic world drove Williams back to that genre that does not have to have a plot—as indeed, life usually does not—poetry. Yet Ower admits that Williams in his poems "makes concessions to descriptive, narrative or logical coherence," and that much of his meaning is carried by his syntax of images" (622). Taylor, in fact, likens Williams's verses to those of Walt Whitman and D. H. Lawrence because "Williams likes to write two kinds of poems, the open, sprawling, prophetic form and the tight, delicate lyric. He shows a mastering of both techniques" (624). The lines themselves bear out the events of the tale, and they help to create the sense of the lines. A grotesqueness of structure is also evident in some of the poems, a "kind of mixture of farce and comedy" (Taylor 626). In "The Angels of Fructification" from *In the Winter*, "the angels are robots coming off a production line" (612). Williams's poetics include technology metaphors and systems as well.

MAJOR PROBLEMS THE POEMS POSE FOR CRITICS

It is difficult to say whether Williams's poems by themselves would be judged differently had he not written the plays. Tischler concisely raises the issue of how the poems stand on their own and their relationship to the plays, a central problem for the critics (*Rebellious Puritan*). Taylor affirms, though, that "the poems are by no means merely footnotes to the plays, however, but impassioned flights that hover above and around the other works" (624). Critical opinion of them, nonetheless, has varied greatly. For Taylor, Williams's poems pose problems because they do so much: "His imagination is so volatile, his symbols so rich, that the unresponsive reader is likely to be left sitting on the curb after the express has gone" (625). According to Taylor, "Orpheus Descending" illustrates Williams's problem of the "destructive force of materialism and parochialism [triumphing] over the artistic sensibility" (625). For Ower, Williams's problem in the poetry was that of the "integrity of the self": Williams "sees the 'I' as imperiled equally by dissolution into physical flux and by the annihilation of nirvana" (620).

PERFORMANCES

Crandell lists several sound recordings of Williams reading from his works, including the poems (569–71).

CONCLUDING OVERVIEW

The tyranny of time, a favorite Williams theme in the poetry, demonstrates more than a passing interest (perhaps unconsciously) in a universe governed by physical laws, seen or not, and by spiritual forces as well. Astronomical images are plentiful in both *In the Winter* and *Androgyne* and are tempered by references to the world of the physical, or the impenetrable though flawed universe of science. In such a world, humankind occupies a precarious place, according to poet Tennessee Williams. Williams refers to the "cosmic circus" in "Carrousel Tune" from *In the Winter* and claims that the "freaks" there are "men." This view of humanity as not only imperfect, but made to be ridiculous as well, is echoed in other poems, such as "Orpheus Descending," in which Orpheus is told to "cringe" because he must learn that we "are not stars." In "The Ice Blue Wind" in *Androgyne*, Williams refers to merging with "The Absolute," a presence that appears to be slightly more indebted to quantum mechanics than to Judeo-Christian mythology.

Williams metaphorizes the "brains' dissection" in the poem by the same name in *Androgyne*, and in this same poem, he includes lesions. In "A Liturgy of Roses," he mentions "wombs" whose warmth "hums" like an electrical current (52). These are all images of physical forces at play upon the lost and the lonely; the different characters who people Williams's poems are caught and acted upon by such forces, both benign and otherwise.

Williams invented a self in which "space" and "cosmic" are leading topoi, as illustrated in the cosmology of Winter in "Carrousel Tune" and in "The Jockeys at Hialeah." In *Androgyne*, he elaborates on an almost personal space-time continuum in "One Hand in Space" by comparing a "nameless place" to a moment. In "Stones Are Thrown" in *Androgyne*, he mentions the "huge Black Man" who may cast into space beyond space "a diadem of stars," and he calls the space beyond space "the indefinable void." Thrown into this mixture of scientific-medical imagery are his many references to machines, robots, infinity, oblivion, heaven, angels, and the leaders of the church. Science meets spirit in the poetry, as it does in the plays. The poems, no less than the dramas, are testaments to an unfolding, complex autobiography.

It is easy to find in the poems a Tennessee Williams whose symbology reveals an uneasy mix of the workings of a God-in-plan and the indifference of physical forces at work. These uneasy juxtapositions sway with the long and short verses of his mixed and finally uncertain stanzas.

WORKS CITED

Adler, Thomas P. "*A Streetcar Named Desire*": *The Moth and the Lantern*. Boston: Twayne, 1990.

———. "Tennessee Williams's Poetry: Intertext and Metatext." *Tennessee Williams Annual Review* 1 (1998): 63–72.

Atkinson, Brooks. "*Streetcar* Tragedy—Mr. Williams's Report on Life in New." *New York Times* 14 Dec. 1947, sec. 2: 1.

Bloom, Harold, ed. *Tennessee Williams's A Streetcar Named Desire*. New York: Chelsea, 1988.

Boxill, Roger. *Tennessee Williams*. New York: St. Martin's, 1987.

Clurman, Harold. "Tennessee Williams: Poet and Puritan." *New York Times* 29 Mar. 1970, sec. 2:5.

Crandell, George W. *Tennessee Williams: A Descriptive Bibliography*. Pittsburgh: U of Pittsburgh P, 1995.

Debusscher, Gilbert. "Minting Their Separate Wills: Tennessee Williams and Hart Crane." *Modern Drama* 26 (1984): 455–76.

Devlin, Albert J., ed. *Conversations with Tennessee Williams*. Jackson: UP of Mississippi, 1986.

Falk, Signi. *Tennessee Williams*. 2nd ed. Boston: Twayne, 1978. 53–62.

Fedder, Norman J. *The Influence of D. H. Lawrence on Tennessee Williams*. The Hague: Mouton, 1966.

Fitts, Dudley. "Talking in Verse." *New York Times Book Review* 8 July 1956: 10.

Fritscher, John J. "Some Attitudes and a Posture: Religious Metaphor and Ritual in Tennessee Williams' Query of the American God." *Modern Drama* 13 (Sept. 1970): 201–15.

Gunn, Drewey Wayne. *Tennessee Williams: A Bibliography*. 2nd ed. Metuchen, NJ: Scarecrow, 1991.

Hale, Allean. "Tennessee Williams's St. Louis Blues." *Mississippi Quarterly* 48 (Fall 1995): 609–26.

Hirsch, Foster. *A Portrait of the Artist: The Plays of Tennessee Williams*. Port Washington, NY: Kennikat, 1979.

Holditch, W. Kenneth. "Tennessee Williams: Poet as Playwright." *Xavier Review* 3.2 (1983): 21–27.

Jackson, Esther Merle. *The Broken World of Tennessee Williams*. Madison: U of Wisconsin P, 1965.

Jennings, C. Robert. "Interview with Tennessee Williams." *Playboy* Apr. 1973: 69–84.

Kolin, Philip C. " 'Isolated': Tennessee Williams's First Extant Published Short Story." *Tennessee Williams Annual Review* 1 (1998): 33–40.

———. " 'No Masterpiece Has Been Overlooked': The Early Reception and Significance of Tennessee Williams's 'Big Black: A Mississippi Idyll.' " *AN/Q* 8.4 (1995): 27–35.

Leverich, Lyle. *Tom: The Unknown Tennessee Williams*. New York: Crown, 1995.

McCann, John S. *The Critical Reputation of Tennessee Williams: A Reference Guide*. Boston: Hall, 1983.

Ower, John. "Erotic Mythology in the Poetry of Tennessee Williams." *Tennessee Williams: A Tribute*. Ed. Jac Tharpe. Jackson: UP of Mississippi, 1977. 609–23.

Rader, Dotson. *Tennessee: Cry of the Heart*. Garden City, NY: Doubleday, 1985.

Skloot, Robert. "Submitting Self to the Flame: The Artist's Quest in Tennessee Williams, 1935–1954." *Educational Theatre Journal* 25 (May 1973): 199–206.

Spoto, Donald. *The Kindness of Strangers: The Life of Tennessee Williams*. Boston: Little, Brown, 1985.

"Talk with the Playwright," *Newsweek* 23 Mar. 1959: 75.

Taylor, William E. "Tennessee Williams: The Playwright as Poet." *Tennessee Williams: A Tribute*. Ed. Jac Tharpe. Jackson: University Press of Mississippi, 1977. 624–30.

Tischler, Nancy M. *Tennessee Williams: Rebellious Puritan*. New York: Citadel, 1961.

———. "Tennessee Williams: Vagabond Poet." *Tennessee Williams Annual Review* 1 (1998): 73–79.

Williams, Edwina Dakin, as told to Lucy Freeman. *Remember Me to Tom*. New York: Putnam's, 1963.

Williams, Tennessee. *Androgyne, Mon Amour*. New York: New Directions, 1977.

———. *Battle of Angels*. Pharos 1–2 [Murray, UT] (1945).

———. *The Glass Menagerie*. New York: New Directions, 1945.

———. *In the Winter of Cities*. New York: New Directions, 1956.

———. "Let Me Hang It All Out." *New York Times* 4 Mar. 1973, sec. 2: 1.

———. *Memoirs*. Garden City, NY: Doubleday, 1975.

———. *The Night of the Iguana*. *The Theatre of Tennessee Williams*. Vol. 4. New York: New Directions, 1971. 247–346.

———. "Preface to My Poems." *Five Young American Poets*. Ed. James Laughlin. Norfolk, CT: New Directions, 1944. 122–26.

———. *Something Cloudy, Something Clear*. New York: New Directions, 1995.

———. *Suddenly Last Summer*. New York: New Directions, 1958.

———. *Sweet Bird of Youth*. New York: New Directions, 1962.

Woods, John. "Tennessee Williams as a Poet." *Poetry* 90 (July 1957): 256–58.

Tennessee Williams's Films

DAVID H. GOFF

BIOGRAPHICAL CONTEXT

Tennessee Williams's work is rich in cinematic techniques and references to films. In his production notes for *The Glass Menagerie*, Williams issued a call for a "new plastic theatre" that has been hailed as "a manifesto of the cinematic stage" (Boxill 68). The playwright had a lifelong love of motion pictures. "When I was little I used to want to climb into the screen and join the action" (quoted in Maxwell xii). Williams was so engrossed in movies that he even experienced "heart palpitations" on the way home from *The Scarlet Pimpernel* (Kalson 779). Because of rejection by his father and peers, Williams sought refuge in writing and in the movie theatre as two avenues of escape. His first paid writing venture was a review of the silent film *Stella Dallas*, which earned the teenaged Williams a $10 prize from the Loews State Theater. At the age of thirty-three Williams was on Broadway, but only earning $17 a week as an usher at the Strand Theatre. Later that same year, he spent six months in Hollywood under contract to MGM as a scriptwriter, but was fired after writing material deemed "too literate" (Jennings 242) for Lana Turner, and for expressing his thoughts about a script for child star Margaret O'Brien (Murray 48). Nonetheless, MGM honored its six-month contract with the writer, and Williams used the time to work on his own projects, one of which was a screenplay, *The Gentlemen Caller*, that was later adapted into *The Glass Menagerie* and became the first Williams motion picture.

Kalson and Leverich discuss the autobiographical significance of motion pictures in Williams's works. The cinematic qualities of Tennessee Williams's plays are analyzed by Brandt, Phillips, and Yacowar. Phillips comments extensively on the relationship between Williams's works and the fifteen major films of his works and on the cinematic qualities of the original plays. The cinematic techniques of Williams and other post–World War II playwrights, according to Boxill, helped make theatre "more of a director's medium, like film" (68).

BIBLIOGRAPHIC HISTORY

Fifteen major motion-picture adaptations of Tennessee Williams's works were produced between 1950 and 1969, including adaptations of thirteen plays, an original screenplay (*Baby Doll*) adapted from two one-act plays, and one film adapted from a novel (*The Roman Spring of Mrs. Stone*). Several adaptations have also been produced for television and the large screen; the newer versions (after 1980) are more faithful to Williams's original material. Yacowar and Phillips survey each major film, and Phillips discusses subsequent large- and small-screen productions released prior to 1980. Both Yacowar (149–54) and Phillips (328–31) include a filmography. Gunn lists the major films and television adaptations as well as some more obscure television presentations that are often overlooked in other sources.

Published screenplays are available for only two of the films, *A Streetcar Named Desire* (Williams, *Streetcar* 330–484) and *Baby Doll*, first published in 1956 (Williams, *Baby Doll: The Script for the Film by Tennessee Williams*; Williams, *The Script for the Film Baby Doll*). Subsequent versions were published in 1957 (Williams 5–140), and 1991 (Williams 1–116).

MAJOR CRITICAL APPROACHES

Themes

Both Phillips and Yacowar survey themes in the fifteen films. Essentially, Williams's themes involve the conflict between illusion or fantasy and reality, especially in *Streetcar* (Crowther 37; Yacowar 15) and *Suddenly Last Summer* (Yacowar 50); and loneliness, developed in *The Glass Menagerie* (Phillips 49–61) and *The Night of the Iguana* (Yacowar 111). Crowther similarly described *The Fugitive Kind* as an "account of loneliness and disappointment in a crass and tyrannical world" (13). Loneliness is also at the core of *The Rose Tattoo* (Crowther 55; Phillips 107) and *Summer and Smoke* (Crowther 41; Knight, "Dissertation" 32).

A third central theme is the conflict between civilization and savagery, broadly explored in *Suddenly, Last Summer* (Phillips 178–80, 189; Yacowar 52–53), and *Sweet Bird of Youth* (Tube 6; Yacowar 93–94). In the xenophobic world of the predatory savagery of distinctly uncivilized local citizens, Williams's outsiders, such as Vacarro in *Baby Doll* and Val in *The Fugitive Kind* (Crowther 13), are the truly civilized forces. Crowther finds in *Baby Doll* the "degeneration and inadequacy of old Southern stock, as opposed to the vital aggressiveness of intruding 'foreigners' " (40). But perhaps the most common Williams theme pits the old against the new, running strongly in *Baby Doll, The Rose Tattoo*, and *The Last of the Mobile Hot Shots* and underscored by the age differences of Baby Doll and Archie, the degeneration of Archie's home and possessions, and the changing business of ginning cotton (Kahn 292–309; Yacowar 25–31, 34–35, 132–35).

Characters

Many of Tennessee Williams's films offer "another helping from [the author's] seemingly inexhaustible closet of mixed-up southern skeletons" (Pyro 6). Knight states that characterization is Williams's forte and that with his characters it is possible "that perfectly outrageous ideas can come from . . . completely acceptable people, or that completely outrageous people can mouth perfectly acceptable ideas" ("Where There's Williams" 22). Despite the vitality of Williams's characters, many have been substantially changed for the screen ever since Laura was "normalized" in the unfaithful adaptation of *The Glass Menagerie* (Yacowar 13). Princess in *Sweet Bird of Youth* became more glamorous (Kinney 2389), and Chicken in *The Last of the Mobile Hot Shots* was played by a white actor on stage but by a black actor, Robert Hooks, in the film (Phillips 218).

Foremost among Williams's film characters are Blanche DuBois and Stanley Kowalski, "just about the best feminine performance you're ever going to see, as well as an interpretation by Brando that is just about perfection" (Kael 352). Phillips hails Blanche as one of the most significant characters in American popular culture (67). In the introduction to the screenplay of *Streetcar*, the editors assert that Brando's method acting is "probably the major explanation of the movie's success" (Williams, "*Streetcar*" 331). Consistent with Williams's original purpose, Blanche is lonely, tormented and illusory, while Stanley, as played by Brando, is the force of reality, crude and direct. Rose describes Stanley as a "nightmare feminist critique of maleness: brutish and infantile" (2).

Big Daddy, played by Burl Ives in the filmed *Cat*, became another pop-culture icon. Like other insistent patriarchs (Jabe, Boss Finley), Big Daddy propels his favorite son Brick (Paul Newman) into responsible adulthood. Brick is the focal point of the story, and the divergence of the film from the play's treatment of Brick's latent homosexuality is significant (Phillips 146). Eliminating the idea of homosexuality from the film created confusion about the reasons for Bricks's avoidance of sexual relations with his wife, Maggie (Crowther 24; Ron 6).

Silva Vacarro, the "Other" in *Baby Doll*, has been discussed at length (Kahn 296–306; Kolin 6–10; Phillips 90–91, 101–02). Brandt places him in a category formed by "Williams's private myth of the Latin lover whose sensuality puts to shame the patently inadequate White Anglo-Saxon Protestant" and includes Lady Torrance (*The Fugitive Kind*) and Rosa Gonzalez (*Summer and Smoke*) in this group (167). More than Archie's antagonist, Vacarro, played by Eli Wallach, exudes sexual symbolism (Brandt 167; Kahn 296). Val in *The Fugitive Kind* has been described as masculine and as "alien and unprepossessing" (Crowther 13). Chance Wayne of *Sweet Bird of Youth*, although a former member of the community, has become an outsider through absence and behavior (Yacowar 93–95). In *The Night of the Iguana*, Shannon is described as "difficult," "a part without glamour yet touched with magical significant force" (Whit 6). Knight believes that Shannon has been extended from the role of a "catalyst" in the play to the central figure of the film and "a vivid illumination of the cross-currents of prudence and carnality that tear his soul" ("Where There's a Williams" 22).

Symbols

The films borrow many of the symbols from the plays yet afford filmmakers opportunities to expand Williams's symbolism through camera work and new locations. Phillips discusses symbolic camera shots foreshadowing rape in *Streetcar* and describes the phallic significance of an overflowing soda glass and a spurting beer bottle (84). Yacowar labels a shot of a squirting hose in the gutter outside the apartment building "an outrageous visual pun" (20). Light is used for symbolic aims in *The Rose Tattoo*. Scenes of Serafina's withdrawal from the world are dark, while sequences outside her cottage are bathed in bright sunlight (Phillips 111–12). Of course, the film, like the play, is full of rose symbols, homage to Williams's beloved sister Rose (Phillips 108–9).

In opening out stage productions for the screen, films symbolically extend a sense of place. In a basement scene unique to the film, *Cat*, Brick smashes belongings that symbolize the wealth of the Pollitts (Phillips 146). As the scene shifts outdoors, a shot of the wheels of Brick's car spinning in the mud points to his inability to escape his problems (Phillips 146). In *Suddenly Last Summer*, the Venables's lush tropical garden symbolizes the savage forces in the world in more frightening visual detail than the play (Yacowar 52). Director Joseph L. Mankiewicz used scenes at the mental institution to convey the savage ugliness that lurks just below the surface of the "wonders of science" (Crowther 22; Phillips 185, 187).

Not unexpectedly, Williams's films are rich in religious symbolism. Crowther comments on the Christ symbolism of Chris Flanders's name in *Boom* (56), and Phillips describes both the symbolic parallels between Flanders and Christ (301–2) and a scene that recalls the ascent of Calvary (306). Hartung finds the symbolism to be largely ineffective (385). *Iguana* is rich in Christian symbols.

Plot

By far the most detailed explication of the plots of Tennessee Williams's films is in Phillips. Most notably, the films deviate in major ways, some successful, some not, from the plays. The changes made to Tennessee Williams's plays in crafting them as motion pictures stemmed from the creative interpretation of directors, the screenplay writers who adapted them, and the internal and external censorship of Hollywood motion pictures that existed in the 1950s and 1960s (Pauly 130–37, 217–19; Walsh 244–45, 274–77, 293–94).

The very first adaptation, *The Glass Menagerie*, succumbed to the studio's desire for a traditional happy ending. Jim, the first Gentleman Caller, has departed, but another soon appears, and both Laura's lonely life and Amanda's hopes for her daughter will be fulfilled, in total violation of Williams's script (Yacowar 13–14). Hollywood also changed *Suddenly Last Summer* by linking Catharine in love with Dr. Cukrowicz (Yacowar 54–56). Because the Motion Picture Association of America (MPAA) protested the topic of venereal disease and the castration of Chance, the film version of *Sweet Bird of Youth* finds a pregnant Heavenly forced into an abortion by her father and ends with Chance savagely beaten (Phillips 163–64; Yacowar 95). The sanitizing of the film version weakens the story (Tube 6). Yacowar calls the film "an imposter" (96).

MAJOR PROBLEMS THE FILMS POSE FOR CRITICS

Though Williams's name "eased his acceptance in film" (Yacowar 138), the films by no means escaped critical censure. As Yacowar notes, adaptation of a stage work for the screen involves compromise, and virtually all films adapted from other forms change the original material; however, "insensitive compromises can ruin an adaptation" (9). This problem has undone many of Williams's adaptations, beginning with *The Glass Menagerie* (Phillips 50–61; Sinyard 164; Yacowar 9–14).

In addition, the Code Authority of MPAA and the Catholic Legion of Decency forced significant changes on the film adaptations of Williams's plays. *Baby Doll*, for example, was the target of a church-led boycott that reduced bookings by 75 percent (Phillips 97–99; Walsh 274–77). In *Streetcar*, Williams and Elia Kazan compromised with the code by punishing Stanley for the rape by having Stella take their newborn baby to Eunice's apartment, vowing never to return (Pauly 132–34). Important dialogue that gave Stanley "complexity and recognizable humanity" (Rose 1) was removed from the sequence preceding the rape (Pauly 132, 136). The MPAA-assigned film rating of X of *The Last of the Mobile Hot Shots*, the screen version of Williams's *Kingdom of Earth*, quickly pulled the film from theatres (Phillips 224).

Screenplay adaptations earned critical ire. Alpert described the work of Francis Coppola (who would later distinguish himself as a director) in *This Property Is Condemned* as "ersatz" Williams (40), and Crowther termed the development of the main characters as "wholly implausible" (24). Of Isobel Lennart's *Period of Adjustment* script, *Variety* stated that "the lapses, inconsistencies, and unlikelihoods of Williams' stage comedy-drama have not been eradicated" and evaluated the film as "uneven" and "lower case Williams" (Tube 6). Gore Vidal penned two film adaptations. Crowther characterized his script of *Suddenly Last Summer* as "sheer verbal melodramatics which have small effect on the screen" (22). Of the seriously flawed production of *The Last of the Mobile Hot Shots*, *Variety* kindly described Vidal's screenplay as "the least defective artistic element" (Murf 6).

CHIEF PRODUCTIONS

The Glass Menagerie, released in 1950 by Warner Brothers, was directed by Irving Rapper from a screenplay by Williams and Peter Berneis (Friedlich 25–26; Hartung 631–32; Phillips 49–64; Yacowar 9–14). Television adaptations were produced by CBS in 1966 and ABC in 1973 (Phillips 61–64; 312–13). A second film version, directed by Paul Newman, was released in 1987 ("Glass Menagerie" 1).

A Streetcar Named Desire was directed in 1951 by Elia Kazan from an adaptation by Oscar Saul (Corliss 44–47; Phillips 64, 74–87; Reisz 170–71; Yacowar 15–24). The 1951 film was reissued in 1994 with the censored footage restored, especially significant in showing just how sexualized Kazan's directing made the script (Rose 2). Subsequent television versions of *Streetcar* have been produced in the United States (1984 and 1995) and Sweden in 1981 as *Linje Lusta* with Bibi Andersson as Blanche and Krister Hendriksson as Stanley ("Linje Lusta" 1).

Williams's own adaptation was the basis for *The Rose Tattoo*, a 1955 black-and-white Paramount film directed by Daniel Mann (Phillips 110–20; Sarris 19–20; Yacowar 25–31; Zinsner 20). The following year Kazan returned to direct the Warner Brothers release of *Baby Doll*, based on Williams's original screenplay (Corliss 44–47; Dyer 21–22; Phillips 87–103). *Cat on a Hot Tin Roof*, the first color adaptation, was released in 1958 by MGM and was directed by Richard Brooks, who co-wrote the screenplay adaptation with James Poe (Downing 454–55; A. Johnson 54–55: McManigal 36; Phillips 142–54; Yacowar 38–48).

Suddenly Last Summer was released in 1959 by Columbia Pictures and was directed by Joseph L. Mankiewicz (Hart 39–41; Hartung 396; A. Johnson 40–42; Phillips 173–96; Yacowar 49–59). The screenplay is credited to Gore Vidal and Williams, but Vidal claims the work as his own (Phillips 184). Sidney Lumet directed the 1960 United Artists film *The Fugitive Kind*, adapted from the play *Orpheus Descending* by Williams and Meade Roberts (Kuhn 290–92; Phillips 197–213; Prouse 144–45; Whitehall 23–24; Yacowar 60–66). *Summer and Smoke* and *The Roman Spring of Mrs. Stone* were both released in color in 1961. *Summer and Smoke* was a Paramount release directed by Peter Glenville from an adaptation by James Poe and Meade Roberts (Armitage 22; Phillips 226–42; Rhode 95; Wharton 621; Yacowar 67–75). *The Roman Spring of Mrs. Stone* was adapted by Gavin Lambert from a novel by Williams and was directed by José Quintero (Fitzpatrick 42–43; Gill 97–98; Phillips 249–66; Yacowar 84–92). Two more MGM adaptations followed in 1962. Richard Brooks wrote the screenplay adaptation and directed *Sweet Bird of Youth* (Gill 148–50; Kauffmann 28; Phillips

154–72; Rothschild 233–34; Yacowar 93–98). *Period of Adjustment* was directed by George Roy Hill from an adaptation by Isobel Lennart (Gill 234–35; Phillips 266–79; Whitehall 38; Yacowar 99–104).

The Night of the Iguana, released in 1964, was directed by John Huston, who collaborated with Anthony Veiller on the screenplay adaptation of the MGM release (Phillips 280–98; Rothschild 439–41; Sussex 198–99; Taylor 50–52; Yacowar 105–12). Sidney Pollack directed *This Property Is Condemned*, a 1966 Seven Arts color release (Adler 88–90; Durgnat 68; Farber 61; Phillips 120–32; Yacowar 113–21) with a screenplay by Fred Coe, Edith Smith, Francis Ford Coppola (of *Godfather* fame) "and [an] additional dozen script doctors" (Phillips 123). An earlier version of *This Property Is Condemned* aired on NBC in 1958 as a "Kraft Television Theater" presentation (Gunn 162; Phillips 123, 311). The 1968 Universal color film *Boom* (also listed as *BOOM* or *Boom!*) was directed by Joseph Losey from an adaptation by Williams of his play *The Milk Train Doesn't Stop Here Anymore* (Gow 43; W. Johnson 52–55; Phillips 298–320; Rothschild 454; Yacowar 122–30). Sidney Lumet also directed *The Last of the Mobile Hot Shots*, a 1969 Warner Brothers/Seven Arts adaptation of *Kingdom of Earth* and the last of the fifteen major film adaptations of Williams's works (Canby 38; Overbeck 75; Phillips 213–25; Yacowar 131–36).

Phillips terms the influence of the twelve directors of the major Williams film adaptations "undeniable" but notes that they ranged in talent from "first class artists" such as Kazan, Brooks, Huston, and Losey to the "more pedestrian," naming Mann and Rapper (309). Kazan's social and political statements in his films are widely noted (Ciment, Pauly, and Michaels); Kolin focuses on Kazan's opposition to racism and support of civil rights in *Baby Doll*. Brooks (see Kantor, Blacker, and Kramer) directed the most successful adaptation, *Cat on a Hot Tin Roof* (Crowther 24), as well as the less successful *Sweet Bird of Youth*, which Phillips believes "reconfirmed [Brooks's] status as one of Williams's foremost screen interpreters" (154). Recent biographies of Huston include those of Brill and McCarty, and Losey's films have been examined by Palmer and Riley. Lumet received mixed reviews for *The Fugitive Kind* and the disastrous *The Last of the Mobile Hot Shots* (Hartung 127; Kael 70). *Variety* hailed Glenville's directing of *Summer and Smoke* as having "successfully disengaged film from its stage format" in the first half (Hawk 6). Yacowar names *This Property Is Condemned* (Pollack) and especially *The Night of the Iguana* (Huston) and *Boom* (Losey) as the three works that "have sparked the film director's intelligence and a lively, different work emerges" (142).

Some of the world's leading actors and actresses starred in Williams's films. Vivien Leigh established the film standard for Blanche in *Streetcar* and performed admirably in *The Roman Spring of Mrs. Stone* (Molt). Marlon Brando (Stanley) also starred as Val Xavier in *The Fugitive Kind* (Manso). Williams wrote the role of Serafina in *The Rose Tattoo* for Anna Magnani, who also starred as Lady Torrance opposite Brando in *The Fugitive Kind* (Zinsner 20). Geraldine Page appeared as Alma Winemiller in *Summer and Smoke* (Crowther 41) and as Alexandra del

Lago in *Sweet Bird* (Gill 148–50). Paul Newman gave powerful performances as Brick in *Cat* and in the role of Chance Wayne in *Sweet Bird* (see Quirk). As Maggie the Cat (*Cat on a Hot Tin Roof*), Elizabeth Taylor appeared in the first of three starring roles in Williams films. She also portrayed Catharine Venable in *Suddenly Last Summer*, and Flora Goforth in *Boom* (see the biographies by D'Arcy and Leclercq). Then husband Richard Burton appeared as Chris Flanders opposite Taylor in *Boom*, then as Shannon in *Night of the Iguana* (see Cottrell and Cashin).

CONCLUDING OVERVIEW

Tennessee Williams's films occupy an important place in the history of American filmmaking. No other American dramatist has had as many film adaptations made from his works, and few writers can claim that the film versions of their works retain as much of their original vision. From the perspective of the playwright, though, this outcome was a mixed blessing. The transition from stage to screen was not always easy for Williams's plays. Williams wrote for the stage and its smaller, focused audience. Ironically, the mediated film versions that reach millions are often significantly different from the original material. His bold material and troubled characters, acceptable on the Broadway stage, did not easily fit the Hollywood vision of family entertainment. The visual material and subject matter of the fifteen films hardly seem shocking by today's standards, yet *Streetcar*, *Baby Doll*, and *Cat* challenged the Hollywood establishment as few other films had. While the bold *Baby Doll* ultimately succumbed to censorship, *Streetcar* broke codes in presenting adult themes despite the work of industry censors. The rape in *Streetcar* was allowed to remain because Kazan and Williams fought for it. Beyond doubt, the film adaptations of Williams's works contributed immensely to the maturing of motion-picture content in the 1950s and 1960s.

When the first adaptations of Williams's works appeared on the motion-picture screen, television's impact on film attendance was already being felt in Hollywood. The rigidity of the MPAA Code was starting to buckle to the changing nature of the film marketplace. Hollywood was losing its customers to television and could only survive by adapting its product. In the 1950s and 1960s, the idea of films for adults gained currency in the film industry and with the filmgoing public. *Streetcar*, *Baby Doll*, *Cat*, and *Suddenly Last Summer*, as well as works by other creative talents, were driving forces in this important transition. The artistic freedom enjoyed by filmmakers today was obtained through the efforts of Williams and the writers, producers, and directors who bravely brought his work to the large screen with creativity and sensitivity.

WORKS CITED

Adler, Renata. Rev. of *This Property Is Condemned*, dir. Sidney Pollack. *New Yorker* 27 Aug. 1966: 88–90.

Alpert, Hollis. "Instant Tennessee Williams." *Saturday Review* 25 June 1966: 40.

Armitage, Peter. Rev. of *Summer and Smoke*, dir. Peter Glenville. *Film* 32 (Summer 1962):
22.

Boxill, Roger. *Tennessee Williams*. New York: St. Martin's, 1987.

Brandt, George. "Cinematic Structure in the Work of Tennessee Williams." *American
Theatre*. Ed. John Russell Brown and Bernard Harris. New York: St. Martin's, 1967.

Brill, Lesley. *John Huston's Filmmaking*. Cambridge: Cambridge UP, 1997.

Broeske, Pat H. Rev. of *Baby Doll*, dir. Elia Kazan. *Magill's Survey of Cinema*. Vol. 1. 2nd.
series. Ed. Frank N. Magill. Englewood Cliffs, NJ: Salem, 1981.

Canby, Vincent. Rev. of *The Last of the Mobile Hot Shots*, dir. Sidney Lumet. *New York
Times* 15 Jan. 1970: 38.

Ciment, Michael. *Kazan on Kazan*. London: Secker and Warburg, 1973.

Corliss, Richard. "*A Streetcar Named Desire* and *Baby Doll*." *Film Comment* 4 (Summer
1968): 44–47.

Cottrell, John, and Fergus Cashin. *Richard Burton, Very Close Up*. Englewood Cliffs, NJ:
Prentice-Hall, 1971.

Crowther, Bosley. Rev. of *Baby Doll*, dir. Elia Kazan. *New York Times* 19 Dec. 1956: 40.

———. Rev. of *BOOM!*, dir. Joseph Losey. *New York Times* 27 May 1968: 56.

———. Rev. of *Cat on a Hot Tin Roof*, dir. Richard Brooks. *New York Times* 19 Sept.
1958: 24.

———. Rev. of *The Fugitive Kind*, dir. Sidney Lumet. *New York Times* 15 Apr. 1960: 13.

———. Rev. of *The Rose Tattoo*, dir. Daniel Mann. *New York Times* 13 Dec. 1955: 55.

———. Rev. of *Summer and Smoke*, dir. Peter Glenville. *New York Times* 17 Nov. 1961:
41.

———. Rev. of *A Streetcar Named Desire*, dir. Elia Kazan. *New York Times* 20 Sept. 1951:
37.

———. Rev. of *Suddenly, Last Summer*, dir. Joseph L. Mankiewicz. *New York Times* 23
Dec. 1959: 22.

———. Rev. of *This Property is Condemned*, dir. Sidney Pollack. *New York Times* 4 Aug.
1966: 24.

D'Arcy, Susan. *The Films of Elizabeth Taylor*. New York: Beaufort Books, 1982.

Davis, Louise. "That Baby Doll Man: Part I." *Tennessean Magazine* 3 Mar. 1957: 12–13,
30– 31. Rpt. in *Conversations with Tennessee Williams*. Ed. Albert J. Devlin. Jackson:
UP of Mississippi, 1986. 43–49.

Downing, Robert. Rev. of *Cat on a Hot Tin Roof*, dir. Richard Brooks. *Films in Review* 9
(Oct. 1958): 454–55.

Durgnat, Raymond. Rev. of *This Property Is Condemned*, dir. Sidney Pollack. *Films and
Filming* Nov. 1966: 68.

Dyer, Peter John. Rev. of *Baby Doll*, dir. Elia Kazan. *Films and Filming* (Feb. 1957): 21–
22.

Farber, Stephen. Rev. of *This Property Is Condemned*, dir. Sidney Pollack. *Film Quarterly*
20 (Winter 1966–67): 61.

Fitzpatrick, Ellen. Rev. of *The Roman Spring of Mrs. Stone*, dir. José Quintero. *Films in
Review* 13 (Jan. 1962): 42–43.

Friedlich, Ruth K. Rev. of *The Glass Menagerie*, dir. Irving Rapper. *Films in Review* (Oct.
1950): 25–26.

Gill, Brendan. Rev. of *Period of Adjustment*, dir. George Roy Hill. *New Yorker* 10 Nov.
1962: 234–35.

———. Rev. of *The Roman Spring of Mrs. Stone*, dir. José Quintero. *New Yorker* 3 Jan. 1962: 97–98.

———. Rev. of *Sweet Bird of Youth*, dir. Richard Brooks. *New Yorker* 7 Apr. 1962: 148–50.

———. "The Glass Menagerie." *Internet Movie Database*. 1997. http://www.us.imdb.com/cache/title-exact/48635 (28 Sept. 1997).

Gow, Gordon. Rev. of *Boom*, dir. Joseph Losey. *Films and Filming* Mar. 1969: 43.

Gunn, Drewey Wayne. *Tennessee Williams: A Bibliography*. 2nd ed. Metuchen, NJ: Scarecrow, 1991.

Hart, Henry. Rev. of *Suddenly Last Summer*, dir. Joseph L. Mankiewicz. *Films in Review* Jan. 1960: 39–41.

Hartung, Philip T. Rev. of *Boom*, dir. Joseph Losey. *Commonweal* 88 (14 June 1968): 385.

———. Rev. of *The Fugitive Kind*, dir. Sidney Lumet. *Commonweal* 72 (29 Apr. 1960): 127–28.

———. Rev. of *The Glass Menagerie*, dir. Irving Rapper. *Commonweal* 52 (6 Oct. 1950): 396.

———. Rev. of *Suddenly Last Summer*, dir. Joseph L. Mankiewicz. *Commonweal* 71 (1 Jan. 1960): 39–41.

Hawk. Rev. of *Summer and Smoke*, dir. Peter Glenville. *Variety* 6 Sept. 1961: 6.

Jennings, C. Robert. "*Playboy* Interview: Tennessee Williams." *Playboy* Apr. 1973: 69–84. Rpt. in *Conversations with Tennessee Williams*. Ed. Albert J. Devlin. Jackson: UP of Mississippi, 1986. 224–50.

Johnson, Albert. Rev. of *Cat on A Hot Tin Roof*, dir. Richard Brooks. *Film Quarterly* 12 (Winter 1958): 54–55.

———. Rev. of *Suddenly Last Summer*, dir. Joseph L. Mankiewicz. *Film Quarterly* 13 (Spring 1960): 40–42.

Johnson, W. Rev. of *Boom*, dir. Joseph Losey. *Film Quarterly* (Winter 1968–69): 52–55.

Kael, Pauline. *Kiss Kiss Bang Bang*. Boston: Little, Brown, 1968.

Kahn, Sy. "*Baby Doll*: A Comic Fable." *Tennessee Williams: A Tribute*. Ed. Jac Tharpe. Jackson: UP of Mississippi, 1977. 292–309.

Kalson, Albert E. "Tennessee Williams at the Delta Brilliant." *Tennessee Williams: A Tribute*. Ed. Jac Tharpe. Jackson: UP of Mississippi, 1977.

Kantor, Bernard R., Irwin R. Blacker, and Anne Kramer. "Richard Brooks." *Directors at Work*. New York: Funk and Wagnalls, 1970. 3–58.

Kauffmann, Stanley. Rev. of *Sweet Bird of Youth*, dir. Richard Brooks. *New Republic* 16 Apr. 1962: 28.

Kazan, Elia. *A Life*. New York: Knopf, 1988.

Keith, Don Lee. "New Tennessee Williams Rises from 'Stoned Age.'" *Times Picayune* 18 Oct. 1970, sec. 3: 6 Rpt. in *Conversations with Tennessee Williams*. Ed. Albert J. Devlin. Jackson: UP of Mississippi, 1986. 147–60.

Kinney, Nancy S. Rev. of *Sweet Bird of Youth*, dir. Richard Brooks. *Magill's Survey of Cinema*. Ed. Frank N. Magill. 2nd series. Vol 3. NJ: Salem, 1981. 2387–90.

Knight, Arthur. "A Dissertation on Roast Corn." Rev. of *Summer and Smoke*, dir. Peter Glenville. *Saturday Review* 11 Nov. 1961: 32.

———. "Where There's a Williams." Rev. of *The Night of the Iguana*, dir. John Huston. *Saturday Review* 18 July 1964: 22.

———. "The Williams-Kazan Axis." *Saturday Review* 29 Dec. 1956: 22–23.

Kolin, Philip C. "Civil Rights and the Black Presence in *Baby Doll*." *Literature/Film Quarterly* 24.1 (1996): 2–11.

Kuhn, Helen Weldon. Rev. of *The Fugitive Kind*, dir. Sidney Lumet. *Films in Review* 11 (May 1960): 290–92.

Leclercq, Florence. *Elizabeth Taylor*. Boston: Twayne, 1985.

Leverich, Lyle. *Tom: The Unknown Tennessee Williams*. New York: Crown, 1995.

"Linje Lusta." *Internet Movie Database*. 1997. http://www.us.imdb.com/cache/title-exact/ 66182 (28 Sept. 1997).

Manso, Peter. *Brando: The Biography*. New York: Hyperion, 1994.

Maxwell, Gilbert. *Tennessee Williams and Friends*. Cleveland: World, 1965.

McCarty, John. *The Films of John Huston*. Secaucus, NJ: Citadel, 1987.

McManigal, John. Rev. of *Cat on a Hot Tin Roof*, dir. Richard Brooks. *Sight and Sound* 28 (Winter 1958): 36.

Michaels, Lloyd. *Elia Kazan: A Guide to References and Resources*. Boston: Hall, 1985.

Molt, Cynthia Marylee. *Vivien Leigh: A Bio-bibliography*. Westport, CT: Greenwood, 1992.

Murf. Rev. of *The Last of the Mobile Hot Shots*, dir. Sidney Lumet. *Variety* 31 Dec. 1969: 6.

Murray, Edward. *The Cinematic Imagination: Writers and the Motion Pictures*. New York: Ungar, 1972.

Overbeck, S. K. Rev. of *The Last of the Mobile Hot Shots*, dir. Sidney Lumet. *Newsweek* 26 Jan. 1970: 75.

Palmer, James, and Michael Riley. *The Films of Joseph Losey*. Cambridge: Cambridge UP, 1993.

Pauly, Thomas H. *An American Odyssey: Elia Kazan and American Culture*. Philadelphia: Temple UP, 1983.

Phillips, Gene D. *The Films of Tennessee Williams*. Philadelphia: Art Alliance, 1980.

Prouse, Derek. Rev. of *The Fugitive Kind*, dir. Sidney Lumet. *Sight and Sound* 29 (Summer 1960): 144–45.

Pyro. Rev. of *The Fugitive Kind*, dir. Sidney Lumet. *Variety* 13 Apr. 1960: 6.

Quirk, Lawrence J. *The Films of Paul Newman*. Secaucus, NJ: Citadel, 1971.

Reisz, Karel. Rev. of *A Streetcar Named Desire*, dir. Elia Kazan. *Sight and Sound* 21 (Apr.– Jun. 1952): 170–71.

Rhode, Eric. Rev. of *Summer and Smoke*, dir. Peter Glenville. *Sight and Sound* 31 (Spring 1962): 95.

Ron. Rev. of *Cat on a Hot Tin Roof*, dir. Richard Brooks. *Variety* 13 Aug. 1958: 6.

Rose, Lloyd. Rev. of *A Streetcar Named Desire*, dir. Elia Kazan. *washingtonpost.com*. 21 Jan. 1994. http//www.washingtonpost.com/wp-srv/s . . . astreetcarnameddesirenrrose__ a09e20.htm (28 Sept. 1997).

Rothschild, Elaine. Rev. of *Boom*, dir. Joseph Losey. *Films in Review* 19 (Aug.–Sept. 1968): 454.

———. Rev. of *The Night of the Iguana*, dir. John Huston. *Films in Review* 15 (Aug.–Sept. 1964): 439–41.

———. Rev. of *Sweet Bird of Youth*, dir. Richard Brooks. *Films in Review* 13 (Apr. 1962): 233–34.

Sarris, Andrew. *Confessions of a Cultist*. New York: Touchstone, 1971.

Sinyard, Neil. *Filming Literature: The Art of Screen Adaptation*. New York: St. Martin's, 1986.

Sussex, Elizabeth. Rev. of *The Night of the Iguana*, dir. John Huston. *Sight and Sound* 33 (Autumn 1964): 198–99.

Taylor, Stephen. Rev. of *The Night of the Iguana*, dir. John Huston. *Film Quarterly* (Winter 1964): 50–52.

"Tennessee Williams." *Mississippi Writers' Page*. 9 Sept. 1997. http://www.olemiss.edu/depts/english/m . . . ters/dir/williams_tennessee/index.html (28 Sept. 1997).

Tharpe, Jac, ed. *Tennessee Williams: A Tribute*. Jackson: UP of Mississippi, 1977.

Tube. Rev. of *Period of Adjustment*, dir. George Roy Hill. *Variety* 31 Oct. 1962: 6.

———. Rev. of *Sweet Bird of Youth*, dir. Richard Brooks. *Variety* 28 Feb. 1962: 6.

Vidal, Gore. Introduction. *Tennessee Williams: Collected Stories*. New York: New Directions, 1985. xix–xxv.

Walsh, Frank. *Sin and Censorship: The Catholic Church and the Motion Picture Industry*. New Haven: Yale UP, 1996.

Wharton, Flavia. Rev. of *Summer and Smoke*, dir. Peter Glenville. *Films in Review* 12 (Dec. 1961): 621.

Whit. Rev. of *The Night of the Iguana*, dir. John Huston. *Variety* 1 July 1969: 6.

Whitehall, Richard. Rev. of *The Fugitive Kind*, dir. Sidney Lumet. *Films and Filming* Aug. 1960: 23–24.

———. Rev. of *Period of Adjustment*, dir. George Roy Hill. *Films and Filming* Mar. 1963: 38.

Williams, Tennessee. *Baby Doll and Tiger Tail: A Screenplay and Play*. New York: New Directions, 1991.

———. *Baby Doll: The Script for the Film by Tennessee Williams. Incorporating the Two One-Act Plays Which Suggested It: 27 Wagons Full of Cotton; The Long Stay Cut Short, or The Unsatisfactory Supper*. New York: New Directions, 1956.

———. *Baby Doll: The Script for the Film*. London: Secker & Warburg, 1957.

———. *The Script for the Film Baby Doll*. New York: New American Library, 1956.

———. "A Streetcar Named Desire." *Film Scripts One*. Ed. George P. Garrett, O. B. Hardison, Jr., and Jane R. Gelfman. New York: Appleton-Century-Crofts, 1971. 330–484.

Yacowar, Maurice. *Tennessee Williams and Film*. New York: Ungar, 1977.

Zinsner, William K. Rev. of *The Rose Tattoo*, dir. Daniel Mann. *New York: Herald Tribune* 13 Dec. 1955: 20.

Bibliography

BIOGRAPHIES AND INTERVIEWS

Devlin, Albert J. *Conversations with Tennessee Williams*. Jackson: UP of Mississippi, 1986.

Hayman, Ronald. *Tennessee Williams: Everyone Else Is an Audience*. New Haven: Yale UP, 1993.

Leavitt, Richard. *The World of Tennessee Williams*. New York: Putnam's, 1978.

Leverich, Lyle. *Tom: The Unknown Tennessee*. Vol. 1. New York: Crown, 1995; Vol. 2. *Tenn: The Timeless World of Tennessee Williams* (forthcoming).

Pagan, Nicholas. *Rethinking Literary Biography: A Postmodern Approach to Tennessee Williams*. Rutherford, NJ: Farleigh Dickinson, 1993.

Spoto, Donald. *The Kindness of Strangers: The Life of Tennessee Williams*. Boston: Little, Brown, 1985.

Van Antwerp, Margaret A., and Sally Johns, eds. *Tennessee Williams*. Detroit: Gale, 1984. Vol. 4 of *Dictionary of Literary Biography. Documentary Series: An Illustrated Chronicle*. 12 vols. 1982–94.

Williams, Dakin, and Shepherd Mead. *Tennessee Williams: An Intimate Biography*. New York: Arbor House, 1983.

Williams, Edwina Dakin, and Lucy Freeman. *Remember Me to Tom*. New York: Putnam's, 1963.

BIBLIOGRAPHIES

Arnott, Catherine M. *Tennessee Williams on File*. London: Methuen, 1985.

Crandell, George W. *Tennessee Williams: A Descriptive Bibliography*. Pittsburgh: U of Pittsburgh P, 1995.

Gunn, Drewey Wayne. *Tennessee Williams: A Bibliography*. 2nd ed. Metuchen: Scarecrow, 1991.

Kolin, Philip, ed. *American Playwrights Since 1945: A Guide to Scholarship, Criticism, and Performance*. Westport, CT: Greenwood, 1989.

McCann, John S. *The Critical Reputation of Tennessee Williams: A Reference Guide*. Boston: Hall, 1983.

CRITICAL STUDIES

Adler, Thomas P. *"A Streetcar Named Desire": The Moth and the Lantern*. Twayne's Masterwork Studies Series, no. 47. Boston: Twayne, 1990.

Bloom, Harold, ed. *Tennessee Williams*. Modern Critical Views. New York: Chelsea, 1987.

———. *Tennessee Williams's A Streetcar Named Desire*. Modern Critical Interpretations. New York: Chelsea, 1988.

———. *Tennessee Williams's The Glass Menagerie*. Modern Critical Interpretations. New York: Chelsea, 1988.

Bigsby, C. W. E. *Modern American Drama, 1945–1990*. Cambridge: Cambridge UP, 1994.

———. *Tennessee Williams, Arthur Miller, Edward Albee*. Cambridge: Cambridge UP, 1982. Vol. 2 of *A Critical Introduction to Twentieth-Century American Drama*. 3 vols. 1982–85.

Boxill, Roger. *Tennessee Williams*. Macmillan Modern Dramatists. New York: Macmillan, 1987.

Crandell, George W. *The Critical Response to Tennessee Williams*. Westport, CT: Greenwood, 1995.

Falk, Signi Lenea. *Tennessee Williams*. 2nd ed. Twayne's United States Author Series. 10. Boston: Twayne, 1978.

Fedder, Norman J. *The Influence of D. H. Lawrence on Tennessee Williams*. Studies in American Literature. 5. London: Mouton, 1966.

Fleche, Ann. *Mimetic Disillusion: Eugene O'Neill, Tennessee Williams, and U.S. Dramatic Realism*. Tuscaloosa: U of Alabama P, 1997.

Griffin, Alice. *Understanding Tennessee Williams*. Understanding Contemporary American Literature. Columbia: U of South Carolina P, 1995.

Hirsch, Foster. *A Portrait of the Artist: The Plays of Tennessee Williams*. Port Washington: Kennikat, 1979.

Jackson, Esther Merle. *The Broken World of Tennessee Williams*. Madison: U of Wisconsin P, 1965.

Kolin, Philip C., ed. *Confronting Tennessee Williams's A Streetcar Named Desire: Essays in Cultural Pluralism*. Westport, CT: Greenwood, 1993.

———. *A Streetcar Named Desire*. Plays in Performance Series. Cambridge: Cambridge UP, forthcoming.

Londré, Felicia Hardison. *Tennessee Williams*. New York: Ungar, 1979.

Miller, Jordan Y., ed. *Twentieth Century Interpretations of A Streetcar Named Desire: A Collection of Critical Essays*. Twentieth Century Interpretations. Englewood Cliffs: Prentice-Hall, 1971.

Murphy, Brenda. *Tennessee Williams and Elia Kazan: A Collaboration in the Theatre*. Cambridge: Cambridge UP, 1992.

Nelson, Benjamin. *Tennessee Williams: The Man and His Work*. New York: Oblensky, 1961.

O'Connor, Jacqueline. *Dramatizing Dementia: Madness in the Plays of Tennessee Williams*. Bowling Green: Bowling Green State U Popular P, 1997.

Parker, R. B., ed. *The Glass Menagerie: A Collection of Critical Essays*. Twentieth Century Interpretations. Englewood Cliffs: Prentice-Hall, 1983.

Phillips, Gene, S. J. *The Films of Tennessee Williams*. Philadelphia: Art Alliance, 1980.

Presley, Delma E. *The Glass Menagerie: An American Memory*. Twayne's Masterworks Studies. 43. Boston: Twayne, 1990.

Roudané, Matthew C. *The Cambridge Companion to Tennessee Williams*. Cambridge: Cambridge UP, 1997.

Savran, David. *Communists, Cowboys, and Queers: The Politics of Masculinity in the Works of Arthur Miller and Tennessee Williams*. Minneapolis: U of Minnesota P, 1992.

Schlueter, June, ed. *Feminist Rereadings of Modern American Drama*. Rutherford, NJ: Fairleigh Dickinson UP, 1989.

Shaland, Irene. *Tennessee Williams on the Soviet Stage*. Lanham, MD: UP of America, 1987.

Sievers, W. David. *Freud on Broadway: A History of Psychoanalysis and the American Drama*. New York: Cooper Square, 1955.

Stanton, Stephen S. *Tennessee Williams: A Collection of Critical Essays*. Twentieth Century Views. Englewood Cliffs: Prentice-Hall, 1977.

Taylor, William E., ed. *Modern American Drama: Essays in Criticism*. DeLand, FL: Everett/Edwards, 1968.

Tharpe, Jac., ed. *Tennessee Williams: A Tribute*. Jackson: U of Mississippi P, 1977.

Thompson, Judith. *Tennessee Williams's Plays: Memory, Myth, and Symbol*. New York: Peter Lang, 1987.

Tischler, Nancy. *Tennessee Williams: Rebellious Puritan*. New York: Citadel, 1961.

Vannatta, Dennis. *Tennessee Williams: A Study of the Short Fiction*. Twayne's Studies in Short Fiction Series. 4. Boston: Twayne, 1988.

Weales, Gerald. *Tennessee Williams*. Minneapolis: U of Minnesota P, 1965.

Yacowar, Maurice. *Tennessee Williams and Film*. New York: Ungar, 1979.

Index of Actors, Choreographers, Composers, Designers, Directors, Librettists, and Producers

Index of Commentators, Critics, and Reviewers

Index of Tennessee Williams's Works

About the Editor and Contributors

PHILIP C. KOLIN, Professor of English at the University of Southern Mississippi, is the founding coeditor of *Studies in American Drama, 1945–Present* and the general editor of the Garland Shakespeare Criticism Series. He has also edited *Confronting Tennessee Williams's A Streetcar Named Desire: Essays in Critical Pluralism* (1993), *American Playwrights Since 1945: A Guide to Scholarship, Criticism, and Performance* (1989), and *Conversations with Edward Albee* (1988), and coedited *Speaking on Stage: Interviews with Contemporary American Playwrights* (1996). He has published extensively on Williams, including articles in *Modern Drama, Journal of Dramatic Theory and Criticism, Tennessee Williams Annual Review, Journal of American Drama and Theatre, Missouri Review,* and *Theatre Survey.* He is currently preparing a volume on *A Streetcar Named Desire* for Cambridge University Press. He has also published *Successful Writing at Work* (1998), now in its fifth edition.

THOMAS P. ADLER is Professor and Head of English at Purdue University, where he has taught dramatic literature for almost three decades. His over thirty publications and presentations on Williams include a monograph, *"A Streetcar Named Desire": The Moth and the Lantern* (1990); two lengthy chapters in his book, *American Drama, 1940–1960: A Critical History* (1994; paperback 1997); and an essay on *Summer and Smoke* and *The Night of the Iguana* in *The Cambridge Companion to Tennessee Williams* (1997).

ROBERT BRAY, Professor of English at Middle Tennessee State University, is the editor of the *Tennessee Williams Annual Review* and serves as the chief organizer for the Tennessee Williams Scholars' Conference, held in New Orleans each March. He has published widely on Williams's plays and has written a full-length study of Williams's works entitled *The Delta Cycle*.

CASSIE CARTER is a lecturer in American Thought and Language at Michigan State University, where her current work centers on experimental theater and performance art by contemporary American women and the popular/mainstream reception of abject feminist art. She has published articles on women's performance art, science fiction, and African American literature and also on New York poet/diarist/performer Jim Carroll, including the authoritative primary and secondary bibliography of Carroll (1990). She maintains the award-winning Jim Carroll Website <http://JimCarroll.forbin.com>.

GEORGE W. CRANDELL is Associate Professor of English and Assistant Head of the English Department at Auburn University. He has published articles on American humor and modern drama as well as *Tennessee Williams: A Descriptive Bibliography* (1995) and *The Critical Response to Tennessee Williams* (1996). He is currently working on a descriptive bibliography of the works of Arthur Miller.

LANELLE DANIEL has published essays on Mamet and Williams, and has recently compiled a bibliography of American drama. She teaches at Floyd College in Rome, Georgia.

LESLIE ATKINS DURHAM is completing her dissertation on the drama of Gertrude Stein at the University of Kansas, where she has also worked on the *Journal of Dramatic Theory and Criticism*.

JAMES FISHER, Professor of Theater at Wabash College, has authored four books: *The Theatre of Yesterday and Tomorrow: Commedia dell'arte on the Modern Stage* (1992); *Al Jolson*; *Spencer Tracy*; and *Eddie Cantor*. He has held several research fellowships and has published articles including " 'The Angels of Fructification': Tennessee Williams, Tony Kushner, and Images of Homosexuality on the American Stage" for the special Tennessee Williams issue of the *Mississippi Quarterly* (Winter 1995–96). He edits *The Puppetry Yearbook* and is the book review editor for the *Journal of Dramatic Theory and Criticism*. Fisher was named "Indiana Theater Person of the Year" by the Indiana Theater Association.

MARILYN CLAIRE FORD teaches at the University of Southern Mississippi, where she is completing her dissertation in Renaissance literature. She is the author of "Parodying Fascism: *Suddenly Last Summer* as Political Allegory" in *Publications of the Mississippi Philological Society* (1997).

DAVID H. GOFF, Professor of Radio, Television, and Film at the University of Southern Mississippi, has research interests in media history and the relationships among media, culture, and society. His publications include the chapter on Paddy Chayefsky in *American Playwrights Since 1945: A Guide to Scholarship, Criticism, and Performance* (1989) and articles in *Journal of Broadcasting* and *Journalism Quarterly*.

PATRICIA GRIERSON, Professor of English at Jackson State University, is the editor of *The Researcher* and a widely published poet. She recently has edited collections of essays on Hank Williams and southern writers.

JOHN GRONBECK-TEDESCO is Chair of the Department of Theater and Film at the University of Kansas and editor of the *Journal of Dramatic Theory and Criticism*. His articles on Tennessee Williams have appeared in *Publications of the Mississippi Philological Association*, *Mississippi Quarterly*, and *Studies in American Drama, 1945–Present*.

CATHY HENDERSON is the Associate Librarian at the Harry Ransom Humanities Research Center at the University of Texas at Austin, the principal repository of Tennessee Williams's papers. She has curated exhibitions on "Tennessee Williams in New Orleans," "Twentieth-Century American Playwrights," and postwar British theatre. She was a panelist at the 1997 Tennessee Williams/ New Orleans Literary Festival.

FRANCESCA OGLESBY HITCHCOCK teaches at Stamford University. Her dissertation, "In Search of Brother Adam and Sister Eve: The Quest for the Androgynous Ideal in the Works of Tennessee Williams," received the University of Alabama Arts and Sciences Outstanding Dissertation Award for 1994. She has published "Tennessee Williams's 'Vengeance of Nitocris': The Keynote to Future Works" in *Mississippi Quarterly* and is at work on other essays dealing with Tennessee Williams and androgyny.

RICHARD E. KRAMER, actor, director, theatre and writing teacher, dramaturg/ literary manager, reviewer, and editor of two theatre newsletters, is completing his dissertation in Performance Studies at New York University. His writing appears in, among others, *The Drama Review, Theatre History Studies, The Cambridge Guide to American Theatre, The Cambridge Guide to World Theatre,* and *Speaking on Stage.*

COLBY H. KULLMAN is Professor of English at the University of Mississippi, where he teaches courses in "The World of Tennessee Williams," "Modern American Drama," and "Drama of the American South." He is coeditor of the two-volume reference work *Theatre Companies of the World* (1986) and of *Speaking on Stage: Interviews with Contemporary American Playwrights* (1996). He is also coeditor of *Studies in American Drama, 1945–Present.* His article "Rule by Power:

'Big Daddyism' in the World of Tennessee Williams's Plays" appeared in *Mississippi Quarterly* (1996).

NEAL A. LESTER, Professor of English at Arizona State University, teaches African-American literature and African-American cultural studies. He has published the first comprehensive examination of the theatre of poet-playwright Ntozake Shange, *Ntozake Shange: A Critical Study of the Plays* (1996), and articles on Alice Walker, Zora Neale Hurston, and Lonne Elder III. His publications appear in such journals and books as *African American Review*, *The Oxford Companion to African American Literature*, *The Oxford Companion to Women's Writing in the United States*, *Reference Guide to American Literature*, *Alabama Literary Review*, *Diversity: A Journal of Multicultural Issues*, *Modern Black Writers*, *South Atlantic Review*, and *Journal of Popular Culture*.

MARK W. ROCHA is Dean of the College of Arts, Humanities, and Social Sciences and Professor of English at Humboldt State University in Arcata, California. He has published essays on A. R. Gurney, Luis Valdez, and other twentieth-century American playwrights, including an interview with August Wilson and chapters in two recent volumes on Wilson: *August Wilson: A Casebook* and *May All Your Fences Have Gates*.

JÜRGEN C. WOLTER is Professor of English and American Studies at Universität Wuppertal, Germany, where he teaches courses in American literature. He has published numerous articles, predominantly on American drama and culture, and books on Thomas Deloney and the American drama from its beginnings to O'Neill. His special fields of interest are American drama and southern literature.

ISBN 0-313-30306-1

HARDCOVER BAR CODE

Krouen